Great Small FIATs

Phil Ward

Other Veloce publications:

SpeedPro Series
4-Cylinder Engine – How to Blueprint & Build a Short Block for High Performance (Hammill)
Alfa Romeo DOHC High-Performance Manual (Kartalamakis)
Alfa Romeo V6 Engine High-Performance Manual (Kartalamakis)
BMC 998cc A-Series Engine – How to Power Tune (Hammill)
1275cc A-Series High-Performance Manual (Hammill)
Camshafts – How to Choose & Time them for Maximum Power (Hammill)
Cylinder Heads – How to Build, Modify & Power Tune Updated & Revised Edition (Burgess & Gollan)
Distributor-type Ignition Systems – How to Build & Power Tune (Hammill)
Fast Road Car – How to Plan and Build Revised & Updated Colour New Edition (Stapleton)
Ford SOHC 'Pinto' & Sierra Cosworth DOHC Engines – How to Power Tune Updated & Enlarged Edition (Hammill)
Ford V8 – How to Power Tune Small Block Engines (Hammill)
Harley-Davidson Evolution Engines – How to Build & Power Tune (Hammill)
Holley Carburetors – How to Build & Power Tune Revised & Updated Edition (Hammill)
Jaguar XK Engines – How to Power Tune Revised & Updated Colour Edition (Hammill)
MG Midget & Austin-Healey Sprite – How to Power Tune Updated & Revised Edition (Stapleton)
MGB 4-Cylinder Engine – How to Power Tune (Burgess)
MGB V8 Power – How to Give Your, Third Colour Edition (Williams)
MGB, MGC & MGB V8 – How to Improve (Williams)
Mini Engines – How to Power Tune on a Small Budget Colour Edition (Hammill)
Motorsport – Getting Started (Collins)
Nitrous Oxide High-Performance Manual (Langfield)
Rover V8 Engines – How to Power Tune (Hammill)
Sportscar/Kitcar Suspension & Brakes – How to Build & Modify Enlarged & Updated 2nd Edition (Hammill)
SU Carburettor High-Performance Manual (Hammill)
Suzuki 4x4 – How to Modify for Serious Off-Road Action (Richardson)
Tiger Avon Sportscar – How to Build Your Own Updated & Revised 2nd Edition (Dudley)
TR2, 3 & TR4 – How to Improve (Williams)
TR5, 250 & TR6 – How to Improve (Williams)
TR7 & TR8, How to Improve (Williams)
V8 Engine – How to Build a Short Block for High Performance (Hammill)
Volkswagen Beetle Suspension, Brakes & Chassis – How to Modify for High Performance (Hammill)
Volkswagen Bus Suspension, Brakes & Chassis – How to Modify for High Performance (Hammill)
Weber DCOE, & Dellorto DHLA Carburetors – How to Build & Power Tune 3rd Edition (Hammill)

Those were the days ... Series
Alpine Trials & Rallies 1910-1973 (Pfundner)
Austerity Motoring (Bobbitt)
Brighton National Speed Trials (Gardiner)
British Police Cars (Walker)
Crystal Palace by (Collins)
Dune Buggy Phenomenon (Hale)
Dune Buggy Phenomenon Volume 2 (Hale)
MG's Abingdon Factory (Moylan)
Motor Racing at Brands Hatch in the Seventies (Parker)
Motor Racing at Goodwood in the Sixties (Gardiner)
Motor Racing at Oulton Park in the 1960s (McFadyen)
Three Wheelers (Bobbitt)

Enthusiast's Restoration Manual Series
Citroën 2CV, How to Restore (Porter)
Classic Car Bodywork, How to Restore (Thaddeus)
Classic Car Electrics (Thaddeus)
Classic Cars, How to Paint (Thaddeus)
Reliant Regal, How to Restore (Payne)
Triumph TR2/3/3A, How to Restore (Williams)
Triumph TR4/4A, How to Restore (Williams)
Triumph TR5/250 & 6, How to Restore (Williams)
Triumph TR7/8, How to Restore (Williams)
Volkswagen Beetle, How to Restore (Tyler)
Yamaha FS1-E, How to Restore (Watts)

Essential Buyer's Guide Series
Alfa GT (Booker)
Alfa Romeo Spider Giulia (Booker)
BMW GS (Henshaw)
Citroën 2CV (Paxton)
Jaguar E-type 3.8 & 4.2-litre (Crespin)
Jaguar E-type V12 5.3-litre (Crespin)
Jaguar/Daimler XJ6, XJ12 & Sovereign (Crespin)
MGB & MGB GT (Williams)
Mercedes-Benz 280SL-560SL Roadsters (Bass)
Mercedes-Benz 'Pagoda' 230SL, 250SL & 280SL Roadsters & Coupés (Bass)
Morris Minor (Newell)

Porsche 928 (Hemmings)
Rolls-Royce Silver Shadow & Bentley T-Series (Bobbitt)
Triumph Bonneville (Henshaw)
Triumph TR6 (Williams)
VW Beetle (Cservenka & Copping)
VW Bus (Cservenka & Copping)

Auto-Graphics Series
Fiat-based Abarths (Sparrow)
Jaguar MkI & II Saloons (Sparrow)
Lambretta LI series scooters (Sparrow)

Rally Giants Series
Big Healey – 100-Six & 3000 (Robson)
Ford Escort MkI (Robson)
Lancia Stratos (Robson)
Peugeot 205 T16 (Robson)
Subaru Impreza (Robson)

General
1½-litre GP Racing 1961-1965 (Whitelock)
AC Two-litre Saloons & Buckland Sportscars (Archibald)
Alfa Romeo Giulia Coupé GT & GTA (Tipler)
Alfa Tipo 33 (McDonough & Collins)
Anatomy of the Works Minis (Moylan)
Armstrong-Siddeley (Smith)
Autodrome (Collins & Ireland)
Automotive A-Z, Lane's Dictionary of Automotive Terms (Lane)
Automotive Mascots (Kay & Springate)
Bahamas Speed Weeks, The (O'Neil)
Bentley Continental, Corniche and Azure (Bennett)
Bentley MkIV, Rolls-Royce Silver Wraith, Dawn & Cloud/ Bentley R & S-series (Nutland)
BMC Competitions Department Secrets (Turner, Chambers Browning)
BMW 5-Series (Cranswick)
BMW Z-Cars (Taylor)
British 250cc Racing Motorcycles by Chris Pereira
British Cars, The Complete Catalogue of, 1895-1975 (Culshaw & Horrobin)
BRM – a mechanic's tale (Salmon)
BRM V16 (Ludvigsen)
Bugatti Type 40 (Price)
Bugatti 46/50 Updated Edition (Price & Arbey)
Bugatti T44 & T49 (Price & Arbey)
Bugatti 57 2nd Edition (Price)
Caravans, The Illustrated History 1919-1959 (Jenkinson)
Caravans, The Illustrated History from 1960 (Jenkinson)
Chrysler 300 – America's Most Powerful Car 2nd Edition (Ackerson)
Chrysler PT Cruiser (Ackerson)
Citroën DS (Bobbitt)
Cobra – The Real Thing! (Legate)
Cortina – Ford's Bestseller (Robson)
Coventry Climax Racing Engines (Hammill)
Daimler SP250 New Edition (Long)
Datsun Fairlady Roadster to 280ZX – The Z-car Story (Long)
Dino – The V6 Ferrari (Long)
Dodge Dynamite! (Grist)
Drive on the Wild Side, A – 20 extreme driving adventures from around the world (Weaver)
Ducati 750 Bible, The (Falloon)
Dune Buggy, Building a – The Essential Manual (Shakespeare)
Dune Buggy Files (Hale)
Dune Buggy Handbook (Hale)
Edward Turner: the man behind the motorcycles (Clew)
Fiat & Abarth 124 Spider & Coupé (Tipler)
Fiat & Abarth 500 & 600 2nd edition (Bobbitt)
Fiats, Great Small (Ward)
Ford F100/F150 Pick-up 1948-1996 (Ackerson)
Ford F150 1997-2005 (Ackerson)
Ford GT – Then, and Now (Streather)
Ford GT40 (Legate)
Ford in Miniature (Olson)
Ford Model Y (Roberts)
Ford Thunderbird from 1954, The Book of the (Long)
Funky Mopeds (Skelton)
GT – The World's Best GT Cars 1953-73 (Dawson)
Hillclimbing & sprinting – The essential manual (Short)
Honda NSX (Long)
Jaguar, The Rise of (Price)
Jaguar XJ-S (Long)
Jeep CJ (Ackerson)
Jeep Wrangler (Ackerson)
Karmann-Ghia Coupé & Convertible (Bobbitt)
Lambretta Bible, The (Davies)
Lancia 037 (Collins)
Lancia Delta HF Integrale (Blaettel & Wagner)
Land Rover, The Half-Ton Military (Cook)
Laverda Twins & Triples Bible 1968-1986 (Falloon)
Lea-Francis Story, The (Price)
Lexus Story, The (Long)
little book of smart, The (Jackson)
Lola – The Illustrated History (1957-1977) (Starkey)

Lola – All the Sports Racing & Single-Seater Racing Cars 1978-1997 (Starkey)
Lola T70 – The Racing History & Individual Chassis Record 3rd Edition (Starkey)
Lotus 49 (Oliver)
MarketingMobiles, The Wonderful Wacky World of (Hale)
Mazda MX-5/Miata 1.6 Enthusiast's Workshop Manual (Grainger & Shoemark)
Mazda MX-5/Miata 1.8 Enthusiast's Workshop Manual (Grainger & Shoemark)
Mazda MX-5 Miata: the book of the world's favourite sportscar (Long)
Mazda MX-5 Miata Roadster (Long)
MGA (Price Williams)
MGB & MGB GT – Expert Guide (Auto-Doc Series) (Williams)
MGB Electrical Systems (Astley)
Micro Caravans (Jenkinson)
Microcars at large! (Quellin)
Mini Cooper – The Real Thing! (Tipler)
Mitsubishi Lancer Evo, the road car & WRC story (Long)
Montlhéry, the story of the Paris autodrome (Boddy)
Moto Guzzi Sport & Le Mans Bible (Falloon)
Motor Movies – The Posters! (Veysey)
Motor Racing – Reflections of a Lost Era (Carter)
Motorcycle Road & Racing Chassis Designs (Knoakes)
Motorhomes, The Illustrated History (Jenkinson)
Motorsport in colour, 1950s (Wainwright)
Nissan 300ZX & 350Z – The Z-Car Story (Long)
Pass the Theory and Practical Driving Tests (Gibson & Hoole)
Peking to Paris 2007 (Young)
Plastic Toy Cars of the 1950s & 1960s (Ralston)
Pontiac Firebird (Cranswick)
Porsche Boxster (Long)
Porsche 356 (2nd edition) (Long)
Porsche 911 Carrera – The Last of the Evolution (Corlett)
Porsche 911R, RS & RSR, 4th Edition (Starkey)
Porsche 911 – The Definitive History 1963-1971 (Long)
Porsche 911 – The Definitive History 1971-1977 (Long)
Porsche 911 – The Definitive History 1977-1987 (Long)
Porsche 911 – The Definitive History 1987-1997 (Long)
Porsche 911 – The Definitive History 1997-2004 (Long)
Porsche 911SC 'Super Carrera' – The Essential Companion (Streather)
Porsche 914 & 914-6: The Definitive History Of The Road & Competition Cars (Long)
Porsche 924 (Long)
Porsche 944 (Long)
Porsche 993 'King of Porsche' – The Essential Companion (Streather)
Porsche Racing Cars – 1953 to 1975 (Long)
Porsche Racing Cars – 1976 on (Long)
Porsche – The Rally Story (Meredith)
Porsche: Three Generations of Genius (Meredith)
RAC Rally Action! (Gardiner)
Rallye Sport Fords: the inside story (Moreton)
Redman, Jim – 6 Times World Motorcycle Champion: The Autobiography (Redman)
Rolls-Royce Silver Shadow/Bentley T Series Corniche & Camargue Revised & Enlarged Edition (Bobbitt)
Rolls-Royce Silver Spirit, Silver Spur & Bentley Mulsanne 2nd Edition (Bobbitt)
RX-7 – Mazda's Rotary Engine Sportscar (updated & revised new edition) (Long)
Scooters & Microcars, The A-Z of popular (Dan)
Singer Story: Cars, Commercial Vehicles, Bicycles & Motorcycles (Atkinson)
SM – Citroën's Maserati-engined Supercar (Long & Claverol)
Subaru Impreza: the road car and WRC story (Long)
Taxi! The Story of the 'London' Taxicab (Bobbitt)
Toyota Celica & Supra, The book of Toyota's Sports Coupés (Long)
Toyota MR2 Coupés & Spyders (Long)
Triumph Motorcycles & the Meriden Factory (Hancox)
Triumph Speed Twin & Thunderbird Bible (Woolridge)
Triumph Tiger Cub Bible (Estall)
Triumph Trophy Bible (Woolridge)
Triumph TR6 (Kimberley)
Unraced (Collins)
Velocette Motorcycles – MSS to Thruxton Updated & Revised (Burris)
Virgil Exner – Visioneer: The official biography of Virgil M Exner designer extraordinaire (Grist)
Volkswagen Bus Book, The (Bobbitt)
Volkswagen Bus or Van to Camper, How to Convert (Porter)
Volkswagens of the World (Glen)
VW Beetle Cabriolet (Bobbitt)
VW Beetle – The Car of the 20th Century (Copping)
VW Bus – 40 years of Splitties, Bays & Wedges (Copping)
VW Bus Book, The (Bobbitt)
VW Golf: five generations of fun (Copping & Cservenka)
VW – The air-cooled era (Copping)
VW T5 Camper Conversion Manual (Porter)
VW Campers (Copping)
Works Minis, The Last (Purves & Brenchley)
Works Rally Mechanic (Moylan)

First published in June 2007 by Veloce Publishing Limited, 33 Trinity Street, Dorchester DT1 1TT, England. Fax 01305 268864/e-mail info@veloce.co.uk/web www.veloce.co.uk or www.velocebooks.com.
ISBN: 978-1-845841-33-1/UPC: 6-36847-04133-5

Great Small
FIATs

FIAT ABARTH 595

Phil Ward

VELOCE PUBLISHING
THE PUBLISHER OF FINE AUTOMOTIVE BOOKS

Contents

*I*NTRODUCTION

This book is about great small Fiats. When considering the huge inventory of cars built by Fiat over the last 100 years, I had to decide which of the Fiats were both great and small. It is fairly easy to determine greatness – a car with character that was well-respected and sold well. Let's look at small. It could be reasoned that a small car would be one with an engine capacity that is not more than 1000cc. Our starting point is the Topolino because it is without doubt Fiat's first great small car.

So we have great Fiats and small Fiats, though not all small Fiats were great. Take, for instance, the lack-lustre 126 which must be included because it tidies up the 500 story. This brings us to a subsidiary of greatness – character. The 500 had it but the 126 didn't. The customers' love of the 500 was so strong that Fiat even reintroduced it and today, years after production finally ceased, Italian cities are still full of them. Character is an attribute that is bestowed on a car by people. It is a magic ingredient that car manufacturers would love to be able to keep in a jar on a shelf in its design departments to be sprinkled liberally on every new project.

Other small Fiats that satisfy most of our criteria, though with not quite so much character as the 500, are the 127 and the first Panda. The 127 sold very well and many readers of this book will be familiar with the model and some may have cut their motoring teeth with one. The same applies to the Panda – the car that wouldn't die. The Italians liked it so much, mostly I suspect because of its sheer practicality, that Fiat continued to build it years after its sell-by date because of public demand. Basically, the Panda is a box with a wheel at each corner but, like the 127, it is appreciated if a bit utilitarian.

The 600 and its successor, the 850, easily fall within our remit. Of the millions that were built, most have faded away and some of the ones that do remain have been cannibalised to fuel the Abarth

replica industry. Then there's the Millecento, every Italian's family car through the 1950s into the 1960s, 1970s and – in India – well into the 1990s. We have the top selling 128, it's a bit on the big side and not particularly charismatic but the Coupé and 3P were very pretty. The Uno sold fantastically well which makes it one of the greatest Fiats ever. The small theme continued with the cheeky Cinquecento and sober Seicento, the latter another exercise in how to design character out of car. Finally, we have the excellent Nuova Panda and a glimpse into the future with the promising new 500.

The reader will have noticed that I have had to stretch the 1000cc engine limit a bit so we can talk about a model range in its entirety, and in my defence, Fiat no longer make cars below 1-litre – its lowest capacity currently being 1108cc.

So, what do we have? Small Fiats that are mostly less than 1000cc, but some are a bit bigger than others with more or less character. Well, not quite because there are the spin-offs, Abarths in particular, most versions of which, because of its rarity and high value, are likely to be beyond the means of most of us but are interesting nonetheless. Anyway, no self-respecting book on small Fiats could ignore Carlo Abarth, the man who made great small cars even greater. I have included some of the efforts created by Carlo Abarth's modern day contemporaries and enthusiasts who can't leave things alone without improving their cars beyond recognition.

For additional interest, I have included chapters on the coach-built derivatives based on small Fiats and versions built under licence under different banners. Autobianchi receives a mention, too, because it was a Fiat-owned subsidiary that produced small cars using shared mechanical components out of Turin's vast parts bin.

I have attempted to establish some separation between the various Fiat models since we effectively have three models the Italians call 'Cinquecento'. The 500A is referred to by its adopted name 'Topolino', while the 500D onward is the 'Nuova 500'. The 1991 Polish-built car is the 'Cinquecento'. The original 600 is known as the 'Six Hundred', while the modern version is the 'Seicento' – not helped at all by the fact that the final edition has the letters '600' on the rear hatch – would that be the 'Seicento 600'? I have called the forthcoming car the 'New Fiat 500' to avoid titles like 'Nuova 500' or 'Nuova Cinquecento'.

While this book tells the story of production Fiats from the Topolino to the New 500, the final chapters cover the multitude of derivatives popularly referred to as 'Etceterini', the various international companies that built Fiats under license, and Autobianchi. I have reported on the better known coachbuilders who used small Fiats as a basis to demonstrate their design talents. This is only scratching the surface as there were countless artisans hammering pieces of metal in small sheds all over Italy during the 1950s and 1960s. Again, the more prominent licensees are described. Autobianchi is a bit of an anomaly, but it was a subsidiary of the Fiat empire and played an important role in the company's history.

FOREWORD
It is inevitable that some of the cars in this book will have appeared in the pages of *Auto Italia* magazine, of which I am Editor. *Auto Italia* is an international publication dedicated to the owner, admirer and enthusiast of all things Italian. The space constraints of a monthly magazine don't allow the full story of a particular model to be told, so this book is a useful opportunity to expand on the subject. Many books of this nature do not include driving impressions as some authors do not have the necessary reporting skills or, indeed, the direct personal access to such a wide variety of machinery. Where some of the feeling for the cars on these pages are those of the author, the more in-depth analysis is based on the intuitive driving skills of Roberto Giordanelli, the magazine's Chief Test Driver. Equally, at home in a Ferrari 512S or a Topolino, Roberto has test-driven a huge range of Italian road and racing cars. His driving experience is backed up by many years as a racing driver, racing instructor and as an accomplished race preparation and restoration engineer. He is also a good friend.

ACKNOWLEDGEMENTS
Thanks to Puneet Joshi at Fiat Auto UK's Press Office for his valuable time, patience and assistance in sourcing many of the wonderful archive photographs from Fiat's Centro Storico. Other information and photography was volunteered by my co-founder at *Auto Italia*, Peter Collins and photographers Michael Ward and Andrew Brown. Additional inspiration came from Tony Castle-Miller, Tony Berni, John Simister, Andrea Sparrow, Andy Heywood, Alessandro Sannia, Tony Soper, Roland Ellison, Simon Park, Richard Dredge and Mrs Ward.

Phil Ward
Letchworth, England

FABBRICA ITALIANA AUTOMOBILI TORINO

an empire is created

Fabbrica Italiana Automobili Torino (FIAT) was founded in Turin on 11 July, 1899, at a time when the city was enjoying a period of vigorous industrial expansion. The first plant, inaugurated in 1900 at Corso Dante, had 35 employees and produced 24 automobiles. The Chairman was Ludovico Scarfiotti, with Emanuele Cacherano di Bricherasio serving as Vice Chairman and Giovanni Agnelli as Secretary to the Board. Thanks to his determination and strategic vision, Giovanni Agnelli, a former cavalry officer, gained a prominent position among the original investors and was made Managing Director in 1902. One of his promotional ideas, a tour of Italy by automobile, was successfully carried out, with the finish line situated at the Milan Fair.

An oval logo on a blue background, designed by Carlo Biscaretti, was adopted in 1904, and the first automobile to bear the Fiat brand name was the Model 3½ HP. The company implemented a two-pronged growth strategy – diversification of production, and focus on the most promising markets – which has characterised its development through its entire 100-year plus history.

In 1903, after listing its shares on the Stock Exchange, Fiat established a number of new companies serving specific functions: Societa Carrozzeria Industriale, Fiat Brevetti and SA Garages Riuniti Fiat-Alberti-Storero. As a result, Fiat factories produced not only passenger and racing cars, but also commercial vehicles, marine engines, trucks, trams and taxicabs. The company's approach to the market was guided by a strategic and international vision. Fiat Automobile Co was incorporated in 1908 in the United States. It manufactured Fiat cars under licence at a plant built in Poughkeepsie, New York, in 1909. Relationships established with other partners led

Senator Giovannia Agnelli. His family name was synonymous with Fiat for several generations.

7

The first of millions. Remarkably, three of the eight 3½ HPs built still exist – two in Turin and one in the USA.

Agnelli's vision of a great future for Fiat, based primarily on automobile manufacturing.

After several trips to the United States by Agnelli, Barnardino Maraini and Guido Fornaca, the company started to plan what was described at the time as "a great new, American-style factory". In 1916, construction of the Lingotto plant started at Via Nizza, in a mixed farming and proto-industrial district of Turin. Giacomo Matte Trucco was the project manager. The Lingotto factory, the largest in Europe, quickly became a symbol of Italian industry, and one of Turin's best-known architectural icons. During that time, Fiat expanded its activities to the steel, railway and electrical industries, and entered the public transportation market with an exclusive contract to supply buses to SITA, a company based in Florence. The end of the First

to exports to France, Austria, Great Britain and Australia. Ten years after its foundation, Fiat had increased its capital stock to twelve million lire, had 2500 employees and had manufactured 1215 automobiles. The start of the First World War meant increased output of trucks, aircraft, ambulances, and engines. However, the conversion to military production did not alter

FIRT
Sezione Automobili
Officine del Lingotto

Built in 1916, the Lingotto plant is a famous Turin landmark. It continues to be used today as a training and conference centre.

Fiat commenced large-scale production in 1919 with the 501. Over 45,000 of these versatile small cars were made.

World War ushered in a decade of complex and profound social changes. Fiat was not spared the turmoil, and in September 1920 its factories were taken over by the employees. In November 1920, Giovanni Agnelli was appointed Chairman of the Board of Directors and Guido Fornaca was named Managing Director.

During the following two years, the company cut costs, downsized its workforce and lowered salaries. Growth resumed in 1923, when the new Lingotto plant went on stream. The launch of the Fiat 501 was followed by the introduction of the 505, 510 and 519 models. The four-seater 509 was launched in 1925. Fiat's management understood that the company's future growth had to be based largely on the development of mass production

A first series 510 complete with a back seat passenger. The 510 was Fiat's first post-war six-cylinder model.

The 519 Berlina had an overhead valve engine, a feature previously reserved for competition cars.

The Balilla three-speed, a small capacity Fiat; popular, it seems, with ladies who lunched in the 1920s …

in Italy, since higher production would generate better living standards, improve social conditions and increase consumer spending. With this in mind, Fiat established SAVA, a consumer credit company created to promote instalment purchases of cars. The company's far-sighted advertising message, delivered through posters, newspapers and corporate publications,

The desirable Balilla 508S Sport is also quite valuable. This well-known example is owned by a cheerful UK Fiat Register member.

been and continue to be a constant reference point in the company's existence.

The number of investments in Italian and foreign companies continued to increase. Management of this complex portfolio was entrusted to the newly created IFI (Istituto Finanziario Industriale). A plan to construct a factory that would build automobiles and trucks in Moscow under Fiat licence had been on the drawing boards since 1913 and the plant went on stream in 1924. The 1930s were characterized by remarkable technological development for trucks and other commercial vehicles, some of which began to be equipped with diesel engines, and by growth for the Group's activities in the fields of aviation and railway products. The world's first self-propelled electric and diesel trains, manufactured using an assembly line system, were produced for Italian State Railways. In 1928, Vittorio Valletta was appointed General Manager of Fiat.

In 1934, Fiat designed the 508, a new economy car known as the Balilla and referred to as Minimum Rate, because of its low fuel consumption of eight litres for every 100km. The company produced 113,000 of these cars. It also introduced a sports version (the 508 S) and a four-speed model (71,000 units).

succeeded at targeting women as potential buyers of new cars.

Fiat's motorsport victories, including the crossing of the Sahara and the 'raids' in Latin America, significantly increased interest in this new mode of transportation. During that time, the company founded employee health services, a central school for Fiat apprentices, and several other employee organisations, including a Fiat sports group, an Alpine children's resort and an employee association. Adjusting to changing social conditions, these entities have

FIAT

FIAT TOPOLINO

a star is born

In 1936, Fiat launched the 500 'Topolino', our starting point for the range of small Fiats covered by this book. To tell the Topolino story we must first consider the man behind this and many more Fiat projects, Dante Giacosa. We owe a lot to Giacosa for the insight into Fiat's manufacturing between 1928 and 1970. In fact, we owe even more to Giacosa's secretary, Wanda Vigliano Mundula, who kept meticulous records of his work from 1946 until his retirement. It is unusual to find someone so forthcoming in providing detail and, even rarer, the politics behind the Italian motor industry.

Giacosa's work is catalogued in great detail in his book *40 Years of Design with Fiat*. This book is something of a bible for the historian because the information comes directly from the author and has not been diluted or interfered with by a third party. Giacosa was both an engineer's and an accountant's friend. He had an infatuation

with making a car as light as possible without compromising structural integrity and at the same time kept material costs down. He was also keen on mechanical simplicity, using as few components as possible and which ideally had a dual purpose or integrated function. In reading Giacosa's book, the reader can pick up some of his frustrations with certain senior management figures. He was a great innovator and had many pioneering ideas that would have kept Fiat at the forefront of automotive engineering if they had been implemented in time. However, Fiat's management was quite conservative and when presented with Giacoas's 'radical' ideas, often defaulted to traditional concepts of engine location, configuration, drive train and body style. Giacosa was responsible for a large number of models, some of which, conveniently, fall within the scope of this book.

For the purposes of this book our story begins in 1934, when a young Dante Giacosa presented Fiat management with the sketches of a small, affordable car that would mobilize transport-deprived Italy. Fiat's brief had been a challenging one: produce a small car that was inexpensive to manufacture, cheap to run and maintain, but that could carry two adults plus either two children or 50kg of luggage. A suitable boot should be included too. The budget for the car was set at a mere 5000 lire.

Dr Antonio Fessia was in charge of the project, the bodywork and styling was to be handled by Rodolfo Schaeffer, while the chassis and engine design were to be the responsibility of the bright young engineer still in his twenties, Dante Giacosa. The project was called Zero A and the finished car was to become known as the Cinquecento – five

Dante Giacosa, the engineering genius responsible for many ground-breaking Fiats over a period of 40 years.

Dr Antonio Fessia was in charge of the Topolino project.

simplicity. The chassis was a simple A-frame design. The longitudinal front-mounted four-cylinder engine was straight forward and uncomplicated, with gravity fuel feed and no need for a water pump. Drive was through the rear wheels. Front-wheel drive had been considered but was not favoured by Senator Agnelli following his personal involvement in an accident with a car of that configuration – we had to wait another thirty years before front-wheel drive was generally accepted.

Rodolfo Schaeffer had produced a design that was stylish, but provided little working space; Giacosa overcame this problem by placing the 569cc water-cooled engine ahead of the front wheels. The first prototype was tested in October 1934 and was successful. The second prototype had slightly altered bodywork, and an annoying noise problem was cured with a redesigned crankshaft.

TOPOLINO 500A

Fiat's huge factory at Lingotto was built to produce the 500, and following the car's official launch on June 15th 1936, production quickly reached 100 cars per day. Although the sale price was 8900 lire – well over the original budget – it was still good value and sold well from day one. With its simple, practical design, a respectable top speed of 53mph and

hundred to non-Italians – and was eventually launched in 1936.

Giacosa was born in Rome in 1905, and studied engineering in Turin where he made his first contacts with the developing motoring industry. At the age of twenty-three, he joined Societa Piemontese Automobili (SPA), where he soon made a name for himself, thanks to his natural talents for design and engineering, and a unique ability to assess a problem from every angle and create inspired solutions. The year after he joined it, SPA was absorbed into the Fiat empire, and Giacosa found himself looking for challenges within his new company.

The idea of a small car had been discussed at Fiat for a long time, and the Zero A project appeared an ideal opportunity to realize its plans to adopt the cost-effective mass production techniques used so successfully in the USA. Within a couple of months, Giacosa and his team produced the final drawings of the Zero A. The key to this rapid development was

The best preserved example of a Fiat 500A in the UK.

fuel consumption of 48mpg, it satisfied a need for enjoyable, inexpensive motoring, and it had style and personality, too.

The 500 was launched initially only in saloon form, although a coupé-style version with a full-length folding sunroof soon appeared – and proved to be the most popular shape. At the end of the year, a commercial van version was also introduced with a single rear door, and then two years later with two rear doors. There were a few minor revisions to the 500 in 1938, including the upgrading of the rear suspension from quarter-elliptic (Balestra Corta) to semi-elliptic (Balestra Lunga). Apart from this, the car remained in production in the same form for twelve years, with 112,016 being produced during this time.

Billed as the world's smallest four-cylinder production car, the diminutive vehicle quickly became famous all over the world and achieved huge fame. Originally called Cinquecento because of its 569cc engine, the name Topolino appeared for the first time in an English magazine where a poem on the car was published with the title 'Mouse-like', inspired no doubt by its resemblance to Walt Disney's cartoon character, Mickey Mouse. In 1937, Rolando and Valabrega, two contemporary Italian songwriters, wrote a song especially for this car with the title *Sulla mia Topolino* (In my Topolino). The Topolino's image was exploited by advertising agencies and it was often chosen as the first prize in competitions. The recipe for the 500A's huge success was its good performance, high reliability, very low fuel consumption and low cost of spare parts.

In 1937, Fiat reaffirmed its commitment to mass production by starting construction of the Mirafiori plant in Turin. This facility, which was inaugurated on 15 May, 1939, enabled the company to introduce in Italy the most sophisticated models of industrial organisation. It was designed to accommodate 22,000 workers in two shifts, a truly remarkable number considering that, at that time, Fiat had a total of about 50,000 employees. Outside Italy, customer assistance centres, workshops and special industrial projects were created in Spain, Egypt, Poland and France. During the

Owned by Italian collector Loris Crispino, this superb Giardiniera is one of 70 final edition 500Bs painted in metallic colours.

war and its aftermath, employee services provided directly by Fiat supplemented the limited assistance offered by the public administration. The company's Assistance Office provided linen, shoes and firewood to working people, while Fiat soup kitchens distributed 100,000 meals per day.

Senator Giovanni Agnelli died in 1945 and in March 1946 Vittorio Valletta became Chairman of Fiat. Matching US technology and developing an Italian way to mass motor transport was the task at hand for Fiat. By 1948, thanks to financing provided by the Marshall Plan, its factories had been rebuilt. The payroll increased from 55,674 to 66,365 employees. Company earnings, which had remained flat during the war, disappeared entirely after 1943. In 1946, the company reported a loss. However, an upward trend resumed in 1948.

As manufacturing output recovered after the war, Fiat introduced the 500B – which was available as a sedan or a station wagon – the 1100E and 1500E models, and the Fiat 1400 – a car with unitary body construction characterized by innovative styling and engineering.

TOPOLINO 500B

With the exception of a few minor cosmetic differences, the 500B, which made its debut at the Geneva Motor Show in 1948, looked the same as its predecessor, except for modified bonnet catches, a new steering wheel and revised instrument panel. However, the technical specification was generally revised. The engine's power output was increased from 13bhp to 16.5bhp. The gearbox, clutch, brakes and suspension were all upgraded. Later that same year, the Giardiniera estate version was introduced. For the first time four people could be carried plus

13

car with great practical style. The 500B range lasted for one year.

TOPOLINO 500C

The 500 was completely restyled in 1949 and was launched at the Geneva Show on 19 March that year. Designated 500C, the frontal appearance of the new model was distinctly American. Even though the car now looked nothing like a little mouse, the Topolino acronym remained. The more modern body shape had practical advantages such as extra space for luggage, and the spare tyre found its way into the boot. The car also had a new efficient internal heating system and a windscreen demisting system, the first time this feature was to be fitted as standard equipment on a Fiat car. Technical modifications to the engine brought more power and even less fuel consumption.

50kg of luggage, which made it an ideal choice for families. The downside was that it was slightly slower, with increased fuel consumption. Another plus point though was the styling; the Giardiniera was a true 'woodie' in polished ash with masonite panels – an extremely characterful

Within three years, two Belvedere versions had joined the saloon – the Giardiniera estate, and an

Based on a 1936 500A chassis, this barchetta was built by Nuccio Bertone in 1947.

all-metal version, with coloured panels echoing the shape and style of the woodie. A van version was produced too, with a front bench seat and grille divider between the passenger and load compartments. The Topolino estates and vans made excellent vehicles for small businesses; they were not huge load carriers, but they were a relatively inexpensive

This Topolino-based Marinella Testudo 750 remains in as-raced condition as driven by Elio Zagato in 1949.

Fiat England Ltd launched the 500 four-seater Saloon, although only a few hundred were produced. In the USA, Topolinos did not achieve great fame as they were too small for American tastes. However, there was a version with the compulsory front and rear bumpers with white wall tyres.

In Poland, Polski Fiat built a special version of the 500 in 1938 with a big boot. In France, the original 500A and 500B were built as the Simca 5 from 1936 and then the 500C as the Simca 6 in 1948. Meanwhile in Holland, Mulder Cars built 2600 500C models between 1949 and 1955. In Austria, Steyr-Puch built its version and in Germany, NSU-Fiat produced a coupé and a beautiful two-seater sports car, which was later copied in Italy by Siata.

option, and could lead a double life as a family car, too. The more spacious and comfortable Belvedere version outlived the saloon and remained in production until 1955; it was the best-selling Topolino 500. A total of 376,368 500Cs were produced.

TOPOLINO TAKES ON THE WORLD
From 1936 to 1955, a total of 519,646 Topolinos rolled off the Fiat production line. Fiat's reputation as a successful maker of small cars was established beyond doubt. The model proved to be very popular internationally and was produced under licence in several countries. In 1937, a modified version was launched on the English market and two years later

IMPROVING THE TOPOLINO
Motorists did not have to be wealthy to buy and modify a Topolino, and racing car enthusiasts had plenty of tuning opportunities. The most common modifications made to the cars were the fitting of special inlet manifolds with twin carburettors and a mechanical water pump (Topolinos were cooled by a thermosyphon system). For the 500B and 500C, there were performance exhaust manifolds and a company called Abarth was developing improved silencers. Overdrives were made by the Monviso factory, and light alloy components by Modauto. For the 500C racing version, Monviso supplied a modified differential.

The original 'Z car', its title longer than the bodywork – 750 Berlinetta Panoramica Zagato.

examples of the famous 1949 Panoramica. They used the same mechanics and body as the 500C version, whilst the corners were rounded off and the rear window became half-moon shaped, typical of the Zagato style of that period.

SIATA (Societa Italiana Applicazioni Techniche Autoaviatorie) of Turin presented its Fiat 500 Gran Sport in 1937, a spider with a rocket-shaped body, similar to the Topolino built under

There were also many changes in bodystyling but unfortunately few have survived. In 1938, two Turinese coachbuilders, Chiabra and Bertolino, patented a Cabriolet Aerodynamic and a four-seater cabriolet. Another Torinese coachbuilder, Montescani, put its efforts into the convertible version, whilst Garavini introduced a version with an open roof and another with an American-style bonnet, the Matford.

Ernesto Accossato transformed the 500A and 500B berlina into a comfortable four-seater and the van version into a four-seater station-wagon. In the late 1940s, Autorama did the same conversion followed by Bruna in Genova. Francis Lombardi from Vercelli, starting from the 500C 2+2 model and taking inspiration from the Studebaker Champion designed by Loewy, built a four-seater with a longer roof and a larger rear window. New modified versions were made by De Pietri of Turin and coachbuilder Ticinum of Milan, who also proposed an American-style four-seater. Mario Riva & Sons in 1949 created a tall and square station-wagon based on the 500C.

Ugo Zagato created a 500A Sport with a very aerodynamic body, and a 500B with a distinctive shape which was called Uovo di Pasqua (Easter Egg). Zagato also produced one thousand

A beautifully restored 1939 Siata Amica Bertone Cabriolet based on the Topolino 500C.

Fiat supervision in Germany by NSU. In 1939, it built the Pescara and Monza versions, which could reach 125 and 135km/h respectively, followed in 1946 by a two-seater version with an open body which had the Supertesta Siata (special cylinder head). Perhaps the most famous Siata 500 was the Amica of 1939, a very elegant and original cabriolet with superior technical characteristics. It was produced in limited numbers and every car was personalised, becoming popular among people who demanded customized distinction.

Ten years later, following fashion trends, Siata commenced the series production of the Amica 49, a real sportscar which, in 1951, was also produced in very limited numbers for the American market, with a 721cc Crosley engine and three-speed gearbox.

TOPOLINO GOES RACING

It would be impossible to describe all the racing Topolinos, but the record breakers require a special mention. Raffaele Cecchini won four world titles in 1938 in the up to 500cc category. Another fast Topolino was the Supertesta Siata which at Monza, again in 1938, established the world record for 3000km in the 750cc category and the Italian twenty-four hour record for Class H.

Topolino cars competed successfully in the Mille Miglia. In 1937, a modified 500A won its class and a Siata Barchetta, modified and driven by Piero Dusio, won the up to 750cc sports category. A Topolino model managed to finish eighth in class at the Le Mans 24-Hours in 1938. In 1947, on the Montenero circuit of Livorno, Carlo Pesci won at the wheel of a single-seater Fiat 500 Siata, a similar car to the Cisitalia D46.

TOPOLINO RESTORATION

Steve Denning is a Topolino enthusiast who lives in South Wales, and is something of a UK authority on the little car. Steve knows the whereabouts of many of the Topolinos in the UK and reckons that there are about 100 left, though many are not running. He has five cars himself in varying condition; at the time of writing one of them was fully restored and operational. According to Steve, the Topolino "has a pace only marginally quicker than a professional racing cyclist, snail-like acceleration, is awkward to work on because of its diminutive size, and replacement parts that are breathtakingly expensive."

Original, new panels are now very rare, so the cost of restoration is high due to the reclamation of used panels or the fabrication of new ones. However, there are some reproduction parts around, namely floorpans, lower door sections and sills from Holland, and Topolino Casagrande which operates from Emmen-Waldibrücke in Switzerland. Run by Ezio Casagrande for the last thirty years,

A Topolino in action at the Mille Miglia retro event. A lot of miles to cover in a very small car.

this company seems to be the world source for Topolino parts, and spares for other rare cars, too.

Engine parts are also hard to find, in particular new pistons and head gaskets. Topolino engines do wear out, not due to poor quality, but because they are only 570cc and are driven flat out most of the time. There is some good news in that kingpins can be made up, bearings are not a problem, brakes and clutches can be relined, and exhausts are made in Holland. Fortunately, Topolino windscreens are not a problem because the glass is flat and is relatively easy to make up. Tyres can be obtained via sources in Uruguay or, nearer to home, from the Citroën 2CV.

Topolino values, like most old small cars, are determined by condition. The very best cars will cost between £8000 and £9000, while working cars are worth around £4000. Restoration projects will be less than £1000.

500B GIARDINIERA TEST DRIVE

Collector Loris Crispino, founder of the Club Amici del Topolino Milano, owns a very rare 500B Giardiniera 'woody'. The model was only in production for seven months and it is thought that just 70 were built. In March 1949, the extensively restyled 500C series arrived, with an all-steel-bodied estate, called the Belvedere, replacing the 'woodie' in 1951. It took Crispino 25 years to find a 500B Giardiniera as they are extremely rare, with only seven or eight thought to still exist. The Giardiniera is Crispino's eighth Topolino and was bought, already largely restored, in January 2004. He has now finished it off completely, and it is a superb example.

This particular version of the Giardiniera was available in six metallic colours – unusual for inexpensive cars in the 1940s. As well as this 'beige' metallic, other choices were amaranto (dark red) and grey or green, light or dark. Even the wipers were painted in body colour – unique to the 500B. The wooden battens are ash and the panels are unglamorous hardboard. Behind each front wheel, badges proclaim 'Fiat Torino Lingotto, carrozzeria speciale', and the bodywork was certainly inspired – possibly even made – by coachbuilders Viotti, who specialised in 'woody' estates. The paired rear lights in the centre of the tailgate are original, while the lower, outer units were added in 1959 to comply with new Italian regulations. Local summers were catered for by fresh air vents either side, in front of the 'suicide' doors, and by the full-length sunroof. Catching the eye, too, are the mechanical indicators in their neat housings on the screen pillars and the two louvred panels on the bonnet, both of which hinge open to reveal, respectively, the petrol tank – complete with beautifully machined brass cap – and the fuel and oil-gauge senders.

The smart interior is narrow, but with the engine in front of the axles, there is plenty of legroom. The driving position is comfortable and there is a light and airy feel to the interior. Everything the driver needs is easily accessible, though the 110km/h speedometer is cleverly sited at the passenger end of the painted dash, where the parallax error convinces you you're going faster than you actually are. In the back, the simple folding bench seat boasts a stylish-looking chrome folding mechanism.

The engine starts easily and ticks over quietly and not at all like its frantic twin-cylinder successor. On the move, the Topolino is surprisingly quiet and refined for so basic and ancient a machine. It rides well, even over paved surfaces, and feels nicely responsive, with very direct steering giving crisp turn-in and a good lock. The pedals are light, the brakes reassuring and the gearbox, with four speeds in a conventional H, generally easy to use.

TOPOLINO HOT ROD

The Fiat Topolino might seem an unlikely candidate for customisation, but one UK hot rod enthusiast decided that's exactly what he would do.

Although very cute, the original Topolino had a maximum speed only marginally quicker than a racing cyclist with acceleration measured more in minutes than seconds. This car is much quicker than that.

Peterborough-based Simon Glenn has been building hot rods for many years and also has a passion for Italian cars that was passed down from his father who had also owned a Topolino. By day, Simon is a design technology teacher as well as a talented engineer. In his spare time Simon builds hot rods.

Simon purchased a sorry-looking Topolino in 1989 which was little more than a shell with some boxes of parts. The car was one of those often dreamed about barn finds and was also fortunate in having retained its original registration number. This modified mouse is not a hugely tuned V8-engined street machine but is fitted with a more sensible 140bhp Alfa Romeo GTV 2.0 Twin Spark. This was coupled to the Alfetta drive train using a shortened prop shaft and the rear-mounted transaxle.

At the time of writing, the Topolino's revival had taken about thirteen years to get to this stage, but like all projects there are always elements to improve and details to finish. The mechanical layout, which offers an ideal weight distribution, does have some practical problems. For example, the transaxle sits very high up in the chassis which has forced the seats to be mounted well off the floor. This means that the driver's head is very likely to touch the roof on uneven roads. Currently, the Topolino sits on Alfa steel wheels, but a set of Fiat Coupé Turbo alloys with remachined offsets are planned.

The chassis was built from scratch by Simon as the original just would not have coped with the modifications. It feels very solid and in a straight line the car goes rapidly as the power to weight ratio is very favourable. More surprisingly, the car actually corners rather well, with a minimal amount of body-roll. There are still some adjustments to be made to the camber of the front wheels but, on the whole, the car is very well set up.

The body is mostly original 1937 Fiat steel and not fibreglass. The front wings are original, just widened, and the rear arches are from a VW Beetle but again widened to take the wide 15in rear wheels. The doors are Topolino but from a later car as the originals were beyond repair.

Just for fun. This eyecatching custom Topolino has two-litre Alfa Romeo twin-cam power.

Under the bonnet, the 2-litre Alfa power unit fills the engine bay. This engine was a second choice as an Alfa V6 was originally sourced for the project but was later sold to pay for other parts. The twin-cam engine breathes through twin 40mm carburettors and uses a Ford Popular radiator for cooling – the Topolino radiator would have sat behind the engine, fairly useless for a modern 140bhp engine.

All door handles and instrument detailing inside were cast in aluminium by Simon. The solid mounted nudge bars were also homemade and were cut from steel boiler plate machined smooth, and chromed – a mammoth task when you look at the thickness of them.

If the reader performs a search on the internet for Topolino Dragster, a plethora of interesting links from car clubs to enthusiasts' pages will be found and, of course, the hot rods which are very popular in America and Australia. The bodies vary in size and shape as do the engines. Some of

It might not suit the purist but it is cleverly engineered and attracts lots of attention.

these cars are amazing but one thing they have in common, apart from being out and out racers, is that they no longer use Italian engines. Simon Glenn's Topolino is refreshing in that it is almost entirely Italian and very well engineered, too.

FIAT 600

a fresh approach

Post-war Italy saw a rapid development in the Fiat empire, which was mainly funded by loans from America to repair its bomb-damaged factories. The main driving force behind this rebirth was Vittorio Valletta, who became president of Fiat following the death of Senator Agnelli in December 1945. From 1948, Fiat assumed a major role in the Italian economy, playing a decisive part in the development of the country.

Destined to become a decisive figure in the history of Fiat, Valletta studied in Turin, taking his degree from the Scuola Superior di Commercio in

1909. On the staff of Giovanni Broglia, he started a university career but simultaneously enjoyed some important professional successes: as the expert defence witness for Giovanni Agnelli and Fiat who were accused of false balance sheets in a trial in 1912, he played a significant part in winning their absolution. In 1921, he entered Fiat: he was invited to succeed Broglia as Executive Vice President for administration, but his role was actually much more extensive, starting with reorganisation of the plants after occupation. His great ability took him rapidly up the management ladder: in 1928 he was General Manager and Managing Director in 1939. Purged and dismissed from Fiat after liberation, he returned 10 months later: he was nominated Chairman, and became the architect of the company's reconstruction and its great expansion. Valletta also guided Fiat, a protagonist of the Italian economic miracle, towards the markets of the East. He resigned in 1966, and later that year he was nominated Life Senator.

During this period of prosperity, Valletta was able to repay the American loans. To capitalise on the American offer of aid, Fiat officials went off to visit General Motors, Ford and Chrysler to see how the Americans built their cars. Armed with new knowledge on mass production techniques, Turin's Mirafiori factory was transformed into the most modern in Europe.

However intellectually stimulating, the multi-storey Lingotto building imposed an excessively rigid manufacturing cycle. Once it had achieved an output of three hundred cars a day, the Lingotto could handle no further expansion in demand. That was why, in the 1930s, the Fiat management started to discuss a ground floor, horizontal factory organised around the final assembly line, the aim being to simplify the flow of material around the plant and make those flows as direct as possible.

Vittorio Valetta. Fiat's Chairman from 1946 to 1966.

The idea was to achieve total coordination between all the various lines and internally on each individual line. In other words, the same approach as the Lingotto's but improved to go beyond the limitations of that earlier experiment. The designers aimed to minimise the transportation of materials in the course of the machining process and to achieve a seamless, uniform, uninterrupted flow of production.

The basic layout involved three car assembly lines with mechanical processing lines set parallel to each other and at right angles to the assembly line. Meanwhile, all these lines were to be arranged in a sequence that reflected the sequential delivery of subassemblies to the line. That horizontal factory concept was to develop into the Mirafiori plant which was officially opened in 1939. The figures were genuinely impressive for their day: a site covering 1,000,000 square metres housing an array of workshops covering 300,000 square metres; 22,000 workers in two shifts; its own power station and outdoor test track.

Production of the new 500 was immediately transferred from Lingotto to the new plant, but then World War II broke out, slashing car production as Fiat converted, as it had in World War I, to military vehicles. After the war, Mirafiori began to be used as originally planned but expanded by the addition of Mirafiori South to reach the impressive size of 1,200,000 square metres under cover. By 1967, Mirafiori was employing 54,000 people and had become a city within the city of Turin. Manufacturing was also reorganised, Mirafiori was automated by the introduction of transfer lines that were gradually extended throughout the plant. There were 110km of the lines in 1962 and 223km in 1968.

With a range composed of four main models (the 500, 600, 110 and 1400, the latter also available with a 1900cc engine), Fiat had finally endowed itself with a manufacturing facility that could turn out the volumes required to bring mass motoring to Italy. By 1960, Mirafiori was turning out 2000 completed cars a day, a figure that rose to 4000 in 1965 after the launch of the 850, and to 5000 in 1967.

Back in 1948, when Mirafiori was upgraded, new design offices were also set up for Dante Giacosa who was gearing up to replace the 500C. Ultimately, the 500C would be replaced by two cars, one a four-seater, the 600 and the other a two-seater, the Nuova 500. The 500C was a two-seater, although a larger passenger carrying capacity was available in the form of the 500C Giardiniera with its wood and masonite coachwork. It was a successful car and sold well but its construction was not suited to the emerging techniques of mass production.

With mass production came the monocoque chassis which cut down the amount of time, manpower, materials and cost that it took to construct a complete car. The decision to discard the separate chassis and body construction was a milestone in Fiat's history and one that required Giacosa to convince Agnelli, who believed that the most sensible technical and commercial policy was to copy the successful developments of the older and more experienced foreign companies. Since the Americans were world leaders in car production at the time, and most of their cars had a chassis, Giacosa, who was a supporter of the load bearing coachwork system, had a hard time. Cost and the fact that a chassis-less construction method was ideal for small cars, won the day.

Giacosa's brief was to produce a small four-seater car that would not exceed the weight of the two-seater 500 using a 'radical' new build concept. With this apparently technically impossible task in mind, Giacosa set about his challenge. However, now that he could use the new style of construction, he soon found that his new car would be lighter, stronger, more space-efficient and it seems above all, cheaper to build.

To maximise interior space, it was decided that the engine and transmission would have to be all in the front or all in the rear of the new car. The new series of cars would be designated the Type 100.

Other projects in progress at this time were the 101 and 102 series, which would later become the 1100 and 1400 saloon ranges. It is worth noting that to rationalise Fiat's model designations '1' would be used for automobiles, '2' for trucks, '3' for coaches, '4' for town buses, and later '5' for tractors and '6' for engines with special purposes.

Tests were carried out on the '102' series of prototypes and one of them, the '102E2' looked promising. It had a four-cylinder water-cooled engine and front-wheel drive. Valletta had misgivings about front-wheel drive and decided that while research into the concept would continue, efforts should be directed into producing a more 'orthodox' vehicle.

Giacosa was left with the decision to choose where the engine was to be placed and carried out a number of tests in order for him to arrive at a satisfactory conclusion. It was known at the time that there was a noise problem with chassis-less

FIAT 600

In Giacosa's pursuit of maximising the 600's interior space, the engine was mounted behind the rear axle line.

eliminated the need for an inlet manifold by casting it as part of the cylinder head. To maximise interior space, the engine was mounted longitudinally behind the gearbox and transmission, and the radiator placed at the side of the engine instead of directly behind it. This required the water pump to also be mounted alongside the engine and the end of its impellor shaft was employed to run the cooling fan. Hot air from the radiator was channelled into the car for heating and demisting purposes, so a separate heater radiator was not required.

It was decided that a 570cc engine would be underpowered, so capacity of 633cc was decided upon that developed 22bhp. This simple and reliable engine design was to power millions of cars and be developed for use in the subsequent Fiat 850, Autobianchi A112 and Fiat 127 models.

Every detail of the 100 was new, including the transverse leaf independent front suspension later used on the 126 and on the rear of the 128. A simple transleaf design was adopted because it doubled up as an anti-roll bar, and it saved on construction and running costs.

Much consideration was given to the weight distribution of the 600. On the plus side, the rear-engined layout assists by not affecting the centre of gravity when the number occupants is a varied. The headlamps also maintain a level beam. However, the handling is affected and oversteer becomes a problem. Giacosa spent much effort in keeping the roll centre as low as possible by designing in-board driveshaft couplings and developing the steering and suspension geometry. Intended to benefit the safe handling of the car, this work was ultimately to be useful when competition-minded people chose the 600 as a basis for a racing car.

While the 600 project was underway, Fiat was continuing its research on marine and aircraft engines. The G80, Italy's first jet aircraft, was produced in 1951; while the

cars, which was exaggerated by a front-mounted engine and especially if it was air-cooled. The decisive element turned out to be cost.

Although the front-wheel drive arrangement was attractive because of the perceived technical advantages, it would have needed a much bigger body and the intended economy model would prove to be too expensive. Also, at this time, CV joint technology for front-wheel drive installation was in its infancy and efficient reliable units would also have been an unacceptable cost. So, the new car was to be rear-wheel drive and rear-engined.

An air-cooled engine was first considered because of its practical nature. Giacosa looked at a twin-cylinder unit with a wide, space-saving V of 150 degrees. A working prototype car was built and was even fitted with an automatic gearbox. However, inefficient combustion, heat deformities and sheer lack of development time led to this design being dropped.

The brief of the project 100 engine was to be a 570cc water-cooled unit made of the smallest number of parts, producing 16bhp and have a top speed of 88km/h in a body weighing about 515kg.

Giacosa set about designing his new engine using the smallest possible number of parts. He even

FIAT 600

An illustration of how to fill interior space – and everyone seems to be having a nice time.

The Multipla found its vocation as a people carrier and was adopted as a taxi for use in many of Italy's narrow city streets.

with rear-wheel drive, and a car that offered comfortable seating for four people at a cost of 590,000 lire – about £4000 at the time of writing.

Fiat celebrated the start of mass production in Italy with a multi-coloured cavalcade of 600s through the streets of Turin. A year later, the six-seater Multipla arrived. Fiat 600s were to be made under licence throughout the world and collectively over 4,000,000 were produced.

FIAT 600D

Fiat introduced the 600D in the autumn of 1960, which incorporated mechanical and body changes compared with its predecessor. Up to 1960,

company broke new ground with the prototype of a turbine-powered car and with its work in the field of nuclear technology. In 1956, the Fiat G91 was chosen for production as a NATO tactical fighter aircraft.

In Spring 1953, the first Fiat equipped with a diesel engine (the 1400) rolled off the assembly line. By the middle of the year, the final version of the 100 project was nearing completion and work was then concentrated on producing a 'familiare' version which was to become the Multipla. Giacosa had put so much time and effort into the saloon version that he had not considered the complications of creating an estate version of a rear-engined car. To solve the problem, he moved the driving position forward and over the front wheels, thus creating a very compact vehicle that could carry six people. Was this the first MPV?

The 100 project became the '600' at the Geneva Show in 1955, replacing the two-seater Topolino and even selling at a lower price. Dante Giacosa had fulfilled his design brief and had created the first Fiat to have a rear-mounted engine

production of the 600 had exceeded 890,000. The major changes in the 600D were an increase in engine capacity to 767cc and a different final drive ratio. Performance was considerably improved. Bodywork modifications included the addition of swivelling quarter lights on the doors and a large number of louvres on the engine cover. Multipla and Taxi versions acquired the same changes. From 1964, the 600D was produced with front-hinged doors.

FIAT 600D FINAL SERIES

From the time of the 1965 Turin Show, the 600D incorporated further modifications. A new fuel tank with a capacity of 311 litres (6.8 gallons), larger headlamps, a new badge on the front panelling

FIAT

Including licenced production, over 4,000,000 Fiat 600s were built. Though few original cars survive today, many live on as Abarth replicas.

At the time of writing, panel availability was still reasonable, but is in decline. Original panels are becoming scarce and are no longer in production. There were parts available from Zastava, floorpans in particular, but following recent hostilities in the Eastern Bloc it is reported that most of this has been destroyed. South America may be a possible source but transportation costs will make parts extremely expensive. Middle Barton Garage, who have converted many 600s to 850TC specification, suggest that some original panels are being stored by racing drivers in case they need them to repair accident damage.

Lighting is becoming another problem, especially for UK-owned cars, because of the lack of right-hand drive headlight units. Laminated windscreens are still available but front and rear bumpers are hard to source. Reproduction exhausts systems are still available.

From a servicing point of view, the 600's brakes are difficult to maintain. Although the drum brakes can be relined, setting them to work efficiently requires four different adjustments to be carried out. With alloy drums on the rear and cast iron on the front, problems with seized components caused by dissimilar metal corrosion have to be overcome. Single circuit brake master cylinders are now unobtainable.

The best prospect for ownership is the 600D, anything pre-1960 is mechanically inferior and really not worth the effort. For example, the original 633cc engine was quite weak and did not have the benefit of a counter-balanced crankshaft. The later 767cc engine was much more robust and more practical to tune for increased performance. Starter motor access is difficult on this power unit.

Care should be taken with the engine's cooling system which is governed by a wax thermostat that is prone to failure. This seizes and the car will never warm up at one extreme or overheat at the other. Carburation was by Weber, Holly or Solex units and

and the elimination of the bright trim on the sides were accompanied by the elimination of the cartridge type oil filter so that oil filtering depended on the centrifugal filter.

RESTORATION ADVICE

The 600 was a better car than the later 500, it was stronger, bigger and had the benefit of a 'proper' four-cylinder water-cooled engine. Unfortunately, the body build quality suffered, mainly because it was built to a cost, necessary for a cheap economical car intended for owners with limited means. Today, the 600 is not as fashionable as the cheeky 500 and often the primary interest in the model is its suitability for conversion into a replica of the Abarth 850TC.

In 2006, a working 600 in good overall condition could be worth between £3000 and £3500. Restored examples, which are quite rare, would only be worth about £4500, so the reader can see that there is little equity in restoring a standard 600. However, an 850TC replica based on a donor 600 would be valued at between £6000 and £8000. This might seem like a more attractive proposition although the cost of an uprated engine, chassis, and suspension components adds considerably to the overall build cost.

are generally efficient, except that Solex parts are now unobtainable.

The 600D gearbox is quite strong, though parts are now rare. As with the Fiat 500, care should be taken when selecting first gear to avoid excessive wear and double declutching up and down the ratios is advisable. The transmission is also robust and well-engineered with boots and couplings still available. Steering boxes can be reconditioned but right-hand drive steering idlers are now scarce.

THE FIAT 600 AND CARLO ABARTH

Carlo Abarth was quick to adopt the Fiat 600 as a basis for his own tuned version. Soon after the launch of the 600 at the Geneva Show in 1955, Abarth launched the 210A Boano Spider which used the 600's structure and an uprated 32bhp engine.

In 1956, Abarth used the production 600 bodyshell to produce the Fiat Abarth 750GT, which was the first model in a long and successful run of 600-based cars. By increasing the bore and stroke of the engine from 60mm x 56mm to 61mm x 64mm, Abarth was able to achieve 747cc which allowed the power unit to be tuned to 47bhp. This engine was to be used in many Abarth cars with various body styles created by the Carrozzeria of the day including Bertone, Viotti and Vignale.

Abarth developed a twin-cam cylinder head for the 747cc engine and was later to extend this through various capacities including 847cc to 982cc, thus introducing models carrying the titles 850TC and 1000 Bialbero.

Fairly soon Carlo Abarth found that he wanted more than just a modified stock base and cast around for someone who would collaborate on the production of a complete car utilising the 600 underpinnings and 747cc engine. The task went to Zagato who had to overcome the difficulty of designing a coupé body on the tiny 2000mm wheelbase chassis. Another problem was the elimination of height which is the enemy of any two-door short-wheelbase shape. The result was the 'Derivazione 750' which was an aerodynamic coupé which debuted at Monza in 1956, This tiny aluminium-bodied car weighed just 535kg compared to the production 600's 895kg. Not surprisingly, it was very fast with its 150km/h top speed and won many races. They were reliable, too, as Abarth & C. were to discover when they drove one round Monza for 72 hours covering 6000 miles at over 5500rpm.

Zagato kept the roof-line low and added

Carlo Abarth – an Austrian born under the Scorpio starsign.

a sloping nose that balanced out the rear of the car. The first prototypes appeared in late 1955 and by the end of the model's life in 1959, there had been three distinct series. By early 1956, production was under way and one of these early cars with smooth roof, chrome surrounds to the upright exposed headlights, and no quarter panel vents took second in class on that year's Mille Miglia.

It was discovered that the interior headroom was too restrictive, so the second series cars were provided with two roof bubbles which had become a Zagato trademark. The definitive Series 3 Abarth 750 had more pronounced bubbles, 7in headlights with plastic covers set higher in the wings, 5in tail-lights and bumper overriders. Alloy Amadori wheels were optional.

When Fiat introduced its 600D in 1960, it had an increased capacity of 767cc. Abarth also used this unit and enlarged it to 982cc for use in the 60bhp Monomille Coupé of 1962 and 66bhp 1000 Berlina Corsa of 1963. From 1964, Abarth focussed his attention on the new Fiat 850 range.

600

Abarth 850TC Nürburgring – a quart out of a pint pot.

ABARTH BY VIGNALE

On the Abarth stand at the 1956 Geneva Show stood a small prototype painted in cream and blue and fitted with gull-wing doors. With its abbreviated nose and long tail it soon acquired the name of goccia or teardrop. Designed by Michelotti and built by Vignale, it was an attempt to attract Abarth's attention as they were considering becoming a car constructor. As it happened, Abarth opted for Zagato to build his Derivazione 750.

It has now been established that three of these Vignale cars were produced, the gull-winged prototype and two others built with conventional doors. The latter were used by Abarth to research aerodynamics where Dott. Avidano, Carlo's right-hand man, put much work into developing the Sperimentales as they had become named. The chassis were the same as the Abarth 750 with

Mighty Mouse. A famous ex-works 1000 TCR roars around Monza.

Blue is not a colour normally associated with Abarths but it looks very smart on this 750 'double bubble' Zagato.

modified transverse leaf spring at the front and a wishbone/coil set-up at the rear. Both cars were involved in the tests, with speed being the main criterion, "after which can come reliability", said Mafiodi, Abarth's chief tester at the time. In fact, 150km/h was achieved on the Turin-Milan autostrada by the first car fitted with the 41.5bhp 750 engine. The second received a 46bhp Mille Miglia Gran Turismo Speciale

One of the three Vignale-built 750 Zagatos with bizarre push-me-pull-you styling.

photographed by the author at the Vernasca Silver Flag hillclimb near Piacenza and it has appeared at several Italian shows and events. The whereabouts of the 1956 Geneva car are unknown.

ABARTH BY ALLEMANO

Another Torinese coachbuilder was Allemano. The company entitled Allemano & Tricò, Carrozzeria per Automobili, was founded in 1927 by Serafino Allemano and its early activities were mainly repairs. The firm was transformed in 1935 and dedicated to the construction of special bodies on Italian and foreign chassis, including collaboration with the Japanese

unit which raised top speed first, to 178km/h and then, finally, to 182km/h, but there were problems. Whilst the short nose was very efficient, it was creating a low pressure area over the rear of the car and allowed the air to flow straight over the top of the engine bay causing the unit to overheat. So the Sperimentale was very fast, but not for long. Suspension settings were difficult to finalise and aerodynamics meant that the wing shapes had to be altered. According to Mafiodi, the cars were always quick in a straight line but did not work well in corners.

To get air into the back it was decided to reshape the front. A new windscreen would be needed. It hasn't been recorded quite how the team decided an Alfa Giulietta SS rear window would be just the thing. However, it worked well along with an enlarged air scoop on the engine cover. It was all for nothing, though, as suddenly work ceased and the Sperimentales were consigned to history. In retrospect, this was probably the result of Carlo deciding to pursue the Zagato route.

The cars disappeared into obscurity until, in the early 1980s, a UK Abarth enthusiast purchased one of them that had turned up for sale in Malta. A second car, owned by an Italian collector, was

This superb Abarth 750 Allemano is run by the Aumüllor family, prominent Abarth experts in Germany.

Fuji Motor Company for whom it built two prototypes. Allemano's main period of development was after the Second World War, and it built numerous models for Fiat, Lancia, Renault, Panhard, Ferrari, Maserati, and ATS. The company closed in 1964.

Allemano were one of the few coachbuilders who managed to build a vehicle on the 600 chassis that didn't look like a toy car. Manufactured in

1959, the Abarth 850 Coupé is easily confused with the later Fiat 850s and actually has an engine of just 833cc instead of 847cc. Rated at 52bhp, this is a relatively high output for a road car of this period. The engine is an Abarth unit with special connecting rods, crankshaft and pistons. It has big valves, a lightweight flywheel and oversized carburettor. Though built by Allemano, the steel body was actually designed by Michelotti. The doors, bonnet and engine cover are aluminium. Its 52bhp is developed at 6000rpm, and with a kerb weight of just 600kg, it's not surprising that the top speed was 160km/h.

A group of original and replica Abarths gathered together for Auto Italia *magazine's group test.*

FIAT 600 GROUP TEST

Carlo Abarth's hot 600s are sought after and very expensive if a genuine one comes up for sale, which they rarely do. It is not surprising then that numerous replicas have been built for fast road use and many are raced to good effect in historic club circuit racing and hillclimbs. *Auto Italia* magazine tested four versions based on the 600, two were genuine Abarth cars, another was a replica racer and the final one a restored road car rebuilt using contemporary parts. All the cars exceeded the original 600's 0-60mph time of 54 seconds and 22bhp by a very wide margin.

CAR 1

A white 850 TC competition car made by Abarth & C in 1964. Prepared by Middle Barton Garage, this left-hand drive car was in excellent condition. Its 52bhp engine had remarkable torque characteristics making it easy to drive. The single-choke carburettor helped gas flow at low rpm. An additional front-mounted water radiator and open engine cover aided cooling, together with an engine-driven fan which constantly cooled the standard rear radiator.

With a low-mounted race seat and big steering wheel, the sitting position was 'arms-high' with poor forward visibility below the wheel rim. For purely competition use, the low sitting position was understandable but it was very uncomfortable and impractical when driving the car on the road. At low speeds, the 850TC was safe enough, but at higher speeds cornering capability was extremely limited. The ancient front suspension design combined with the rear-heavy weight distribution destroyed turn-in. The slow steering ratio (3.5 turns) and 4.5 x 13in Dunlop Racing tyres didn't work very well, especially on the road.

CAR 2

This car was an extremely rare Abarth 850TC SS built in 1961 and was one of the last early cars as it

A genuine 850 TC built by Abarth & C in Corse Marche in 1964. Though it only had 52bhp, the torque was remarkable.

One of only 10 examples of the 850 TCSS built in 1961. This is an original right-hand drive 'suicide door' example supplied to UK importers Anthony Crook.

This highly-modified car was also right-hand drive, which is an advantage for circuit racing. Its body had been strengthened, lightened, widened, lengthened and lowered. Despite the addition of a full roll cage, fire system, front-mounted oil and water radiators and various other racing equipment, the car still had a dry weight of just 585kg. The 982cc Abarth engine produces 100bhp and breathes through two huge 40 DCOE Webers. The gearbox is a five-speed unit and the transmission is fitted with a limited slip differential. Front suspension is double wishbone with adjustable dampers and an anti-roll bar. The whole machine sits on 5.5 and 7 x 13in Campagnolo wheels.

Of Car 3, *Auto Italia* magazine's test driver, Roberto Giordanelli, said, "It's like a car, only smaller". By placing a human complete with full-face helmet into this historic racer, there was not much room for anything else. The 100bhp motor was an all-or-nothing 9000rpm screamer which made the car very difficult to get off the line and hard to drive. It was not happy below 5000rpm. The test revealed the car's good grip but did not allow the driver to lift-off near the limit without the risk of a spin. The

has 'suicide' doors. It is one of only ten TC SSs made by Abarth & C and the only genuine right-hand drive car built. Formerly used by Anthony Crook, the then UK Abarth importer, its history, originality and documentation are backed up by letters from the late Carlo Abarth. Standing on its original 4.5 x 13in steel wheels, it has a narrow look compared with the other cars that took part in the test. Still fitted with a single-choke Solex PBIC 32 carburettor, the SS had a higher engine specification than the TC and felt noticeably more powerful and very responsive. The turn-in problem of the white TC is still there with the ivory SS, but reduced and helped, no doubt, by the Michelin MX 135 x 12in tyres.

CAR 3
At the time of the test, black Car 3 was owned and built by Tony Castle-Miller of Middle Barton Garage. It was reshelled in 1987 following a racing accident, and is built to 1966 Abarth 1000 TCR Series 1 specification. In 600 Abarth parlance, 'TC' stands for Testa Corsa and the 'R' for Radiale. In other Abarth applications, 'TC' is an abbreviation for Turismo Competizione.

Built up from a road-going Fiat 600, this replica 850 TC was successfully campaigned for many years by Middle Barton Garage.

wishbone front suspension gave much better turn-in characteristics compared to the other test cars. With only 100bhp (sudden) and low weight, tyre scrub during cornering slowed the vehicle dramatically, and needed a clever driving style to get the most from it.

CAR 4

Restored by Roberto Giordanelli from a remarkably sound 40 year-old shell, this 600 was intended to be used as everyday transport. Rather than using all-original and costly Abarth parts, the intention was to create a

This Panda-engined car was created for everyday use by journalist and engineer Roberto Giordanelli.

car that was in character but was also practical. A 903cc pushrod engine was sourced from a Fiat Panda which fitted straight into the 600's engine bay. It was rebuilt with many new parts including an Abarth cam, twin-choke carburettor and an OMP exhaust system. The head was skimmed and ported, the bores were honed, new piston rings fitted, new bearings, new timing chain and sprockets were also fitted. A rolling road check showed 70+bhp at the flywheel.

Extra engine cooling was required and provided by an under-the-bumper front-mounted radiator and a thermostatically-controlled electric fan for the reconditioned rear-mounted radiator (the original fan was mechanical). An interior override switch and warning light was comforting without having to resort to extra instrumentation which would be out of character. Early trials revealed that the carburettor needed cooler air. Since the car was to be used with the engine lid closed, cool air was ducted to the Weber twin-choke from under the car.

The front brake drums were converted to discs with a larger brake master cylinder. Just about every other brake component was checked or replaced. Wheel bearings, track rod ends, suspension bushes – all were dealt with. Uprated and slightly lower Abarth springs were fitted with 30 per cent uprated dampers. The wheelarches were carefully and precisely reshaped in steel to neatly accommodate 5.5 x 13in period alloy wheels with low profile 175/50VR13 Pirelli

P7000 tyres (safe to 200mph), providing grip that was only bettered by Car 3, the 1000 TCR racer.

The finished car worked reasonably well in London traffic, although speed bumps had to be treated with care to avoid wiping off the front-mounted radiator. It was soon found that the gearing was too low. First gear was almost pointless and a taller crown wheel, obtained from Middle Barton Garage, finally cured the problem. 0-50mph time (8 seconds) was slashed by 27 seconds and the 0-60mph time was reduced from several minutes down to 13 seconds. With the correct gearing fitted, 100+mph top speed would be attainable. Compared with modern machinery, engine and transmission noise were high, especially at speed.

By 1950's standards, handling was excellent and adequate by modern standards. The steering was surprisingly low-geared for such a light car, requiring 3.25 turns lock-to-lock. With a good lock in such a short wheelbase, parking and manoeuvring was a pleasure. Like an early Porsche 911, very hard cornering was first met with understeer followed by sudden lift off oversteer. With all that rubber, big brakes and little weight, the converted car had excellent stopping capability.

Roberto Giordanelli drove the car regularly for a while and it was found that the car attracted great attention and approval from on-lookers. However, concerns over damaging the 600 relegated it to special occasions only.

FIAT MILLECENTO

every Italian's family car in the 1950s

To trace the family tree of the 1950s Fiat 1100 we must go back to 1937 when a revised Balilla, the 508C, was introduced with an uprated 1089cc 32bhp engine. A version of this engine would subsequently be fitted to the Nouva 1100, to become popularly known as the Millecento. The 508C was replaced in 1939 when the first version of the original 1100 was introduced, which was effectively a 508C but with a new corporate grille. Numerous versions were produced including a berlina, cabriolet and one with a long wheelbase.

It was back in 1946 that plans for the Nuova 1100 were laid down, and to differentiate it from the old model it had the numbers 103 added to its description, hence 1100-103. Dante Giacosa's attention to the new model was diverted by several other projects including the 1400, the first project he was wholly responsible for, the 8V (project 104) and the off-road Campagnola (project 105).

Early considerations were given to installing the proposed new car with a 944cc V4 power unit and front-wheel drive, but Giacosa ran out of development time on this interesting concept and defaulted to the tried and tested in-line four-cylinder engine driving the rear wheels. Later, Ford Germany were to 'borrow' Giacosa's idea when it built its V4 Taunus 12M.

A great deal of development went into the 1100-103 with much emphasis placed on keeping the weight down to a minimum. A batch of 50 cars was set aside for final road testing so that the car would be thoroughly sorted by the time of the launch.

The Nuova 1100 was introduced at the Geneva Motorshow in 1953. Despite similar mechanics to the old 1100, the 1100-103 was effectively a new car. The body was all new, using a monocoque, or load bearing construction. The rest was conventional, with the in-line four-cylinder 1089cc engine (36bhp) driving the rear wheels through a four-speed gearbox with a column-mounted shift. Two versions were produced at the launch with different levels of trim and a choice of separate or bench front seats. Overall bodyweight was 810kg and 825kg respectively. Performance was much more lively than the old 1100 and the 1100-103 was quickly considered to be a 'drivers' car', in fact, Giacosa received congratulations from none other than Enzo Ferrari himself.

Later in 1953, at the Paris Motorshow, Fiat released the 103 TV (Turismo Veloce) with a modified engine now producing

Despite Dante Giacosa's reservations about the dimensions of the 1100, over 1.5 million found buyers.

50bhp. Various details were changed, including the trim and a new front grille (incorporating a central foglight), and the bodywork was finished in a special two-tone paint scheme. A coupé was also built by Pininfarina based on the TV.

The following year an estate version was introduced – the 'Familiare'. This was mechanically identical to the saloon with the exception of the tyres. The 103 TV Trasformabile, a spider with a completely new body, emerged at the Geneva Motorshow in 1955. The first series of the 1100-103 continued in production until 1956, by which time a total of over 250,000 had been built.

An 1100D Station Wagon ready for family fun. This version was fitted with the 1221cc engine.

The first major revision to the 1100 range came in 1956 with the release of the second series car, the 103E. This was available in saloon, TV, 'Familiare' and trasformabile versions. A revised engine (power up to 40bhp and 53bhp in the TV) was fitted, the bodywork was modified including a new front

Built from 1956 to 1957, the 1100 TV had a higher trim specification with power increased from 50bhp to a heady 53bhp.

grille. The rear suspension was slightly revised and various smaller detail changes were also made. These models were only produced until 1957, about 115,000 being built.

The next version was the 103D, launched in October 1957. The TV and Trasformabile models

were discontinued, replaced by versions of the Fiat 1200, while the engine in the saloon and estate was further improved to produce 43bhp. The body was significantly modified, with a longer boot (and thus longer overall length) and also included yet another design of grille, while the braking system was improved. The two-tone paint scheme also became available on the normal models. About 150,000 were built up until 1960.

In 1959, the 103D was launched alongside the 103H or 1100 'Lusso'. This was basically the same as the 103D saloon with a 50bhp engine and numerous changes to reflect the 'Lusso' tag. Yet another new grille was fitted. The 'Lusso' was built until 1960 and over 227,000 cars were produced.

Another revision took place in 1960 when the 1100 'Export' and 'Special' models were released (replacing both the 'D' and 'H' models), while the 'Familiare' continued in revised form. The engine in all versions was now a 55bhp (still 1089cc) unit, a while later, an

MILLECENTO

automatic clutch was also available in the 'Special'. The 'Export' and 'Familiare' had a very similar body style to the old 103D model, while the 'Special' had more angular lines. The mechanics followed the layout of the 103H.

In 1962, after 272,067 cars had been built, the next version emerged, the 1100D. Launched at the Turin Motorshow that year, a saloon and an estate were released, both with a more angular bodystyling taken mainly from the previous 'Special' but with a much 'cleaner' and less fussy front end. Despite continuing with the title '1100', a new 1221cc engine was now fitted, still generating 55bhp. These variants were produced for four years, during which about 332,000 were built.

The last version of the 1100 was the 1100R (for 'rinnovata' or 'refurbished'), released in February 1966. Many changes were made both to the mechanics and the bodywork. The main changes included the return to a 1089cc engine (with 48bhp) and the adoption of disc brakes at the front. About 341,000 examples of the saloon and the estate were built until 1969 when they were replaced by the new, front-wheel drive 128.

Though the Millecento was an obvious success with over 1.5 million vehicles produced, Dante Giacosa had his reservations about the car, feeling that some areas could have been improved had he had more development time. In particular, he felt that the width of the body was too narrow and that an extra eight to ten centimetres would have made the car more comfortable and attractive

Though Millecento production spanned 16 years, few examples have survived intact, but this one is alive and well in Turin.

– but then he was a perfectionist.

Like the Topolino, the mechanics of the 1100 were a convenient source of engines for competition car preparers. With little else to choose from in Italy during the 1950s, companies like Stanguellini, Ermini and Siata used these off-the-shelf engines as a basis for building highly-tuned and competitive power units. Indeed, there were race series created around the Millecento power unit, perhaps the most notable being Formula Junior single-seaters.

The stylish 1100 TV Trasformabile was launched in 1955 and became known as the 'Diavoletto' – little devil.

NUOVA 500

impudence on four wheels

At the time of its introduction in July 1957, the Fiat Nuova 500 had a folding roof panel that included the rear window.

had been built. However, everything came to an abrupt halt when the entire design facility, including the prototype, was destroyed in a devastating allied bombing raid. So the Topolino was destined to remain in production until 1955, by which time more than half a million had been sold. The Topolino would be a tough act to follow. Meanwhile, the 600 made its debut in 1955 with huge acclaim from the press

The car was not well-received by the Italian public. To make amends Fiat quickly increased power output and improved the trim level.

By the time Dante Giacosa became Assistant Director of Fiat's car division in 1940, he was already working on two possibilities for replacing the Topolino; a slightly larger model labelled the 700 and a smaller one called the 400. The 400 project was looking very hopeful; initial design and planning were complete, and a single prototype

At launch, the Fiat Nuova 500 was rated at a puny 13bhp at 4000rpm. The engine was air-cooled – a first for Fiat.

A rear-mounted, air-cooled engine would power the car, which would primarily be a two-seater with room in the back for children or luggage. Maximum weight was to be 375kg, fuel consumption about 60mpg, and attainable speed around 53mph. By the end of 1954, Giacosa was working on the details, finalising everything with the aim of testing prototypes within six months. However, the choice of engine was a problem, with each member of the management team rooting for their own solution to the problems of weight, noise and vibration. In the end, Giacosa's reputation and superior knowledge won through, and thoroughly practical solutions to the problems were found. All this procrastination had wasted a lot of time; it was 1956 before the go-ahead was given to begin production the following year. Prototypes were built and tested, and tragically, one of the test drivers was killed in an accident. There were many minor hitches and glitches, too, but Giacosa's team kept going with determination.

In July 1957, the motoring press headed for Turin for the press launch of the 500 Nuova. It was introduced to a tiny car – much smaller than the 600 – fitted with a rear-mounted, two-cylinder, air-cooled 479cc engine, and a four-speed gearbox with reverse. Comparisons with the much-loved Topolino were inevitable, but the newcomer came out rather well. Having made a good impression on the professionals, it was time for the baby Fiat to greet the public. This did not happen conventionally at a show, but by a procession through the streets of Turin.

It was impossible not to fall in love with the cute little shape, and the practicality of it. Its debut was a triumph, and Italy's motorists made a mental note to try out a Fiat 500 just as soon as they could. Unfortunately, all this euphoria did not convert to decent sales. Despite the extended time spent in development, the 500 still suffered severely from vibration, and performance was definitely not up to par. A rethink was in order – a quick rethink, too, for it would be essential to offer the public a better 500 at the Turin show that autumn. Fiat pulled out all the stops. The Nuova did indeed appear at the show, in the guise of the Normale, a much-modified and improved 500 with a price tag 5 per cent higher than the original. The first version was still available, as the Economy, although with the new 479cc 15bhp engine – its original 13bhp unit had been just too underpowered. Both cars were now more pleasant to drive, the Normale very much more so, and top speed increased to 56mph. Fiat took the opportunity to make some sensible improvements that helped the Normale cross that all-important line from crude to basic; windows that opened and upholstery on the rear seats being good examples. The plan

and public alike. It would continue in production until 1969, with sales topping 1.5 million.

Although the 400 would undoubtedly have made a worthy successor to Topolino, there were advantages in having to go back to the drawing board. Post-war Italy was a very different place. Of necessity, trends were towards inexpensive motoring. Scooters were selling in huge numbers, but were no good for families or for carrying loads. Microcars and bubble cars were popular, too, but suffered the same constraints as scooters. Having already completed the primary design work for the 600, Giacosa had a good idea of what would work – and, as importantly, what would not work – in terms of weight, layout and construction. As he intended the new car to be complementary to the 600 rather than its replacement, it is clear that his perception of it was rather different. The new project was known internally as 400 – it appeared that Giacosa was definitely thinking small. In fact, the new project had much in common with its pre-war namesake. The aim was to keep everything simple.

worked. A potential disaster was averted. At last, the Topolino had a replacement worthy of the Cinquecento title.

500 SPORT

Within a year of the launch, another model, the Sport, was added to the range. Its 499.5cc engine delivered 21.5bhp and proffered a top speed of a terrifying 68mph. With its distinctive colour scheme – grey with a broad red side-stripe – the Sport was soon living up to its name, with class wins at Hockenheim and rally successes to its credit, all within its first year. For extra strength the sunroof was omitted on the Sport, although a short sunroof was made available in 1959.

Power at last! The Nuova 500 Sport appeared in 1958 with its 21.5bhp 499.5cc engine.

The 500D was introduced in 1960 to replace the Sport. The fuel tank was reshaped to accommodate a fold-down rear seat.

500D

1960 was an important year for the 500 – out went the Trasformabile and Sport versions, while the Normale was renamed 500D. The major improvement was the adoption of the 499.5cc, 17.5bhp engine. This gave the car much more respectable performance, with top speed increasing to 60mph, and fuel consumption up to a still respectable 46mpg. Importantly, a folding rear-seat back was introduced, which made for increased load-carrying capacity, and the fuel tank was slightly reshaped to give more room up front. Apart from the enlargement of the exterior lights, there were few other changes, although later refinements brought an automatic interior light, windscreen washer, and changes to the instrument panel.

500 GIARDINIERA

At the same time, an estate version of the 500 was introduced, called the Giardiniera (Topolino's estate had been called this, too). Faced with the problems

Sunroofs also helped the other models shake off any lingering embarrassment caused by the false start; the Normale sported a short sunroof, while the Economy's full-length roll-back roof allowed it to transform into the more exotic Trasformabile. Many cars would not have survived the troubles that it had had to face, but the little 500's endearing character and practicality, along with the determination of its creator Dante Giacosa, saw it through.

The engine was laid on its side so that cargo could be loaded into the Giardiniera. This version was built by Autobianchi.

of the 500D by the 500F (what happened to the 500E?). Power was increased to 18bhp, but the major change was the fitting of front-hinged doors – not only safer, but also enabling the door pillars to be thinner and the windscreen deeper. These changes to the 500's outward appearance gave it a much more modern look, without changing its basic character. On the mechanical side, a modified driveshaft and improved clutch were fitted, and the heating system updated.

500L

Three years on, the 500F was joined by the 500L (L for Lusso). The outward differences on the L were subtle. Out went the Nuova 500 badge, since the 500 was no longer new, to be replaced with a discreet Fiat 500. Nudge bars adorned the front and rear, and chrome trim brightened the window surrounds and gutters. Radial tyres were standard, and the wheels were fitted with smart hubcaps. Instrumentation

of getting a quart into a pint pot, Giacosa came up with an inspired solution. He turned the engine on its side, and sited it under the floor area at the rear, where it was reached for maintenance through a hatch in the floor. Access to the large, flat luggage space was through a single, left-hinged rear door. Back seat passengers benefited from sliding rear windows and a long sunroof. The extra weight certainly made the Giardiniera not the quickest 500 around, but it was so practical that it soon became popular, especially with growing families and small businesses. The Giardiniera was produced until 1965, but reintroduced three years later with production passing to Autobianchi, by then part of the Fiat group.

500F

The next major change came in 1965 with the replacement

A nicely restored 500F poses on the Brooklands banked track and shows off its front-hinged doors.

Fiat produced the 500L in 1968 alongside the base model, where 'L' signified 'Lusso'.

594cc unit producing 23bhp. Inside, the 500R was very similar to the 500F, although many of the options from the L could be specified at extra cost. The front badge had now changed to the modern Fiat horizontal strip. The 126 didn't have the charisma of the 500 and was universally unloved during the early stages of its life. It is thought that the 500R was introduced to compensate for the 126's lack of acceptance by the Italian public, a case of giving the customer what they actually wanted. However, when the 126 began to gain ground in the market, sales of the 500R were affected and it did not sell in great numbers. The last unit rolled off the production line in 1975, by which time sales of the 500 had reached a staggering 3.4 million. However, the Giardiniera

was improved, with a fuel gauge fitted for the first time, a redesigned steering wheel, and a speedometer courtesy of the Fiat 850. The fascia was padded, carpets replaced rubber mats, map pockets nestled in the doors and leather was an option for the seats, which reclined. The downside of all this luxury was a 10 per cent higher price for the 500L over the more modest 500F. Together, these two models made a huge impact, offering between them the basics of practical motoring and a well-judged degree of luxury at a sensible premium.

500R

Both 500F and 500L were withdrawn in 1972, to be replaced by the 500R. This had a lot in common with a new Fiat arrival, the 126. The two cars shared a floorpan, and also an engine – a

The 500L had bumper extensions, new hubcaps, extra bright trim and a completely revised interior.

version soldiered on under the Autobianchi name until 1977.

In addition to its outstanding popularity when new, the 500 proved to be a sought-after second-hand choice, and is now a classic of its type. During its production lifetime, the 500 caught the attentions of numerous stylists, coachbuilders, and tuners that recognised its amazing potential. Autobianchi produced more luxurious versions which sold alongside the Fiats. The 500 went racing under the Abarth badge. Neckar (formerly NSU-Fiat) built versions geared specifically to the German market, while Steyr-Puch did the same in Austria. Ghia, Savio, Vignale, Giannini, Fervès, Moretti, Lombardi, Brutsch, Frua, Siata and Viotti – large or small, all were captivated by the little Fiat, and created their own versions from it – a compliment to Giacosa's vision and the 500's unique appeal.

This Abarth 595SS, with its distinctive livery, is immortalised as the subject of a Bburago 1:18 model.

FIAT 500s BY ABARTH
When the Fiat 500 was launched in the summer of 1957, it received a cool reception by the Italian public because of its basic nature and lack of power. Fiat responded quickly by increasing the car's 13bhp engine to 20bhp. Carlo Abarth immediately spotted an opportunity and introduced his own version in the autumn of the same year. Although Fiat had improved the 500's top speed performance from 53mph to 56mph, Abarth was able to extract enough power to run the car up to 62mph.

The coachbuilders also turned their attention to building versions of the 500 Abarth, notably Pininfarina and Zagato, the latter producing another fast, light coupé that was to win the 1958 Italian GT Championship for 500cc cars.

In 1963, Abarth introduced his 595 Berlina which had a capacity of 593cc, achieved by increasing the bore size from 67.4mm to 73.5mm. This substantially modified engine produced 30bhp and was available as a kit for owners to fit to their 500D Normale. A complete Abarth 595 Berlina cost 595,000 lire, only 145,000 lire more expensive than the standard Fiat 500D.

An Abarth 595SS version arrived in 1964, built on the 500D convertible bodyshell, it had a high

compression, and a 32bhp engine capable of propelling this little car to 130km/h. An alternative version, the 695 Berlina, was also available in the same year and was fitted with a less frantic, larger capacity 689cc engine developing 30bhp. In 1965, the model was revised and retitled 695SS, and incorporated some minor improvements including a larger carburettor and altered compression ratio.

When Fiat introduced its 500F in March 1965, Abarth created three versions the following year called the 595, 595SS and 595/34, each with differing performance characteristics to suit owners' requirements. This model is identified in having rearward opening doors. Abarth also turned his attention to building 695 and 695SS models that boasted 38bhp. The racing version of the 695SS could be supplied with big 10in wheels.

THE 500 TODAY
The 500 is still prolific in Italy today. It remains mainly as town transport for commuters and its size allows creative parking in restricted areas. Indeed, some sad looking 500s exist purely as a means of retaining the exclusive ownership of a parking space. The similarly sized 126 is rarely seen, proving that the 500 is still regarded affectionately by the Italians. A recent cull on old cars by the Italian government removed many worthy classics from local roads. Generous trade-ins were offered (about £1000) on any old car against the cost of,

A UK enthusiast's novel way of solving the Fiat 500's luggage space problem.

typically, a new Panda. Since a Panda costs the equivalent of around £4000 in Italy, many motorists elected for this option. Consequently, many good 126s, 127s and 128s were consigned to the scrapyard but, judging by the number of 500s that still exist in Italy, their owners decided they were worth keeping.

In the UK, 500 ownership seems to fall into two categories: that of the enthusiast and that of the sycophant. Enthusiasts of the 500 congregate in groups of like-minded people to share the mutual sympathy of ownership. Many enthusiasts have the urge to drive enormous distances in their noisy and slow 500s as if in search of heroic recognition. The other group of 500 owners consider the car to be a bijoux form of transport, are usually wealthy, sometimes famous, and often live in London. They spend huge amounts of money on customizing their full-scale toys and are likely to be seen in the King's Road and other trendy places. Whatever the motivation, the Fiat 500 owner should be congratulated for making the world a better place for keeping the charismatic 500 in it.

RESTORATION ADVICE

All Fiat 500s have value. At the time of writing, a working car in recoverable condition will cost in the region of £2500 in the UK. A car fully restored to standard specification will cost in the region of £12,000, more if it has been customised. So the prospect of bringing over a truck load of worn out, rust-free, 500s from southern Italy may appear

to have its merits. There are still some decent cars left in Italy, but for how much longer?

Restoration costs for 500s are rising steadily because the sources of new body panels and trim are drying up. Sensible rebuilds will be based on cars that are already in good condition. Deep rebuilds are expensive and will diminish any equity in the project.

The 500 was a cheap, economical form of transport for the masses and, as such, churned out by Fiat almost as a disposable car. On this basis it should be of no surprise that the car's build quality and materials were average at best, and without modern body protection its survival was finite, especially in a damp environment. The 500 was also a model that became progressively cheaper to buy as the years rolled on.

Aftermarket body panels came only from Italy, no doubt created from the original body pressing tools which have now become so tired that their use is no longer viable because the panels they produce are of progressively poor quality. Consequently, bodyshells, wings and doors are no longer manufactured. However, there is a second-hand market but this has obvious limitations.

Body trim is also becoming hard to find. Although items like bumpers – which were poorly chromed when new – are still being reproduced in better quality stainless steel. Headlights are becoming a problem as the original units are no longer available, and nobody is making repro units at the moment. Windscreens are still available but side and rear glass isn't, although there is a second-hand industry of refurbished items. It is said that the glass is the only thing on a 500 that doesn't rust!

Wheels and tyres are not a problem. Standard tyres are still made by CEAT and work out at about £25 each. Supplies of steel 3.5J x 12in wheels are not a problem either, though many owners go for reproduction Campagnolo-pattern alloys

A professionally restored 500 complete with 'suicide' doors and attractive reproduction Campagnolo alloy wheels.

at around £460 for four (plus tax). These are die-cast by Lesmo. Exhaust systems are still available, made by the Italian CSC brand. It should be noted that 500 and 126 units are not interchangeable. This applies to many other components, too.

A beautifully trimmed interior and Nardi steering wheel will finish off your restoration, but hopefully not your bank balance!

quietness and longevity is EP90. The 500's original carburation was very primitive and lacked the benefit of an accelerator pump which adversely affects performance, after all, the 500 was intended as an economy car. Replacement Dell'Orto units do have a pump and have a noticeable benefit to the car's acceleration.

One potentially dangerous defect inherent with the 500 is the heating and cooling system. A thermostatically-controlled flap on the engine directs the airflow into the car and around the engine. If these seize, the engine will overheat but the car's occupants will get cold! On early engines, the overheating would cause the head gasket to blow and carbon monoxide gases would be pumped into the car's cabin with potentially lethal consequences. Later engines had sealing rings fitted to prevent the gases escaping.

The best engine choice for a 500 rebuild is the 126's 650 unit which has more torque and more fully developed ancillaries. Original 500 gearboxes are non-synchromesh units and do suffer from inconsiderate driving. It is important not to change into first gear when on the move and double declutching is necessary both up and down the gear ratios. Synchro modification kits are available. The 126 gearbox can be substituted which benefits from a higher differential ratio. The preferred oil for

When deciding which 500 model is the most suitable choice, Middle Barton Garage suggest that the most sensible version is the 500F from the late-1960s. They have a purity in design, having the classic round speedometer and overrider-less bumpers. Least desirable models are the 500R and

Owners of Fiat 500s ought not to have an introverted personality. The little car draws many admiring glances from passers-by and other motorists. The fear element comes in when you realise that there is very little space between your 500 and the massive HGV truck wheel spinning furiously at eye level next to you. More unnerving moments occur when the traffic comes to an abrupt halt and your front and rear vision is dominated by the starting handle of the red London bus behind, and the back axle detail of the lorry in front.

The owner of this bespoke 500 requested it be painted the same colour and trimmed in the same leather as his Aston Martin V8.

500L. The 500R had the inferior 600cc 126 engine and was built in Sicily (poorly) in left-hand drive form only. The 500L had problematic universal joints in the steering column.

DRIVING IMPRESSIONS
Driving a Fiat 500 is a mixture of fun and fear. There is no doubt that there is a high grin factor when rushing about in one of these little cars; which is pretty harmless because the car is moving much slower that the driver thinks it is. The short suspension, small wheels and direct steering mean that that car is leaping about on all but billiard table-smooth road surfaces. With the engine buzzing away, a glance in the rear-view mirror will result in a fuzzy image caused by the noise and vibration.

Gear changing needs some care because it is easy to damage the non-synchromesh first gear by selecting it while still on the move. The lack of flywheel effect from the little power unit will mean that unless you balance the throttle between changes, the car will lurch forward because the revs take time to fall on the overrun – this is uncool and will make the driver appear incompetent. Braking needs thought, too. Even though speeds will not be stratospheric, arresting progress needs a good shove on the brake pedal to get the drums working properly.

Abarth badges everywhere, and enough instruments to keep an eye on what the 51bhp 800cc engine is doing in the back.

AN EXPENSIVE FIAT 500
One example of a very expensive Fiat 500 has been built by UK specialists, Middle Barton Garage. Cost was of secondary importance to the car's owner whose involvement with Formula 1 and Indycar technology left no room in the project for cutting engineering corners. His plan was to have the world's ultimate Fiat 500 with modifications in keeping with the original design. It also had to be painted in the same colour as his Aston Martin V8 – light metallic green – and have matching Connolly leather and Wilton carpets. Consequently, this unique car cost over £22,500 and took a year to build.

ENGINE
Type: Flat twin
Capacity: 800cc
Bore/stroke: 82mm x 76mm
Max power: 51bhp at 6000rpm

TRANSMISSION
Gearbox: Five-speed with reverse
Final drive: 3.7 :1
Speeds at 6500rpm: 1st gear 14mph
                   2nd gear 30mph
                   3rd gear 58mph
                   4th gear 86mph
                   5th gear 108mph

DIMENSIONS
Weight : 500kg

PERFORMANCE
Top speed: 108mph
Acceleration: 0-30mph 4.1 sec
               0-60mph 14.5 sec

Middle Barton Garage located a 1972 car from a retired schoolmistress and stripped it to a bare shell. New body panels were fitted with Group 2 wheelarches, the chassis strengthened at its known weak points and then rust-proofed. A roll cage was tailored to fit, and the floor was modified to allow for special seats to move back and forth, accommodating both the tall owner and his shorter wife.

An Abarth dashboard was fitted, together with special equipment, such as an extra electronic speedometer, push button starter, two-way radio equipment, intercom with head sets, portable satellite navigation, internal and external temperature gauges, clocks, timers and more. The Abarth dash houses a 160mph speedometer, a tachometer red-lined at 6250rpm and all the usual minor instruments. Abarth suspension, disc brakes, big master cylinder and 5J x 13in Cromodora wheels with 175/50 13 Yokohama A 008s, all do their best in keeping the 500's wheels firmly on the ground.

Power was increased from 21bhp to 51bhp, which was achieved by increasing the capacity from 500cc to 800cc and then uprating everything to suit. New bore and stroke measurements are 82mm x 76mm. The steel crankshaft has special bearings and connecting rods. Other modifications include forged pistons, a very special four-port cylinder head, side draught 40mm Dell 'Orto carburettor, big valves, titanium retainers, double valve springs, an oil cooler, special fan,

competition clutch and a big aluminium sump. This specification is very close to a full race set-up, except for the camshaft. Although power would be significantly increased by installing a camshaft with a racing profile, tractability for road use would have been sacrificed. The transmission was uprated by installing a five-speed, close-ratio, straight-cut gearbox and a 3.7:1 final drive crown wheel and pinion.

Auto Italia magazine test drove the car and found that the twin-cylinder motor started and ran much better than the standard noisy 500 unit. It revved freely with quite a bit of torque, pulling from low rpm, yet was still able to run up to 6500rpm on the tachometer. The competition clutch was not heavy and the gearchange excellent, apart from the shift from fourth to fifth, which took a little practice. A newcomer could easily make a mistake and select third. While it was still no match for a performance car, it could make quite a nuisance of itself with more mundane traffic and attracted a lot of attention. The 0-30mph time of 4.1 seconds was particularly useful. Top speed is estimated to be 108mph but no one has been brave enough to find out if this is accurate.

Handling and grip were way ahead of the standard car. However, its wheel camber changes, tail heaviness, small overall footprint, and its high centre of gravity relative to its track, had their limitations. Low-speed tight turns were fun but high-speed corners needed to be treated with respect. Initial understeer was quickly followed by terminal oversteer lifting-off near the limit. Nevertheless, the object of the exercise had been achieved. Here is a Fiat 500 that is great to drive and doesn't get in the way of the modern man who is always rushing about. The car drives very capably and looks expensive – which indeed it is.

A MAD FIAT 500
Auto Italia magazine tested another modified Fiat 500, this one could certainly be described as radical and not quite what Dante Giacosa had in mind when he designed the original car.

If you can't afford to pay someone to build your dream Fiat 500, then you can always create one yourself assuming, of course, that you have the necessary skills. This machine took its motor engineer owner nearly three years to transform his 1974 18bhp Fiat 500 into a roadgoing 187bhp rocket.

The rear-mounted air-cooled Fiat unit was replaced by a Honda Blackbird motorcycle engine mounted ahead of the rear wheels. This water-cooled 1100cc four-cylinder unit produces 187bhp at 12,000rpm – ten times the power of the original. The gearbox is also Honda, with the six-speed sequential lever mounted on the steering column and chain drive to the rear wheels. There is a green neutral indicator light on the dash. Pull back a click for first gear, and then click forward for the other five. For reverse, you just get out and push. Not difficult as the whole car weighs only 650kg – that's 288bhp per tonne.

A new engine bulkhead was fabricated in steel, level with the B-posts. The four double wishbone suspension system utilizes gas dampers, also from a motorcycle. The owner also made the driveshafts, the Perspex windows, the roll cage, the dramatic steel body panels and the pedal box. Braking is provided by four drilled discs with Fiat calipers and a hydraulic handbrake. The water radiator is front-mounted, venting out through the bonnet. Wheels and tyres are Camanatura Alfa Romeo wheels 5.5J x 13in, with Dunlop SP Sport 175/50 13 tyres.

Climbing in over the door bars, the driver settles into Sparco race seats tipped up and forward with a near vertical backrest resting against the engine bulkhead. The engine occupies the space once used for rear seats, and the radiator and fuel tank fill what was once the front luggage area. The folding sunroof is one of the few standard features left. A battery master switch is dead centre on the dash, together with a couple of other switches to make it go. The Honda unit is so responsive, making outrageous racing car/motorcycle noises despite the big silencers.

Motorcycle engines are rarely successful when fitted to cars because of their relatively poor torque characteristics, but with just 650kg to move around, the big 1100cc Blackbird engine worked well. *Auto Italia* magazine's test driver found that the motorcycle engine in the car was successful because a Fiat 500 is only just a car and the four-cylinder 1100cc Honda Blackbird engine is almost a car engine. Without accurate instruments, acceleration was estimated to be about six seconds for the 0-60mph dash and top speed was thought to be around 120mph. The car felt stable considering its short wheelbase. Cornering at the limit brought on initial understeer, then a period of neutral handling followed by lots of lift-off tuck-in and eventually lift-off oversteer. With good mid-engined traction, power slides in the dry were impossible.

Extreme customisation. Powered by a 1100cc motorcycle engine, this machine will cover 0-60mph in six seconds.

Christened the Mad 500, this car provides its owner with huge enjoyment and it is probably as radical as you can get while still being road legal – in some countries at least.

ABARTH 595SS REPLICA

With genuine Abarths being rare and expensive, building your own from a basic 500 is quite appealing. Abarth specialists Middle Barton Garage, were commissioned to build a replica 595SS for one of its customers and the author was fortunate enough to test-drive the result.

Abarth offered the 595 and 695 models in basic, SS and Assetto Corsa (competition-prepared) forms. The most popular by far was the 595 of which many thousands were produced. Both models were offered with uprated suspension, brakes, wider wheels, Abarth steering wheel, exterior and interior badging and very attractive Jaeger-Abarth instrumentation. The bigger-engined 695 was considerably more expensive and more fickle – increasing the original engine size by nearly 40 per cent was a big leap. The 695 had a reputation for speed and being somewhat temperamental.

The Fiat 500 engine is an in-line air-cooled twin with a single carburettor and no apparent aspirations to performance. A standard 500 wheezes out around 18bhp, giving the standard version an official top speed of 58mph. This does not sound like the basis for anything remotely fast. Enter Abarth.

Sublime customisation. A fully specified Abarth 595SS replica with a Fiat 126-based power unit.

Carlo Abarth recognised that size was important. Consequently, he calculated that the lowly 500 engine could be bored out from 67.4mm to 73.5mm, while retaining the standard Fiat 70mm crankshaft. This produced a capacity of just over 594cc and the '595', as the model became known, was born in 1963.

It only remained for Abarth to add a larger carburettor, sports exhaust, camshaft and alloy oil-sump. The enlarged engine now boasted 27bhp at 5000rpm. This is hardly gut-wrenching horsepower but when you start with just 18bhp, a 50 per cent power increase is significant. The top speed went up to 75mph (a 29 per cent increase) and the acceleration was hugely improved.

The 595 engine was further developed and later cars produced 32bhp at 5000rpm, still utilising the standard Fiat 500 crankshaft. This resulted in a Fiat 500 capable of over 80mph. In 1964, Abarth introduced its 695 version of the Fiat 500.

The 695 is rather more radical than the 595. With this model, Abarth abandoned the Fiat 500 crank in favour of an Abarth steel version with a longer stroke of 76mm. He also increased the piston size to 76mm, resulting in a capacity of 689cc. Abarth knew that it was impossible to bore the standard Fiat 500 barrels from 67.4mm to 76mm, so he designed a siamesed barrel set-up which dropped into the Fiat 500's crankcase. The rest of the 695 engine was similar to the 595 engine and produced 38bhp in

standard form. Abarth had now increased the power by 90 per cent, propelling the little car to over 90mph. Anyone who has experienced 90mph in a Fiat 500 remembers it!

Competition-tuned examples boasted over 40bhp due to higher compression and more extreme camshafts, while still retaining the single-choke 34mm Solex carburettor. It is interesting to note that the 695 produced its maximum power at only 5350rpm. Abarth realised that the longevity of the little two-cylinder engine would be compromised at higher revs.

The final development of the 695 included four-port downdraught cylinder heads and 'Radiale' (crossflow) heads. Both these heads utilised a sidedraught 40DCOE Weber. Abarth only offered these heads as aftermarket parts and does not appear to have manufactured cars with them fitted. Power was certainly increased and excellent torque characteristics were obtained. It is probable that Abarth was exploiting a marketing opportunity with the introduction of the 695 Radiale head and indeed the four-port head that looked similar. The European Touring Car Championship was being dominated by the fabled Fiat Abarth 1000TC Radiale and the name Radiale achieved quite some cache among the Abarth fraternity. The under-bonnet appeal of the big sidedraught carburettor is obvious, particularly with the engine held open in Abarth racing style.

THE 'MIDDLE BARTON' ENGINE
This particular engine, as it arrived for rebuild, was a good example of an engine built with some very good parts and some glaring omissions. The unit was based on a Fiat 126 engine, itself being an evolution of the original 500 – outwardly almost identical but with the advantage of a useful 650cc.

The engine had been built up with a very rare Abarth four-port cylinder head, Weber 40DCOE, hot cam, Abarth exhaust, Abarth sump and oil-cooler set-up. The pistons employed were no less than 85mm (1mm larger than a 2-litre Fiat twin-cam engine!). The resulting capacity was 795cc, top-heavy, and capable of producing significant power.

The Achilles heel in the specification was the retention of standard 126 conrods and lack of accurate balancing. When the whole thing 'grenaded', a long-suffering connecting-rod broke. The piston made a bid for freedom, vertically through the cylinder head, the flailing con-rod slicing through the barrel, crankcase, camshaft and lovely Abarth cast-alloy sump.

TECHNICAL SPECIFICATION

Middle Barton Garage has a proven 695 engine specification that is both powerful and safe.

This specification was enhanced for this engine by utilising the Abarth four-port head that was resurrected from the damaged engine. The resulting engine produces over 40bhp without the need to exceed 6000rpm. The little engine has very friendly torque characteristics and should experience a long life.

The need for accurate balancing of this type of engine (indeed, any engine) cannot be over-emphasised. Many tuned 500 engines can be seen expending significant power in their attempts to remove themselves from the engine compartment by ripping the rear mounting apart. Much better to transmit this power to the back wheels. Although the bore and stroke differ from the original 695, the capacity seems to suit the air-cooled twin. Experience over the years has often reaffirmed that Carlo Abarth knew exactly what he was doing.

The featured car is based on a rebuilt Fiat 500 shell. Though fitted with the 695 engine, it is badged as a 595 and has Group 2 wheelarches as used by Abarth for its Assetto Corsa specification. The car looks and performs just as Abarth 500s did back in the 1960s.

To extract 40bhp from the tiny twin-cylinder engine, you have to fit lots of Abarth goodies. The result – a pocket rocket.

126/650 crankcase
650 barrels bored out to 79.5mm
Forged flat-top pistons
Steel rods (Ferrari Dino)
New Fiat 126 crank
40/80/80/40 camshaft
Abarth oil-sump
Sports exhaust
Lightened flywheel
Uprated clutch
Electronic balancing
Gas-flowed and ported cylinder head

DRIVNG IMPRESSIONS

The author had the opportunity to drive the Middle Barton 595SS and found it to be much more rewarding experience than a basic 500.

It does help if you are friendly with your passenger as the interior accommodation is best described as cosy. But the driving position behind those lovely Abarth instruments is fine, with excellent visibility, though you do have the feeling of vulnerability in such a small car.

When driving this car, it is immediately apparent that some excellent engineering has gone into its construction. The gearbox is positive and easy to use, the steering is direct, the brakes work and nothing rattles. Acceleration is quite rewarding with loads of torque. In fact, running the engine beyond the 6000rpm red line is pointless, as it has all happened well before then. There is a satisfying deep boom from the exhaust to remind you that all the exotic mechanical components have been well put together and work well without flat-spot or fuss from the engine.

FIAT 850

something for everyone

Developed from the 600, the boxy 850 saloon arrived in May 1964.

to the squared-off treatment that became fashionable on the 850 and Fiat's other saloon and coupé designs of that period.

The Fiat 850 was something of a revolution for Fiat, in that it was able to produce a wide family of attractive body styles on the same platform. Each model was completely different; there was the cute saloon, the sleek Spider, the sporty Coupé and a range of utility vehicles which included van, pick-up and camper versions.

Fiat decided to look outside of its empire for someone to design and build the 850 Spider, which has been and still is one of its traditions when it comes to open-top cars. Bertone picked up the contract for the design and manufacture of the Spider, the styling being attributed to Marcello Gandini of Lamborghini Miura fame. The 850 Spider was a great success for Bertone with over 140,000 built, mainly for the US market where it was very good value, even though it was inflicted with an 817cc engine to creep under the anti-smog regulations.

The Coupé was designed in-house at Centro Stile by father and son team, Felice and Gian Boano. It followed design cues from its big brother, the 124 Coupé, also styled by the Boanos. There were to be three developments of the Coupé and eventually a total of 380,000 were constructed in Italy. An amazing 2,203,380 Fiat 850 saloons rolled out of Turin, making it an all-time success for the company.

The 850 project was intended as a replacement for the 600 and was generated back in 1959, as project types 119 and 122. Prototypes were produced of both projects and the 119 variation used a 1-litre destroked Fiat 1100 engine. The 122 had an engine derived from the 600D, which was enlarged to 843cc. The 119 engine was fitted to the 122 body but the project was not adopted by Fiat management.

Several design prototypes were built including the 122/540, design 1a, which had more than a passing resemblance to the 600. The more angular 122/540, design 4a, was later chosen by the president of Simca as the basis for the Simca 1000.

The chassis chosen for the 850 is essentially stock 600 and designated 100G – G for Grande, the 850 prototypes continued the 600 prototype numbering sequence. It was discovered during development, that by adding a horizontal surface under the rear window of the 122/540 4a prototype's 600-derived body, a further 6mph could be extracted. This lead

Bertone won the contract to build the 850 Spider. This is the production line at Grugliasco in Turin.

The headlights are currently expensive to replace as they are shared with the Bertone-built Lamborghini Miura.

The 850 Coupé and Spider fitted into Fiat's range of similarly paired sports cars produced from the mid-1960s. Depending on the size of your pocket, you could choose between the exotic and expensive Dino Coupé and Spider, or the more popular 124 versions. A wide range of bright and vibrant colours were available for all the sporting Fiats, consistent with the swinging

sixties. In the 850 Coupé and Spider, Fiat had for the first time made available a stylish pair of sports cars for the younger driver, where previously these kind of cars were only within the reach of the wealthy.

The Fiat 850 departed from Fiat's conventional technical

To accommodate the wider 850 radiator the transaxle input shaft had to be moved, thus requiring the engine to be reverse-rotated.

procedure by having reverse rotation engines. Curiously, the reason for this was to improve the cooling system. To allow for a wider radiator, the transaxle input shaft had to run down the left of the gearbox centreline to create the space. This meant having the pinion gear also on the left, which reversed the drive rotation. To prevent the car from having one forward and four reverse gears, the engine rotation was changed to suit. The engine was then tilted 5 degrees to the left to enable the number four spark plug to clear the radiator to allow easy access.

850 BERLINA

It would be convenient to say that the 850 replaced the 600, but it didn't because the 600 ran in parallel production in Italy until 1969 and continued to be built for many years in Spain and Yugoslavia.

Very few 850 saloons live on. This one has managed to survive the British climate which was not kind to 1970s Italian metal.

Introduced in May 1964, the first 850 saloon variant, which lasted until 1968, had a four-cylinder, 843cc water-cooled engine and all-round independent suspension. Two versions were announced, the standard saloon with 40bhp (designated 100G.000) and the Super with 42bhp (100G.002). From 1966, the saloon was available with semi-automatic, Idroconvert transmission which had a pedal-less manual gearchange. Weighing in at just 670kg, the little car had drum brakes, transverse leaf and upper wishbone suspension and a 4.625:1 final drive ratio.

850 COUPÉ AND SPIDER SERIES1

In 1965, the sporty Coupé and Spider were both presented at the Geneva Show. The models inherited the saloon's power unit but the Coupé (100GC.000) was

The 'oh-so-pretty' 850 Coupé took the styling of much more expensive cars to an affordable level.

uprated to 52bhp and the Spider (100GS.000) to 54bhp. Front disc brakes appeared and the final drive ratio was raised to 4.875:1. For the first time since the 1920s, the circular Sport badge with bronze laurel leaves was reintroduced. The Coupé weighed in at 720kg but the Spider was substantially heavier at 920kg. Also, in 1965, the Station Wagon

Built in left-hand drive form only, the 850 Spider was another great Fiat sports car that was denied to the UK market – Dino, 124 Spider, Barchetta …

version was launched. It was available with the 40bhp 843cc engine until 1976. However, an uprated version fitted with the 903cc engine was introduced in 1970.

850 COUPÉ AND SPIDER
SERIES 2

Revised in March 1968, the new Mk2 Coupé and Spider had Sport added to their titles, in-line with their 124 big brothers. Both cars had the bigger capacity 903cc engine (100GBC.000) although it was still rated at the Mk1 Coupé output of 52bhp. Main changes for the Coupé were a higher tail, a four headlamp front end, revised tail lamps, bumper overriders, an alternator to replace the old dynamo, and radial tyres. Weight was now up to 745kg. The Spider also received new lighting in the form of headlamps that stood vertically, overriders and a Giugiaro-designed hardtop became available. In 1968, the Bertone-built Racer Team was sold directly by Bertone in USA, but not in the UK.

A second series Spider is identified by the upright headlights. The Coupé sprouted inset driving lights.

A rare '850 Racer' fixed-head coupé spotted at a Belgian club event at Zolder.

850 COUPÉ SERIES 3

The saloon was not left out in the 1968 revisions and became available as the 850 Special. Main improvement were the installation of the 52bhp power unit from the Mk1 Coupé, front disc brakes and an improved level of trim. A Mk3 Coupé appeared in 1971 at the Geneva Show, featuring new

Fiat must have been really annoyed when it were required to raise the inner driving lights on the 1971 'Mk3' to comply with regulations.

front lighting, which was raised to comply with export regulations. This had the effect of increasing the front overhang. The model was short-lived as it was replaced by the 128 Coupé, announced at the Turin Show during the same year. Italian production of the 850 saloon also ceased in 1971 to be replaced by the 127, although it continued in other countries, notably Spain where Seat built a four-door version. The 850 range was to soldier on until 1985, with the 900E camper version which

The bodyshell of the Abarth OT 1000 was basically a stock 850 Mk1.

The OT 1300/124. Abarth's philosophy well demonstrated, a big engine in a small car.

had the 903cc 127 unit rated at a derisive 35bhp.

THE 850 ABARTHS

The Fiat 850 was an ideal platform for the attention of Carlo Abarth, and the saloon and Coupé, but not the Spider, received the master's attention. There were a few Spider prototypes built for show purposes by Pininfarina and Ellena, but it was the saloon and coupé versions that became an excellent base from which to build rapid competition cars. Abarth built numerous models with enlarged power units including 982cc, 1324cc, 1600cc and even 2-litres.

The OT range of 850s were the last complete Abarth-modified cars to carry the Fiat badge. From this point on, Abarth was to concentrate on building competition cars and his own engines. It wasn't until Fiat bought out Abarth in 1972 that its cars would once again carry the scorpion logo.

Carlo Abarth built numerous hot versions of the 850 Coupé for the model's homologation into touring car and GT racing; hence the title OT – Omologato Turismo. Four of the versions were based on the original Fiat 850 power unit. These were the OT, OTS, OTR and OTSS. Power outputs were 62bhp, 68bhp, 80bhp, and 90bhp, respectively.

The 'basic' OT 1000 was very similar in appearance to the stock Mk1 1965 Fiat 850 Coupé, except

An even bigger engine in a small car. The Abarth-built 2-litre, 185bhp, OT 2000 America guided missile.

for the mock radiator grille on the front panel. The more powerful OTR and OTSS were of more radical specification and had front-mounted radiators. All engines were based on the 850 block but with a longer stroke steel crankshaft that provided 982cc. The block was extensively modified to accept bigger main bearing journals, line boring was carried out, and the oil system was uprated. The R in OTR refers to the complicated Radiale cylinder head that has modified combustion chambers; this innovation allowed 80bhp to be extracted from the engine. In road trim, the OTR Coupé was somewhat under-stressed with a 9.5:1 compression ratio and twin 32mm Solex carburettors. However, the OTR could be uprated to full race specification if required and, being under-stressed, the engine was effectively bombproof.

The OTSS Group 3 racer used the single inlet 850-based cylinder head. It developed over 90bhp at 6400rpm (some say 100bhp), and ran on a 13:1 compression ratio with a single 36DCD carburettor. The OTSS also had special manifolding, big fuel tank and a five-speed gearbox. It is said to be the most powerful 1000cc unit ever produced. Fifty were supposed to have been built – but who knows?

Carlo Abarth elected not to fit a twin-cam cylinder head to the 850 block to further increase power, which he could have done by using one of his 600-derived cylinder heads as they are interchangeable. The reason for not going twin-cam was essentially to comply with racing regulations, which insisted on production-based

engine blocks with the original camshaft location. This is why Abarth's ingenious Radiale system was developed. Instead of the conventional eight rocker installation with a single rocker shaft in the 850 cylinder head, Abarth devised an eight rocker system that had twin rocker shafts, while still operated by pushrods from the single block-mounted camshaft, allowing for a more advantageous valve layout. The head was now effectively a crossflow unit that could produce over 100bhp in full race trim.

In 1966, to further develop the 850 Coupé, Carlo Abarth took the unusual step (for him) of fitting a larger capacity, basic specification power unit he borrowed from the then new Fiat 124. Perhaps as a halfway house between modifying a small Fiat engine to provide high specific power output at the cost of torque, and the need for high revs, the OT 1300/124 represents a radical departure in that extra performance was obtained by substituting a relatively unmodified engine of larger capacity. Foreseeing the future, perhaps?

Abarth took the stock 124 1197cc block out to 1324cc, fitted 10.5:1 pistons and achieved 88bhp – without making any changes to the top end. The 124 installation required reverse engine rotation which involved replacing the timing chain with gears. Modifications were made to the engine mountings by Ing Colucci who designed a tubular frame to carry the unit. A special bellhousing was made to mate up the transmission. Performance was quite rapid, with a top speed of 100mph

FIAT

850

possible. The US magazine *Road and Track* tested one in October 1969 and liked it, but significantly mentioned that it was one of those cars that become increasingly difficult to import as Federal standards tighten. Some refer to the model as the OT 1300/124, others the OT 1300 S. It is known that there was also an SS version that had a hot camshaft and twin-carburettors.

Hottest of all Abarth 850s was the extraordinary OT 2000 America of which, apparently, only three were made. It was fitted with the twin-cam Simca-Abarth engine that had a capacity of 1946cc, 10:1 compression, and breathed through twin 45 DCOE carburettors. The OT 2000 developed 185bhp at 7200rpm – a lot of power for a very small car.

Auto Italia magazine featured a white OTR that was sold to its first East Coast USA owner in 1965, but was promptly returned to Italy because it was the wrong colour! The car arrived again in the US and lived there for many years before eventually resurfacing at a classic car dealer in Holland.

In 1966, *Motor* magazine tested an OT 1000 and suggested it was a pocket rocket GT. The OTR was expensive when new and it is expensive to buy one now, so the reader might not be surprised to learn that they could buy a very good Ferrari 308 for the same money.

RESTORATION ADVICE
The Fiat 850 range offers a selection of eminently practical classics for not a lot of money. Low mileage, well-cared-for examples still come up for sale in Fiat club magazines and the classic car press. Obviously, these cars are a much better prospect than having an existing car restored, so a purchaser would be well advised to be patient in sourcing a well-preserved example in the first place.

It would appear that running a Fiat 850 is a very practical prospect. Mechanically, the car is quite simple and nothing should be beyond the capabilities of the owner who wants to throw spanners around. The engine, gearbox and clutch are considered to be bombproof. The 850 engine (apart from a few first series cars) doesn't have a canister-type oil filter, so problems can arise if the centrifugal filter mounted on the crankshaft pulley is not cleaned every 5000 miles.

As with most classic Fiats, the supply of original body parts is rapidly diminishing and there are no aftermarket panels available save, perhaps, for outer sills. It is possible to locate some panels in Italy or Spain, but items like saloon bonnets are certainly

impossible. Coupés and saloons have survived better than the Spider. It is a fact that the Bertone-built cars did not endure well in a European climate but fared better on the US west coast. Spider body panels are the proverbial hen's teeth, certainly in the UK where the model was not available when new. Some parts are particularly expensive, like series one Spider headlamps that are shared by the Lamborghini Miura, and door handles that come from something exotic, too. The supply of right-hand drive headlights is also a problem. Although reflectors for the 850's circular rear light units are available, the casings are not. This is due to the demand for this design by the Stratos and Ford GT40 replica market which adopted the units as a convenient source of supply.

Exhausts systems are available as an aftermarket product and many owners opt for one of the Abarth-type performance systems as supplied by specialists suppliers.

Although new 850 engines are a thing of the past, there are plenty of mix and match opportunities. For example, the crankshaft from a 965cc Panda 4 x 4 mated to a 127 block will provide a useful 1050cc. Until recently, a convenient choice for improved performance was the 1050cc Autobianchi A112 engine, but even these are drying up, although plenty of second-hand units can be found in Italy. It is essential that the 850 flywheel is retained and that the correct 850 starter motor is also fitted. Best clutch choice is the unit as fitted to the 900T Camper. The all-synchro gearboxes are strong, although, like most gearboxes, replacement parts are expensive.

The heating and cooling system works well in the 850 series as it has a conventional thermostat (same as the 124) mounted on the cylinder head. The car's occupants are able to enjoy heating and windscreen demisting, unlike most 500 and 600 owners. However, overheating is not unusual if the radiator and cooling system are not fully clear. A new radiator core and continuous use of antifreeze should keep everything running cool.

First series 850 brakes with narrow discs and calipers are now rare. Fitting the more effective later series discs is a sensible alternative. A popular conversion is to modify the hub carriers to accept the more powerful, and more obtainable, 124 units. Kingpins on the front hubs will wear quickly if not regularly greased, there is a nipple provided for the purpose.

The 850 fuel tank is mounted in the engine bay and has obvious safety hazards when it comes to refuelling. The same applies to the 30DIC

Strong five-bearing crankshaft ready for regrinding and balancing.

Pistons, con-rods and big ends laid out for inspection.

Rebored cylinders and a resurfaced block await installation of components.

efficient and reliable, although any leaks should be attended to without delay. The mechanical fuel pump can pack up if the diaphragm dries out and splits; there's one in the carburettor, too, that needs checking out.

Since leaded fuel is no longer available in most countries, a practical alternative is to use normal unleaded fuel combined with a suitable additive. Apparently, satisfactory results have been obtained with the product manufactured by Miller Oils. It is possible to fit hardened valve seats to most Fiat cylinder heads, although, damaging the casting is always an expensive risk

The quick and nimble Fiat 850 range is currently considered to be undervalued. The best 850 saloon in the world is not going to be worth much more than £1000. A very good Coupé will be around £3000. Naturally, the open-top Spiders command a higher value and a good Mk1 will be worth £5000 plus. The Mk2 is not as pretty, but is better built and has a better specification – value about the same as a Mk1.

Sample parts prices
Stub axle assembly: £120.00
Shock absorbers (4): £100.00
Clutch kit: £99.80
Brake master cylinder: £28.90
Brake pads: £18.13
Track rod end: £14.85
Engine gasket set: £28.50

Tuning parts
Adjustable gas shocks (4): £258.00
Reverse eye leaf spring: £85.00
Uprated rear springs: £82.83
Recon Cromodora wheel: £80.00
OT type exhaust: £165.00
Leather steering wheel kit: £120.00

twin-choke carburettor which sits immediately above the exhaust manifold. This unit is said to be

FIAT 128

Fiat's first transverse-engined, front-wheel drive car

There was a lot going on at Fiat in the mid-1960s and Ing Dante Giacosa was juggling several very different projects at the same time. The boxy 124 family arrived in 1966, quickly followed by the boxy 125 and the svelte Fiat Dino – an unconventional model for Fiat and built mainly to benefit Ferrari's racing interests.

There were a number of concepts that that Giacosa felt he would like to pursue, in particular, the adoption of diesel engines based on the 1500 and 2300 power units, but his senior management were not as far-sighted as he and diverted his attention from what would have been a ground-breaking venture. Giacosa's boss, Vittorio Valletta, was interested in project X1/3, later to become the 130 Berlina, which Fiat intended to be its flagship

to compete with Mercedes. Giacosa was not fully in support of the big X1/3 and he felt that too much effort devoted on this specialist top-end model would divert attention away from a more important bread and butter model, project X1/1, eventually to be known as the 128. With the wonder of hindsight, we now know that the 130 was a blind alley, not only because a Fiat badge on the front of a prestige car just does not have the same cache as the Mercedes star, but also because building big cars is not what Fiat is best at doing. Fortunately, Giacosa's energies to mobilise the 128 project were justified and he was rewarded with one of the most significant of all the small Fiats.

In the late 1950s, Giacosa arranged for a number of working prototypes to be built called the 123 projects. These cars had a variety of configurations including front-wheel drive and rear engine layouts. He also experimented with three and four-cylinder power units mounted vertically, horizontally, in-line and transverse. It was from these prototypes that the production Autobianchi Primula (A109), A111, A112, Fiat 124, 127 and 128 were to be derived.

The 128 was intended to replace both the 1100 and 850 saloons. It was to be Fiat's first front-wheel drive production car; though this concept was not new to Fiat as Giacosa had experimented with it way back in 1943. The all-

The 128 was launched in 1969, three years into Fiat's 'boxy' styling period. Easy times at Centro Stile!

new transverse engine drove through the front wheels via unequal driveshafts, allowing the gearbox to be mounted at the side of the engine. Though front-wheel drive had been on the cards for some time, Fiat's management considered that the world wasn't yet ready for it. When it did decide it was time, it quietly introduced it was on the home market in the form of the Autobianchi Primula which, of course, never achieved international recognition. It seemed that Fiat was expecting a public outcry over the front-wheel drive concept and did not wish to risk its reputation by using its own logo on the new car, preparing instead to sacrifice that of its subsidiary, Autobianchi. In the meantime, in England, BMC had launched the Austin Seven and Morris Mini Minor in 1959 and stole the march on Fiat by some 10 years.

Fiat's first transverse-engined car had an unburstable Lampredi-designed overhead camshaft power unit.

At launch, the 128 model range comprised two- and four-door saloons and three-door estate versions.

Giacosa originally envisaged two sizes of power units for the 128, one of between 850 and 900cc and the other 1100cc. His first prototype ran with a converted 850 engine with a power output uprated to the equivalent to an 1100. Aurelio Lampredi was commissioned to build the new engine for the 128. Lampredi had already created the superb sporting twin-cam unit for the 124 and 125 ranges and was also developing a V6 for the 130. All three engines had overhead camshafts driven by toothed rubber belts, alloy cylinder heads, inverted bucket-type tappets and had similar, and in some cases, interchangeable components. Lampredi's 1116cc 128 engine was obviously intended as a base version as there was considerable engineering reserve for increased capacities. With an 80mm bore and a very short 55mm stroke there was plenty of room for expansion. Unlike the 124 and 130, Lampredi's 128 engine was not a crossflow design, the inlet and exhaust manifolds both being at the rear of the engine. This configuration was likely to have been chosen as a space-saving consideration as Giacosa wanted optimum cabin space. However, the engine was easy to maintain in that it had the spark plugs and distributor within easy reach at the front of the engine.

The Rallye was worthy of a scorpion in the badge but Abarth was never involved in the 128 range.

in that it had a sloping rear boot that was part of a rear hatchback. At the time, Fiat considered the hatchback was acceptable for the Autobianchi Primula but too risky to put into production on a new Fiat, though no one seems to know why. So, the 'risky' 128 hatchback was farmed out to Zastava to build in Yugoslavia out of the sight of Western European eyes. Fiat successfully passed over another great marketing initiative and it was to be another three years before the hatchback appeared on the 127 and later on the 128 3P.

The 128 was launched in March 1969. The range comprised a two and four-door saloon and a three-door estate with a 55bhp 1116cc power unit. It was immediately awarded 'Car of the Year' by international journalists. In 1971, the two-door Fiat 128 Rally was introduced with a more powerful 1290cc 67bhp engine. It had revised gearing, a brake servo and sporty trim. The increased capacity was achieved by installing 86mm pistons in the block but the 55mm stroke was retained.

At the Turin Motor Show, also in 1971, Fiat introduced the 128 Sport Coupé which was fitted with an uprated 1116cc (64bhp) unit and the 1290cc Rally engine, now with 75bhp. With the latter

The 128's transmission was inherited from the Primula which had proved to be reliable. It was a two-shaft, all-indirect, all-synchromesh four-speeder mounted below and behind the main gearbox. This set-up required the use of unequal driveshafts which might not appear to be ideal in engineering terms but worked well in service.

Giacosa chose MacPherson struts for the front suspension and attached the anti-roll bar to the lower wishbones. The rear suspension was Giacosa's preferred transverse leaf arrangement as used on the Fiat 600 and 850 which saved weight and space. It effectively provided an all-independent suspension which provided an excellent set-up in terms of both handling and ride. Steering was by rack and pinion, the first time the system had been adopted by Fiat.

Paolo Boano was entrusted with the 128's body styling, a designer who was noted for his work on the very attractive 850 and 124 Coupés. He inherited styling mock-up E4 from the 123 project which was notable

Rectangular headlamps identify the 'S' version of the pretty 128 Sport Coupé.

An excellent restored example of the 128 Sport Coupé in 'SL' trim with circular twin headlights and different grille.

engine, the 128 Coupé was capable of 100mph. There were two trim levels, easily differentiated as the 128S had single square headlights and the 128SL twin round units. The mechanical components remained the same as in the saloon, but the superb Paolo Boano-designed body was new, based on a shortened saloon floorpan. In the meantime, Fiat commissioned Bertone to design and build the 128 Spider, which retained its project number right into in production – the Fiat X1/9.

In 1972, the models were mildly revised by fitting a brake servo. Trim, the grille and other small changes were also made. In 1974, the 'Special' arrived which had the four-door saloon body with the 'Rallye' engine (in this application rated at 60bhp) and numerous other minor changes.

Initially, the 128 Coupé sold well but when the open-top X1/9 became available, sales started to drop off. Since Fiat had to pay Bertone a commission on X1/9 sales, it was within its interest to promote its own car. So to counter the X1/9 invasion, in 1975, Fiat introduced the 128 3P (*tre-porte* – 3-door) to replace the Sport Coupé. This was a clever move because not only did it economise on

tooling costs but it also produced a very pretty car. The most significant difference was a new rear end which incorporated a hatchback. The rear seats could also be folded flat to provide a larger load area. Several other details were changed at the same time (new grille, lights), while in order to meet more stringent emissions standards, the engine was modified by increasing the compression ratio from 8.8:1 to 9.2:1, but the overall power dropped from 75bhp to 73bhp. The 3P was available with both the 1116cc and 1290cc engines.

The second series 128s were introduced in 1976 and included many changes. Externally, there were new bumpers, lights and detail trimmings, while the engines were also modified as were the gear ratios, the driveshafts, brakes and electrical system. Internally, the dashboard, trim and seats were all updated.

The Strada (Ritmo) was introduced in Spring 1978 and 128 production was cut back to just the 1100 engine version, the Panorama was

Some UK 128 3P hatchbacks were adorned with go-faster stripes which were popular at the time.

A Fiat 128 with a difference. The South African-built 'Bakkie' was basically a pickup with a bolt-on top.

PROJECT 128
A STORY OF THE ROCKY ROAD TO RESTORATION

Auto Italia magazine's Deputy Editor, Michael Ward, is a 128 enthusiast. His very first car was a 128 1100 CL. Influenced by the exciting 1970s Scuderia Filipinetti competition 128s, he quickly set about modifying his car with big wheels and wide arches to replicate the racing cars.

Michael was also impressed by a highly-modified Fiat 128 owned by Giovanni di Gennaro, who raced his car in the UK's Auto Italia Championship during the 1990s. Not only did this lightweight car look good but it had a powerful 175bhp engine.

dropped from the range in 1980. Production finally ceased in 1985. Total production was 2,776,000 saloons and estates, and 330,800 coupés and 3Ps.

Of all Dante Giacosa's projects, he considered the 128 to be one of his finest achievements and the best value for money.

THE 128 UNDER DIFFERENT FLAGS

A true world car, the Fiat 128 was built or assembled in many different countries including Spain, Eire, South America, South Africa and Egypt. In Yugoslavia, the 128 formed the basis of the Zastava Skala range of cars made by the Zastava company in Serbia. The 128-based Zastavas remained in production until very recently, as a three (Zastava 311) or five-door hatchback (Zastava 511) and four-door sedan (Zastava 101).

Based on a 128 two-door shell, this effective club racer is powered by a 1600cc, 175bhp Fiat Tipo engine.

Inspired by these extreme cars, Michael set about building his own. In 1998, the opportunity arose to buy a 'race-prepared' four-door 128. In reality, the car was full of rust with hand-painted stripes, blue Hammerited interior, a roll cage and some Koni suspension parts. Despite the car's condition, he bought it and 'Project 128' had begun.

The lack of inner wings, rear suspension turrets and scuttle panel led Michael into the search for parts. He discovered that there was a network of 128 enthusiasts who traded spares but the ones he needed simply did not exist because they were integral to the basic original bodyshell and not available individually.

Admitting that his purchase was actually scrap, it was back to the drawing board. He salvaged the roll cage and suspension parts and set about looking for another donor car. While waiting for the right 128 to appear, Michael optimistically purchased a set of 8 x 13in Revolution wheels and painted them Sprint Blue in preparation for fitting to the completed car.

Finally, a two-door Mk1 128 appeared in *Parliamo*, the Fiat Motor Club magazine. This time the advert said 'drive away' but the car had no windscreen. However, the bodyshell was in sound condition and worthy of restoration.

The search for new body panels resulted in the discovery of numerous ultra-rare '128 Rallye' parts including a front grille and the rear panel which carries the desirable circular rear lights. Some Uno Turbo brake calipers were found and mated to Red Dot discs, and the wheelarch extensions came from 124 Abarth mouldings.

Many moons and much money came and went until a shining, Sprint Blue, Group 4-style 128 body emerged from the workshop. The car needed an engine. It was again through *Parliamo* that Michael spotted an advertisement describing a highly-modified 160bhp 1500cc engine and five-speed gearbox for sale. The specification included a high lift cam, vernier cam wheel, newly-assembled and dyno-tested, twin 40DCOE Webers, lightened and balanced throughout – it sounded fantastic.

True to Michael's experience with advertisers being economical with the truth, the boxes

Michael Ward's do-it-yourself 128 Rallye was built from spare parts gleaned through the network of UK Fiat enthusiasts.

of unmated engine parts did not bear much resemblance to the 'recently dyno-tested' engine that had been described – especially when it finally turned out to be a 1301cc unit. Roberto Giordanelli dry-built the engine to discover that the valves touched the pistons. After much fettling, the engine was finally installed in the car.

Five years after the project was started, the blue machine was finally rolled out and fired up. Early testing revealed that there was still much work to be done in order to make the car run and behave properly, but then this is normal for a highly-modified car based on 30 year-old parts.

The car drives as well as it looks, like a racer for the road. Hard suspension with no roll, lots of noise from the straight-through exhaust and masses of torque-steer. The 1300 motor loves to rev but is only happy if it is running above 3000rpm.

The cost of 'Project 128' was high and not easy to justify, but if you want a personalised car that provides enormous satisfaction, then you have to pay the price, the price for fun.

FIAT 127

the hatchback arrives

Though it retained the engine from the 850, the 127 shared many components with the revolutionary 128.

In 1971, Fiat launched the 127, its first front-wheel drive model, which featured innovative technology. It was extremely well-received, and by the end of 1974, over one million 127s had rolled off the assembly line.

Cheap to buy and insure, the Fiat 127 appealed to millions of motorists throughout Europe and also in the more remote and less affluent countries of the world. Like the Panda that was to follow, the 127 sold very well and was a huge commercial success for Fiat.

Beyond the basic models, which were fairly utilitarian, Fiat introduced some sporting versions that were actually quite quick and many current Italian sports car enthusiasts had their first taste of Italian brio with a 127 Sport. The basic 127 is another one of those little Italian cars that many young drivers will have borrowed from their parents or owned a cheap second-hand example as their first car. Though many were built, the 127 has not achieved classic status and very few remain that have been cherished as a collector's car.

The Sport models were quite impressive performers, and very popular with younger drivers.

FIAT 127

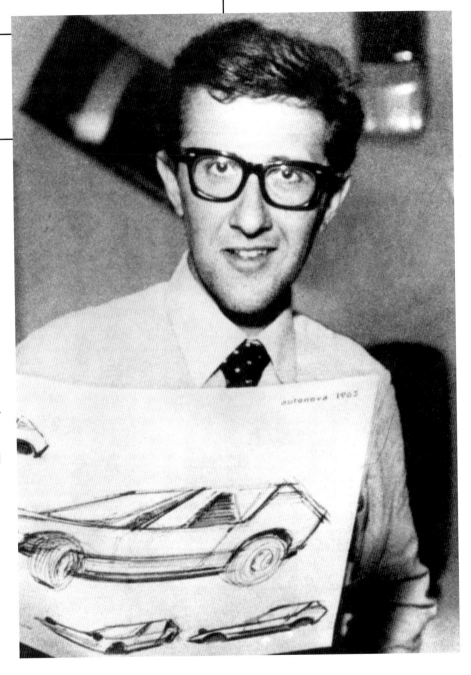

Sadly, young rising star Pio Manzu died as the result of a traffic accident before he could see his 127 design completed.

The 127's styling was the work of Pio Manzu, who was also responsible for the G31 project, a study into a small rear-engined coupé – later to be realised as the Lombardi Grand Prix. Manzu preferred simple, minimalist designs and his preliminary 127 sketches were well-received by Dante Giacosa. Giacosa arranged for Manzu to present his work to Fiat's presidential committee on 26 May 1969. Sadly, Manzu died at the wheel of his Fiat 500 in a traffic accident on the way to the meeting in Turin and failed to benefit from the accolades that his highly successful design would ultimately receive.

In describing the various versions of the 127 range, it should be noted that the information relates to models available on the Italian market, and may vary in specification when distributed elsewhere.

127 FIRST SERIES

The two-door 127 was introduced in 1971 as the replacement for the 850. The model was to play a significant role in the growth of Italian car sales. Its front-wheel drive layout was a development of the Autobianchi Primula, introduced in 1964 and embodied lessons learned from production of the 128 and Autobianchi A112, incorporating many of the mechanical components from these models. The 127 also inherited the basic mechanical layout of the 128 in terms of the suspension, brakes and steering while the 47bhp 903cc engine was derived from the 850 Sport.

In Spring 1972, a three-door version was introduced at the Geneva Show with a tailgate and fold down rear seat. The basic two-door model had a boot lid for rear access. From 1973, the 127 became the biggest selling car in Europe. The two-door and three-door 127 Special made its debut at the 1974 Paris Show. It had a higher level of body finish, a new front grille, and rubber fittings to the bumpers and body side trims. The interior trim was also updated, including an improved steering wheel and dash layout. Anti-pollution treatment to the engine in 1976 reduced the power output to 45bhp. It was nominated as 'Car of the Year'.

A 127 Special shows off its tailgate. The first Fiat hatchback had arrived.

127 SECOND SERIES

In May 1977, the 127 was updated and the new models introduced were known as the 127C, 127L and 127CL. The 903cc engine was complemented by the Fiat Brazil-built, single overhead camshaft 1050cc unit. Output was increased to 50bhp. A four-door version of the 127 was also available in Spain under the Seat banner.

127 SPORT

The 127 Sport arrived in 1978 and had styling improvements and a higher compression (8.8:1) 1050cc engine that was rated 70bhp at 5600rpm, more powerful brakes, an anti-roll bar uprated from 19mm to 21mm, wider section tyres on 4.5J rims and a lower final drive ratio of 13/58.

The circular Fiat Sport logo was adopted on this version. Front and rear spoilers, side rubbing strips, and a new interior with double rear seats, were also part

From 1977, the 'New 127' was available in L, C and CL versions, the latter having the Brazilian-built 1050cc engine.

A 'Special Series' was introduced in 1979 as the 127 'Top' – marketed as the 'Palio' in the UK.

of the increased specification. The Sport was capable of achieving a top speed of 100mph. By 1979, 4,000,000 127s had been manufactured.

127 'TOP' AND 'PALIO'

In June 1979, the limited edition 127 Top (Palio in the UK) arrived. It had a 50bhp engine, tinted windows and special wheels with 155 tyres instead of the usual 135s. The bodywork was available in just two colours; metallic blue or bronze.

63

The 'Top' or 'Palio' was available in just two colours: metallic blue and bronze. The blue version also had a sunroof.

The 3-door Panoramica was derived from the Brazilian-built 127, where it was known, curiously, as the Fiat 147.

One rather odd version of the 127 was the Rustica. It was developed from the 147 Brazil (the 127 built in South America) and intended for rough road use. The reinforced body, finished in beige only, was 45kg heavier than the standard model and it and a 55bhp 1050cc power unit. The transmission ratios were lower and the suspension and brakes were uprated to suit rough terrain. Other features were a front guard rail, mesh-covered headlamps, heavy duty bumpers and a large fuel tank. The interior was designed by Lamborghini and the model is thought to have been constructed at Sant'Agata Bolognese between 1979 and 1981.

127C FIVE DOOR

In April 1980 the 127C five-door arrived, a model derived from the four-door Seat version. The trim was similar to the 127 Comfort and it also had a 903cc engine. In 1981, with the introduction of the third series 127, the model replaced the five-door Super. An estate version, the 127 Panorama, was introduced at the end of 1980. Derived from the Brazilian-made 127, the Panorama had a single overhead camshaft 1050cc engine and a final drive ratio of 13/53. It replaced the outgoing 128 Panorama. A 127 pick-up was also available.

127 DIESEL

From 1981 to 1983, the 127 Diesel was introduced and it inherited the body style from the second series 147 Brazil. It had thicker steel body panels which increased the weight from 835kg to 1255kg. The final drive ratio was 17/64. The engine was the 127A 5000 unit derived from the single overhead camshaft 1050cc engine and enlarged

Not all markets received the 127C 5-door in 1980, a design first produced by Seat in 1976.

or 1050cc engines. The Special was the new basic model and the Super replaced the top 1979 model.

127 THIRD SERIES

At the end of November 1981 the third series of 127 was introduced. The car had a major facelift inside and out. A new carburettor and improved clutch were also part of the update. The 127 Special was the 903cc-engined two- and three-door version, the Super was also available in three- or five-door

to 1301cc. It developed 45bhp at 5000rpm, had a 20:1 compression ratio and featured a Bosch injection system. The Panorama also received this engine in 1982.

127 SPECIAL, SUPER AND SPORT

From 1981, the new 127 Special, Super, Sport replaced the old L, C, and CL models. At this time, the 127 had become the biggest selling car in many European countries, including Italy and almost 5,000,000 units had been constructed. The body style was improved yet again and the 127 was available with either 903cc

The 127 Diesel was fitted with the '147' 1050cc sohc engine. Note the different frontal styling of this Brazillian-built model.

The quick one! The 3rd Series 127 Sport, built from 1981 to 1983, had a 1301cc engine that developed 55bhp.

versions; the three-door having the 1050cc engine and a five-speed gearbox. The 127 Sport received the 1301cc (127A 3000) 55bhp engine, a 34 DMTR carburettor and 155/70 tyres on 13in wheels.

The diesel 1301cc, 45bhp 127 saloon and Panorama were introduced in 1983. The Panorama soldiered on until 1987, mainly because there wasn't an estate version of the incoming Uno (the Duna) at that time. Both models had the final 'look' which had slanting bars on the grille and wrap-around headlamps to mirror the contemporary corporate appearance.

127

FIAT

FIAT 126

competent but unloved

The 126 engine was derived from the 500 unit with capacity increased from 499cc to 594cc.

Not all small Fiats are perceived as having been successful, the 126 is one of those. The fact that it was in production for almost 20 years and a lot of them were built, is largely ignored. It was labelled as the 500 replacement, but the fact that the model was designed to accommodate four people more comfortably meant that it was never going to fill the gap left by its predecessor.

The 500's transformation was another task for Dante Giacosa whose brief was to build a four-seater car with negligible increases in cost. Even for Giacosa, who had been faced with many apparently impossible briefs in the past, this was a tough one. Despite discussions with senior Fiat management, including Agnelli, the project went

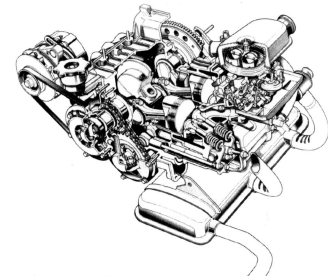

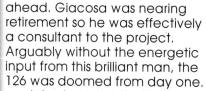

ahead. Giacosa was nearing retirement so he was effectively a consultant to the project. Arguably without the energetic input from this brilliant man, the 126 was doomed from day one.

Introduced at the Turin Show in 1972, the 126 retained the basic engineering layout of the 500 in a completely new four-seater body. It was improved in two particular features, the engine and gearbox. The engine was slightly increased in capacity from 499cc to 594cc, and had

With the fuel tank located under the rear seat and the engine lying on its side, there was plenty of room for luggage.

Mechanical features were more powerful brakes inherited from the 128, a higher output alternator and softer suspension. Prices ranged from 11,988,000 to 2,024,000 lire for the version with a sunroof.

126 650

From July 1977 the 126 was equipped with a 650cc engine. At the end of 1978 there were a series on limited editions including the Black and the Silver. At the beginning of 1980 came the Red and the Brown. In 1983, only one standard version was offered and from May 1985, production was moved to the FSM works in Poland.

A proposal for a multi-purpose small car of 126 descent, the Cavalletta (Grasshopper), was presented at the 1976 Turin Show. It was a diminutive 'Torpedo' with the possibility of fitting a hardtop. The engine was that of the 500 Giardiniera with horizontal cylinders. A power take-off was linked to the primary shaft of the

To hedge its bets, Fiat introduced an updated version of the 500 at the same time as the 126 was launched.

a higher power output of 23bhp instead of 18bhp. Performance was improved by about 10km/h (6.2mph). The gearbox had synchromesh on the three upper ratios. Another engineering innovation worthy of note is the relocation of the fuel tank under the left-hand side of the rear seat instead of under the bonnet.

126 PERSONAL

In 1976, the base model was accompanied by the 126 Personal which had a higher level of body finish and some mechanical improvements. The main body changes were black bumpers, side rubbing strips, an external rear-view mirror and new wheels. Interior changes included a new steering wheel, dash panel and interior carpeting. There were two versions, the Personal and the Personal 4 (four seats with a rear bench).

It might have been modern and functional but the 126 was not loved like the cheeky old 500.

gearbox. Engine capacity was increased to 594cc, maximum power output to 21.5bhp.

126 BIS

In September 1987, the 126 underwent a series of technical modifications the most important being the adoption of a water-cooled engine with an increased cylinder capacity of 704cc. The flat configuration of the unit allowed a luggage compartment to be created behind the rear seat that, with the seat back lowered, has a useful load capacity. Access to the new compartment was via a rear hatch. Other changes included revised interior fittings, new and more complete instrumentation, a more efficient climate control system and better cabin sound proofing. The model was known as the 126 BIS. A special edition called the UP became available in June 1990. Production of the 126 ended in 1991, just prior to the introduction of the Cinquecento.

In 1987, the 126 was substantially revised and received a water-cooled 704cc engine and a fully opening rear hatch.

The 126-based Cavaletta was the prototype for a more rugged 126. Fortunately, it didn't reach production ...

While the 126 may have been a competent vehicle, the world did not warm to it like they did with the original Topolino and Nuova 500. Public perception of a vehicle must not be ignored and while senior management and accountants look at profitability, production costs and a car they want to build, it is very easy to miss the point. The fact that an inanimate mechanical device made of metal, plastic and rubber should somehow obtain the human qualities of personality, charisma and charm is magical, a remarkable achievement that is a marketing dream. Fiat designers did actually regenerate some degree of 'cuteness' when they built the Cinquecento, but lost it again with the replacement Seicento. By combining retro elements with modern technology, it is possible to build character back into a

This Italian car club event provided a rare opportunity to compare the early and late rear opening design.

car, take for instance, the Fiat Barchetta and Coupé.

Travelling through Italy, it is remarkable how many Fiat 500s are still around, especially in the cities. Despite incentives from the government for owners to trade in their old cars, the 500 is jealously preserved. The technically superior 126 is seen less frequently. Thankfully Fiat have – eventually – recognised the passion for the 500 and we will see a new small car with retro features in 2007.

Although the 126 was a much better car than the 500 in every way, it just didn't have the same charisma.

FIAT PANDA

the car that wouldn't die

Fiat was very fortunate that the Panda was one of those models that was still selling beyond the point where it was expected to be replaced. The motoring public would not let it die, a rare situation where the consumer rules over the manufacturer. The Panda has become a bestseller in motoring history and ranks among other icons like the Volkswagen Beetle and Austin Mini. It is popular, not because it has huge charisma – which it hasn't – but because it just does the job it was intended to do perfectly well, and it was very cheap.

In 1982, the Panda 34 – with its 843cc engine – joined the 30 and the 903cc 45 in the model range.

The 1980 Panda 30 inherited the air-cooled 652cc engine from the 126. Note the air intake on the left.

Design master, Giorgetto Giugiaro, built a simple box-like structure, maximised interior space and put a wheel on each corner; car design doesn't get any simpler than that. A four-wheel drive version was built so that people of limited means and those who live up mountains can afford practical utility transport without having to resort to a huge, expensive, off-road 4 x 4. Public utility companies and airport operators bought the Panda in great numbers because frills didn't matter, but cost and function did.

Giugiaro's original clean design was somewhat compromised when Fiat decided to add its latest corporate front grille.

Spain – the Spanish version being known as the Seat Marbella.

At the Paris Show in 1982 the Panda Super was revealed. This had numerous improvements, most significant being the availability of a five-speed gearbox. Out went Giugiaro's original grille design and in came the full-width plastic grille carrying Fiat's slanted corporate emblem, as fitted to most models during this period.

The Panda 4 x 4 was introduced in 1983, featuring a four-wheel drive system developed by Steyr-Puch and a 965cc engine (112B1.054) with 48bhp derived from that in the Autobianchi A112. Intended for light off-road use, the 4 x 4 became standard equipment for many Italian utility companies and airlines. A number of companies, including Moretti, offered a Furgonico version of the Panda that had the rear windows

The Panda also served another function. It was cheap, and even cheaper second-hand, proving it a sensible choice for young drivers as their first car. With low insurance rates and a little bit of cheekiness, many owners of more ambitious Italian cars cut their motoring teeth on a Panda.

At the beginning of 1980 Fiat presented the Panda, a new and important type of car. For the first time, Fiat chose an outside stylist to design a mass production car, Giorgetto Giugiaro of Italdesign fame. Initially, the Panda was available in three versions; the 30, 34 and 45. Engine options included a 126-derived twin-cylinder air-cooled 652cc unit for the 30; the four-cylinder water-cooled 903cc from the 127 range for the 45; and, in 1982, the 850-derived 843cc unit for the Panda 34. Panda production was based in the Autobianchi factory at Desio, near Milan; Termini Imerese in Sicily and Pampiona in

The Panda 4x4 arrived in 1983 and became an instant hit with Italians living in rural areas.

A UK version of the 4x4. These cars were fitted with a 965cc A112 engine mated to Steyr Puch transmission.

blanked off and a small plastic extension attached to the rear.

Fiat restructured the Panda range in time for the Turin Show in November 1984. Improvements were aimed mainly at the 30 range which now had 30L, 30CL and 30 CL College versions, and included a heated rear window as standard equipment, a rear screen wiper, head restraints and hinged rear windows.

A special limited edition of 5000 examples was presented

Panda interiors were quite basic, which helped to keep the purchase price very low.

in September 1985 and was known as the Nuova Panda 4 x 4. The model featured long-range headlamps, a roof rack and decorative stripes. One and a half million Pandas later, in 1986, major changes were made to the range. One of the most significant developments was the implementation of Omega rear suspension which utilised coilover springs in place of the earlier, single-leaf variety. As a result, road holding was significantly improved. The old engines were replaced with 769cc and

999cc versions of Fiat's new Fire engine, the latter already installed in the Uno. Power output was now 34bhp and 45bhp respectively, though the 4 x 4 version was rated at 50bhp. Also in 1986, the Panda Diesel was introduced with a 1301cc engine with 37bhp based on a detuned 127/Uno unit. Trim was basic but the model had the benefit of a five-speed gearbox.

During 1987, the Panda Young was equipped with a 769cc engine which used the basic 903cc block and had the same output of the Fire family. Catalysed versions of the 999cc Fire arrived fitted with single-point fuel injection and electronic ignition.

From 1989, a plethora of limited editions commenced that were available mainly for the home market, and using the old 903cc unit. These were the Bella and Dance. They were followed in 1990 by the Fun and Sergio Tacchini, the latter having the 999cc Fire engine. Most recognisable

The one to collect! A limited edition 'Italia '90' liveried Panda with 'football' hubcaps.

was the Italia 90 which had patriotic trim and 'football' hub caps. At the same time, the New Dance replaced the Dance of the previous year. In June 1990 the 1000 Top Ten, the 750 Bianca and 750 Nera were available, the last two for the French market. To confuse the issue even further, the 750cc pushrod Young was replaced by the Young 2 in March 1990, but in October 1990 reverted to Young following a slight facelift.

Another limited edition. This one is the Panda Bianca with white everything.

A man fitting an outboard to an amphibious Panda or just someone demonstrating the versatility of the final version of the 4x4?

The 4 x 4 was also subjected to special editions with the Sisley in 1987 and Trekking in 1990. At the end of 1990, the Trekking was also offered with the Europe series of ecological engines with the 44bhp 'ECO Box' unit and 45bhp electronic fuel injection engine fitted with a three-way catalytic converter.

The two-seat Panda Elettra introduced in 1990, had only two passenger seats because the batteries to power the car occupied all the space behind the front seats, plus some space under the bonnet where the 18bhp DC motor was installed.

The Panda Elettra was only a two-seater because of all the batteries it needed to carry. Initially, its range was 100km with a top speed of 70km/h.

The weight significantly increased to 1150kg, necessitating stiffer suspension and uprated brakes. In 1982, the power went up to 23.8bhp and the weight dropped slightly.

From May 1991, there were no fewer than thirteen versions of the Nuova Panda with seven different petrol engines, three of which were Fire engines fitted with electronic fuel injection, three-way catalytic converters and Lambda sensors. This final version had another new corporate grille and revised colour choices. A CLX version had a standard five-speed gearbox, tinted glass and a right-hand rear-view mirror. Function and comfort were enhanced with the use of illuminated dash board switches and sound-deadening materials. Also, introduced in 1991 was the Selecta with its CVT transmission and choice of 999cc or 1108cc FIRE engines (45bhp and 50bhp). This latter engine replaced the 1000 unit in the 4 x 4 during the following year.

In 1992, the Cafe was presented with a choice of either a 750cc or 899cc Fire engine, the latter having fuel injection, a catalyst, hydraulic tappets and servo-assisted brakes. The 899cc engine was, in fact, the new unit fitted to the incoming Cinquecento. In 1993, the Cafe was updated to include the 999cc Fire engine and the Regimental had the 899, this model had a robust roof rack, diagonal side badges, metallic green or blue paint and an optional sunroof. There were other special editions intended for the export market; the 750 Perfect in March 1992, the Estivale in May 1992, 1000ie Pop in summer 1992, and Bluebay, Brio and Malicia in summer 1993.

In 1994, a further and final revision was made and the 769cc engine was discontinued, the 903cc unit was reduced to 899cc (for tax reasons) and both that unit and the 1108cc unit were fitted with injection and catalysts across the range. The model range consisted of the Young, L, CLX, 1.1 Selecta, 4 x 4 Trekking and Country Club.

Panda sales were further boosted by the Italian government's ecological initiative to assist in the disposal of the country's old small cars by offering owners generous trade-in allowances. So, from Autumn 1996, all Pandas benefited from a price reduction of 13 per cent and the 900 Jolly was introduced. The Jolly had electric windows, opening rear windows and roof bars. A further price reduction occurred in 1998 making the Panda 900 Young the only car in Italy priced below 10,000,000 lire. The 900 Hobby replaced the Jolly.

The final Panda range consisted of five versions; the Young, College, Hobby, 4 x 4 Trekking and 4 x 4 Climbing. All versions have the 54bhp 1108cc engine. Prices range from 6521 to 11,481 euro.

MODIFIED FIAT PANDAS

There will always be someone who wants to make small cars go faster, even if the sensible option is to buy a bigger one in the first place. It is fortunate that there are people with this infatuation otherwise Carlo Abarth might not have become so well-known. The Panda has not escaped the attention of enthusiasts who wish to run them in competitive events, although the model is not such a popular choice as, say, a Fiat Uno.

Auto Italia magazine tested two modified Pandas on a karting circuit. 'Pandamonium' was originally

PANDA

'Pandamonium'. A very rapid, lightweight, well-prepared car built to compete in UK club racing.

mid-turn brought the nose in and, occasionally, the back-end out.

The second car in the test, a white Panda 1000S, had been prepared to compete in sprints and hillclimb events. It had an OMP cage bolted and welded to the shell. Much weight was trimmed from the doors and the tailgate, and the bonnet was made out of glassfibre. All trim was removed and Perspex windows were installed. The inside of the car was kitted out with a multi-coloured Benetton-style Momo wheel, Sparco pedals, a Cobra seat and Elliot and Stewart Warner gauges with a gearchange light. Overall weight with a full tank was 643kg.

The suspension had been lowered by almost four inches and fitted with Leda front adjustable struts with 400lbs front springs and 350lbs rears. Braking was assisted by OMP grooved discs. During the test, the Panda was fitted with Firestone F 560 165/65 x 13in tyres on MSW wheels, although for competition, Yokohama A008R on TSW 6J x 13in wheels are used.

The power unit in this car was originally from an Autobianchi A112 Abarth (1050 cc and 70bhp) and had been further enlarged to 1149cc. With a special camshaft and a standard 32 DMTR Weber carburettor, a rolling road test produced 100bhp at 7400rpm at the flywheel (about 80bhp at the wheels). The A112 layout was quite efficient with the induction at the front and the exhaust on the bulkhead side. Transmission was standard A112 four-speed.

The white car did not handle as well as 'Pandamonium' because of its average condition road tyres which, even though they were noisy, built up little heat during the test. The red car with its wide track managed to get some heat into the tyres and they worked reasonably well.

Despite giving away 150cc to the white car, the red car also had the sweeter power unit. Not only was the red car more torquey, it also had a higher rev range. The white car had the power but its four-speed gearbox had to be worked quite hard. However, both cars had similar performance figures of 0-60mph in eight seconds with about 120mph top speed.

a roadgoing, red Panda 1000S. The engine was modified by Avanti Tuning to produce 95bhp at 7000rpm (73bhp at the wheels). Four carburettors came from a Kawasaki 1000 motorcycle and were fitted to a one-off aluminium inlet manifold. One of the heater intakes below the windscreen was ducted for carburettor air supply. A performance camshaft and a four-into-one tubular exhaust manifold with a side tailpipe were fitted. The steel sump was extended to carry more oil and to combat surge. Avanti also fitted a five-speed close-ratio gearbox.

The bodyshell was seam-welded, a full roll cage fitted, and a homemade strut brace welded in. Additional strut bracing ran back to the bulkhead. All this provided a rigid structure necessary for strong springs. Suspension front and rear was rose-jointed, with adjustable front spring platforms, stiffer springs and adjustable dampers.

Body weight was reduced from 750kg to about 620kg. Apart from stripping out the interior and the heater, weight was reduced by fitting a glassfibre bonnet and tailgate, and installing perspex windows. An alloy petrol tank was fitted under the boot floor. Braking was provided by Tar-Ox grooved discs with a brake bias adjuster. The wide wheelarches housed 7J x 13in Superlight wheels. During the test, it was immediately obvious that the car was rose-jointed and very rigid. On the really tight corners the car understeered, but lifting-off

FIAT UNO

modern, versatile and efficient

The design brief for a new small Fiat to replace the 127 was technically quite difficult to fulfil and presented a dilemma for the project engineers. The car had to comfortably seat five people, be goodlooking and aerodynamic to reduce fuel consumption. This criteria meant that one aspect of the requirement had a direct affect on the others.

The basic solution that the project team came up with was to increase the cabin height. However, in choosing this route they created a new problem, the increase in the frontal area of the car created resistance to progress forward and thus, increased fuel consumption. To solve this issue, the engineers took their prototype to a wind tunnel and managed to reduce the drag coefficient

The Uno was the product of intensive research into aerodynamics – and the design genius of Giorgetto Giugiaro.

down to an impressive 0.34cd. With a little help from Giorgetto Giugiaro and Italdesign, Fiat came up with an attractive car that had a very low drag coefficient, was fleet of foot and economical. The Fiat 146 – better known as the Uno – was born. It was launched in January 1983.

What Fiat had also done was to go against the fashion in the 1980s for low sporty cars which looked good but had cramped interiors. They had set a trend. Fortunately, the Uno captured the public's imagination who saw it not just as an evolution of the popular 127, but as a fresh design with lots of glass area and interior space. It was not until during their ownership of the new car that the benefits of the wind tunnel testing and the extensive development

Swift and economical, the Uno also had lots of glass area and interior space.

The Uno 45 base model was fitted with the ubiquitous 903cc engine inherited from the old 850 and 127.

An 'energy saving' ES model was also available and had some detail changes, such as wheel trims, to reduce the drag further (down to 0.33), while mechanically it had different gearing to improve fuel consumption as well as a higher compression ratio and different engine management systems. A shift-light informed the driver of the optimum time to change gear while a consumption meter showed efficiency. Overall, this version returned 12 per cent better fuel consumption figures.

The range was enhanced in mid-1984 by the introduction of the range-topping Uno SX. Using the 1300 '70' engine in both three and five-door bodies, the SX added external visual details of bumpers, side skirts, wheelarch extensions and a chrome tailpipe. Interior improvements included new front and rear seats, front

of the car became fully appreciated. It didn't escape the attention of the press either, as the Uno was voted 'Car of the Year' in 1984 by a narrow margin over its key competitors, the Peugeot 205 the Mk2 Volkswagen Golf.

The Uno range was extensive and for ease of manufacture, both the three and five-door versions were based on the same bodyshell. The first versions were named according to their bhp; the 45, 55, 60 and 70. Several engine versions were available at the launch; the overhead valve 903cc (45), the overhead cam 1116cc (55) and 1290cc (70) units inherited from the earlier 850 and 128/Strada models. In 1985, the 55 was replaced by the 60 with its more powerful 58bhp engine. Both three and five-door bodystyles were produced in two trim levels, 'normal' and 'Super'. Fifteen exterior colours were available, including five metallics. In May 1983 the Uno 45D joined the range, it had the same trim levels but was fitted with the 1301cc 45bhp diesel unit from the 127.

Another corporate identity change, another grille. This is the home market utility Uno Van.

headrests, new cloth and trims and a new steering wheel design. Various items previously offered as options became standard; a rev counter, digital

During its production life, the Uno was fitted with a wide variety of power units ranging from 903cc to 1929cc.

SX versions of the Uno were very well-trimmed and added a touch of class to the model range.

clock, foglights, heated rear window and rear wiper.

By March 1985, one million Unos had been built. In April, the Uno Turbo was released with a 105bhp 1299cc engine and was priced to compete with the Peugeot 205 GTI. Numerous details differentiated this version from the rest of the range, including alloy wheels, a unique trim, new bumpers and new instrumentation. Shortly after launch, the capacity was increased to 1301cc with the same power output. Later, in 1987, it became available with a catalyst, and ABS was also introduced on the 'Antiskid' model.

An all-new 999cc power unit arrived in 1985 called the FIRE (Fully Integrated Robotised Engine). Built on a fully automated production line using less parts than its predecessor, this lightweight engine provided new levels in performance, economy and reliability.

The following year, in 1986, the Uno Turbo D was introduced. Using a 1367cc 70bhp sohc turbocharged and intercooled engine derived from the 1929cc Ritmo unit, it also featured external trim similar to the Turbo ie model, a deeper front bumper with extra air-intakes, fog lights and plastic wheelarch extensions. Around this time, a 1697cc diesel engine (58bhp) was made available in certain markets. The next new model to appear was the 75ie cat which was fitted with the 1498cc sohc (75bhp). It was fitted with electronic fuel injection (Bosch L-Jetronic) and a three-way catalytic converter. In October 1986, the two millionth Uno rolled off the production line.

In 1987, the Uno Selecta was introduced using a CVT gearbox developed by Fiat and Van Doorne in Holland. It utilised the 58bhp 1116cc engine attached to the new transmission, and was available in three or five-door form in 'super' trim. By March 1988, the three millionth Uno had been built.

In September 1989 the Uno was given a mild facelift, which saw revisions to the bodywork and an even greater improvement to the drag coefficient which was down to an even more impressive 0.30cd. The interior was also revised. At this time, the old 1.1 engine was replaced by a new FIRE version, and a new Tipo-derived 1.4 engine replaced the Strada-based 1.3 in both naturally aspirated and Turbo versions.

The Duna was effectively an Uno with a boot. This Brazillian-built model was available on the Italian home market.

In 1990 another diesel joined the range, a 1929cc (60bhp) unit with EGR (Exhaust Gas Recirculation) in order to reduce the emissions. In 1991 the 1498cc unit was also catalysed, becoming the 1.5ie. In 1993, the Brazilian 994cc engine was used in some limited editions.

During its life, numerous special edition cars were produced, including the Suite with full leather upholstery and air-conditioning, the Hobby, Rap, Rap Up, Turbo ie Racing, Formula, Estivale, Cosy, Seaside, Targa and Brio. Most featured revised colour schemes or normally optional equipment offered as standard.

UNO UNDER DIFFERENT FLAGS

Following the introduction of the Fiat Punto Mk2 in 1994, Italian Uno production was phased out and ceased completely in 1995 after at total of over 6,032,911 examples had been sold. After Western European production and sales came to an end, the Uno continued to be manufactured and sold in other parts of the world.

In Brazil, the Duna, a four-door saloon version was introduced in 1987 alongside the Weekend, a four-door estate. These models had Ritmo single transverse leaf spring rear suspension, 1116cc and 1301cc petrol, and 1697cc diesel engines. Revised

Another home market Duna, this one the popular Weekend version. Note the clam shell bonnet design of the Brazillian models.

After mainstream Italian Uno production ceased, the cars were marketed under the Innocenti banner. This is the Elba.

in 1990 to follow the frontal styling of the new Uno range, the saloon was dropped in 1991 and the estate became the Innocenti Elba with a 1301cc power unit. In April 1992, a 1498cc fuel-injected and catalysed unit (75bhp) was introduced and in October, a 1697cc diesel (57bhp) became available. Development continued, with a three-door version released in 1993 and later that year, two new fuel-injected engines. The 1.3 was replaced with a 1372cc (67bhp) unit and the 1.5 by a 1581cc (75bhp) unit. Other small changes were also made.

In 1994 the Innocenti Mille was released. Based on the Fiat Uno CS, the car was built in Brazil in three and five-door form and had single transverse leaf spring rear suspension. It was easily identified in that it had a clamshell bonnet and roof bars. In 1995, the model was renamed Mille Clip when production moved to Poland. The clamshell bonnet was dropped and Punto-style independent rear suspension was adopted. Engines included the 994cc, fuel-injected 1372cc and 1697cc diesel units. When production ended in 1997, the sale price of

Uno hatchback production continued until 1997 with the Polish-built Innocenti Mille. Note the straight-sided 'Italian' front wings.

A pre-owned Uno Turbo was a popular choice for the younger driver with a limited budget.

the Mille Clip started at 12,700,000 lire (about £4000) which made it a very cheap economy car.

At the time of writing, the Brazilian-built entry-level Fiat Mille continues in production and received its most recent facelift for the 2004 model year. The 2005 Brazilian range has received a Flex Fuel system, enabling the car to use ethanol or gasoline as

The Mk2 came very nicely trimmed as standard, but many Turbos were 'improved' by their owners and few survive in this condition.

Internationally, the Uno has been replaced by the Palio 'World Car' and elsewhere by the Nuova Panda.

RUNNING A FIAT UNO

Once very popular, the Fiat Uno numbers are now in decline. However, it is still possible to buy good low mileage quality cars that have led a quiet life, often owned by elderly drivers. Every new 'small' car that is launched has increased size and weight due to ever more stringent safety requirements. When compared to Fiat's current model range, the Uno is both small and light. Performance is brisk and the larger capacity models in the range are actually quite fast.

fuel, both pure or in any proportion mixture. There is also a toughened-up version for off-road use which has heavy duty suspension, larger wheels and side protection trim. The Uno Prêmio saloon and an estate version are also still available.

Though production in the Europe had ended, the Uno was still being built in Poland until 2002. It also continued to be built in South Africa where the second series bodies were assembled under licence by Nissan and marketed it as the Uno Up until 2005.

With over 30 models to choose from, the Uno offered something for everyone and had a fairly classless image, except perhaps for the rapid Turbo versions which became popular with younger drivers who were out to impress.

Though the thin body panels are easily dented, the Uno was actually quite a tough car and

With lots of good, cheap roadcars around, the Uno was adopted as a budget club racer and became highly competitive on UK and Irish circuits.

capable of a very high mileage. Some say that it is one of the most reliable Italian cars built. It was certainly well-made, in particular the interior trim which was hard-wearing with all the switches, handles and trim remaining intact.

The overhead camshaft engines are developed from the 128 and are pretty bulletproof providing they are properly serviced and the cambelts changed at specified intervals; a trouble-free 100,000 to 180,000 miles is possible. The pushrod 903cc engines, carried over from the old 850 range, develop rattly timing chains and tappets at high mileages, but this can be easily rectified. Clutches are good for 70,000 miles before replacement is required.

Of the faults that do occur, the most common are intermittent mechanical fuel pump failures on overhead camshaft carburettor engines and blocked idling jets on older cars. Gearbox life is variable depending on how swiftly attention is given to leaking oil seals. Front brake calipers can stick giving uneven braking, and handbrakes can become ineffective if the self adjusters seize on the rear brake drums.

Corrosion has never been an issue on the galvanised Uno bodywork, though stone chips and body-stressing will ultimately have an effect. The bolt-on front wings have protective plastic liners. However, the running gear can be a different matter and some cars suffered corroded bottom wishbones and rear suspension turrets. One cause of irritation is the electrical contact to the rear lights via the spring connectors on the tailgate.

IMPROVING A FIAT UNO
The Uno is tall and narrow, so improvements can be made by increasing the width of the car and lowering the centre of gravity. The cheapest way to do this is to remove slightly less than one coil from each spring which will lower the car by about 1in all round. Alternatively, buy a sports handling kit which has four springs and uprated dampers.

Front suspension geometry will benefit from around 1 to 1.5 degrees of negative camber. Fitting the front anti-roll bar from a Turbo model will help and a rear anti-roll bar will sharpen the handling dramatically. As an alternative to fitting a rear anti-roll bar, welding up the U-section on the rear suspension beam works wonders. Wider wheels, or spacers with standard wheels, will help produce serious cornering power.

Various tuning options are available from aftermarket specialists, though an up to 30 per cent power increase can be obtained by simply machining 50 thou from the cylinder-head face. For significant power increase, fitting a 1498cc Ritmo/Delta engine can provide up to 130bhp. With this conversion, a 0-60mph time of under eight seconds and a top speed of 120mph are possible.

UNO GOES RACING
The Fiat Racing Challenge is run in the UK by the British Racing Sportscar Club (BRSCC). It is a well-established racing series aimed at drivers wishing to enter motorsport with a limited budget. The grids are predominantly made up of Fiat Unos, though the occasional classic 127 and 128 make up numbers. As age and attrition take their toll on the Uno entry, Puntos are expected to become the budget racer's choice.

Regulations in the Fiat Racing Challenge are strict to ensure close racing and to keep costs down. Within the regulations it is possible to build an engine that produces 90bhp, with a bodyshell that can be trimmed down to under 800kg, providing a power to weight ratio of around 126bhp per

A survivor! The Uno Turbo was very much a classic of its era and this Mk1 has been painstakingly restored by its enthusiastic owner.

The Uno Turbo arrived in July 1985, with a 1299cc engine that gave 105bhp, which was enough to take the car to a decent 127mph. Less than three years later, the engine grew by all of two cubic centimetres, but the big change came in January 1990 with the appearance of the Mk2 car. With a restyled nose that housed a 1372cc powerplant, there was also multi-point fuel injection to give a slightly more palatable 114bhp. Things were looking up – except this larger unit has proved less reliable than its predecessor and the catalytic converter fitted from June 1992 inevitably took the edge off the free-revving engine.

While the Uno Turbo was based on a Uno 70, it was far more than just a standard car with a turbo bolted on. Alongside water-cooled cylinder liners there was an intercooler and oil cooler. Also new, was a redesigned cylinder head, electronic ignition, a knock sensor and Bosch LE Jetronic fuel injection. There were all sorts of other tricks up the Turbo's sleeve, too, so it was no surprise that the car out-performed most of its rivals when new.

Auto Italia magazine had the opportunity to test drive both Mk1 and Mk2 versions, but finding unmodified examples proved to be impossible. Having attained banger status years ago, most Uno Turbos were worn out by uncaring owners who wanted some cheap fun. Those owners who cherished their cars treated them to fresh alloys and bodykits that frequently breached the rules of good taste.

UNO TURBO MK1

At the time of *Auto Italia* magazine's test (2006), Bobby Holder's Mk1 Uno Turbo was just as it left the showroom and probably the best original example in the UK. Resplendent in its Rosso Corsa paintwork, Bobby bought his car from the proverbial one elderly lady owner who had cherished it all its life, covering just 47,000 miles.

Original down to its factory-fitted radio, despite its apparently perfect condition, as soon as Bobby bought it he started taking it apart. He had the car repainted and the engine rebuilt, and the car has covered just 3000 miles since.

The Uno felt just like it must have done when it left the factory and was great to drive. The steering

tonne. Apart from the obvious benefit to speed and acceleration, this desirable power to weight ratio also vastly improved the braking and cornering ability.

The secret of a successful racing Uno is in the suspension set-up, the correct spring-rates and damper choices are critical. The correct settings will help send the tail out on lift-off to reduce understeer and improved corner-exit traction.

Low-powered cars, like the Uno, are a good basis to learn race driving techniques, as speed must be carried through the corners and the engine kept in the power band to produce good lap times

FIAT UNO TURBO – THE 'CLASSIC' HOT HATCH

Is there anything that sums up the 1980s better than hatches of the hot variety? Maybe the Rubik's Cube, padded shoulders or Filofaxes would make it to the shortlist, but when it comes to the very essence of the 1980s, breathed-on hatchbacks have to be top of the list.

Twenty years ago the hot hatch ruled the roost; it had taken a decade from VW launching its Golf GTi to catch on, but once the trend had started, there was no stopping it. Suddenly, every city car received fuel injection or a turbocharger to pep things up (sometimes both), and while the French and the Germans often hogged things, the Italians didn't miss the party. Lancia had its long-forgotten Y10 Turbo while over in the Fiat corner came the Strada Abarth, along with the boosted Uno – Fiat's first ever turbocharged production car.

was perfectly weighted and beautifully direct, and at speed the car was surprisingly refined. The ride was also good considering how the small the wheels were.

Writing for *Auto Italia* magazine, journalist Richard Dredge expected that there would be horrific turbo lag, but this was not the case. The engine was very tame until 3000rpm, and from there on the power and speed just built, right through to the red line.

The Uno felt so sprightly because of its low weight, tipping the scales at just 895kg, which was why the car handled so well in tight corners. However, it did oversteer on the limit, but exercising some restraint in the bends, the car just went where it was pointed.

UNO TURBO MK2

Owner Michael Alexiou decided to modify the engine on his Mk2 Turbo following the demise of the original unit. Although the Mk2's engine has a greater displacement than its predecessor, Michael overbored his engine to almost 1500cc.

Every component was upgraded in some way, with both the top and bottom ends being thoroughly overhauled. The specification sheet is extensive and includes a gas-flowed head complete with oversized matched valves. The bottom end has forged low-compression pistons, con-rods that have been balanced and shot-peened, plus hardened bearings for the big ends. To prevent the engine from overheating, a larger oil cooler was installed together with a Cosworth Sierra intercooler. The Cosworth also donated its wiring loom, ECU, throttle bodies and distributor.

Though not fully run-in, at the time of the test it was expected that the modified engine would produce 250bhp. The Mk2's performance was completely different from the Mk1 tested and the two cars didn't feel remotely related. The quickshift gearchange felt more like a Subaru Impreza Turbo than a 16 year-old Fiat. The 4in Scorpion exhaust was also rather vocal in comparison. The ride was hard, thanks to the adjustable Koni shock absorbers set on a stiff rate. The cross-drilled and grooved discs made the brakes highly efficient.

The almost standard appearance of this car disguises the significant modifications to its performance and surprises many BMW drivers around the roads near the owner's home in North London.

CINQUECENTO

the Polish Italian

The author was invited by Fiat UK to test drive the Cinquecento at London's Chelsea Harbour prior to the model's UK launch in May 1993. At the time, the Cinquecento was the latest in a long line of imaginatively styled and well-engineered city cars – the type of vehicle that Fiat is synonymous with building. Fiat are good at building small cars with big hearts and the new Cinquecento fulfilled the criterion exactly.

The Cinquecento project followed exactly the same design ethic that was applied to Topolino and later the Nuova 500; compact dimensions, fuel frugality and an accessible purchase price. The new Cinquecento was the result of a project that started in the mid-1980s, under the designated code X1/75, to develop a Fiat 500 for the nineties. Early comments from insiders and the press referred to the new car as the 'Topolino', emphasising a return to Fiat's traditions. However, the Turin company decided to call it 'Cinquecento', thus neatly forging a historical link with the car's ancestry.

The validity of the Cinquecento project was proven when the car was driven in city traffic, where the experience was made much less depressing than usual. The car instills confidence in the driver by giving the impression that it will fit into gaps in the traffic that were previously unavailable. The high seating position and large glass area provided excellent visibility that encouraged the driver to drive progressively, creating space in the mayhem. The sharp cut-off rear body

styling was a great aid to reversing and made parking that much easier, another city nightmare. The firm ride and nippy handling were reassuring and it was soon discovered that speed ramps could be attacked with great flair.

The 899cc engine was a more sophisticated version of Fiat's established 903 that has seen many

The Polish-built Cinquecento was launched in 1991.

Styling followed the 'house style' of the time established by the Uno.

The upholstery was bright, smart and serviceable, and the deep door pockets ideal for maps and oddments. The see-through adjustable front seat head rests also contributed to the general feeling of space. All the driving controls were light, but effective, especially the brakes. Two great plus points were the readily located external bonnet release and the engine oil dipstick that was immediately obvious and accessible. The whole Cinquecento package was good value with prices (1993) that started at a very reasonable £5254.

CINQUECENTO 700ED, CAT ED

Although launched in the UK in 1993, the heir to the 126 had already been presented in Rome in late 1991. Two power units were offered, the 704cc flat-twin (two parallel, horizontal cylinders) and the 903cc pushrod four. The 704cc unit was fitted to ED (Economy Drive) version in catalysed and normal forms. This unit was derived from that of the 126 BIS, but had been considerably modified so that it could be mounted at the front of the car. It was more powerful and smoother, thanks to counter-rotating balancer shafts. In both cases, the engine was fitted with a carburettor but the catalysed version featured electronic management. The car was assembled in the FSM factory at Bielsko Biala in Poland where the twin-cylinder engine and the gearbox were built. The bodyshells were brought in from the Tychy factory, also in Poland.

CINQUECENTO 903i CAT, 899 CAT, S AND SUITE

The 903cc pushrod engine (now built by Zastava Yugo at Kragujeva, Yugoslavia) is one of the most thoroughly developed Fiat power units. For use in the Cinquecento, hydraulic tappets were adopted that eliminated periodic valve adjustment. As well as the carburettor version, the unit was also

years of reliable service in several models. With distributor-less ignition, the engine ran efficiently and helped minimise maintenance costs. Coupled to a five-speed gearbox with well-chosen ratios, the engine produced enough power to make the car effective and highly manoeuvrable. With only 41bhp available, the engine was ideal in town but had to be driven quite hard to be rewarding on the open road.

Fiat's psychologists must have had a hand in the design of the Cinquecento because they achieved the impression of a car that felt small when being driven without the penalty of a claustrophobic interior. Considering its overall dimensions, the roominess of the interior was remarkable. Excellent use of interior space, aided by split rear seating, provided a decent fold down area big enough for the odd washing machine. The trade-off was a very small boot when the seats are upright.

The Cinquecento Elettra was Fiat's first rear-wheel drive car since the Argenta in 1985.

standard accessories. At the end of 1993, the Cinquecento range was mildly face-lifted, one of the modifications being the concealing of the fuel filler cap behind a hatch.

CINQUECENTO ELETTRA
The Cinquecento was also available with an electric power unit. The front-mounted unit had recharging equipment that could be hooked up to any 220 volt socket to recharge the batteries. With respects to the petrol-engined model, the structure of the car was unchanged. The rear seat was removed to gain access to the choice of lead-gel or NICAD batteries.

With the back of the car full of batteries, there was only room for two people. Luggage went in the space vacated by the petrol engine.

CINQUECENTO SPORTING
The 1108cc Sporting arrived in 1994 and was an instant hit with young drivers who wanted a smart car with sporting appeal, but without a high

available with Weber single-point fuel injection, a three-way catalyst and a Lambda probe. In the Spring of 1993, the engine's displacement was reduced from 903cc to 899cc for fiscal reasons in some countries like Germany, where the taxation system is based on 100cc increments. The same period also saw the launch of the 900i Suite, a model that included air-conditioning among its

purchase price, insurance and running cost. The 54bhp overhead camshaft engine performed well and the gearbox was much improved over the original version. The car was 20mm lower than the base version and it had stiffer suspension and an anti-roll bar. The body was finished in yellow, red, black or silver and featured colour-coded bumpers with contrasting beading and body-coloured rear-view mirrors. Alloy four-spoke wheels were fitted with wider tyres. The interior was brightened up with red safety belts and sporty seats. A leather-rimmed steering wheel, a rev counter and drilled accelerator pedal were also fitted.

The Sporting arrived in the UK during January 1995 and cost £6200. In June 1995, an immobiliser was added along with a new washer/wiper and height adjustable seatbelts. The model was discontinued

Bright colours and alloy wheels helped create the sporty image.

Broom Yellow was very much the colour during the early 1990s.

in June 1998, by which time metallic purple and 'redder' red body colours had been introduced. It is said that the very last cars were fitted with the more desirable Seicento gearbox.

CINQUECENTO TROFEO
It was inevitable that the Cinquecento would find itself in competition events,

The overhead cam 1100 engine put brio into the car's performance.

Italian engineers extracted 160bhp at 9500rpm from this Trofeo.

Below: The Cinquecento Trofeo was a great entry level rally car.

considering the history of small Fiats and its connection with motorsport; the Balilla Coppe d'Oro, 1100 Mille Miglia Coupé,

carried out by Fiat Auto Corse and the Trofeo cars put out about 65bhp. They proved to be valid competition cars giving their crews invaluable first experience of rally driving.

Fiat Auto Corse announced its participation in the 1996 European Rally Championship with a specially prepared version of the Cinquecento Sporting entered in the 'Martini Cup Europa'. Multi-point fuel injection was installed and the engine's power output was increased to 90bhp. The brakes were sourced from the Uno Turbo ie. In January 1997, 14 of

500/600 derivatives and the Uno Turbo are notable examples. Turin lost no time in producing a rortier Cinquecento and its efforts were first made public after the Monte Carlo rally in 1993. This was the Cinquecento Trofeo, which was based on the standard car with its 899/903cc engine. It looked the part in rally trim with a roll cage, altered suspension, alloy wheels and a very neat front light pod. Initial preparation was

The revised range included the Soleil, which had a sunroof.

The Abarth bodykit added a premium to the price of the Cinquecento Sporting.

Below: All show and no go. The scorpion logos were purely cosmetic.

side rubbing strips and wheel trims. In Spring 1996 the Soliel was introduced, which had an

these Group A cars were entered in the Monte Carlo rally.

CINQUECENTO REVISED RANGE

Revised in the summer of 1995, the new models featured a new rear hatch without a horizontal channel between the tail lights, a shrouded rear wiper and wider wheels. The cabin featured grey instrument dials and height adjustable seatbelts. A space-saver wheel was provided. Five models were offered, the ED, S, Suite, Sporting and SX – the ED and Suite were not available in the UK. The SX had body-coloured bumpers,

electric sunroof and chequered interior trim. Finally, the 900 Young replaced the twin-cylinder 700ED on the home market in January 1997.

CINQUECENTO ABARTH

In May 1996, Fiat Auto revived the Abarth logo and applied it to a range of bodykits for its then current Cinquecento, Bravo and Punto models. The scorpion logo had not been seen since it had been applied to the

Abarth branding was appealing to young pretenders but not the purists.

Though launched with the familiar 903cc engine, the capacity was quickly reduced to 899cc for fiscal reasons.

Below: The Italian market endured the twin cylinder 700ED version from 1991 to 1995.

wheel centres of the Uno Turbo in 1989, a car that was not officially recognised as an Abarth, but at least it did qualify in the spirit of the name.

There was much grumbling among purists that the revived Abarth title was being devalued because it was being employed purely for cosmetic purposes and none of the models had any performance enhancements. It was argued that Fiat was missing a marketing opportunity by not applying the Abarth tag to performance versions of its popular model ranges. The rapid Punto GT would have been an ideal candidate. So, too, would the Bravo HGT, an excellent car that was being undersold because nobody could tell it apart from the lesser-powered versions. The Cinquecento Sporting could also have carried the Abarth logo even without the bodykit because it was already a performance version of the basic model. Fortunately, Fiat had a change of heart in 2002 when the Abarth title was applied to a performance car, the 2.4-litre version of the Stilo.

CINQUECENTO VAN
Launched at the Barcelona Show in May 1997, the Cinquecento Van was reserved for the Spanish and Polish markets. The interior had plenty of room for a comfortable cabin

Cinquecento

One of the first batch of UK press fleet Cinquecentos.

Below: The Cinquecento was well-suited to London traffic.

of 39bhp and top speed of 140km/h.

CINQUECENTO: THE UK VERSIONS

Available in 1993, the Cinquecento was very well-received by the small car buying sector and effectively replaced the Fiat Panda – in the UK at least. Supplied with the 899cc and 1.1 engines, three models were offered in the UK; the 900S, 900SX and later the Sporting. The S and SX were equipped with the 899cc 41bhp engines and five-speed gearboxes.

The cars came fairly well-equipped with tinted glass, washer/wiper on the heated rear screen, cloth interior trim, remote tailgate release and stereo. The SX came with extra goodies such as remote central locking, electric front windows and a glass sunroof. In February 1994, some small revisions were made to the fascia, and the interior trim was made from brighter materials.

February 1995 saw the now standard VIN security etching on all models. The face-lifted versions were launched in June 1995, giving the S

and generous load space: 980dm3 and 385kg payload (in addition to the driver). The rear area was protected with trim designed for goods transport and fitted with a partition to separate the driver's cabin plus retaining hooks to secure loads safely. The Fiat Cinquecento Van was fitted with the 899cc petrol engine, with a power output

The bizarre Zagato Z-Eco was one of the Cinquecento design studies shown at London's Design Museum.

wider tyres, side protection strips, reworked trim and an immobiliser (also supplied on the Sporting). The SX on the other hand, came with colour-coded bumpers and a centre console. The 900 Soleil special edition was introduced in June 1996.

DESIGN PROTOTYPES

An exhibition held at the London Design Museum during 1993 celebrated the Fiat 500 legend and heralded the arrival of the new Cinquecento. Fiat offered eight of Italy's internationally renowned design houses the opportunity of creating their own interpretations of the Cinquecento. The exercise was not intended to create works of art, but genuine feasible industrial designs.

Bertone made an off-road spider, Boneschi a minicab, Pininfarina a pick-up, Zagato a city car and ITCA a mini-cabrio. Coggiola went for a streamlined coupé, while Italdesign opted for a tailgated people carrier and the I.DE.A. Institute opted for a high-tech three-seater. The Bertone, Zagato and I.DE.A. designs were chosen for the exhibition at the Design Museum and presented interesting alternatives on the Cinquecento base.

Bertone's effort was a "spectacular and emotional interpretation of the objective and rational original project". Entitled the Toy-car, the design was based on the remote-controlled models that fascinate the young and not-so-young of today.

I.DE.A. attempted to match a racy lifestyle with the changing needs of the motorist. In doing so, its research went into maximum utilisation of all available interior living space. I.DE.A did this by opting for seating for three occupants and their luggage. It was called the Grigua, or lizard, the detailing was extremely effective, even down to a reptilian imprint in the tyre tread pattern.

Zagato, traditionally radical in its creations, went for a bicycle-carrying car named the Z-Eco. According to Zagato, its Cinquecento was a vehicle for those who had no intention of giving up the freedom provided by individual transport

The ITCA mini-cabrio seemed to be a sensible interpretation.

and would like to expand its range, while caring for the environment and overcrowding.

RUNNING A CINQUECENTO

When the Cinquecento was replaced by the Seicento, there was a surplus of traded-in nearly new and used cars that became available on the supermini market. These low mileage cars offered good value for someone looking for a good starter car, second car or just cheap reliable transport. With low insurance rates and now, in the UK, cheaper road tax, the Cinquecento offered a lot of fun per pound.

Cinquecento buyers list the size of the car high in their criteria. With a small turning circle, short wheelbase and track, this is the perfect city

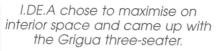

I.DE.A chose to maximise on interior space and came up with the Grigua three-seater.

There were three problems with the Cinquecento that were dealt with by the manufacturer on a recall basis. A properly maintained service history that should accompany a second-hand car will record the work carried out. The first problem affected Cinquecento S, SX and Soleil models. The brake servo unit could become inoperative after extended high-speed running. Loss of brake servo-assistance was caused by petrol contamination of the servo diaphragm. The affected vehicles were recalled for replacement of the servo brake vacuum pipe and checking of the brake servo efficiency. Vehicles affected were within the chassis number sequence 862082 to 957625 with build dates from November 1996 to April 1997. The second recall concerned steering column weld fractures on non-airbag models caused by a manufacturing fault resulting in possible failure of the steering column universal joint. Vehicles affected were between chassis numbers 1081337 and 1086344. Finally, corrosion of the welded seam on the fuel tank led to an improved tank being fitted. This defect affected virtually all S, SX, Sporting models and derivatives from the start of production.

There were reports of poor gearboxes on the base model 899cc Cinquecento but this was generally unfounded as it was more about the feel of the gearchange than an actual mechanical defect. However, the Sporting version does have a much more pleasant gearchange than the base model. Such items as the widely reported ticking speedometer is a minor irritation, apparently caused by a vibrating cable, this can be cured by fitting a cable from an Uno. The central locking motor on early cars was claimed as a fault and was found to be a 'lazy' solenoid. There were also reports of knocking coming from the rear of the car which is blamed on the shock absorbers, not actually failing, just making noise.

Initially, Pirelli were the only manufacturer to produce tyres in the correct size for the Cinquecento, this is said to have produced an unusual shortage, requiring some owners to fit 175/50 Mini tyres, with 14in or 15in wheels where the tyre choice was much better. To avoid rubbing on the bodywork, some inner wheelarch modification

runabout. Ranging from insurance groups 2 to 4, with impressive fuel consumption figures (43-60mpg for the 900cc and 38-60mpg for the 1108cc), the Cinquecentos are certainly cheap to run.

Auto Italia magazine's Deputy Editor, Michael Ward, ran a Cinquecento Sporting as an everyday car and was also a member of the UK's enthusiastic Clubcento. The following information is based on his own experiences and those of the club members. Although numerous problems were encountered, it should be noted that the Cinquecento was built to a price and that any small car that has survived since 1995 has done well.

The Cinquecento Sporting quickly achieved cult status among the UK's Fiat enthusiasts.

may be required if 15in tyres are fitted. Goodyear, however, currently manufactures the correct size so there are now more tyre choices.

Under the bonnet, a minor niggle comes from the hydraulic tappets. Apparently, sediment builds up which can cause the tappets to rattle on some engines that are only driven on short journeys without the car being fully warmed through. Cars used in this way should have the engine oil changed more frequently. The single-point fuel injection system benefits from occasional cleaning. Inefficient fuel injection will shorten the life of the Lambda sensor and the condition of the rear tailpipe on the exhaust system.

Some owners have expressed concern over the cost of servicing the Cinquecento. However, the schedule requires more than simply an oil change every 12,000 miles, with fuel filters, air filters and spark plugs all being necessary. Although a small car, the Cinquecento still requires the same basic service items that much bigger cars do. Some original equipment replacement parts are expensive, in particular exhausts systems, but these can be sourced from various aftermarket suppliers. Plastic covers are also a good idea to protect the costly headlight units.

At 69,000 registered miles, Michael Ward's car was fitted with its third replacement radiator, the first two having sprung leaks. Head gaskets have been known to fail, at as little as 40,000 miles on some cars, Michael's failed at 68,000 miles. This may be due to undetected overheating caused by a leaking radiator.

Other reported faults were fractured frames on drivers' seats, ineffective handbrakes, clutch cable breakages, wiper blades that lift off the windscreen at high speeds, and rust in the boot floor on the inner arches and behind the rear bumper.

MODIFIED CINQUECENTOS

It is likely that Fiat's decision not to uprate the Cinquecento beyond Sporting specification has a lot to do with practicality and economics. The car was made in Poland, no doubt to keep costs down. To produce an off-the-shelf performance version would have increased costs considerably and required additional skilled staff to set the cars up. Fiat is in the business of mass production and does not have the infrastructure to build low production specialist cars. Having said that, its tuning department did build the Cinquecento

Trofeo for budget rallying and could have made performance kits available direct to owners or through the dealer network. The problem is that buying real performance costs money and then it has to be competently installed, probably at dealer level. High cost of extreme tuning components might be justified when building a competition car, but could make a road car impossible to drive during everyday use.

Making little cars go quickly instead of buying a bigger faster one in the first place doesn't make much sense. This insensibility is justified in the name of enthusiasm and without enthusiasts the world would be a boring place, and there would never have been someone called Carlo Abarth. It was obvious from the day that the Fiat Cinquecento Sporting arrived that some owners would want to make their cars go faster. Naturally, there are tuning specialists who would provide the necessary products and services to profit from this need.

In true Abarth fashion, the small Fiat received attention from the tuning fraternity.

In the days of Carlo Abarth, it wasn't that difficult to make small cars go quickly. Four branch manifolds, multiple carburettors, high lift camshafts, and straight-through exhaust systems couldn't fail to produce huge power gains when fitted to an otherwise agricultural standard engine. Today it's different. Modern electronics allow very high compression ratios, highly efficient metered fuel injection has replaced carburettors, and variable valve timing provides a wider power band and higher revs. The modern combustion engine is already a highly-tuned device, so how do you build on that?

Carlo Abarth could do his magic with mechanical hardware and dexterous spanner work. Of course, the modern mechanic also needs these skills, but now he must also have electronic talents to reprogramme ECUs and tune the engine via a laptop computer. When the Cinquecento Sporting arrived on the scene, understanding the engine management technology was in its infancy and the results were variable. For the owner with a limited budget, tuning a small Fiat could be a costly exercise and some were left with a car that only worked well, and anti-socially, at high rpm.

TRACK TEST
Auto Italia magazine tested two modified Fiat Cinquecentos. Van Aaken Developments (Car 1) went the turbo route, while owner Jonathan Sage (Car 2) went the conventional route and topped it off with a six-speed gearbox.

CAR 1
VAD offered several upgrades for the Cinquecento. The version tested was fitted with a Garrett T15 turbo, intercooler, thicker head gasket, cone air filter, additional injector, electronic mappable fuelling and injection system, and Bosch Super 4 spark plugs. The power output was claimed to be 110bhp and the conversion cost £1920.

Sitting on larger diameter, wider wheels and tyres, the Van Aaken car looked to have a firm hold on the ground. The Minilite-style 6J x 14in alloys were fitted with Yokohama A509185/50VR14 tyres. Wheels apart, the only other outward sign of tuning was a big twin pipe Novitec exhaust. The interior was standard apart from a calibrated boost gauge and an air/fuel ratio meter, the latter being disconnected. This is a row of lights which gives instant read-out of how the fuel is burned

Some engine tuners were able to extract more power from the overhead cam power unit.

With power up from 54bhp to 75bhp, this car could carry the scorpion with pride.

– i.e. rich or lean. These are useful instruments for modified cars, they weigh nothing and warn of impending melt down.

Auto Italia magazine's chief test driver, Roberto Giordanelli, had reservations about this conversion believing that doubling the power would lead to handling problems. This was not the case, and apart from being able to spin the wheels on tight first gear turns, the power and its delivery did not upset the chassis. Hard acceleration whilst turning did not bring on understeer followed by lift-off oversteer as had been predicted. Even on/off power inputs mid-turn did not confuse the suspension, steering or tyres unduly. Torque steer was absent. In the dry, traction could only be broken by full power, full lock, first gear take-offs.

The turbo supplied a mild/safe 0.7 bar of boost, enough to produce 110bhp at 5300rpm. Unfortunately, below 3000rpm the acceleration was slower than a standard car; the lower 8.5:1 compression ratio (9.6 standard) and additional plumbing reducing low-speed efficiency. Once the tacho needle was passed 3000rpm, the power surge was healthy without being alarming. Some turbo lag was present but could be compensated for by driving technique. VAD claimed a 0-60mph time of 9.2 seconds with a top speed of 113mph.

CAR 2

The car's owner elected to go the non-turbo route with his then six month-old Sporting. Power output was increased from the standard 54bhp to 75bhp, accomplished by fitting a special air filter, rechipped ECU, special camshaft, bigger injector and a gas-flowed cylinder head and inlet manifold. The catalytic converter had been removed and a 4-2-1 tubular exhaust manifold and a free-flow big-bore one box system fitted. The cost of modification was £1275 and carried out by Abarth specialists Middle Barton Garage.

The six-speed gearbox was sourced from a Punto. Its top gear ratio is virtually the same (slightly shorter) as the standard Cinquecento Sporting five-speed unit. Having six speeds means that through the range there are more gears to choose from, ensuring that instant response was always available. Using the speedometer and tachometer fitted, fifth

Thankfully, there will always be someone who wants to make fast Fiats go faster.

gear gave 15mph per 1000rpm and sixth provided 18mph per 1000rpm. With the rev-limiter raised to 7500rpm, top speed was increased despite the lower gearing.

Predictably noisier than Car 1, Car 2 suffered from a lumpy tick-over. Further work on the ECU was planned. Blipping the throttle in neutral, it was also more responsive than turbocharged Car 1. With six gears to choose from, the best was made of the available 75bhp. The 0-60mph time took 11.5 seconds (fourteen standard) and the top speed was 110mph (95 standard). The power delivery was smooth enough, but it did seem lacking at low rpm. Up to 4000rpm progress was nothing special but after 4000rpm was noticeably quicker than standard. Combined with six gear ratios, the unit made the most of its 1108cc. It was good fun too.

Other modifications included vented front discs, a strut brace and special Fiat wheels (standard size, painted black). Standard size, grippy Pirelli 165/55 13 P700Zs were fitted. Inside, only a Momo steering wheel and floor mats were non-standard. The handling was slightly improved by shorter, stiffer springs without ruining the ride comfort. Minor low-speed understeer was still present but dialling it out could bring on high-speed oversteer. Being a brand new car, the original dampers were retained. Further handling

	Cinquecento	Sporting	MBG/mod	VAD/mod
Cubic cap:	899cc	1108cc	1108cc	1108cc
Comp ratio:	9.1:1	9.6:1	9.8:1	8.5:1
Power bhp:	41bhp at 5000rpm	54bhp at 5500rpm	75bhp at 6500rpm	110bhp at 5300rpm
0-60mph:	17.7sec	14sec	11.5sec	9.2sec
Top speed:	87mph	95mph	110mph	113mph

improvements could be achieved by fitting dampers which matched the stronger spring rates and by fitting an uprated anti-roll bar.

Roberto Giordanelli found comparing the two cars difficult. Power freaks would be likely to opt for Car 1. Roberto's own engineering experience with turbos had taught him that much more development work is required than with naturally aspirated modifications. There was some concern over the turbocharged engine's long-term reliability. As for the conventionally modified Car 2, long-term reliability was expected, but it was considered that a lower-stressed higher capacity engine would be a better option. In conclusion, it would seem that the most sensible option would be to fit a larger unmodified engine, either a 1242cc or 1388cc eight-valve unit.

Cinquecento

THE FIAT SEICENTO

smoothing off the corners

Fiat has been present in Poland for 76 years. Its involvement in the country has grown continually: the first sales were made at the beginning of the century, the first sales outlet (Polski Fiat) dates back to the 1920s, and the first cars were produced in the 1930s.

After a break due to World War II and the Cold War, relations were resumed in the 1960s with two major licensing contracts: the Fiat 125P in 1965 and the 126P in 1971. FSM (Fabrika Samochodûw Malolitrazowych) was set up in Bielsko Biala to produce the 126P, and was joined a few years later by the Tychy plant and the Skoczow foundry.

A third licensing contract was signed in 1987 for production of the Fiat Cinquecento at the FSM, and all the other plants were extended (particularly the Tychy plant, where the Cinquecento was produced until mid-1998). On May 28th 1992, FSM was converted from a state company to a limited company with 90 per cent of its share capital held by Fiat Auto and 10 per cent by the State Treasury. On this occasion, the company took the name by which it is known today: Fiat Auto Poland SA. The agreement between Fiat Auto and the Polish state is the most important privatisation agreement so far drawn up in the state, and one of the biggest ever made anywhere in Eastern Europe.

BUILDING A SEICENTO

The Fiat Seicento is produced at Tychy and the engines are made in Bielsko Biala. The high-tech Tychy complex employs nearly 6000 people and occupies an overall area of 1,895,000 square metres, 380,000 of which are covered. At the peak of production, a new Fiat Seicento rolled off the lines every 90 seconds. In the panel shop, the various body parts are assembled on a robotized rig known as a Robogate. The system is equipped with gates that can be replaced automatically without interrupting the chain of production when changing from one model to the next.

All main body sub-units (floorpan, front frame, chassis, sides and roof) are first tacked by hand on mechanised lines, and then completed by robots to ensure maximum precision. Then the body is put together. The operation takes place in a special robotized centre where gates are used to ensure body

The Seicento was another product of Fiat's highly efficient Polish operation.

101

The Seicento was better built and better finished than the Cinquecento, but was it better looking?

The car then passes through stations for door removal, insulation application, electric wiring and installation of heater, pedal unit, roof panel, fascia and windows. Underbody units, body parts, bumpers, headlights and wheels are installed on the second section. The assembled Seicento undergoes other operations during the final section: fluid filling, seat

geometry is correct, while robots apply about eighty weld spots.

Eighty-five robots work in the panel shop altogether. Machines check subunit and whole body dimensions after each process to ensure they have been carried out correctly. The newly-assembled bodies are then taken to the paint shop, the most advanced in Europe. The level of automation is extremely high (particularly in the spray booth) to ensure consistent quality standards. The paint shop is also designed to be completely environmentally sound.

The newly-assembled bodyshells firstly undergo pre-treatment to ensure the paint sticks more effectively to the panels. They are then submerged in phosphating and passivating tanks. This is followed by cataphoresis, another immersion process. An electric current is passed between the body and a bath containing paint suspended in water. This process deposits a layer of protective paint over all interior and exterior surfaces. The paint is then stoved at a temperature of 170 degrees celsius in ovens with gas burners. Sealant is then applied along the panel joints and a thick layer of protective agent is sprayed onto the underbody and into the wheelarches to protect surfaces from abrasion and corrosion. Both products are supplied from a centralised system.

The interiors were well-trimmed and, overall, a nice place to sit.

installation, door refitting, battery positioning and engine bay completion. At the end of the line, the suspension is adjusted, the electrical system and engine are tested, wheel toe-in is checked, headlight alignment is adjusted, the brakes are tested on rollers and a watertightness test is carried out. Quality is assured by the way the entire manufacturing cycle is organised and also by a series of tests that the car undergoes before it leaves the factory.

THE FIAT SEICENTO RANGE
SEICENTO 900, S, SX, YOUNG AND CITYMATIC
The Seicento set new standards for the great small Italian car, in particular the Sporting version,

which achieved something approaching cult status among enthusiasts in the UK.

A car intended to replace the Cinquecento would have a tough act to follow. Launched in Spring 1998, Fiat took the Seicento one step further and improved on the earlier car. However, although the Cinquecento was not as well-made and more basic than the Seicento, it did have more charisma.

The Seicento gained refinements, but put on weight, cost more and managed to lose some character in the process. The Cinquecento's angles were softened up and replaced by rounded corners and the Seicento's goldfish bowl rear window doesn't really work, the car had become cuddly rather than cheeky. This may be because Fiat had made a big effort to broaden the appeal of the Seicento and attempted to make the car heterogeneous – all things to all people. In the highly competitive compact car segment, potential owners are young students, pensioners, housewives, working women, professionals who only ever use their car around town, and commuters who travel many miles a year. It even claims to be a family car and is officially approved as a five-seater – over-stretching reality, perhaps.

To be fair, the Seicento did have an impressive range of equipment for such a small car. A total of six versions represented the most varied range in the category. Choices varied from the versatile S, to the sporty Sporting, from the stylish SX to the sophisticated, comprehensively equipped Suite. The conventional Seicento range was supported by two special versions, the Citymatic and the Elettra. Also, to suit all tastes, an impressive array of 13 young, lively colours with matching trim were also on offer.

The Seicento Suite came with the 1100cc overhead cam engine and air-conditioning.

As with other Fiat models, the variety of standard equipment (which varied slightly from market to market) on the Fiat Seicento range was joined by a wide selection of options including ABS, air-conditioning and an air recirculation facility. Other standard features included tailgate opening from the inside, integral wheel trims, lockable fuel filler cap, central console, right-hand door mirror, tinted windows and electrically-operated windows.

SEICENTO SUITE
The Suite was top of the range. Equipped with a 1108cc Fire engine, its long list of equipment was unique in the world of super-compact cars. The SX specification included central locking, air-conditioning and a front anti-roll bar. Other finely judged details gave this car a charmingly sophisticated appearance. Such features included body-coloured door handles and trimmed central pillars. This model was aimed at the owner who required comfort and refinement in a small car.

SEICENTO CITYMATIC
Available in SX specification, the Citymatic was particularly well-suited to people who drive regularly

in town traffic. The car was fitted with an electronically-controlled clutch which automatically-controlled starting, stopping, low speed manoeuvres and driver-controlled gearchanges.

SEICENTO ELETTRA

The S specification Seicento Elettra was a noiseless, environmentally-friendly car, intended to transport people and goods through town centres. Designed using state-of-the-art battery technology, the Elettra's range and performance was impressive. The Elettra, the 899cc Young base model, and the Hobby 1.1, were also included in the home market Seicento range but were not part of the UK line-up.

When introduced in 1998, the Seicento Elettra was the smallest four-seater zero emissions car available on the market. By locating the batteries in the tunnel between the seats, it was possible to provide two comfortable seats at the rear plus a roomy luggage compartment.

The motor offered excellent performance for its category. Maximum power output was 30kW (a direct current engine delivers 15kW). The maximum torque of 130Nm (13.02 kgm) was available at start-up. Acceleration from 0 to 50km/h took just 8 seconds and top speed in excess of 100km/h was possible.

The ultra-silent Fiat Seicento Elettra was equipped with two different horns. One indicated the car's presence to pedestrians, the second to other cars. A black button on the right of the steering wheel controlled the traditional horn, while a special green pedestrian horn button on the right emits a softer sound.

A special electric car park was made available for the Elettras in Piazza Vittorio Veneto in Turin. At the time, the Fiat Seicento Elettra was the only rear-wheel drive Fiat in production.

SEICENTO SPORTING

The Sporting was intended for the driver who preferred a touch

The 'goldfish bowl' rear window was perhaps the least pleasing aspect of the Seicento's design.

of compact car sportiness. The car was lively and came with a youthful, appealing specification. The body-coloured bumpers had a broad air intake giving the car a more distinctive and aggressive look. Other differences included fog lights, alloy wheels and wider 165/55 tyres.

Inside, the rev counter was not located on the dashboard but high up on the central console. The

Abarth wheels and side skirts were dealer-fitted options.

performance enhancements. Exterior fitments included a roof spoiler, side skirt kit, exhaust tailpipe and choices of two alloy wheel designs. The Abarth interior options were; a leather steering wheel and gear lever knob, aluminium handbrake grip, gear lever frame and sporty pedal unit with footrest, and Abarth sill strips.

Writing for *Auto Italia* magazine, Andy Heywood felt that Fiat had undoubtedly unleashed extra zest from the revised 1108cc four-cylinder engine by giving it multi-point fuel injection, and although the output is only 54bhp, the engine

steering wheel and gear lever knob were leather-trimmed, the pedals were drilled and the seats were anatomical with a sporty configuration. An optional Abarth bodykit was also available and consisted of a rear spoiler, side skirts, wide 14in wheels and tyres, and a special sporty interior.

SEICENTO SPORTING ABARTH
Fiat developed an Abarth styling kit for the Seicento Sporting and, like the previous Cinquecento version, it did not have any

The Abarth treatment wasn't extended to the power unit.

The illusion of interior space was a clever achievement.

now had the ability to rev smoothly all the way to 6000rpm. The Sporting was certainly more sprightly than the base model, but purely because it had that closer set of gear ratios for the five-speed box with the same final drive ratio and shares the same top speed of 93mph as the rest of the range.

The interior of the car was a step forward from the Cinquecento in terms of quality, but the Seicento offered a great deal more. The instrument layout was much improved with its shiny silver panel in the centre of the dash housing all the switchgear for fog lights, heating and ventilation. The rev counter was mounted on a semicircular binnacle in the centre of the dash.

The Seicento was able to cruise in-line with other motorway users. With 80mph equating to 4200rpm in fifth gear, cruising at this speed was relaxed and stable, and there was very little noise from the engine. However, there was considerable wind noise from around the A pillars.

The other major addition across the revised range was the adoption of the EPAS system from the Punto. It was found that Fiat's new electronic power steering gave maximum assistance for ultra-light parking, and above 30mph added the relevant weight and excellent feel to the steering. Unlike the Punto, there is no City button on the Seicento, which seems largely unnecessary anyway. The Sporting Abarth that *Auto Italia* magazine tested also came with ABS and air-conditioning, options that together with the Abarth sports kit, pushed the on-the-road price to over £9000, against a normal Sporting at £7525. A lot of money for a little car, but it's actually a lot of car for your money and is exhilarating to drive aided, no doubt, by the scorpion logo. The Abarth kit added some masculinity to an otherwise slightly cute and cuddly Seicento image.

Black bumpers identify this car as the revised range Seicento S.

REVISED UK RANGE

A mild facelift in 2000 was most easily distinguishable by the new front bumper and the adoption of the new round Fiat badge. From October 2000, the Seicento S and SX became available with the multi-point injection 1108cc unit in order to become Euro 3 compatible. This engine replaced the old single-point injection 1108cc engine, while the 899cc was dropped altogether.

The pushrod 899cc engine was dropped in favour of the unburstable overhead cam 1100.

The limited edition Seicento Schumacher used rebadged Abarth trim.

The Maestro's signature meant everyone wanted to race you.

SEICENTO S

The Seicento S represented a no-frills motoring option without sacrificing style or comfort. It was fun to drive and a very useful car around town where cheeky antics are tolerated. On the motorway it's a different matter because some drivers of much larger cars were often surprised to see a tiny Seicento S wanting to overtake. The Seicento S is a bit of a Q-car because, although it looked like a base model, it now had the 1108cc engine of its sportier brother with the smarter clothes. With just 54bhp, obviously it was never going to be called a super-fast car, but it was nippy and cruised quite happily at high speed.

The original 899cc power unit was discontinued (in the UK) in favour of the superb multi-point fuel-injected 1108cc Fire engine which is even better than old Sporting unit. The maximum power was still 54bhp but produced at 5000rpm instead of 5500rpm. Likewise, torque was up to 65lb ft from 63lb ft at a lower 2750rpm instead of 3250rpm. The mechanical difference between the S and the Sporting was the gearbox. The Sporting had slightly shorter ratios giving a faster 0-62mph time of 13.5sec compared with the S at 14.5sec.

Auto Italia magazine road tested the Seicento S and found that the fuel consumption around town was 34mpg and out of town about 60mpg with a combined figure of 47mpg, very frugal; but driven with a heavy foot as little Fiats often are, these figures suffered. During the test, the driver was aware of high speed wind noise from the front pillars. The car's high sides were also a factor in a crosswind. Although the little wheels and tyres cut through the water on the roads, the car felt a little

nervous and twitchy at high speeds. Even without ABS, which was not available of the S, the brakes were superb. All around visibility was excellent, making parking easy. The interior trim was much improved along the model's life compared to it's more basic older sister, the Cinquecento S. A very low insurance group and high fuel economy make this an ideal first car for the new driver or a city/town runabout for a small family. Definitely a small car with big car capabilities for just £6526 (SX is £6825), the Seicento S has spades full of practicality.

SEICENTO SCHUMACHER

Michael Schumacher's first car was a Fiat 500, so it is appropriate that the Formula One World Champion should have a special version of its spiritual successor, the Seicento, named after him. The Fiat Seicento Sporting 'Michael Schumacher', of which a limited edition of just 5000 were manufactured, had its world preview at the 2000 Bologna Motor Show.

The limited edition Seicento Schumacher takes its styling cues from the Seicento Sporting

Group A Challenge cars had power output doubled to a significant 108bhp at 7800rpm.

trained in this way. The popularity of the Cinquecento Trofeo bears witness to its value as a school for aspiring drivers.

The Fiat Seicento replaced the Cinquecento as an entry level rally car. Standard production versions were joined by a Group A version for use in the Regional Fiat Seicento Rally Challenge races. Challenge races were fought out between 20 cars, one representing each Italian region. The six races counted towards the national championship, the European championship and – in the case of the San Remo rally – the world championship. Drivers were selected by dealers in each region requiring each driver to be under 25 years of age and born in the region represented.

The Fiat Seicento Group A was derived from the Sporting version. The 1147cc engine produced 108bhp at 7800rpm and included special engineering features such as multi-point injection, intake manifold with twin throttle body and steel split exhaust manifold. The transmission system included a six-speed gearbox derived from the Fiat Punto. The differential benefited from a controlled slip Viscodrive-type system derived from the Fiat Coupé 2.0 20v Turbo. The chassis was strengthened for rally use and the front and rear suspension was rose-jointed. The upgraded braking system was fitted with discs on all four wheels (self-ventilated at the front) in addition to the Fiat Punto GT servo pump and distributing valve.

Abarth kit. Standard features included ABS, side skirts with Michael Schumacher logos, and 14in alloy wheels with low profile tyres featuring new Fiat wheel centres. Other features included aluminium sports pedals, gear lever frame and handbrake lever, limited edition plate, Michael Schumacher logo and signature on the tailgate spoiler, Michael Schumacher branded kick plates, and a leather steering wheel with red stitching.

Standard equipment also included a driver's airbag, manual sunroof, electronic steering, electric windows, central locking, front seat belt pre-tensioners, a Sony single CD player/RDS stereo radio unit and a Fiat CODE immobiliser. Available in two colours, Tiziano Red and Broom Yellow, the Seicento Schumacher was priced at £7894 on-the-road.

The author has test driven one of these cars and found that on numerous occasions other road users would have an irresistible desire to demonstrate their driving abilities in a rather over-competitive manner.

FIAT SEICENTO – GROUP A RALLY VERSION
Small Fiats have enjoyed a long history of racing success. Innumerable past category victories have been achieved by 500 and 600 cars prepared by tuners such as Abarth and Giannini – to name the two most famous. For many years, Fiat's Trofeo series has allowed hundreds of young drivers to race on a limited budget. Many rally champions have been

SEICENTO SPORTING KIT
Another competition version of the Seicento, the Seicento Sporting Kit, was built around the regulations for rallying and was without a doubt the most potent of the official versions. With the engine capacity increased marginally to 1146cc and the use of four 38mm throttle bodies, it produced 128bhp at 7800rpm. With Uno turbo ventilated discs at the front and 227mm solid

seicento

600

discs at the rear also stopped, while fully rose-jointed suspension, limited slip differential, six-speed gearbox and weight of only 810kg meant it also handled. A complete cost of only 29000 Euro (in 2002) also made it somewhat of a bargain!

SEICENTO 600

With the New Panda taking most of the limelight, early 2004 saw a revised Fiat Seicento range released, with new interiors and a very slightly changed exterior. Only the 1100cc engine with basic trim levels remained, other versions ceased production, including the Sporting.

The final version of the Seicento appeared on the Italian home market in 2004.

A special edition was introduced to mark the 60th anniversary of the original 600.

The smart interior trim of the commemorative Fiat 600.

To mark the fiftieth anniversary of the Fiat 600, Fiat decided to update the Seicento with a number of styling changes and to rationalise the range. The new car features some stylistic elements of one of the most emblematic Italian products of all time, starting with the name, which reverts to the historical version written in figures, and is repeated in a chromed logo on the rear of the car.

The new range also includes a special limited edition known as the Fiat 600 '50th' which is a tribute to the legendary 600, the forefather of an entire class of cars. These cars are all finished with 'classic' beige paintwork.

In addition to these obvious historical references, the new Fiat 600 confirms the winning features that have enabled the Fiat Seicento to reach an output of over 1,100,000 units since 1998: good performance, excellent handling and very low running costs. Plus, an excellent quality/price ratio and a high residual value on the second-hand market. A market success, which shows that the model has earned itself a significant position in its highly competitive market bracket.

Today, to reinforce and improve this position in relation to its many competitors, the 'super-mini' receives a facelift that underlines its role as an advantageous alternative in the lower part of the segment. At the time of writing, the 600 was the smallest four-seater on the market. Seicento production is expected to end by the time the New Fiat 500 arrives in September 2007.

A German Italian. The Novitec turbocharged Seicento.

MODIFIED FIAT SEICENTOS
NOVITEC

Based at Stetten in Germany, the Novitec tuning company is renowned for its work on tuning current range Italian cars and supplying aftermarket styling products. In 1999, Novitec turned its attention to the Seicento. The conversion was based on a turbocharged version of the Seicento Sporting. Novitec dismantled the engine and lowered the compression ratio to 8.3:1 with modified pistons.

The compact turbo unit, made in the UK by Schwitzer, had an integral wastegate and provided a 0.5 bar boost. An intercooler was positioned low down in the front of the car. The Seicento uses single-point injection and its ECU is a very basic one, so Novitec have installed its own ECU which is placed in-line between the factory unit and the engine. A single, larger injector replaces the original installation.

Power from the 1108cc engine was increased from 54bhp to 101bhp at 5500rpm, with 115.9lb ft (157Nm) of torque at 4600rpm. Performance figures included an impressive 0-62mph time of 8.1 seconds and a top speed of 120mph (192km/h). To optimise on this power capability, Novitec have re-engineered the five-speed gearbox to accept a sixth ratio. The extra ratio also provided a good cruising ability of 70mph (112km/h) at 3000rpm. The good spread of torque and the light weight of the Seicento reduced the

A six-speed gearbox made sure that the turbo was kept on boost.

Engine tuners were quick to adopt the Seicento as a means of selling their wares.

Commissioned by its owner, the smart yellow and blue-themed Seicento started life as a 1108cc 54bhp standard car but was converted by UAD to accept an eight-valve 1242cc engine from a Punto 60. The compression ratio was increased to 11.5:1 and the cylinder head was gas-flowed

UAD doubled the Seicento's power by fitting a Punto 60 engine.

amount of gearchanging normally required to keep a tuned small engine 'on the cam'.

The small turbo was on boost almost at idle, and provided strong and linear acceleration. The engine revved smoothly and enthusiastically to the redline, with such energy that each of the first five standard gear ratios seemed that much shorter. Without the sixth gear, the driver would simply run out of ratios, even on country roads.

To cope with the extra power safely, Novitec uprated the suspension with sports springs, dampers and an uprated front anti-roll bar. Ride height was lowered by 45mm. A front suspension strut brace helped stiffen the bodyshell. The 7J x 15in alloy wheels were fitted with 195/45ZR15 tyres for additional grip. Although the standard Seicento braking system was adequate, Novitec offered an uprated brake kit.

Novitec also marketed a 1242cc turbo conversion with 118bhp, and also developed a twin-turbo version, the SeiBi, that developed a massive 190bhp with 282Nm of torque.

UNIQUE ACTIVE DESIGNS

Unique Active Designs (UAD) adopted the Abarth tradition of putting big engines into small cars. Tony Soper, writing for *Auto Italia* magazine, tested two of UAD's converted Seicentos, one a yellow car which was normally aspirated, and the other a silver turbocharged version.

and ported. High lift, high duration camshafts were fitted and the balanced crankshaft assembly was matched to a 50 per cent lightened flywheel. The ECU was remapped and Magnecour KV85 leads, an ITG filter, a UAD tuned induction kit, and Trofeo group N 4-2-1 exhaust were also installed. Braking effort was improved with Red Dot 20 groove discs/drums and linings as well as braided brake hoses. The finishing touch was a set of Skyline 6.5J x 15in alloys fitted with 195/45 Goodyear Eagle F1s, which just fitted under the standard wheelarches. Although it was not fitted to the test car, UAD also offered a custom suspension package.

More ambitious options included a 1388cc big bore motor, carbon-fibre induction kit and a variety of body styling. UAD's philosophy was to bring together the best engine with a combination of other components that represented the ideal

When you run out of tuning options, fit a bigger engine. This one has a Punto 1242cc, 8-valve unit.

Seicento conversion, and was packaged as the 600M (the M stands for Modificata – Seicento Modified).

Despite being slightly taller than the 1108cc powerplant, the 1242cc Punto engine slotted

Aftermarket seats and full harnesses for driver – and passenger – confidence.

The silver car started life as a 1108cc Sporting and UAD used the car as its development prototype. At the time of the test, it was fitted with an experimental 1242cc eight-valve turbocharged engine, a full body kit (custom bonnet, rear venturi and flared arches), a Cadamuro front splitter and spoiler, 7J x 15in wheels, Red Dot grooved discs/drums, Novitec 50mm lowering springs, strut brace, special front strut top mounts and a motorsport-inspired interior.

At the time, the engine was operating on single-point injection (albeit with a bigger injector) although a multi-point conversion was being developed. The turbo was by Schwitzer and feed through an intercooler. Performance produced was about 120bhp with 100lb ft torque. Further development has been hampered by the constraints imposed by chipping a standard ECU, however, with the planned multi-point injection and a fully mappable ECU, UAD was confident that the final conversion would offer in excess 150bhp.

Hard acceleration was rewarding and power built up from 3000rpm and every gear change was accompanied by a cacophony of popping and puffing from the wastegate. The engine was good to 6000rpm, giving a useful power band and real overtaking ability. Most striking was the big car feel of this Seicento and its confident high-speed stability. With much less body roll than the yellow car, it put its power down without drama.

straight into the Seicento. Starting it up, the Trofeo exhaust sounded purposeful with it's Peco big bore exhaust. Once rolling, this small car had a big car feel. When fitted to the Punto or Brava, the 1242cc motor needs lots of revs and gear changing, but the lightweight Seicento was transformed with generous torque compared to the standard set-up, this little car was a pleasure to drive in traffic yet would also perform well on the open road. UAD predicted 105 to 110bhp was possible from this conversion, tangible power built from 4000rpm and the engine revs seemed to be unlimited.

While fine for urban use, the suspension on this car needed some adjustment for fast road work. Lower and stiffer springs at the front, combined with standard equipment elsewhere, seemed to result in tail-happy high-speed antics, and the generous body roll allowed loss of traction through tight corners, but it hung on gamely.

NUOVA PANDA

Fiat's supermini

The Ecobasic concept car laid the foundations for the new Panda.

The Nuova Panda story began with the Ecobasic concept, a car which aroused much interest when a static version was presented to the press at the end of 1999.

Making its first appearance at the Turin Show in September 2000, the car evoked similar emotions to the first sighting of the controversial design of the Multipla MPV. Having redefined the MPV, Fiat turned its attention to the small car concept. The innovative Ecobasic concept car was highly acclaimed by the press and it immediately won several environmental awards during 2000. Ecobasic was essentially a research and development vehicle used to experiment on new concepts, some of which found their way into the Nuova Panda.

Fiat contracted Zagato to design and build the first Ecobasic prototype. Zagato's brief was build a low cost, light, yet strong steel chassis for a three-door hatchback car that would have one specification. The intention was that the shell would have modular components 'hung' on it, including extra doors in self-coloured recyclable plastics that could be fitted at dealer level as options. Employing the latest CAD CAM design technology, Zagato designed and built the first car in just four months.

To achieve its aims, Fiat were forced to rethink the small car concept, the way it was built, distributed and sold. A light car with excellent aerodynamics was required to keep fuel consumption down. Hence, the Ecobasic weighed just 750kg and displayed a long shape tapering off at the rear that more than hints at the classic teardrop configuration. This innovative design provided uncommonly good visibility and lighting for such a small car and offered a record-breaking Cx of 0.28.

To achieve outstanding fuel consumption, an ultra-frugal engine was essential. Fresh from its experience in the field of diesel engines, Fiat's research department continued to delve into the further possibilities of common rail injection systems and came up with a small four-cylinder second-generation 1.2JTD turbodiesel engine. A maximum power output of 45kW (61bhp) at 3500rpm, enabled the Ecobasic to achieve160km/h (electronically limited) and accelerate from 0 to 100km/h in 13 seconds. Maximum torque is 16.3kgm (160Nm) at 1800rpm.

It was to take Fiat three long years to begin Panda production.

to fuel returns. Fuel consumption dropped by 10 per cent over the combined ECE plus EUDC cycle, and no less than 20 per cent over the ECE urban cycle. The Ecobasic consumed less than 3-litres of fuel per 100km.

The driver could also select sequential operating mode, when speeds were engaged directly using a gear lever. However, the best fuel consumption benefits were enjoyed when the gearbox operated in fully automatic mode. In this case, two programmes were available. 'Standard' offered a more lively drive while 'Economy' was geared for fuel economy. A stop-and-go strategy came into play at traffic lights when the car was in economy mode. After about four seconds at a standstill, the engine was switched off, and restarted automatically when the accelerator is pressed again. This function was important in reducing fuel consumption since 10 per cent of all fuel used during an urban cycle is burnt when the engine is idling.

The five-speed robotized gearbox made very good use of this torque, particularly at low speeds, to ensure very low fuel consumption. The real breakthrough on this gearbox was its software, which was able to integrate engine control unit strategies at a deep-seated level. The software coordinated the actions of both by simultaneous selection of the gear to be engaged and the engine service point (rpm and load). The driver informed the system of power requirements via the accelerator and the system satisfied this requirement by choosing the option most beneficial

One rather cynical aspect of the Ecobasic was the sealed engine compartment. A small cover on the bonnet allowed access to Inspect lubricant and coolants levels. The reader may speculate that any servicing work on the engine would involve its removal from the vehicle and only at a Fiat approved service centre.

'Small' was the project title during design for the new car that was originally intended to be named Gingo.

INTO PRODUCTION
Nuova Panda was presented to the gathered international press in Lisbon in September 2003. The narrative of Fiat's Italian advertising campaign for Nuova Panda, which coincided with the launch, insisted that its new car should not be referred to as a 'baby' Fiat. Fiat wanted its new car to be called a supermini

This new Panda was test driven by the author on the Lisbon press launch.

Panda

which aligned it closer to the Punto.

The title of Panda was a real last minute affair, as the car was originally to be named Gingo. However, Renault complained that Gingo was too close to its Twingo and that confusion would arise. Fiat had already produced its launch merchandising adorned with 'Gingo' and the author has some launch presentation items that were hastily overprinted with 'Panda'. Arguably, Gingo was not the best name anyway for this important new car as it sounds rather trivial. The fact remains that Fiat had to quickly throw all its marketing might at finding a new name, and they came up with 'Nuova Panda'.

Inevitably, reusing the Panda title will encourage people to make comparisons with the original version, which is unfair because where the first Panda was distinctly utilitarian, Nuova Panda is stylish and refined.

Nuova Panda replaced the Panda 'originale' on September 5th 2003. The outgoing model had plenty of orders right to the end, and it is said that some of the last remaining examples in the showrooms were actually sold at a premium. The hint was that the five-door Nuova Panda would also replace the Seicento, too. However, at the time of writing, the Seicento was still in production as the entry level small Fiat and was face-lifted in 2004.

Fiat have big plans for its new car and 70,000 of them rolled out of the Polish plant during the first four months of production. With production in full swing, 200,000 were expected to be on the road by the end of 2004, 20 per cent of which would be diesel-powered. With such a versatile, brand-new platform stock, Fiat parts were used to add lots of engine options with the promise of 4x4, off-road and possible cabriolet models to come.

A lot of development went into project 169, the Fiat 'Small', and visitors to Turin in 2002 might have seen some of the 80 disguised black prototypes running around the city clocking up over 1.6 million

kilometres during testing. The fruits of this work were revealed in Lisbon, where hundreds of the little cars were lined up all painted in refreshing vibrant colours. The overall impression was slightly retro and during the press presentation, smiling people leaped about the stage which was dressed with beach balls and brightly coloured drinks, just like the 1970s ads. The chosen body colours were retro, too, and included a colour close to Mediterranean Blue (ex-124 Spider), a 'proper' crimson red (500), turquoise (similar to the 128), 'Exorcist' green (127) and 'banana' yellow (124 Coupé). Fun colours for a fun car, which it has since proved to be.

Nuova Panda has some of that cheekiness inherited from the Cinquecento – which evaporated when Fiat introduced the Seicento. Use of interior space is remarkable and doesn't feel at all cramped or claustrophobic. Fiat is good at doing this, aided by Bertone who is attributed as the interior designer. The feeling of spaciousness is helped by the glass rear quarter windows which help illuminate the cabin and also assist with easy parking. However, the space illusion is affected when you notice that the door side trim has been heavily sculpted to accommodate your forearms that are quite close to the door glass.

The upholstery chosen for the seat fabric is colourful and cheerful, the 'splash' version being particularly attractive. Split rear seating helps with bulky load distribution and Fiat's publicity informs that the car is a four/five-seater, this is unlikely, even if you are really friendly with your back seat companions. The boot space is reasonable given the size of the car and the interior room on offer.

However, although the back of the rear seat tips forward, the squab is fixed and compromises the load space. Another space saver is the seat elevation lever which is next to the handbrake instead of near the door. Seat elevation is a novelty on a car in this class, so too is the up and down adjustment on the steering. With all these adjustments and low door glass, it would be hard for even the most vertically challenged of drivers to be uncomfortable in this car. Power steering is fitted and a 'City' option gives additional assistance at low speed.

There were three trim levels specified at the launch; Active, Dynamic and Eleganza, and UK prices ranged from £6295 to £8095. Active is the most basic specification but it does include airbags, central locking,

The ever-growing Panda range lines up for a family portrait – and there are more in the pipeline.

Happy workers at Tychy. Half a million Pandas in two years is an impressive achievement.

power steering, immobiliser, sound system, electric windows and a rear screen wiper. The Punto Dynamic has the benefit of a rev counter, trip computer, ABS/EBD and can be specified with air-conditioning, a SkyDome glass roof or uprated six-speaker 100 watt sound system. The Eleganza further adds 14in alloys, full climate control and split rear seats.

Previously a luxury item, air-conditioning has now become essential in modern cars today. There was a time when selecting air-conditioning while driving a small car almost stalled the engine, but this has no detrimental effect on the Panda. HiFi enthusiasts will be delighted with the excellent 100 watt six-stack system option with the CD changer conveniently located to the rear of the glove compartment. The Sky Dome sunroof option provides an almost open-air feeling for the occupants and further adds to the illusion of great interior space.

Earlier small Fiats were noted for their choppy and harsh ride. Fiat's engineers have put a great deal of effort into solving this problem and the result is a well-damped and comfortable ride without undue body roll or understeer. The brakes (with ABS), clutch and five-speed gearbox

Panda

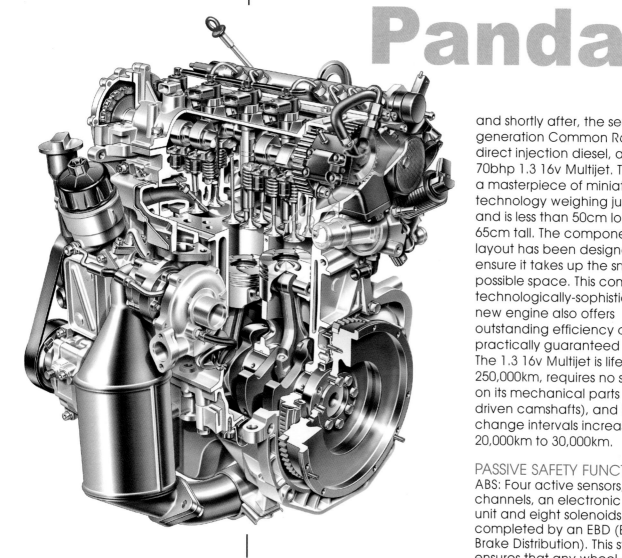

A highly efficient 1.3 16v Multijet is lifed for an amazing 250,000km.

and shortly after, the second-generation Common Rail direct injection diesel, and the 70bhp 1.3 16v Multijet. This is a masterpiece of miniaturised technology weighing just 130kg and is less than 50cm long and 65cm tall. The component layout has been designed to ensure it takes up the smallest possible space. This compact, technologically-sophisticated new engine also offers outstanding efficiency and is practically guaranteed for life. The 1.3 16v Multijet is lifed up to 250,000km, requires no servicing on its mechanical parts (chain driven camshafts), and has oil change intervals increased from 20,000km to 30,000km.

PASSIVE SAFETY FUNCTIONS
ABS: Four active sensors, four channels, an electronic control unit and eight solenoids. It is completed by an EBD (Electronic Brake Distribution). This system ensures that any wheel at the point of locking can brake as effectively as possible. In emergency situations, it also allows full directional control of the car by means of the steering wheel.

EBD: An electronic brake force distributor. This divides braking action over all four wheels to prevent the rear wheels from locking and ensures a balanced car response under all conditions. The system also adapts system operation to wheel grip conditions and pad efficiency. It also reduces front brake temperatures and the brake servo thrust requirement.

ESP: Electronic Stability Programme. The ESP, available from the beginning of 2004, cuts in under extreme conditions when car stability is at risk and also helps the driver to control the car. ESP continually monitors tyre grip in both longitudinal

are all light and easy to operate, making this a very pleasant car to drive. The short gear lever mounted high on the dashboard is similar to the popular arrangement on the Multipla.

One of the most impressive attributes of the Nuova Panda range is the build quality. At no time does the car appear to have been built down to a price, and only the black plastic bumpers on the Active model bring a visual sense of a budget specification, justified by the low purchase price.

ENGINES
There are currently three power units. The established 54bhp 1108cc and 60bhp 1242cc eight-valve petrol engines offered at the launch

A secret Panda Abarth prototype was track-tested by Auto Italia magazine.

and lateral directions. If the car skids, it cuts in to restore directional and ride stability. The ESP is permanently engaged.

ASR: Nuova Panda is fitted with a very sophisticated automatic traction control device to restrict drive wheel slip in the case of reduced road grip. This is known as ASR (Anti Slip Regulation) and comes as standard on all versions equipped with ESP.

MSR: 'Motor Schleppmoment Regelung' cuts in when the gear is changed down abruptly in conditions of low grip. This device restores torque to the engine to prevent the wheel skidding as a result of lock.

HBA: Nuova Panda is fitted with a device to assist with emergency stops. On vehicles with ESP, the function is carried out electronically by the ABS control unit and is referred to as HBA (Hydraulic Brake Assistance). In emergency braking situations, most drivers recognise a situation of danger and press the brake pedal very quickly, however, not with sufficient force. This is because people, unless they are professional drivers, are used to applying a certain load to the brake pedal. People tend to switch to autopilot mode when they carry out repetitive actions, so the same level of force tends to be applied in all circumstances. On the new model, however, the brake-assist devices cut in at this point. Although the pressure on the pedal is unchanged, the car is decelerated by the same amount as it would if it were braked with all the necessary force.

PANDA ON THE ROAD

The Panda does not drive like a small car – merely a smaller version of a 'normal'-sized car. The five-speed gearbox has a slick and precise short throw lever placed high on the dashboard. The gear change is simple to use and alleviates the need for a centre console, in turn, adding to the feeling of space. Steering in all Pandas is of the Dualdrive electric power-assisted type, familiar to anyone who has driven a modern Punto. Ultra-light at parking speeds but with impressive bite and feel at high speed, this steering adds enormously to driver appeal. The handling and ride are also far more sophisticated than you might think, even with a degree of body roll, the car can be hustled along country roads with great verve. When driven hard, the Panda will understeer but it remains a stable, refined and fun car to drive. Motorway cruising is also relaxed, 70mph being reached with the engine running at just 3500rpm.

The 1.1-litre engine is the established Seicento unit producing 54bhp. The 1.2-litre version is the eight-valve FIRE engine used in the Punto, producing 60bhp. The 1.1 engine appears to offer no advantage other than initial purchase price because the 1.2-litre engine offers similar or better fuel consumption and emissions performance. With

Wearing full war paint and ready for the entry level 2007 Italian Trofeo rally championship.

a kerb weight of a mere 860kg, both engines give the car a useful turn of speed.

The undersquare 1242cc engine supplies torque rather than revs, meaning that most of the time it is operating at less than 3000rpm, and this no doubt contributes to the outstanding fuel economy. When mated to the clutchless five-speed sequential 'Dualogic' transmission, the 1.2-litre engine meets the tough Euro IV emissions regulations, but the five-speed manual versions can only manage Euro III.

Pick of the engine options is the 70bhp 16-valve turbo diesel which is also Euro IV compliant with an outstandingly low CO_2 figure of 114g/km. This engine provides brisker initial acceleration than its petrol equivalents and outstanding fuel economy.

FIAT PANDA ABARTH RALLY

With the launch of any new small Fiat, there is always speculation among enthusiasts as to whether a performance Abarth version will become available. Many were delighted to see a prospective rally version of the Panda sporting Abarth badges at the 2004 Bologna Show.

Entitled the Panda Abarth Rally, the car had been built to comply with FIA competition regulations for the 2005 season. Equipment included special spoilers at the front and rear, and side skirts. The wheels are OZ Racing 7J x 16in, with additional wheelarch mouldings incorporated into the front spoiler and side skirts. Inside, the car had a roll cage

bar in steel and chrome-molybdenum alloy and the full safety equipment.

The engine was a development of the 1.3 Multijet tuned to develop 102bhp at just 4200rpm. The engine power has been boosted by the addition of a slightly larger, variable geometry turbo, a racing exhaust complete with catalytic converter, and modifications to the mapping of the standard ECU. The engine is mated to a new five-speed gearbox derived from the Punto JTD. The transmission was modified to accept higher torque and could also accommodate a self-locking differential. Suspension was by Bilstein oil-air dampers, and Eilbach double springs that can be adjusted for the height and camber. The Fiat Abarth Rally was prepared by N-Technology, the company responsible for all the Fiat Group's racing cars.

At the time of writing, Fiat had not announced any plans to enter the Panda Abarth Rally in any competitions or build a road version of the car. The car certainly has the spirit of Abarth in its concept; that of making small cars go very quickly, although purists might scoff at its diesel power.

PANDA 4x4

The 4x4 version of Nuova Panda became available in Italy from September 2004. The model fills a gap in the four-wheel drive market where there is a genuine need for a vehicle with an off-road capability at a budget price.

Initially, the 4x4 was offered with the 60bhp 1.2-litre engine in two specifications, the Panda 4x4 and Panda 4x4 Climbing. Later, the 70bhp Multijet engine became available, though not for the UK market. The Panda Climbing differs from the Panda 4x4 in that it has a more stylish exterior features, 5mm higher ground clearance (165mm against 160mm) and bigger tyres (185/65-14 instead of 165/70-14) .

The rugged bumpers (front and rear) come complete with protective shields, while the side strips are large and coordinate with special strips on the wings and a guard under the engine.

Inside, the Panda 4x4 offers a distinctive and sophisticated interior that benefits from special fabric trims offered in two colour

The highly capable and versatile Panda 4x4 on test during the press launch in Tuscany.

High ground clearance combined with a short wheelbase helps the Panda cope with most terrain.

that has always been one of the strengths of this model. With the one-piece split rear seat folded down, the space increases from a minimum of 200 dm3 to a maximum of 855 dm3 (measured to the roof). If the rear seat is split and also slides, the figures are 230 dm3 (with the seat fully forward) and 780 dm3 respectively.

The Panda 4x4 has a permanent four-wheel drive system with a viscous coupling and two differentials that come into operation automatically, avoiding the need to be stationary to select the drive mode. The high ground clearance combined with the short wheelbase provides high front and rear incidence angles, a measure of the maximum angle that may be undertaken by an off-road vehicle without the body touching the ground. The slope angle, the maximum possible angle without the centre point of the underside touching

matches: grey/red and grey/yellow. The new 4x4 version also retains the big luggage capacity

Old and new: essential 4x4 transport for almost inaccessible Italian mountain locations.

Late in 2003, the New Panda was announced winner of the prestigious 'Car of the Year' award for 2004, judged by numerous European motoring journalists. It has also won a variety of other awards, especially in the UK.

The New Panda went on sale in Italy and various markets around Europe from the autumn of 2003, and got off to a flying start with exceptional sales – the factory had to increase production volumes to meet the demand. The 4x4 and MultiJet diesel versions were launched in the second half of 2004, whilst the MultiJet 4x4 emerged in 2005. A limited edition version developed in conjunction with the famous Italian designer Alessi, the Panda Alessi, was also shown at various shows around Europe in 2004. Also shown, were various two-tone cars with the upper bodywork being a different colour to the lower part. The 500,000th Panda emerged from the factory in Poland in October 2005.

the ground, is also record-breaking for a car in this class. The turning circle is also just 9.6 metres.

On the road, the Panda 4x4 feels somewhat underpowered with a lengthy 0-60mph time of 20 seconds. The raised ride-height also negatively affects the handling and the car is generally much harder work to drive than the Panda 'normale'. Tyre noise is quite high, too. However, this a functional, economical car without being agricultural, and is ideally suited to regular off-road use or where there is restricted access in remote country and mountain regions. It also has style and its occupants can sit in civilised and comfortable surroundings.

Also officially announced is another version, the SUV (Sport Utility Vehicle). This also features the 4x4 transmission with more significant external modifications to differentiate the car. A sporty diesel version is also rumoured, and a diesel-powered rally car prototype was shown in 2003. The latter has a modified 1.3 MultiJet producing 102hp. In 2004 the Panda Kit car was revealed, using the 1242cc engine but now with 120bhp and front-wheel drive. This is used in an Italian rally championship.

Nuova Panda

PANDA 100 HP

When Fiat's Nuova Panda was launched in October 2003, it was considered to be a direct replacement for the venerable, utility Giugiaro box and the uninspiring Seicento. The new car was jollied along by fairly tame 1.1 and 1.2 petrol engines. Later, the more interesting 1.3JTD arrived but the Panda was never regarded to be a performer – that is until the Panda 100 HP arrived.

Developed from the Starjet unit in the Grande Punto, the sparkling new 1368cc 16v twin-cam engine was first spotted in Panda prototypes at the Balocco test track in 2004. This free-revving unit is mated to a six-speed gearbox with superbly chosen ratios.

And it's a real hoot to drive. The engine can be kept on the boil all day with the excellent six-speed gearbox. The engineers have built in some induction roar, which is highly satisfying. On the fast Balocco test track, it was easy to find the point where the ASR cut in and it is quite invasive holding back the engine revs to avoid breaking traction. Switching the ASR off adds another exciting dimension to the sportiness of the car. Ultimately, the ESP will cut in to rescue an over-determined driver by putting braking effort into the front wheel with the most traction to keep the car in shape.

Fiat's engineers have put a lot of effort into the suspension design of the Panda 100bhp. After all, there's no point in having a rapid engine if the car doesn't go round corners properly. It's not easy to develop sporting suspension that doesn't compromise the ride quality, especially on a small car. Well Fiat have found a way of dealing with these issues and the result is a car that has tenacious cornering ability without shaking your teeth out. Understeer is minimal and the rear wheels remain firmly planted on the road under hard cornering. The front and rear discs arrest progress admirably without the need for heavy pedal pressures.

The interior is smart rather than sporting. Gone are the light-coloured dash coverings of the original car to be replaced with more sombre colours highlighted by bright metal trims on some of the controls. Black and grey fabric covers the seats, and are comfortable and supportive to suit the sporting nature of the car. The rear seats backs are split to provide some loading practicality.

Pocket Rocket! Twin cam powered Panda 100HP redefines front-wheel drive road holding.

The Panda Terramare crossing the channel during a Fiat publicity stunt – and it made it!

At £9995, the Panda 100 HP is temptingly priced and with Group 5 insurance, the car will certainly

Panda

The Panda Jolly concept was designed by Centro Stile and built by Stola.

appeal to the younger driver. In terms of performance per pound, it makes a lot of sense and it will also be economical to run and maintain. Italian flair combined with sparkling performance does not normally appear this far down the price ladder.

Fiat is back to doing what it does well, building small, fast, inexpensive cars. With this Panda, it has created a car that people actually desire. Fiat is going to sell a few of these. If a car really deserved to carry an Abarth logo then it is this one, something is in the pipeline we understand.

The Alessi is a brave collaboration between Fiat and the prominent Italian household goods designer.

The New Fiat 500

great expectations

Fiat has ambitious plans for the latest incarnation of its great small cars.

Fiat introduced the 'Trepiùno' concept car at the 74th Geneva Motor Show in 2004. Designed by the Fiat Centro Stile to represent the theme of 'back to the future', the prototype was clearly a modern reworking of the car that marked the first wave of mass motorisation in Italy; the 500.

Trepiùno was the working title for the car shown in Geneva and indicates a 3+1 seating arrangement. Though the production version is likely to have a more conventional seating layout, the prototype was intended to demonstrate the possibilities of easily convertible interior roles in a car that was just 3.3 metres in length.

To make the best use of the limited interior space, the designers created front seats of minimum thickness, intending to offer more comfort than seats with conventional padding. They were made from a layer of soft polyurethane complemented by a more rigid polyurethane structure, creating a flexible, comfortable three-layer configuration able to absorb all loads without detracting from volume and space.

The seats allow so much room in the back that two further places can be created through a clever arrangement of backrests and cushions. For example, the split backrests fold forward to create the customary extended load compartment. They can be turned up to shield the extended boot area from prying eyes. All of this makes it possible to reconfigure the interior to suit the car's various applications, and also to accommodate tall people in the back. In a normal 3+1 configuration, the front passenger seat is moved so far forward that it is almost swallowed up by the fascia. The fascia can be deflated by means of a conversion process to leave room for the front passenger's legs. This, inturn, gives more room for people in the corresponding rear seat.

New 500

This clever blend of modern and retro design deserves to capture public imagination.

The Trepiùno concept car offered some insight into what the Nuova 500 would look like, but images of the real thing were released to the press on March 20th 2007. The retro styling features are quite subtle, the most significant being the bluff front panel with its horizontal chrome strip and circular red badge. The chrome full rear and front quarter bumpers are a nice touch, too.

Built at Tychy in Poland, the Nuova 500 will initially be equipped with three engine choices; a 75bhp 1.3 16v Multijet diesel and two petrol units, a 69bhp 1.2 8v and a 100bhp 1.4 16v. All engines will have the option of five or six-speed manual gearboxes. Ford have collaborated with Fiat on the Nuova 500 and intend to use the new model as a basis for its latest version of the Ka. Ford are likely to have its own power units.

The original 500 was launched on July 4th 1957 in Turin. The new car will be launched 50 years to the day on July 4th 2007. Fiat deserves every success with its new baby, but the question is, have they left it too late and will it still be fashionable? Other manufacturers decided to market the retro appearance several years ago and BMW have enjoyed huge success with its new Mini. Volkswagen tried to capitalise on the massive following by building a car using original styling cues. But some classic shapes do not scale-up very well – like the VW Beetle.

The really small car seems to be a thing of the past as every new model that is launched is bigger that its predecessor due to increasingly stringent structural safety regulations. However, cars can be made to look small and the Mini proves it with the illusion created by clever design. By way of a comparison, the Nuova 500 is 3550mm long, 1650mm wide and 1490mm tall which means that it is longer, wider and taller than the Seicento measuring 3320mm long, 1508mm wide and 1445mm tall.

The original Fiat 500 had great character due to its size and appearance and hopefully Fiat has transplanted the 'cheeky' gene into the new car. Fortunately, Fiat does have an ace card up its sleeve. It is planning a full-scale revival of the legendary 'Abarth' performance division, and a 'hot' version of the Nuova 500 seems likely. The cache of the Scorpion logo is undeniable and at least as glamourous as 'Mini-Cooper'.

Fiat's revival of 1950s colour schemes is promoted by modern fabrics and clever interior design.

FIAT TODAY

Fiat was one of the founders of the European motor industry. Right from its inception in Turin, on July 11, 1899, the company followed a two-prong growth strategy – penetration of foreign markets and focus on innovation – which would continue to guide its future evolution, and was expressed in both the quality of its products and the adoption of cutting edge industrial and organisational systems.

Fiat does not only stand for cars. The company always had an original and almost unique approach to its international mission, revealing a vocation for all forms of mobility: from cars to aircraft, trucks, trains, tractors, marine engines, and even space launching systems. Manufacturing diversification was accentuated by its growing commitment to the sectors of metallurgy and components, later followed by production systems, insurance and services. Throughout Fiat's history, this diversification has certainly contributed to the success of the globalisation that the company has always pursued. Its presence on the markets of the world – a result of a business vision that considered the international market as a challenge to be overcome and won, and an essential part of Fiat Group policy – is now directed towards emerging nations such as India, China, Asia, Brazil and Argentina.

Today, with revenues of more than Euro 57 billion, Fiat is one of the world's largest industrial groups, operating in 61 countries with 1063 companies that employ over 223,000 people – 111,000 of whom are outside Italy.

The Group runs 242 manufacturing plants (167 abroad) and 131 research and development centres (61 abroad). 46 per cent of production is generated outside Italy, while exports account for over 67 per cent of sales.

Fiat Group companies are organised into 10 operating sectors: Automobiles, Agricultural and Construction Machinery, Commercial Vehicles, Metallurgical Products, Components, Production Systems, Aviation, Publishing and Communications, Insurance and Services.

After a particularly difficult period during 2004 and 2005, Fiat has been revitalised thanks to the efforts of its latest Chairman Luca Cordero di Montezemolo and its current CEO Sergio Marchionne. These two dynamic personalities have restructured the Fiat empire and have been responsible for the latest exciting products like the Grande Punto and the forthcoming New 500.

AUTOBIANCHI

Fiats by another name

Autobianchi is virtually unknown in the UK and now defunct in Italy, it was a company title used by Fiat as much more than a mere badge engineering exercise and had a very positive role to play.

Autobianchi started life as just Bianchi, being the brainchild of Edoardo Bianchi, who started manufacturing bicycles in the via Nirone, Milan in 1885, before turning his hand to motorcars in 1899. Full production didn't get underway until 1905, and inevitably the company became involved in motor racing, producing a 11.4-litre sports car in 1907. Apart from this monster, Bianchis tended to be fairly conservative offerings, its most sporting model still clinging to the use of double chain drive as late as 1916.

By the 1920s, sports cars were out and the company had established a bloodline of production based upon one model. The S4, which became the S5 in 1928, kept Bianchi in business through the vintage years but there was nothing remotely energetic about them. This model eventually evolved into a 1500cc car having started life as a competitor to the 1-litre Fiat 509. In 1934, the one model policy was reintroduced with

the S9, another 1.5-litre saloon which kept Bianchi's balance sheet the right side of disaster until just before Italy joined the war in 1940, by which time, production had been mostly turned over to motorcycles and trucks.

Neither particularly innovative or wealthy, Bianchi struggled to get its act together when hostilities ceased. It took until 1950 for an S9 update to even reach the prototype stage – shades of 1905. In fact, the company could have died there and then but the patron saint of the Italian motor industry, Fiat, did a deal with Pirelli and the now comatose Milanese company, to kick start it into action again. The new combine called themselves Autobianchi and started production in a factory that Bianchi had built, but never used, in Desio, north of Milan.

The most interesting and innovative period of the company's life now began. Slowly at first, with the first fruits of the new relationship being introduced at the 1957 Turin Show. This was effectively an upmarket Fiat 500 convertible named the Bianchina. Saloon and coupé versions followed and the little cars sold steadily, if not very spectacularly, to a clientele who wanted a bit more pizzazz from their city motoring. One most notably appeared as the Paris transport of Audrey Hepburn in the film 'How To Steal a Million'.

BIANCHINA
Autobianchi introduced its first production model in September 1957, the Bianchina. Based on the Nuova 500, the Bianchina was an upmarket version of Fiat's tiny economy car, but the Autobianchi marque soon broke free of that mould and became

Three Autobianchis take to the old Abarth test track at Aeritalia.

The Bianchina Trasformabile was the first production Autobianchi. Làunched in September 1957, it was based on the Nouva 500.

an independent producer which, despite sticking to the air-cooled twin and the 500 floorpan, soon boasted a diversified range. *Auto Italia* magazine gathered together a selection of small Autobianchi's in Turin, with the assistance of Lauro Lodi who runs the Italian club for this marque.

BIANCHINA TRASFORMABILE
Among the cars attending the test, was a 1957 Bianchina Trasformabile S1. Owned by Emanuelle Perotti, this car is thought to be the oldest surviving Autobianchi. Beautifully restored, this example retains its early 500 479cc twin-cylinder 13bhp engine.

BIANCHINA CABRIOLET
The Bianchina Cabriolet ran in three series from 1960 to 1969. The car that was featured in *Auto Italia* magazine was a 1967 model owned by Laura Lodi for over 10 years. It had been fitted temporarily with a 24bhp 650cc engine from a Fiat 126 while the 17bhp 500cc motor was being restored. Inside, there was a Nardi steering wheel and a period extra in the form of a wooden centre console. The hood operation was easy and there was only

This Cabriolet is owned by a prominent Italian Autobianchi Club member.

Right: A remarkable 1964 Bianchina Berlina 4 Posti – one owner from new! Below: Utility vehicles don't normally survive to become restored classics, but this delightful Bianchina Furgoncino did.

baggage space behind the front seats.

The Cabriolet was heavy at 854kg but 100-110km/h (62-69mph) was available and, apparently, 200km/h (125mph) downhill. The power to weight ratio worked out at 20bhp/ton.

BIANCHINA BERLINA 4 POSTI

The remarkable point about the white berlina in the group, was that it was bought new by Salvino Bardella in 1964 and he has owned it ever since, although it has enjoyed the luxury of some restoration work in recent years. Powered, as ever, by the ubiquitous 499cc twin engine, Salvino still uses the cheeky little car on a regular basis and it is a genuine four-seater, helped by the high roof line that extends at the same level as far as the back window.

Mechanically, Salvino Bartella's car was the same as Laura Lodi's – a Fiat 500. Salvino has two sets of wheels and tyres: original whitewalls for shows and modern for everyday use. Original, but with an additional electric fan on the radiator and a period lace-on steering wheel glove, this car belies its mileage – 380,000km from new! As was customary at the time, the speedometer face advises on maximum speeds for each gear. Salvino clocked up this huge mileage commuting from Turin to his old home town near Venice to collect the grapes to make his Merlot. That's an 800km (500 mile) round trip with a 17bhp motor.

BIANCHINA FURGONCINO

Any line-up of likable Autobianchis would be incomplete without including the Bianchina Furgoncino. Owned by Giancarlo Arizzi, the little van became famous as being the slowest vehicle that the test driver of *Auto Italia* magazine, Roberto

Giordanelli, had ever driven. Not a surprising accolade since the Furgonico had the frontal aspect of a house-brick – plus weight of goods when loaded – powered by the 17bhp 499cc horizontal twin somewhere under the

than Fiat rebadged offerings, then the great front-wheel drive revolution got underway and the Desio firm was about to be launched into the forefront of the new technology. From 1964, Autobianchi took a major new direction. With the introduction of the Primula that year, it became a means by which Fiat could test public reaction to new automotive technology without committing the parent name to an initial project.

Dante Giacosa, the great Fiat designer of the period, said that although his employer had much faith in him this "clashed with their great fear that in my

Fiat used the Autobianchi banner as a toe-in-the-water exercise for its first production front-wheel drive car, the Primula.

floor at the back. The van weighed in at 55kg more than the saloons at 585kg. They probably didn't sell many of them to express courier service companies.

The gearbox was the usual non-synchro four-speeder, the first three ratios being low with a tall top gear for cruising or for downhill. Given enough time and favourable conditions, the Furgoncino could eventually manage 50mph. After all, it's from an era when nothing got in your way so speed changes were less of an issue.

The engine was based on the 1221cc Millecento unit. Note the resemblance to the BMC Austin/Morris 1100 of the same period.

A steel bulkhead between the cargo area and the driver protects him or her in the event of a collision. Consequently, rear view is through two windows. The steering was good with 3.375 turns between tight locks. The owner had to source the 125SR12 tyres from Rumania.

AUTOBIANCHI PRIMULA
Strictly speaking, the Primula does not fall within the title of this book, but since the model was something of a milestone for Fiat, it is worthy of a mention on historical merit alone.

By the 1960s, it would have been easy to assume that Autobianchis were not much more

enthusiasm, I might ignore the risks." So the Primula was the first result of his experimentation with front-wheel drive, which had taken place over many years. The new car also incorporated features which we take for granted today, such as a hatchback, all-round disc brakes and an electrically-driven engine cooling fan. The engine, based on the use of the 1221cc Millecento block, underlined Fiat's close involvement in the project. The Primula pioneered rack and pinion steering on cars in the Fiat group and, to avoid front/rear pitching under braking, Giacosa introduced an automatic compensatory valve to split braking effort according to load and trim.

AUTOBIANCHI

At the Turin Show in 1964, the Autobianchi Primula was unveiled. The blue saloon at the test session for *Auto Italia* magazine was a breakthrough car for the Fiat group, pioneering front-wheel drive for them whilst keeping the project relatively low-key. The car is powered by what was effectively the Fiat 1100D unit of 1221cc, developing 57bhp, suitably adapted and set transversely. A further enhancement was the employment of a thermostatic fan, one of the first Fiat group cars to utilise this then-new power-saving device.

The Autobianchi A112 – a car that was superior in many ways to the BMC Mini.

Avant-garde for the period were four disc brakes and a hydraulic clutch. Under the bonnet, the Alfasud-style double bulkhead added rigidity and noise suppression. Less avant-garde were the leaf springs, one at the front also acting as a top wishbone, and two at the rear. Dampers were telescopic, none of your ancient donkey's leg items found in some British cars until embarrassingly recent years.

A four-door version was added to the Primula range whilst a year later, at the 1965 Paris show, the Primula Coupé took its bow. This was based on the saloon but with a more stylish fastback coupé style rear. It also had a more powerful engine of 65bhp. March 1968 saw a facelift take place on all models with both the two and four-door saloons receiving more rounded bodywork, and the top of the range Coupé S version appeared at the Geneva Show. New engines accompanied these changes and reflected new models from Fiat itself. The saloons received the 1197cc unit from the 124 saloon, whilst the coupé enjoyed the 1438cc engine from the 124S, both utilising pushrods with the latter producing 75bhp.

Auto Italia magazine was extremely lucky to be able to try one of these Fiat front-wheel drive antecedents, especially as they are now largely forgotten. Their place in Fiat history and development, though, should never be underestimated. However, driving the car owned by Italian enthusiast Franco Garbarini was a disappointment, it felt old fashioned and slow – more like a 1959 car than one from 1969. The steering was heavy and a slow 3.6 turns lock-to-lock (Fiat's first attempt at rack and pinion). Its four-speed gearbox worked well and the Primula was capable of 130km/h (81mph). Handling was stable but the suspension design made the 155/80/13 tyres work hard and protested early.

The verdict was that the Primula was a good effort as a test bed for the Fiat 128 but no match for the BMC 1100 range designed by Alex Issigonis.

AUTOBIANCHI A112

The first standard A112 model in 1970 utilised mechanically the 903cc unit from the Fiat 850 Coupé with its rotation reversed to suit the front-wheel drive application. Developing 44bhp at 6000rpm, this made the 655kg car particularly agile.

With cute, clean, modern lines, the A112 sold well right from the outset. Very little was done radically to change the styling of the car throughout its life – just enough to keep it looking

An Autobianchi A112 family portrait. These are the 3rd series models built from 1975 to 1977.

fresh. The basic shape stayed exactly the same, the nose and rear window being the only parts of the car to receive much attention. For the first few years until the early 1970s, the radiator grill was rectangular in shape, the Nuovo A112 saw this widened and softened and, finally, a full-width, more contemporary slatted grill was used.

A112 ABARTH

At the Turin Show in 1971, a high-performance Abarth version was introduced and subsequently there were as many as seven succeeding series all with detail differences. The first ran from 1971 to 1973, and employed a 982cc Abarth-built version of the standard 903cc unit with power raised from 44bhp to 58bhp which was developed at 6600rpm. The bonnet was painted matt black, as were the sills. The second series was launched at the Geneva Show in 1973, losing the black sills and gaining better lighting and black bumpers. New Cromodora alloy wheels were also fitted.

A112 THIRD SERIES

In 1975 a third series model was introduced, with a new 1049cc engine that was optional until 1976 when the 982cc unit was discontinued. The former was identifiable by a 58hp badge at the rear whilst the latter displayed 70hp. The 1049cc power unit still had pushrods and should not to be confused with the later 'Brazilian' block, overhead cam 127 unit of the same size. Also included in the new 70hp version were interior seating, and a rear with improved lights and a window washer/wiper.

AUTOBIANCHI

A112 FOURTH TO SEVENTH SERIES

The fourth series ran from 1977 to 1979, and incorporated face-lifted styling with altered front and rear, new wheels and side protection strips. From 1979 to 1982, the fifth series incorporated a new front grill and black bonnet air-intake along with Speedline wheels and electrical improvements, whilst the sixth series, introduced at the 1982 Paris Show, revealed another freshening of the styling lasting until the final update of the seventh series in 1984.

From 1974 to 1986 nearly 120,000 A112 Abarths were produced; the earlier cars are now rare and we were lucky to catch up with some at the Red Dot Test Track in Turin, specially arranged by Laura Lodi of the Italian Autobianchi club. As well as these, a special based on the cut-down body of an A112 and used for speed hillclimbing, also came along and gave Roberto Giordanelli an exhilarating ride.

The A112 was eminently tuneable and it was not surprising to see them being entered in motorsport events throughout Europe. Some competed in World Championship rallies, in particular, the Monte Carlo carrying the colours of the French Lancia

A 5th series Autobianchi A112 Elite.

importer, Chardonnet and Aseptogyl (toothpaste). There was an Italian Trofeo A112 Abarth annually from 1977 to 1984 and such future Italian rally stars as Attilio Bettega, Fabrizio Tabaton, Gianfranco Cunico and Michele Cinotto all won this award.

Various other versions of the A112 were produced, such as the more luxurious Elite, but essentially these only varied in detail. In 1986, after fifteen years, production finally ceased to make way for the Y10 that had been launched in 1985, the last Autobianchi model. The factory at Desio eventually ceased production when the Lancia Y was introduced.

So, the little A112 should not be overlooked in the great automotive halls of fame. It was probably its clear success that prompted Fiat to feel confident enough about the release of its second front-wheel drive car, the 127, in 1971. And that was the start of something big.

A112 TEST DRIVE
As Italian enthusiast, Giorgio Vivio, took the test driver for *Auto Italia* magazine, Roberto

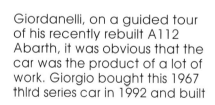

Giordanelli, on a guided tour of his recently rebuilt A112 Abarth, it was obvious that the car was the product of a lot of work. Giorgio bought this 1967 third series car in 1992 and built

Another Autobianchi A112 family portrait, this time 4th series models. A total of seven series were produced over a period of 15 years.

An Autobianchi A112 – the Italian Mini Cooper.

it to Group 3 Rally specification. The shell was stripped of everything, stiffened, fitted with brace bars, a multi-point cage, rally specification wiring loom, Sabelt seats and harnesses and a fire system. Uprated brakes, suspension, quick steering and a geometry set-up followed. The original 1049cc engine and four-speed gearbox have been rebuilt and now develops 70-80bhp at the flywheel, with a rev limit at 7500rpm.

With a 1050cc engine developing 70bhp at 7500rpm, the A112 Abarth was a rapid little mover.

Many A112s were adopted across Europe as entry level track and rally competition cars.

Giorgio uses the bright red little car for historic rallies, hillclimbs and fun events. The black bonnet, big lights, alloy sump guard and 4.5J x 13in Cromodora alloys, all add to the smart spectacle. The little A112 Abarth drove very well indeed. The power delivery was linear with a progressive top end – just what a rally car needs. Lively and positive handling make the car very chuckable.

A112 SLALOM TEST DRIVE
This mad little car started life as an A112. The all-steel body was

AUTOBIANCHI

A somewhat extreme, but indecently quick, A112 converted for driving test competition.

The owner increased the power to 106bhp and reduced the weight to 430kg. Bodywork is adorned with old Italian comics.

chopped about, and the finished article was wallpapered with comics and then lacquered. The big rear spoiler serves no aerodynamic purpose but is a useful advertising hoarding for sponsors. Inside the low-slung machine there are triangulated steel tubes to stiffen the shell and a modified floorpan to allow the exhaust system to pass inside the car, enabling a lower ride height. The steering column is very long so that the driver can sit aft to help balance the otherwise front-heavy 430kg car. The roll-over bar is mounted to the suspension points and there is a fly-off handbrake.

Brakes come from a Lancia Delta 1300 at the front and Uno Turbo for the rear. The suspension has solid top mounts and retains the transverse rear leaf spring. There is a quick rack and the front anti-roll bar is alloy-mounted instead of rubber. This has the effect of making the bar feel 20 per cent stiffer. The near solid mounted 1050cc engine is a real screamer with a 8000rpm limit. The two twin-choke downdraught carbs are lifted from a Ferrari Dino. The claimed 106bhp drives through a normal four-speed gearbox but with a very low final drive ratio. This means a 0-60mph time of six seconds but a top speed of only 142km/h (89mph). The slick-shod wacky-racer is used in slaloms, which are popular in Italy. It drives like a kart.

ETCETERINI

the coachbuilders and tuning houses

The pretty G31 project car was the basis for the Fiat X1/9, but eventually evolved into the Lombardi Grand Prix ...

built by OSI (Officina Stampaggi Industriali). A number of power units were considered for this project, the first being a transverse Autobianchi Primula unit – hence the car's appearance on the Autobianchi stand – and the second a

There were many coachbuilders who adopted Fiat's 500, 600 and 850 model ranges as a basis to produce their own versions, some stylish, others utilitarian. There are so many derivatives that they really need a separate book on the subject. This chapter covers some of the more notable variants.

FRANCIS LOMBARDI
Although the Lombardi Grand Prix was only in production between 1969 and 1972, it was sold under several different titles and has a complicated history. In 1968, a stylish coupé prototype was displayed on the Autobianchi stand at the Turin Show. Built on a Fiat chassis, the bodywork was designed by Pio Manzu and

... and the Lombardi Grand Prix evolved into the Abarth Scorpione.

1438cc Fiat twin-cam. Eventually, the car was to receive a 128 engine and was used to develop the forthcoming X1/9.

A Vignale-bodied Gamine seeks refuge among a selection of classic Fiats.

were produced, the Scorpione S and SS. Unfortunately, when Fiat bought Abarth in 1971, the model was dropped, possibly as it would have been in competition with its X1/9 which, ironically, had been developed from the G31 project …

Our story doesn't quite end there, after the Fiat takeover, Francis Lombardi continued to produce the car which regained its Grand Prix title and was briefly imported into the UK by businessman Frixos Demetriou.

VIGNALE

Alfredo Vignale was born in 1913. During the 1930s, the young Alfredo learned his trade as an all-round technician at Pinin Farina, and would have become well aware of both the technical expertise and the creativity required to clothe the cars that Farina produced. At the end of the war, Vignale bought himself a Topolino, trading in his old motorbike in the process. His Topolino's bodywork left a lot to be desired, and Vignale decided to make it a nice new aluminium replacement. This was very successful and he soon bought another and repeated the process. In 1948, he founded his own company in Turin. Business grew rapidly, and Vignale built up a reputation for excellent craftsmanship and first-class quality. He was soon designing and building cars for most of the major Italian manufacturers. Vignale later began to manufacture cars under his own name; his first Fiat 500-based offering, unveiled in 1958, was called Minnie – as in Mouse, not Minor.

The Vignale Gamine (which means urchin in French), was based on the 500F and was introduced in 1967, remaining in production until 1970. At just three metres in length, and weighing 480kg, the Gamine is a tiny car, and with its large, false radiator grille, has instant appeal. Its proportions make it look young and friendly, rather in the same way as a puppy with large paws. Its toy car

LOMBARDI

Somewhere along the line, the project was inherited by Francis Lombardi who ran a bodyshop in Turin. Lombardi continued work on the project which utilized a Fiat 850 floorpan and mechanics. It appeared at the 1968 Turin Show entitled the Francis Lombardi Grand Prix. Enter Giannini who agreed to supply Lombardi with its 982cc G2 engine. This arrangement led to the renaming of the car as the OTAS Grand Prix 1000. OTAS (Officina Trasformazioni Automobili Sportive) being the acronym for Giannini's Turin-based tuning outfit.

Meanwhile, Mr John Rich, an American Fiat and Abarth dealer, thought he would import the car into the US fitted with a 817cc power unit. This capacity was arranged to avoid the current US anti-smog regulations. As might be expected, the engine performed poorly. At this point, the attention of Carlo Abarth was attracted. Out went the 850 engine and in went an over-bored (1280cc), 'Americanised' version of Fiat's 1197cc pushrod 124 unit.

The car's title was changed yet again, this time becoming the Fiat Abarth 1300 Scorpione Coupé Francis Lombardi. Thankfully, the car was commonly known as simply the Abarth Scorpione. It proved to be quite successful and two versions

VIGNALE

SAVIO

appeal is plain – it *is* Noddy's car! In addition to plain bright colours, Vignale offered a range of novel two-tone colour schemes; blue with yellow interior, yellow with aquamarine, coral with black. The little softtop was much-loved by the yachting fraternity, although a hardtop was available for winter motoring. At the end of 1969, Vignale sold his business to De Tomaso, which was part of the Ford empire at the time. Sadly, just a few days after the sale, Alfredo Vignale was killed in a car accident, at the age of 56.

SAVIO

Yet another Turin-based coachbuilder that was unable to resist Fiat 500 possibilities was Savio. The company was founded in 1919 by brothers Antonio and Giuseppe Savio, and made bodies for many of the major Italian manufacturers. It had a good relationship with Fiat from the early days, and in 1965 unveiled the Fiat 600-based Jungla, which later evolved into a 126-based model. Savio also utilised the 500 in the same way, producing the Albarella. This is a cute, angular car, again in jeep-style, with wicker seats and a fold-up hood.

FERVÉS

Perhaps one of the oddest manifestations of the Fiat 500 was the Fervès Ranger. The Turin-based Fervès company (full name Ferrari Veicoli Speciali) introduced the Ranger at the Turin Show in 1966. Although on first appearances the little Ranger might have been a fun car, it was in fact an extremely rugged and practical vehicle which soon became very popular for utility work, especially in inaccessible areas where a full-sized vehicle would

Variations on a theme. The 500-based Savio Albarella and the very odd Fervés Ranger.

FERVÉS

A very rare Millecento-based Stanguellini 1100TV Bertone Coupé owned by an Italian collector.

or offering them as roadgoing performance cars. Some built their own bodywork, while others added their own badges to tuned versions of Fiat's model ranges.

STANGUELLINI

Number 751, via Emilia, is the address for the Fiat dealer in Modena. The sign over the showroom frontage carries the name of the proprietor – Stanguellini. In a private museum behind the showroom, resides a carefully arranged collection of small red competition cars, all bearing the Stanguellini logo. Also in the museum, is a 1910 Fiat Zero bearing the number plate MO1 – the very first car registered in Modena.

Stanguellini is well-known for its competition

have problems. Fire and forestry departments, electricity and water companies all took to the little Ranger, which was especially popular in Southern Italy.

Mechanically, the Ranger was essentially a Fiat 500 with a few modifications, although the suspension owed a good deal to the 600, and the drive assembly came courtesy of the 600 Multipla. The original Ranger was two-wheel drive, with a four-wheel drive version appearing in 1967. This model had a slightly longer wheelbase (1.55m instead of 1.33m), and was fitted with a specially manufactured five-speed gearbox and drive assembly. Two years later, the Ranger Rallye made its debut. It was fitted with many improvements, including a roll-bar and fog lights. Depending on the work that the Ranger was expected to do, it came either in four-seater form or as a two-seater with space for goods and luggage. Production of the Fervès Ranger was short-lived, ending in 1970, with approximately 1000 units in total having been built.

THE TUNING HOUSES

A number of independent companies established themselves as manufacturers of small Fiat-based cars for the purposes of using the cars in motorsport events

The 1961 Delfino Formula Junior pictured at Stanguellini, which is still an official Fiat dealership in Modena.

activities which started with tuning small Fiat-based cars. Prior to 1900, its business had been in musical instruments. In 1925, after an involvement with bicycles, Scuderia Stanguellini was created to race motorcycles made by a local Modenese firm called Mignon. By 1929, Stanguellini had become the first Fiat agent in Modena and immediately began to modify and tune the cars for competition.

Following success with a Balilla, Stanguellini developed a 500 Topolino with teardrop body which won its class in the 1939 long-distance race from Tripoli to Tobruk. Stanguellini fitted a special filter to the carburettor to keep out the desert sand and the little car averaged a remarkable 102.8km/h.

Stanguellini's Campana-bodied 750 Sport was raced successfully between 1952 and 1956.

twin-cam power unit rated 70bhp at 8500rpm, enabled the little machine to to cover 0-60mph in about 13 seconds and return a top speed of 180km/h (112.5mph); quite exceptional for a fifty year-old 750cc car. Cars made in 1953 almost invariably came with heavy steering, no brakes, no handling, and no performance, but this car was quick and had light positive controls.

Despite its small capacity, the long-stroke engine gave excellent torque characteristics and pulled happily from surprisingly low rpm. At the top end, the engine sounded great and turned many heads during the road test.

STANGUELLINI

By the time the war brought racing to a halt in Italy, Squadra Stanguellini consisted of two 750-engined Topolino barchettas, a modified 1100 Sport with special bodywork, and a 2800 Sport. Once the war was over, Stanguellini's agency in Modena grew and so did its development of competition-prepared Fiats. To make the Topolino engine competitive, Stanguellini manufactured twin-camshaft heads that were fitted to Topolino blocks and enlarged to 750cc.

Throughout the 1950s, Stanguellini turned out many small-capacity sports racing cars including the 750 Sport Bialbero residing in its collection. *Auto Italia* magazine was able to drive this car on the streets in Modena. Jewel-like in every respect, this car represents the most successful and prolific of all Stanguellini sports racing cars.

The aerodynamic body, in aluminium over a tubular chassis, is by Onorio Campana and has a dry weight of only 360kg. This, together with a tiny

SIATA

Siata is another marque that is not well-known outside Italy, and yet it built around 13,000 cars. Siata is an acronym for Societa Italiana Auto Trasformazioni Accessori, a company founded in 1926 by Giorgio Ambrosini, a Torinese motoring journalist and engineer.

Siata's early work included supercharging the Fiat 514, but was more notable for a similar conversion on the Fiat Balilla in 1932. In 1936, Siata turned its attention to the Topolino with its powerless 13bhp engine and fitted an OHV head that offered a 'powerful' 18bhp.

Siata also built cars based on Fiat components. This is one of its larger offerings, the 208S 'Otto Vu'.

Up to 1937, Siata had relied on the intuition of its founder and the talent of its mechanics. There were no engineers. That year, however, a trained engineering draughtsman by the name of Aldo Leoni was taken on, and Ambrosini set his sights on making complete cars in series, rather than conversions and one-offs. With backing from Fiat in 1938, Ambrosini built his first car, the Amica, which was modified with Topolino mechanicals. It debuted in 1939 and only fifty were made before

Though rear-engined, the Siata 850 Spring had a disproportionately large false front radiator.

Despite its odd appearance, 3500 examples found owners. The Spring was to be Siata's finale as a manufacturer.

the onset of the Second World War when Siata was required to build military equipment and was subsequently bombed as a result.

In post-war Italy, Siata built 48cc motorised bicycles and over 100,000 units were sold by 1949. With the Fiat 500B and later the 500C as a base, Siata revived the Amica, which in its post-war form was built by Bertone and others. In 1950, the Fiat 1400 was announced and provided another opportunity for Siata with its Daina series and then the Fiat 8V 'big car' project for which it built the

chassis. While Siata was making a name for itself on the USA market with its 208S, it continued to supply tuning parts through seventeen outlets around Italy. A liaison with Abarth was established in 1959 with the 600-based Siata-Abarth 750 Coupé and Spyder.

Into the 1960s and Giorgio Ambrosini's son, Renato, began to take the reigns. New coupé models were built using Fiat's 1300/1500 range, and then a Michelotti-designed coupé based on the Fiat 850 was introduced – the Siata Spring.

The Spring was a rather odd looking machine but proved to be very popular. In just one month, Renato Ambrosini took orders and deposits for 3600 cars. Unfortunately, industrial problems in Italy seriously affected production and the company was forced to cease trading even though 3500 Springs were made. Carrozzeria Siata closed down in 1970.

SIATA

GIANNINI

Giannini Automobili is an unusual company in that it is located in Rome when most of the Italian motor industry is to be found in the north. It is also the only coachbuilder whose entire business is dedicated to the construction and sale of its own products based entirely on the Fiat model range.

Like many Italian tuning companies, Giannini's origins can be found in motorsport. Following the post-war boom in Italy, motorists began to look at motorsport again and road races like the Mille Miglia began to attract huge entries. Before the war, there were just a few tuning firms that had become established and one of them was the Giannini company formed by brothers Attilio and Domenico.

Rome-based Giannini will build you one of its 590GT replicas to order.

They had opened an Itala agency back in 1920, in Rome, near Villa Torlonia, north-east of the centre of town. When the Fiat 500A arrived in 1936, it was immediately adopted as a basis for a competition car. Giannini added a third bearing and alloy connecting rods to the little engine, fitted this unit into a super-light frame clothed in an aerodynamic body and took the result to Monza where, in 1938, it set up twelve new world records. The flying kilometre was covered at 151.2 km/h – remarkable for a 500cc car.

After the war, ambitions ran high with the introduction of Giannini's own engine, the G1, which was a single overhead camshaft unit of 660cc, later available also as a 750. During the late 1940s, Attilio Giannini went into partnership with Berardo Taraschi to build small sports cars that would utilise G1 engines. The cars were called Giaur, taking the first letters of Giannini and Urania which was a company Taraschi had previously been involved in. These tiny cars were very successful and won the national 750 title several times.

By 1954, Giannini had come up with the G2 engine which was a 750 topped with twin overhead camshafts. In supercharged form and developing 115bhp, this was used in a Giaur chassis with sports racer style body for record-breaking and driven by a Frenchman named Grousset. Another car connected with Giannini was the bizarre Nardi Bisiluro Giannini, which took part at Le Mans in 1955. The car consisted of twin booms connected only by

chassis tubes. On one side sat the driver and on the other was the engine. A 1000cc version of the G2 was installed in a Lotus 23, enabling Giannini to win the 1-litre sports car championship.

When the Nuova 500 arrived, Giannini adapted it to produce its own performance versions that included the 500 Montecarlo, 590 Vallelunga, 650 Modena and Imola. On the track, these cars met Carlo Abarth's interpretation of the model and achieved sixteen class championships in Italian Group 2 during the 1960s and 1970s.

Because the 500-based Giannini cars are now quite rare and very collectable, to capitalise on the interest Giannini decided to make a number of replicas. Entitled the Giannini 590GT Corsa Replica, the cars are constructed from strengthened 500 shells and are fitted with balanced 650 engines and five-speed gearboxes. Tuned to develop 35bhp at 6000rpm, the 590GT is capable of 135km/h. The specification includes an alloy sump, oil cooler, roll cage, Koni dampers and Eibach springs, and period style leather-trimmed bucket seats. At the time of writing, one of these built-to-order mini marvels costs around £8500.

From 1969/1970, Giannini turned its attention to making improved versions of Fiat production cars, particularly the 850 range which included the Giannini 1000 Grand Prix, and a Francis Lombardi

GIAN

Top to bottom; Giannini 590 Corso Replica, Giannini Seicento Sport GTO and a Giannini Cinquecento Corsa.

850 Grand Prix fitted with a version of the G2 1000cc engine. This body style, developed from Dante Giacosa's abandoned G31 project, was also known as the OTAS Grand Prix and Abarth Scorpione.

Giannini was responsible for its own performance and restyled versions of many Fiat production cars including the 127, 128, 132, 126, Panda, Strada, Uno, Tipo, Punto, Cinquecento and Seicento.

Currently it is still possible to have your Cinquecento or Seicento modified by Giannini.

GIANNINI TEST DRIVE

Writing for *Auto Italia* magazine, Peter Collins travelled to Rome to test drive three of Giannini's current models including the Seicento Sport GTO, Cinquecento Corsa and 590 Corsa Replica. The Seicento had a Giannini-developed engine and engine management system, bringing power up from the standard 54bhp to 72bhp. Giannini had managed to increase the power without sacrificing any of the original car's torque characteristics, making the car feel like a normal Cinquecento Sporting but much quicker in every way.

Optional Bilstein dampers were fitted to the car which helped make it feel much more precise than the standard version. Top speed was up to just over 170km/h. The 13in wheels and higher profile tyres provided an increase of about 7km/h more than a 14in wheel option. The 0-100km/h time was about 10.5 seconds. On the autostradas, fifth gear acceleration from 70km/h

143

In the late 1970s, Moretti employed a house style for its 128, 125 and this, the 127 Coupé.

MORETTI

Moretti was a lesser-known Turin-based coachbuilder that built its own stylish versions of the cars covered in this book, namely the 500, 600 and 850 models.

In 1925, Carrozzeria Moretti was formed by Giovanni Moretti as a motorcycle constructor. Its first car was built in 1928 and it went on to enjoy

to 130km/h had improved to just 27.3 seconds compared to the standard car's 41.5. Complete with leather retrim, the price for the improved Seicento is around £7500 to £8000.

The Cinquecento Corsa was effectively a stripped out racer with an extra seat fitted. With stiff racing suspension, hand-cut slicks, and competition exhaust the car was noisy, harsh, had kart-like responsiveness, but was great fun.

Out on the autostrada in the 590 Corsa, with the engine sounding like a pneumatic drill, it was possible to run in the outside lane most of the time. The gearchange was more like a switch but the drum brakes needed care. Handling and steering were very direct.

Although the Giannini name is not quite so well-known in an international context as Abarth, the cars it has been responsible for and those it still builds are very much an important and integral part of the history of motoring in Italy. Giannini is regarded by some as the poor man's Abarth which is certainly not true. Its competition successes might not be as well-recorded as Abarth's, but at least it still exists. Giannini can be contacted at Via Idrovore della Magliana, 57, 00148 Roma.

Moretti's oh-so pretty coupé must surely be the world's best-looking 500.

MORETTI

considerable competition success in the 1950s with its 750S, fitted with a bespoke overhead camshaft engine. Moretti gained international fame when, in 1952, two Italian journalists competed in the 120,000kms Giro del Mondo. Morettis achieved outright wins and class wins in several international events. The cost of producing its own models in relatively small numbers was huge, especially when compared to the mass-market models that Fiat was building. Giovanni Moretti and Giovanni Agnelli were friends, however, and they came to an arrangement whereby Moretti could put its own bodies on Fiat's chassis and mechanical components.

FIAT 500 MORETTI

The first Fiat 500-based Moretti went on sale in 1958. It was a station wagon which was joined three years later by a cabriolet and, in 1961, the first version of the elegant Moretti Coupé. Some front-engined estate models were also built, and at least one electric-powered 500. The Morettis, especially the

This car was presented at the 1966 Turin Show under the Caprera logo, though it is considered to be the Moretti Coupé prototype.

Coupé, were very stylish cars, boasting beautiful finish and attention to detail.

The 500 Coupé was updated In 1968 with a new shape, and a sporty version based on the 595SS was also introduced. Only a few hundred Coupés were ever made, so they are very rare, the earlier model being particularly sought-after. In

1971 Moretti introduced the Minimax, a small jeep-style car with optional canvas sides and roof. It was originally based on the 500, with the 126 taking over from 1973.

FIAT 850 MORETTI – SERIES ONE

Fiat launched its 850 range in May 1964 to replace the 600. Of course, most of the Italian coachbuilders immediately made their own special versions of the 850 and Moretti was no exception. It prepared an upgraded version with additional chrome trim, better upholstery, detailing and finish.

Control of the company was handed over to Giovanni Moretti's sons, Sergio and Gianni who, from 1965, decided to design cars in-house. They approached the famous freelance stylist, Giovanni Michelotti, to draw a new shape for some sports cars based on the new Fiat. The result was a traditional design, very neat but not as innovative as many people expected.

In 1966, the whole Moretti 850 range was completely revised. The bodywork of a new coupé, the 'Mk1' 850 Sportiva, was a more ambitious

Moretti was less successful with its 850 Coupé S4 – '4' indicates a four-seater.

This first series 850 Coupé shared the Fiat Dino-like front of the early Sportiva Coupé.

design by Michelotti. Looking at the 850 Sportiva to think that Coupé today, it's easy the prolific designer was Inspired by the Fiat Dino Spider, but Pininfarina's design was not unveiled until November 1966 – while the Moretti was launched in the summer. However, the new shape was wonderful: elegant, light, slender; just the right styling to change a mundane Fiat saloon into a real sports car.

The Moretti 850 Sportiva was offered with two different bodies and with three levels of engine tuning. The bodies offered for all the versions were the Coupé and 'Convertibile', which had two removable plates in the roof, as with some contemporary 'T-roof' American sports cars.

The entry-level version was the 850 Sportiva, fitted with the standard 843cc 42bhp engine from the Fiat 850S. Standard equipment included vinyl upholstery and a tachometer. Optional extras included a wood rim steering wheel, power windows, metallic paint, whitewall tyres and a choice of different wheels – steel, chrome wires or Campagnolo light alloy. The second version was the 850SS Sportiva, which had a 50bhp engine. Equipment was the same as the basic version but with the wooden steering wheel fitted as standard. The top-of-the-range model was the 1000SC Sportiva, boasting 982cc – obtained by increasing the stroke from 63.5 to 74mm. This engine developed 62bhp at 6500rpm and provided a top speed of more than 165km/h. The prices were, respectively, 1,050,000 lire, 1,300,000 lire and 1,500,000 lire. As a comparison, a normal Fiat 850 Coupé cost 950,000 lire, a Ford Cortina GT 1,350,000 lire and an Alfa Romeo 1300 Sprint 1,550,000 lire.

A pair of later series Sportivas with the revised 246GT-like front end. Apparently, Michelotti was not best pleased with Danny Bravand's alteration to his first design.

FIAT 850 MORETTI – SERIES TWO

The Series 2 Coupé was unveiled at the Geneva Motor Show in 1969. It had the same engine options as the earlier car but with a significantly redesigned front end that improved the car's appearance to echo the Ferrari Dino 246GT. The redesign was undertaken by Swiss-born Danny Bravand, who had served his apprenticeship at Michelotti and Vignale. Bravand had left Michelotti's studio to work at Moretti, something Giovanni Michelotti was not very happy about. It has to be said, the new Moretti S2 was even better than the former 850 Sportiva.

It is thought that about 700 Sportivas were built, most of which remained in Europe, though some found their way to Argentina and the USA. Of the total Sportiva production, about 300 were Series 2 cars, none of which were officially exported with the exception of an example that was owned by the author. Production of the 850 Morettis continued until early 1971 when they were replaced by the new 127 and 128-based variants.

Moretti was proud of being an independent car maker and originally all the mechanical modifications to its cars were made directly in its factory. Over the period from the late 1950s to the early 1980s, this became increasingly unviable and gradually the engine and chassis building died out, soon to be followed by tuning and the manufacturing of new bodywork. Ultimately, Moretti was reduced to cosmetic upgrades of Fiat's small car range. The 850 Sportiva was half-way along this descending path, at the point where Moretti built the bodies but farmed out the engine work. The tuning parts were bought from a company called CMG, a performance components factory near Rome. CMG was established by Attilio Giannini following a split with his brother Domenico who ran the parent company Giannini Automobili. The engine modifications were implemented at Edoardo Zen's workshop, the Turin-based branch of Giannini Automobili, managed by Domenico's son, Franco.

It's easy to see how all the specifications of the Moretti 1000 match exactly those of Giannini's own model range. The cooperation between the two companies also appears clearly in the Moretti 850 Sport Competizione. This car was a coupé unveiled at the Turin Racing Car Show in 1966, fitted with an experimental 70bhp Giannini engine using the 850 cylinder block and an all-new cylinder head with an overhead camshaft. Only a few were actually built.

MO

The author's restored Moretti 850 Sportiva in action on the Val Saviore Hillclimb.

MORE FIAT-BASED MORETTIS

Moretti was also responsible for some highly desirable coupé versions of the Fiat 124, 125, 127 and 128. A prototype 132 Coupé was also built but did not enter production. With Fiat producing its own range of sporting 124 and 850 coupé designs, Moretti was unable to compete on price and concentrated its activities on light commercial and utility vehicles instead. Special cabriolet Pandas, Unos and personalised Tipos were among Moretti's final work before it ceased operations during the mid-1980s

FIAT 850 MORETTI RESTORATION

According to Fiat UK, the author's car started life as a Fiat 850 saloon chassis in March 1970. The original UK log book records that it was sold new in early 1971 to a British serviceman in Malta called John Steven Ward (no relation) and bore the Maltese registration 66335. So the

A brand new 1050cc Autobianchi Abarth A112 was installed.

Above right: A complete interior refit by Italian Abarth expert Berni Motor.

first owner was a Ward, the author's daughter subsequently owned it and later belonged to him. This Moretti has its steering wheel on the right because of Malta's UK links (cars there drive on the left). During restoration, it became evident that the car was built as a right-hand drive by Moretti which makes it very rare indeed, if not unique.

BASIC PRINCIPLES

To stand any good chance of a successful classic car restoration, you really need engineering

Though the Moretti body had survived reasonably well, the Fiat chassis had to be replaced.

skills and resources, time, energy, loads of determination and money. Unfortunately, most of us do not have all of the above, and often any one of these essential attributes is replaced by optimism, which is a very dangerous condition. Optimism is when the sensible part of your brain is locked away to be replaced with a vision: a vision of carefree driving along sunny country lanes in a perfect, affordable classic motor car.

Unless you are very lucky, one of the realities of classic car restoration and ownership is that the car rarely turns out as good as you expected it to be. Even after restoration, there is always something that needs to be done and it might not even be very nice to drive. In England it rains; the car probably lets in water, doesn't like sitting in congested traffic and rewards you by overheating.

Storage is also a big issue. Italian cars like to be driven and sitting around in a damp garage, or even worse in the open, won't do them any good. A dehumidified, heated environment is ideal but it will be costly. At the very least, a classic car should be kept in an air circulation tent that are available on the classic car market. Whichever way is chosen to store a classic, the engine should be warmed through at regular intervals to circulate the oil, and prevent the oil seals from drying out and cracking, causing leaks. If possible, the car should also be driven occasionally to prevent the brakes from seizing up.

And the costs? I doubt that there has ever been a restoration that has been completed within its budget. Very few restoration companies will be able to come up with an accurate figure

Middle: During restoration it was revealed that the car had been factory-built in right-hand drive.

With all the metal work completed, the car received its first coat of new paint at Trentside Classics.

because, to be fair, they will not be able to predict all the problems they will encounter along the way. What is certain, is that you will receive regular invoices for work carried out and if the amounts are beyond the money you have set aside, then you have a problem. This is why part-restored cars are sold-on as 'unfinished projects' or are found hiding under a dust sheet in the back of a garage – because the money ran out. The basic formula for a classic car restoration is to work out roughly how much you think it should cost and then double the final figure!

THE RESTORATION

At first glance, the Moretti seemed to be superficially sound and a realistic prospect, but investigation revealed that the years of mend and make-do welding covered by lashings of underseal were hiding the sad remains of a chassis resembling a used tea bag. If there was any consolation at all, it was that the Moretti's bodywork was in quite good structural order. It was the Fiat part that had disintegrated.

It was at this point that a decision had to be made whether or not to continue with the project, but since the car had already been partially dismantled – without prior consultation regarding the car's suspected condition – the author had two choices: embark on an expensive restoration or scrap a very rare and interesting car.

Having elected reluctantly to continue with the project, a tired but sound Mk3 850 Coupé was located to donate its chassis, onto which the Moretti body was skillfully remounted. Once work on the shell had been completed, it was decided to pack up all the bits and send them off to Italy for the car to be completed. This decision was based on the availability of cheaper Italian labour rates and the fact that all the new parts required for the rebuild were sitting on the shelf at Abarth specialist Berni Motori.

The list of new parts fitted to the Moretti fills several A4 pages and includes a replicated windscreen ($1000 and air-freighted from the USA) and a zero-miles, off-the-shelf Autobianchi A112 Abarth power unit. The engine was reverse rotated to match the drive from the original 850 gearbox. A sidedraught Weber carburettor was mounted on a suitable manifold to add that extra bit of power and torque, though this was later changed to a conventional downdraught A112 instrument. Output

is estimated to be about 75bhp, which is fairly substantial in a car weighing just 660kg.

The rechroming of the bumpers was carried out in the UK, where the quality of work is superior to Italian efforts. The body was readjusted to enable the doors to fit properly which generated the need for another full repaint to be carried out.

The author has attempted to keep the car looking as original as possible and he was lucky enough to obtain some Fergat wheels that were optional equipment on Morettis of the period. One of the few concessions to non-originality was the installation of an additional radiator, mounted discreetly in the front compartment. This was considered to be important, as rear-engined 850s are marginal on cooling at best, and the Moretti was to be driven in numerous Italian hillclimb events – in the heat of summer.

The car went straight from Berni Motori's workshop to an Italian hillclimb event, which was a bit unfair on the largely untested car. It performed reasonably well at its first events, the Silver Flag Historic Hillclimb near Piacenza and the Val Saviore Classic near Brescia. The engine ran cool, thanks to the additional radiator, but the tickover was irregular causing the engine to stall. The new Autobianchi A112 engine created an overgearing situation, so that we were pulling peak revs very early in each gear and top speed was limited. This was fine for hillclimbing but not sensible for general road use. Once the car was back in the UK, a standard A112 carburettor was fitted and the engine immediately settled down to a regular tickover with smooth power delivery throughout the rev range. The gearing issue was resolved by installing a high ratio crown and pinion supplied by Berni Motori.

Other issues were dealt with by the UK Abarth specialists Middle Barton Garage, including the fitting of more effective matched shock absorbers and accurate suspension geometry alignment. The opportunity was also taken to fit a new set of tyres – the originals, though of good appearance, were rather hard being over 12-years-old!

The Moretti was entered in a UK timed sprint, where it performed very well coming second in class behind an Autobianchi A112. Now fully run-in, the engine revs freely and the new gearing is quite fast and rewarding to drive. Displayed regularly at classic car events, the Moretti always attracts much appreciative attention which to some extent offsets the expense of such an ambitious project.

FIATS UNDER DIFFERENT FLAGS

production outside of Italy

The Millecento has an extraordinary production record that spans 40 years.

POLAND: POLSKI FIAT

Fiat has been present in Poland for seventy-six years. Its involvement in the country has grown continually: the first sales were made at the beginning of the century, the first sales outlet (Polski Fiat) dates back to the 1920s, and the first cars were produced in the 1930s.

After a break due to World War II and the Cold War, relations were resumed in the 1960s with two major licensing contracts. The Fiat 125P in 1965 and the 126P in 1971. FSM (Fabrika Samochodûw Malolitrazowych) was set up in Bielsko Biala to produce the 126P and was joined a few years later by the Tychy plant and the Skoczow foundry.

A third licensing contract was signed in 1987 for production of the Fiat Cinquecento at the FSM and all the other plants were extended (particularly the Tychy plant, where the Cinquecento was produced until mid-1998). On May 28th 1992, FSM was converted from a State Company to a Limited Company with 90 per cent of its share capital held by Fiat Auto and 10 per cent by the State Treasury. On this occasion, the company took the name by which it is known today: Fiat Auto Poland SA. The agreement between Fiat Auto and the Polish state is the most important privatisation agreement so far drawn up in the state and one of the biggest ever made anywhere in Eastern Europe.

GERMANY: NSU-NECKAR

In 1929 Fiat bought a factory in Heilbronn, Germany, from the Neckarsulmer Fahrzeugwerke AG (NSU) for two million Reichsmark. The cars built there were to become known as NSU-Fiat and later Neckar.

A Belgian-registered, German-built NSU-Fiat 1100.

The NSU-Neckar 'Jagst' models were produced from 1956 to 1969.

In 1938, Fiat sold a total of 7155 cars in Germany and by 1962 they had exceeded 100,000 units, more than half being locally produced. When the factory was closed down in 1969, 360,000 cars had been built there.

The first model to be produced was the Topolino which continued until 1955. During the intervening war years, commercial and military vehicles rolled off the production lines. Allied bombing caused the factory to be out of action until 1952. The Balilla, 1100, 1500 and 2500 models were also produced in varying volumes during the 1930s.

The German-produced version of the Nuova 500 was available as a coupé and a saloon

Designed by Vignale, this is the attractive NSU Riviera Coupé.

the 767cc engine from the 600D. From around 1961 to 1964, a coupé was produced and a cabriolet version designed by Vignale, the Riviera. Again using a mainstream Fiat as a basis, this time the 1300/1500, the 1500TS was differentiated by minor styling details but this time the engine was also slightly tuned by Siata to give some extra power. More significantly different was

The side lights give away the Riviera's Fiat 1300/1500 underpinnings.

ZASTAVA

You could still buy a new Zastava 600 well into the 1980s.

The former were based on a 767cc engine while the latter had a 848cc unit. The 101 series, still recognisable as a 128, lasted until the 1990s. Potentially, these cars are a source of parts for classic car restorers, in particular 600 floorpans, but it is believed that the stocks were destroyed in the recent war in that area.

In 2005, Fiat and Zastava announced an assembly contract agreement to manufacture the Fiat Punto from CKDs (Complete Knock-Down) at

The Yugo 45 was a heavily disguised, budget Fiat 127 and was available in the UK.

the 1500TS Coupé, basically a Siata car built at Heilbronn. Neckar also built the Fiat 850 and was known as the Adria, whilst the Autobianchi Bianchina Panoramica was known as the Neckar Panorama.

YUGOSLAVIA: ZASTAVA
Based at Kragujevac in the former Yugoslavia, the ZCZ company (Zavodi Crvena Zastava) built a number of Fiats under licence. Zastava was a susbtatial organisation with 40,000 employees and built about 150,000 cars each year. Its model range included the 600-based 750, the 128-based 101 series and a fairly nasty-looking rebodied 127 called the Jugo 45 and, later, the 65. The 750 series was interesting in that it kept the Fiat 600 going well into the 1980s. Ultimately, three versions were available, the 750LE, 750SE and 850.

Zastava inherited the 128 hatchback design that was discarded by Fiat.

Zastava's facility in Kragujevac, Serbia.

SPAIN: SEAT

The Spanish Seat company is an essential part of the small Fiat story, as it built many models under licence during its twenty-seven-year-long association with the Italian company. Even before Seat was created (Sociedad Espanola de Automoviles de Turismo), the Spanish government had reached an agreement with Fiat to build its cars as early as 1941. It was not until 1948 that the Seat company was formed and then it took another five years before the first Seat 1400 was manufactured. Built mainly from locally produced parts, 1345 versions of the 1400 were constructed in 1953. By 1964, it had made 99,000 cars and a further 140,000 with a 1500cc engine between 1963 and 1972. Its next model, the 600, debuted in 1957 and by 1963, 132,000 had been built. The later 600D and 600E versions accounted for almost 200,000 in all.

Seat produced most of the mainstream Fiat model range, adding some of its own versions. The Seat 1500, for example, used Fiat 2300 bodywork with the smaller engine and the 600 had convertible and four-door versions. The 850 arrived in 1966, the 124 (saloon and coupé – but not the spider) in 1968 and the 127 in 1972; the latter was to achieve the production of a record 1.3 million units.

In 1967, Fiat gave Seat freedom to export cars under the names of either company,

Built under licence in many countries, the 128 was a true world car.

something Seat had pre-empted with its 600 which was already being exported to Columbia. Fiat was happy about this arrangement because it increased the company's exposure in areas where its own dealer network was not fully developed. Seat continued to export cars in its own name

A comprehensive model line-up of Seats, perhaps the most prolific manufacturer of Fiat-based cars outside of Italy.

YUGOSLAVIA

A Spanish-built Seat 850 with locally designed four-door bodywork.

Fiat-badged, Spanish-built Seat 600s were exported worldwide.

SPAIN

and established itself in Argentina, Morocco, Finland and Greece. Later, Seat provided knocked down kits to be assembled in Egypt by NASCO from 1977 to the mid-1980s.

Between 1974 to 1979, Seat built the 133 which was mechanically similar to the Fiat 850 but took styling cues from the 127. The design was totally Fiat, with minor reference to Seat. It was sold through the UK Fiat dealer network between 1975 and 1976 for £1239. The car was not greeted with much enthusiasm by UK dealers because of the potentially

No, it's not a 127 but the rear-engined Seat 133. A few of these cars were sold in the UK.

low sales volume and the need to stock body panels which were incompatible with other Fiats. However, 2565 vehicles were registered in the UK. Total production of the 133 was 191,033.

In spring 1980, at the same time that Seat was presenting the new Fiat Panda to its dealers, Fiat announced its withdrawal from Spain. Seat realised that

Another model unique to Seat was the 1200/1430 Sport. Based on the 127, these stylish cars were fitted with 1197cc, and later 1438cc, Fiat 124 engines.

models during 1981 and 1982, reducing to just 50,000 a year from 1983 to 1985 – and then only Pandas. This was a help but not enough to keep the company afloat, so Seat appealed for permission to export other models under its own name. Fiat agreed to this but on the condition that the cars must be modified to no longer look like its own model range.

Seat obtained refunding from the Spanish government and set about creating a new model range to replace those left by Fiat. The 133 was the first to go and the 127, now nine years-old, needed replacing. The 131, Ritmo and Panda would be surgically altered. Seat did some token alterations to the Ritmo, Regatta and 127 to comply with Fiat's desire to have its identity altered. However, cosmetic changes to headlights and grilles and retitling the cars Ronda, Malaga and Fura didn't fool many. Anyway, Fiat seemed to be content and even it admitted that any alteration to the featureless Regatta would be an improvement! Fiat decided the Ronda was too much like the Ritmo and wanted the Panda modified, too. In the

a divorce from Fiat would mean its demise; after all, Fiat was supplying 30 per cent of the parts for the then current range of Panda, 127, 124, Ritmo (Strada) and 131. Also Fiat, through its own dealer network, accounted for a quarter of Seat's turnover and half of the export sales. The Spanish government decided to buy out Fiat's shares and, not surprisingly, managed to do so at a very favourable rate! Seat set about rebuilding bridges. Renegotiations with Fiat achieved an agreement whereby up to 50,000 cars exported from Spain would be under the Fiat name until the end of 1980. Scat then obtained a further, more positive undertaking, whereby Fiat would buy 100,000 cars a year of all

The Seat 1283P hatchback was identical in appearance to the Italian version.

SEAT

SPAIN

spring of 1986, Fiat accepted a settlement from Seat allowing the Spanish company a free reign to sell its cars whilst developing a relationship with its new partners – Volkswagen.

Prior to the Ritmo's revision, less than 27,000 units had been built during 1981. In 1982, production was up to 34,000 and nearly 70,000 a year later. Also, 21,000 Furas (127s) were built. Seat capitalised on Fiat ending its 127 production and exported 40,000 Furas in 1984.

SEAT Volkswagen Group	SEAT MARBELLA 850 'SPLASH'	For further information please contact the Press Office 0293 514141

Seat found itself competing with Fiat for international Panda sales with its Marbella.

NEW ZEALAND: MOTOR HOLDINGS

The Antipodes is an unlikely area to find Italian cars being manufactured, but Motor Holdings in Auckland, New Zealand, did actually build Fiat 500s. About 5,000 Nuova 500s were dispatched from Turin in kit form to be assembled locally. Motor Holdings also assembled Fiat 850s.

PREMIER PADMINI: AN INDIAN ITALIAN

An extraordinary story of automotive longevity is that of the Indian-built Fiat 1100. During the 1950s, the Millecento had become established as a world car with variants being either manufactured or assembled from knocked down kits in Argentina, Poland, Spain, West Germany, Yugoslavia and India. Fiat's involvement with India's motor industry started with Premier Automobiles Ltd of Mumbai – formerly Bombay – and production of the 1100 commenced during 1954. At the time, its nearest competitor was the 'Baby Hindustan', a locally-built version of the Morris Minor. Compared with the Hindustan, the Fiat offered a greater top speed – combined with mechanical simplicity that made it repairable by the remotest of

Fiat required Seat to alter the appearance of its model range so that it did not resemble the Italian product. Is the reader convinced?

rural garage mechanics. Within a few years, the Fiat 1100 had achieved its own niche with both India's middle-class business community and the all-important taxi market.

Production of the Italian-built Fiat 1100 ended in 1970 to make way for the 128, but the model soldiered on in India. In 1968, an agreement had been forged between Premier Automobiles Limited and Fiat to manufacture the 1100D under licence as the 'Premier Padmini', succeeding its earlier Fiat-badged 1100-103 models. The new car was able to be built on a generation of goodwill that had been created by the 1100-103. Indeed, long after fellow European hybrids such as the Standard Gazel (née Triumph Herald) had vanished from the Indian motoring scene, tens of thousands of Padminis were still being sold as recently as the early 1990s – thanks to the archaic government regulation that placed high duties on imported cars, or cars to be assembled from kits of parts.

During the mid-1990s, the restrictions on imported cars were finally being eased, bringing a radical measure of change to the Indian motoring

Strict Indian legislation on importing new cars meant that the Mumbai-built Millecento production soldiered on well into the 1990s.

landscape that had virtually been 'frozen in time' since the mid-1950s. As early as 1993, Premier had entered into negotiations with Fiat to manufacture the Uno, and by the time of the Padmini's demise, only 194 Taxi models had left the production line. When the final Padmini Diesel, still equipped with a four-on-the-column gear change and bench front seat, entered service, its sale price was less than half of that of a new Fiat Sienna; the model currently being built in the old Premier factory alongside the Fiat Palio.

Fiat exported right-hand drive versions of the 1100 to the UK though they were expensive and few have survivied. Today, a right-hand drive 1100 is mainly to be found in India, where countless of them are still employed as taxis. At least one Indian-built 1100 has made the journey overland to the UK.

This Indian-built Fiat Millecento made the ambitious overland trek all the way to the UK.

PADMINI

Technical specifications

FIAT 500A TOPOLINO
1936-1948
Engine: Type 500
Location: Front longitudinal
Capacity: 569cc
Cylinders: 4 in-line
Valves: 8 side valves
Bore and stroke: 52mm x 67mm
Compression ratio: 6.5:1
Power: 13bhp at 4000rpm
Transmission: Four-speed, rear-wheel drive and synchromesh on 3rd and 4th
Final drive: 4.875:1
Suspension: Front – independent, by wishbones and transverse leaf spring, and shock absorbers. Rear – rigid axle. Series 1 – quarter-elliptic springs, radius arms and hydraulic shock absorbers. Series 2 – semi-elliptic springs and hydraulic shock absorbers
Tyres: 4.00 x 15in
Steering: Worm and roller
Brakes: Drums front and rear and a mechanical drum handbrake on transmission
Top speed: 53mph (85km/h)
Fuel consumption: 46.8mpg (6L/100km)
Wheelbase: 2000mm
Track: Front – 1114mm. Rear – 1083mm
Length: 3215mm
Width: 1275mm
Height: 1377mm
Weight: 535kg
Production: 112,016

FIAT 500B TOPOLINO NORMALE
1948-1949
Engine: Type 500B
Location: Front longitudinal
Capacity: 569cc
Cylinders: 4 in-line
Valves: 8 overhead valves
Bore and stroke: 52mm x 67mm
Compression ratio: 6.45:1
Power: 16.5bhp at 4400rpm
Transmission: Four-speed, rear-wheel drive and synchromesh on 3rd and 4th
Final drive: 4.875:1
Suspension: Front – independent, by wishbones and transverse leaf spring and telescopic shock absorbers. Rear – rigid axle, semi-elliptic springs, telescopic shock absorbers and anti-roll bar
Tyres: 4.25 x 15in
Steering: Worm and roller
Brakes: Drums front and rear and a mechanical drum handbrake on transmission
Top speed: 59mph (95km/h)
Fuel consumption: 56mpg (5L/100km)
Wheelbase: 2000mm
Track: Front – 1116mm. Rear – 1083mm
Length: 3210mm
Width: 1273mm
Height: 1375mm
Weight: 600kg
Production: 21,262

500B GIARDINIERA
As the 500B Normale except for:
Final drive: 5.2:1
Top speed: 56mph (90km/h)
Fuel consumption: 43mpg (6.5L/100km)
Length: 3360mm
Width: 1273mm
Height: 1430mm
Weight: 930kg

FIAT 500C TOPOLINO BERLINETTA
1949-1955
Engine: Type 500B
Location: Front longitudinal
Capacity: 569cc
Cylinders: 4 in-line

Valves: 8 overhead valves
Bore and stroke: 52mm x 67mm
Compression ratio: 6.45:1
Power: 16.5bhp at 4400rpm
Transmission: Four-speed, rear-wheel drive and synchromesh on 3rd and 4th
Final drive: 4.875:1
Suspension: Front – independent, by wishbones and transverse leaf spring, and telescopic shock absorbers. Rear – rigid axle, semi-elliptic springs, telescopic shock absorbers and anti-roll bar
Tyres: 4.25 x 15in
Steering: Worm and roller
Brakes: Drums front and rear and a mechanical drum handbrake on transmission
Top speed: 59mph (95km/h)
Fuel consumption: 56mpg (5L/100km)
Wheelbase: 2000mm
Track: Front – 1116mm. Rear – 1083mm
Length: 3245mm
Width: 1288mm
Height: 1375mm
Weight: 610kg
Production: 376,368

500C GIARDINIERA
As the 500C Normale except for:
Final drive: 5.125:1
Top speed: 56mph (90km/h)
Fuel consumption: 48mpg (5.8L/100km)
Length: 3360mm
Width: 1273mm
Height: 1430mm
Weight: 930kg

FIAT 600
1955-1960
Engine: Type 100.000
Location: Rear longitudinal
Capacity: 633cc
Cylinders: 4 in-line
Valves: 8 overhead valves
Bore and stroke: 60mm x 56mm
Compression ratio: 7.5:1
Power: 22bhp at 4600rpm
Transmission: Four-speed with combined final drive, rear-wheel drive and synchromesh on 2nd, 3rd and 4th
Final drive: 4.875:1
Suspension: Front – independent, by wishbones and transverse leaf spring, and telescopic shock absorbers. Rear – independent, semi-trailing arms, coil springs and telescopic shock absorbers
Tyres: 5.20 x 12in
Steering: Worm and roller

Brakes: Drums front and rear and a mechanical drum handbrake on transmission
Top speed: 62mph (100km/h)
Fuel consumption: 49mpg (5.7L/100km)
Wheelbase: 2000mm
Track: Front – 1144mm. Rear – 1154mm
Length: 3215mm
Width: 1288mm
Height: 1405mm
Weight: 585kg
Production: 891,107

FIAT 600 MULTIPLA
As the 600 except for:
Final drive: 6.4:1
Top speed: 55mph (90km/h)
Fuel consumption: 43mpg (6.7L/100km)
Track: Front – 1225mm. Rear – 1151mm
Length: 3530mm
Width: 1450mm
Height: 1580mm
Weight: 1150kg
Production: 76,711

FIAT 600D
1960-1969
Engine:Type 100D.000
Location: Rear longitudinal
Capacity: 767cc
Cylinders: 4 in-line
Valves: 8 overhead valves
Bore and stroke: 62mm x 63.5mm
Compression ratio: 7.5:1
Power: 29bhp at 4800rpm
Transmission: Four-speed with combined final drive, rear-wheel drive and synchromesh on 2nd, 3rd and 4th
Final drive: 4.85:1
Suspension: Front – independent, by wishbones and transverse leaf spring, and telescopic shock absorbers. Rear – independent, semi-trailing arms, coil springs and telescopic shock absorbers
Wheels: 5.20 x 12in
Steering: Worm and roller
Brakes: Drums front and rear and a mechanical drum handbrake on transmission
Top speed: 68mph (110km/h)
Fuel consumption: 48mpg (5.8L/100km)
Wheelbase: 2000mm
Track: Front – 1150mm. Rear – 1160mm
Length: 3295mm
Width: 1378mm
Height: 1405mm
Weight: 605kg
Production: 1,561,000 (Multipla 83,389)

FIAT 1100-103
1953-1969
Engine: Type 103.000
Location: Front longitudinal
Capacity: 1089cc
Cylinders: 4 in-line
Valves: 8 overhead valves
Bore and stroke: 68mm x 75mm
Compression ratio: 6.7:1
Power: 36bhp at 4400rpm
Transmission: Four-speed, rear-wheel drive and synchromesh on 2nd, 3rd and 4th
Final drive: 4.3:1
Suspension: Front – independent, coil springs, wishbones, telescopic shock absorbers and anti-roll bar. Rear – rigid axle, semi-elliptic springs, anti-roll bar and telescopic shock absorbers
Wheels: 5.20 x 14in
Steering: Worm and roller
Brakes: Drums front and rear and a mechanical drum handbrake on transmission
Top speed: 72mph (116km/h)
Fuel consumption: 35mpg (8L/100km)
Wheelbase: 2340mm
Track: Front – 1229mm. Rear – 1212mm
Length: 3775mm
Width: 1458mm
Height: 1485mm
Weight: 825kg
Production: 250,000 (first series 1953-1956)

FIAT 1100-103
Model: 103E (Berlina/Familiare)
Capacity: 1089cc
Power: 40bhp at 4400rpm
Brakes: Drums front and rear
Wheelbase: 2340mm
Track: Front – 1229mm. Rear – 1212mm
Weight: 870kg

Model: 103E (TV)
Capacity: 1089cc
Power: 53bhp at 5400rpm
Brakes: Drums front and rear
Track: Front – 1229mm. Rear – 1212mm
Weight: 850kg

Model: 103D
Capacity:1089cc
Power: 43bhp at 4800rpm
Brakes: Drums front and rear
Wheelbase: 2340mm
Track: Front – 1232mm. Rear – 1215mm
Weight: 880kg

Model: 103H
Capacity: 1089cc
Power: 50bhp at 5200rpm
Brakes: Drums front and rear
Wheelbase: 2340mm
Track: Front – 1232mm. Rear – 1215mm
Weight: 915kg

Model: 1100D
Capacity: 1221cc
Power: 55bhp at 5000rpm
Brakes: Drums front and rear
Wheelbase: 2340mm
Track: Front – 1232mm. Rear –1215mm
Weight: 895kg

Model: 1100R
Capacity: 1089cc
Power: 48bhp at 5200rpm
Brakes: Discs front, drums rear.
Wheelbase: 2342mm
Track: Front – 1232mm. Rear – 1214mm
Weight: 850kg

FIAT NUOVA 500
1957-1960
Engine: Type 110.00
Location: Rear longitudinal
Capacity: 479cc
Cylinders: Air-cooled, 2 in-line
Valves: 4 overhead valves
Bore and stroke: 66mm x 70mm
Compression ratio: 6.55:1
Power: 13bhp at 4000rpm
Transmission: Four-speed with combined final drive, rear-wheel drive and constant mesh on 2nd, 3rd and 4th
Final drive: 5.125:1
Suspension: Front – independent, by wishbones and leaf spring, and telescopic shock

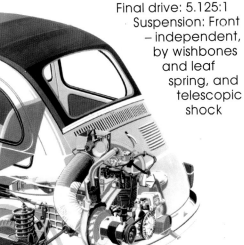

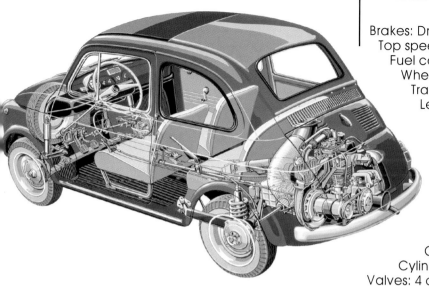

absorbers. Rear – independent, semi-trailing arms,
coil springs and telescopic shock absorbers
Tyres: 125 x 12in
Steering: Worm and roller
Brakes: Drums front and rear and a mechanical
drum handbrake on transmission
Top speed: 53mph (85km/h)
Fuel consumption: 50mpg (4.5L/100km)
Wheelbase: 1840mm
Track: Front – 1121mm. Rear – 1135mm
Length: 2970mm
Width: 1378mm
Height: 1325mm
Weight: 470kg
Production: 181,036

FIAT 500D
1960-1965
Engine: Type 110D.000
Capacity: 499.5cc
Location: Rear longitudinal
Cylinders: Air-cooled, 2 in-line
Valves: 4 overhead valves
Bore and stroke: 67.4mm x 70mm
Compression ratio: 7.7:1
Power: 17.5bhp at 4400rpm
Transmission: Four-speed with combined final drive,
rear-wheel drive and constant mesh on 2nd, 3rd
and 4th
Final drive: 5.125:1
Suspension: Front – independent, by wishbones and
leaf spring, and telescopic shock absorbers. Rear
– independent, semi-trailing arms, coil springs and
telescopic shock absorbers
Wheels: 125 x 12in
Steering: Worm and roller

Brakes: Drums front and rear
Top speed: 59mph (95km/h)
Fuel consumption: 58mpg (4.8L/100km)
Wheelbase: 1840mm
Track: Front – 1121mm. Rear – 1135mm
Length: 270mm
Width: 1322mm
Height: 1325mm
Weight: 500kg
Production: 640,520

FIAT 500F
1965-1972
Engine: Type 110F.000
Location: Rear longitudinal
Capacity: 499.5cc
Cylinders: Air-cooled, 2 in-line
Valves: 4 overhead valves
Bore and stroke: 67.4mm x 70mm
Compression ratio: 7.1:1
Power: 22bhp at 4400rpm
Transmission: Four-speed with combined final drive,
rear-wheel drive and constant mesh on 2nd, 3rd
and 4th
Final drive: 5.125:1
Suspension:Front – independent, by wishbones and
leaf spring, and telescopic shock absorbers. Rear
– independent, semi-trailing arms, coil springs and
telescopic shock absorbers
Wheels: 125 x 12in
Steering: Worm and roller
Brakes: Drums front and rear
Top speed: 59mph (95km/h)
Fuel consumption: 51mpg (5.5L/100km)
Wheelbase: 1840mm
Track: Front – 1121mm. Rear – 1135mm
Length: 2970mm
Width: 1320mm
Height: 1325mm
Weight: 520kg
Production: 2,272,092 (includes 500L)

FIAT 850 BERLINA
1964-1968
Engine: Type 100G.000
Location: Rear longitudinal
Capacity: 843cc
Cylinders: 4 in-line
Valves: 8 overhead valves
Bore and stroke: 65mm x 63.5mm
Compression ratio: 8.1:1
Power: 40bhp at 5300rpm
Transmission: Four-speed with combined final drive
and rear-wheel drive
Final drive: 4.625:1
Suspension: Front – independent, by wishbones and

transverse leaf spring, telescopic shock absorbers and anti-roll bar. Rear – independent, semi-trailing arms, coil springs, telescopic shock absorbers and anti-roll bar
Tyres: 5.50 x 12in
Steering: Worm and roller
Brakes: Front discs and rear drums
Top speed: 75mph (120km/h)
Fuel consumption: 44mpg (6.3L/100km)
Wheelbase: 2027mm
Track: Front – 1146mm. Rear – 1211mm
Length: 3575mm
Width: 1425mm
Height: 1385mm
Weight: 670kg

FIAT 850 COUPÉ
1965-1968
Engine: Type 100GC.000
Location: Rear longitudinal
Capacity: 843cc
Cylinders: 4 in-line
Valves: 8 overhead valves
Bore and stroke: 65mm x 63.5mm
Compression ratio: 9.3:1
Power: 52bhp at 6200rpm
Transmission: Four-speed with combined final drive and rear-wheel drive
Final drive: 4.875:1
Suspension: Front – independent, by wishbones and transverse leaf spring, telescopic shock absorbers and anti-roll bar. Rear – independent, semi-trailing arms, coil springs, telescopic shock absorbers and anti-roll bar
Tyres: 5.50 x 13in
Steering: Worm and roller
Brakes: Front discs and rear drums
Top speed: 84mph (135km/h)
Fuel consumption: 40mpg (7L/100km)
Wheelbase: 2027mm
Track: Front – 1158mm. Rear – 1212mm
Length: 3608mm
Width: 1500mm
Height: 1300mm
Weight: 720kg

FIAT 850 SPIDER
As the Coupé except for:
Engine: Type 100GS.000
Power: 54bhp at 6500rpm
Top speed: 90mph (145km/h)
Fuel consumption: 39.2mpg (7.2L/100km)
Wheelbase: 2027mm
Track: Front – 1158mm. Rear – 1212mm
Length: 3782mm
Width: 1498mm

Height: 1200mm
Weight: 725kg

FIAT 850 COUPÉ
1968-1971
Engine: Type 100GBC.000
Location: Rear longitudinal
Capacity: 903cc
Cylinders: 4 in-line
Bore and stroke: 65mm x 68mm
Valves: 8 overhead valves
Compression ratio: 9.5:1
Power: 52bhp at 6500rpm
Transmission: Four-speed and rear-wheel drive
Final drive: 4.875:1
Suspension: Front – independent, by wishbones and transverse leaf spring, telescopic shock absorbers and anti-roll bar. Rear – independent, semi-trailing arms, coil springs, telescopic shock absorbers and anti-roll bar
Tyres: 155 x 13in
Steering: Worm and roller
Brakes: Front discs and rear drums
Top speed: 90mph (145km/h)
Fuel consumption: 39mpg (7.2L/100km)
Wheelbase: 2027mm
Track: Front – 1170mm. Rear – 1222mm
Length: 3652mm
Width: 1500mm
Height: 1300mm
Weight: 745kg

FIAT 850 SPIDER (1968-1972)
As the Coupé except for:
Top speed: 93mph (150km/h)
Fuel consumption: 38.5mpg (7.3L/100km)
Length: 3824mm
Width: 1498mm
Height: 1220mm
Weight: 705kg

FIAT 128
1969-1972
Engine: Type 128
Location: Front transverse
Capacity: 1116cc
Cylinders: 4 in-line
Bore and stroke: 80mm x 55mm
Valves: 8 valves and a single overhead camshaft
Compression ratio: 8.8:1
Power: 55bhp at 6000rpm
Transmission: Four-speed and front-wheel drive
Final drive: 4.077:1
Suspension: Front – independent, MacPherson struts, coil springs, telescopic shock absorbers and anti-roll bar. Rear – independent, transverse

leaf spring and wishbones, and telescopic shock absorbers
Tyres: 145 x 13in
Steering: Rack and pinion
Brakes: Front discs and rear drums
Top speed: 84mph (135km/h)
Fuel consumption: 35mpg (8L/100km)
Wheelbase: 2448mm
Track: Front – 1308mm. Rear – 1306mm
Length: 3856mm
Width: 1590mm
Height: 1420mm
Weight: 805kg

FIAT 128 RALLY
1971-1972
As above but with:
Engine: Type 128 AR.000
Capacity: 1290cc
Bore and stroke: 86mm x 55mm
Compression ratio: 8.9:1
Power: 67bhp at 6200rpm
Final drive: 4.077:1
Tyres: 145 HR-13
Top speed: 93mph (150km/h)
Fuel consumption: 32mpg (8.6L/100km)
Track: Front – 1308mm. Rear – 1313mm
Length: 3876mm
Height: 1390mm
Weight: 820kg

FIAT 128 SPECIAL
1974-1976
As 1969-1975 but with:
Capacity: 1116cc
Power: 55bhp at 6000rpm
Capacity: 1290cc
Power: 60bhp at 6000rpm

FIAT 128 COUPÉ 1100
1971-1975
As 1969-1975 but with:
Engine: Type 128 AC 5.000
Capacity: 1116cc
Power: 64bhp at 6600rpm
Top speed: 93mph (150km/h)
Fuel consumption: 33mpg (8.6L/100km)
Wheelbase: 2223mm
Track: Front – 1325mm. Rear – 1333mm
Length: 3856mm
Width: 1590mm
Height: 1420mm
Weight: 775kg

FIAT 128 COUPÉ 1300
1971-1975

As above but with:
Engine: Type 128 AC.000
Capacity: 1290cc
Power: 75bhp at 6000rpm
Top speed: 100mph (160km/h)
Fuel consumption: 33mpg (8.5L/100km)
Weight: 815kg

FIAT 128 3P 1100
1975-1978
As the Coupé but with:
Capacity: 1116cc
Compression ratio: 9.2:1
Power: 65bhp at 6000rpm

FIAT 128 3P 1300
1975-1978
As above but with:
Capacity: 1290cc
Compression ratio: 9.2:1
Power: 73bhp at 6000rpm

FIAT 127 FIRST SERIES
1971-1977
Engine: Type 100 GL.000
Location: Front transverse
Capacity: 903cc
Cylinders: 4 in-line
Bore and stroke: 65mm x 68mm
Valves: 8 overhead valves
Compression ratio: 9:1
Power: 47bhp at 6200rpm
Transmission: Four-speed and front-wheel drive
Final drive: 4.6:1
Suspension: Front – independent, struts, coil springs, telescopic shock absorbers and anti-roll bar. Rear – independent, transverse leaf spring, wishbones and telescopic shock absorbers
Tyres: 135 x 13in
Steering: Rack and pinion
Brakes: Front discs and rear drums
Top speed: 87mph (140km/h)
Fuel consumption: 41mpg (6.9L/100km)
Wheelbase: 2225mm
Track: Front – 1280mm. Rear – 1295mm
Length: 3595mm
Width: 1527mm
Height: 1325mm
Weight: 705kg

FIAT 127 SECOND SERIES
1977-1981
Engine: Type 127 A.000
Location: Front transverse
Capacity: 1049cc
Valves: 8 overhead valves

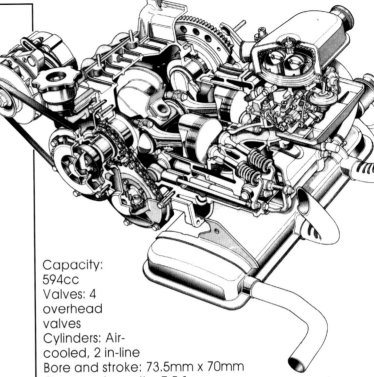

Cylinders: 4 in-line
Bore and stroke: 76mm x 57.8mm
Compression ratio: 9.3:1
Power: 50bhp at 5600rpm
Transmission: Four-speed and front-
wheel drive
Final drive: 4.0:1
Suspension: Front – independent, struts,
coil springs, telescopic shock absorbers and
anti-roll bar. Rear – independent, transverse
leaf spring, wishbones and telescopic shock
absorbers
Tyres: 135 x 13in
Steering: Rack and pinion
Brakes: Front discs and rear drums
Top speed: 87mph (140km/h)
Fuel consumption: 36.5mpg (7.8L/100km)
Wheelbase: 2225mm
Track: Front – 1280mm. Rear – 1295mm
Length: 3645mm
Width: 1527mm
Height: 1358mm
Weight: 730kg

FIAT 127 THIRD SERIES SPORT
1981-1983
Engine: Type 127A. 3000
Location: Front transverse
Capacity: 1301cc
Valves: 8 overhead valves
Cylinders: 4 in-line
Bore and stroke: 76.1mm x 71.5mm
Compression ratio: 9.75:1
Power: 55bhp at 5750rpm
Transmission: Four-speed and front-wheel drive
Final drive: 4.0:1
Suspension: Front – independent, struts, coil springs,
telescopic shock absorbers and anti-roll bar. Rear
– independent, transverse leaf spring, wishbones and
telescopic shock absorbers
Tyres: 135 x 13in or 155/70 x 13in
Steering: Rack and pinion
Brakes: Front discs and rear drums
Top speed: 103mph (165km/h)
Fuel consumption: 37.2mpg (7.7L/100km)
Wheelbase: 2225mm
Track: Front – 1288mm. Rear – 1303mm
Length: 3711mm
Width: 1536mm
Height: 1370mm
Weight: 775kg

FIAT 126
1972-1977
Engine: Type 126 A.000
Location: Rear longitudinal

Capacity:
594cc
Valves: 4
overhead
valves
Cylinders: Air-
cooled, 2 in-line
Bore and stroke: 73.5mm x 70mm
Compression ratio: 7.5:1
Power: 23bhp at 4800rpm
Transmission: Four-speed, rear-wheel
drive and synchromesh on 2nd, 3rd and 4th
Final drive: 4.87:1
Suspension: Front – independent, top wishbones,
transverse-mounted self-stabilising leaf springs and
telescopic shock absorbers. Rear – independent,
semi-trailing arms, coil springs, telescopic shock
absorbers and anti-roll bar
Tyres: 135 x 12in
Steering: Worm and roller
Brakes: Drums front and rear
Top speed: 65mph (105km/h)
Fuel consumption: 54mpg (5.2L/100km)
Wheelbase: 1840mm
Track: Front – 1140mm. Rear – 1203mm
Length: 3054mm
Width: 1377mm
Height: 1335mm
Weight: 900kg

FIAT 126 BIS
1987-1992
Engine: Type 126A2.000, ohv
Location: Rear longitudinal
Capacity: 704cc
Valves: 4 overhead valves
Cylinders: 2 in-line
Bore and stroke: 80mm x 70mm
Compression ratio: 8.6:1
Power: 26bhp at 4500rpm

Transmission: Four-speed and rear-wheel drive
Final drive: 4.3:1
Suspension: Front – independent, top wishbones, transverse-mounted self-stabilising leaf springs and telescopic shock absorbers. Rear – independent, semi-trailing arms, coil springs and telescopic shock absorbers
Wheels: 135/70 x 13in
Steering: Worm and roller
Brakes: Drums front and rear
Top speed: 72mph (116km/h)
Fuel consumption: 56mpg (5.1L/100km)
Wheelbase: 1840mm
Track: Front – 1134mm. Rear – 1169mm
Length: 3107mm
Width: 1377mm
Height: 1343mm
Weight: 620kg

FIAT PANDA 45
1980-1984
Engine: Type 146A. 000
Location: Front transverse
Capacity: 903cc
Valves: 8 overhead valves
Cylinders: 4 in-line
Bore and stroke: 65mm x 68mm
Compression ratio: 9.0:1
Power: 45bhp at 5600rpm
Transmission: Four-speed and front-wheel drive
Final drive: 4.0:1
Suspension: Front – independent, wishbones, coil springs, hydraulic shock absorbers and longitudinal beams. Rear – rigid axle, longitudinal leaf springs and hydraulic shock absorbers
Tyres: 135 x 13in
Steering: Rack and pinion
Brakes: Drums front and rear
Top speed: 87mph (140km/h)

Fuel consumption: 55mpg (5.8L/100km)
Wheelbase: 2160mm
Track: Front – 1254mm. Rear – 1249mm
Length: 3380mm
Width: 1460mm
Height: 1445mm
Weight: 680kg

FIAT PANDA 30 AND 34
General specification similar to Panda 45 but with the following engine differences:
Panda 30
Engine: Type 141 A. 000
Location: Front transverse
Capacity: 652cc
Valves: 4 overhead valves
Cylinders: Air-cooled 2 in-line
Bore and stroke: 77mm x 70mm
Compression ratio: 8.0:1
Power: 30hp at 5500rpm

Panda 34
Engine: Type 100 GL6. 000
Location: Front transverse
Capacity: 843cc
Valves: 8 overhead valves
Cylinders: 4 in-line
Bore and stroke: 65mm x 63.5mm
Compression ratio: 7.8:1
Power: 34hp at 5800rpm

FIAT PANDA 4 x 4
1983-1986
Engine: Type 112B1. 054
Location: Front transverse
Capacity: 965cc
Valves: 8 overhead valves
Cylinders: 4 in-line
Bore and stroke: 67.2mm x 68mm
Compression ratio: 9.2:1
Power: 48bhp at 5600rpm
Transmission: Five-speed and four-wheel drive
Final drive: 14/41
Suspension: Front – independent, wishbones, coil springs, hydraulic shock absorbers and longitudinal beams. Rear – rigid axle, longitudinal leaf springs and hydraulic shock absorbers
Tyres: 145 x 13in
Steering: Rack and pinion
Brakes: Drums front and rear
Top speed: 84mph (135km/h)
Fuel consumption: 38.1mpg (7.4L/100km)
Wheelbase: 2170mm
Track: Front – 1254mm. Rear – 1258mm

Length: 3390mm
Width: 1485mm
Height: 1451mm
Weight: 740kg

FIAT PANDA 1100ie
1994-2003
Engine: Type 176 B2. 000
Location: Front transverse
Capacity: 1108cc
Valves: 8 valve and a single overhead camshaft
Cylinders: 4 in-line
Bore and stroke: 70mm x 72mm
Compression ratio: 9.6:1
Power: 54bhp at 5500rpm
Transmission: Five-speed and front-wheel drive
Final drive: 17/74
Suspension: Front – independent, MacPherson strut with transverse arm and oblique beam, and coil spring. Rear – rigid axle with central link, oblique arm and coil spring
Tyres:135 x 13in or 155/65 x 13in
Steering: Rack and pinion
Brakes: Discs front and drums rear
Top speed: 84mph (140km/h)
Fuel consumption: 38.1mpg (7.4L/100km)
Wheelbase: 2159mm
Track: Front – 1263mm. Rear – 1266mm
Length: 3408mm
Width: 1494mm
Height: 1200mm
Weight: 745kg

FIAT UNO 45
1983-1989
Engine: Type 146 A. 000
Location: Front transverse
Capacity: 903cc
Valves: 8 overhead valves
Cylinders: 4 in-line
Bore and stroke: 65mm x 68mm
Compression ratio: 9:1
Power: 45bhp at 5600rpm
Transmission: Four-speed (Five-speed optional) and front-wheel drive
Final drive: 1/57
Suspension: Front – MacPherson struts, wishbones, coil springs, telescopic shock absorbers and anti-roll bar. Rear – semi independent, longitudinal arms, coil springs and telescopic shock absorbers
Tyres: 135 SR 13
Steering: Rack and pinion
Brakes: Discs front and drums front
Top speed: 87.5mph (140km/h)
Fuel consumption: 46mpg (6.4L/100km)
Wheelbase: 2362mm

Track: Front – 1340mm. Rear – 1300mm
Length: 3644mm
Width: 1548mm
Height: 1432mm
Weight: 700kg

Selected engine variations:
Model: Uno 55 (1983-1985)
Engine: Type 138 B. 000
Capacity: 1116cc (sohc)
Bore and stroke: 70mm x 64.9mm
Power: 55bhp at 5700rpm

Model: Uno 60 (1985-1989)
Engine: Type 138 B.000
Capacity: 1116cc (sohc)
Bore and stroke: 70mm x 64.9mm
Power: 58bhp at 5700rpm

Model: Uno 70S (1983-1989)
Engine: Type 138 B2.000
Capacity: 1301cc (sohc)
Bore and stroke: 86.4mm x 55.5mm
Power: 65bhp at 5600rpm

Model: Uno 45 Fire (1985-1989)
Engine: Type 156 A2. 000
Capacity: 999cc (sohc)
Bore and stroke: 70mm x 64.9mm
Power: 45bhp at 5000rpm

Model: Uno Diesel (1983-1989)
Engine: Type 127 A.5 000
Capacity: 1301cc
Bore and stroke: 76.1mm x 71.5mm
Power: 45bhp at 5000rpm

Model: Uno Turbodiesel (1986-1989)
Engine: Type 146 B. 000
Capacity: 1367cc and a single overhead camshaft
Bore and stroke: 78mm x 71.5mm
Power: 70bhp at 4800rpm

Model: Uno 75ie Cat (1987-1989)
Engine: Type 132 C2.048
Capacity: 1498cc and a single overhead camshaft
Bore and stroke: 86.4mm x 63.9mm
Power: 75bhp at 5500rpm

Model: Uno 60D (1989-1995)
Capacity: 1697cc
Bore and stroke: 82.6mm x 79.2mm
Power: 58bhp at 4800rpm

Model: Uno 60D (1989-1995)
Capacity: 1929cc

Bore and stroke: not known
Power: 60bhp at 4400rpm

Model: Uno 1.0 Trend (1988-1992)
Engine: Type 146 B4.000
Capacity: 994cc
Bore and stroke: 76mm x 54.8mm
Power: 44bhp at 5250rpm

Model: Uno 1.1 Trend CS (1988-1992)
Engine: Type 146 A6.000
Capacity: 1116cc
Bore and stroke: 76mm x 61.5mm
Power: 58bhp at 5500rpm

Model: Uno 60 (1989-1992)
Engine: Type 160 A3.000
Capacity: 1108cc
Bore and stroke: 70mm x 72mm
Power: 56bhp at 5500rpm

Model: Uno 70ie (1989-1992)
Engine: Type 146 C1.000
Capacity: 1372cc
Bore and stroke: 80.5mm x 67.4mm
Power: 71bhp at 5500rpm

Model: Uno 75ie (1989-1992)
Engine: Type 149 C1.000
Capacity: 1498cc
Bore and stroke: 86.4mm x 63.9mm
Power: 75bhp at 5600rpm

FIAT UNO TURBO ie 'Mk1'
1985-1989
Engine: Type 146 A2. 000
Location: Front transverse
Capacity: 1301cc
Valves: 8 overhead valves
Cylinders: 4 in-line
Bore and stroke: 80.5mm x 63.9mm
Compression ratio: 7.7:1
Power:105bhp at 5750rpm
Transmission: Five-speed and front-wheel drive
Final drive: 3.58:1
Suspension: Front – MacPherson struts, transverse arms, coil springs, gas shock absorbers and anti-roll bar. Rear – semi independent, longitudinal arms, coil springs and gas shock absorbers
Tyres: 175/60 x 13in
Steering: Rack and pinion
Brakes: Discs front and drums rear
Top speed: 124mph (200km/h)
Fuel consumption: 32mpg (8.9L/100km)
Wheelbase: 2362mm
Track: Front – 1346mm. Rear – 1309mm

Length: 3644mm
Width:1650mm
Height: 1370mm
Weight: 845kg

FIAT UNO TURBO ie cat
1985-1989
As above except for:
Engine: Type 146 A2. 246
Compression ratio: 8:1
Power: 100bhp at 6000rpm
Top speed: 121mph (195km/h)
Fuel consumption: 31mpg (9.2L/100km)

FIAT UNO TURBO ie 'Mk2'
1989-1995
As above except for:
Engine: Type 146 A8. 000
Capacity: 1372cc
Bore and stroke: 80.5mm x 67.4mm
Compression ratio: 7.8:1
Power: 116bhp at 6000rpm
Brakes: Discs front and rear
Top speed: 127.5mph (204km/h)
Fuel consumption: 9.5L/100km
Wheelbase: 2362mm
Track: Front – 1353mm. Rear – 1309mm
Length: 3689mm
Width: 1562mm
Height: 1430mm
Weight: 925kg

FIAT UNO TURBO ie cat Mk2
1989-1995
As above except for:
Engine: Type 146 A8. 046
Capacity: 1372cc
Bore and stroke: 80.5mm x 67.4mm
Compression ratio: 7.8:1
Power: 111bhp at 6000rpm
Brakes: Discs front and rear
Top speed: 127.5mph (200km/h)
Fuel consumption: 9.8L/100km
Weight: 940kg

CINQUECENTO 899
1991-1995
Engine: Type 1170 A1. 046
Location: Front transverse
Capacity: 899cc
Valves: 8 overhead valves
Cylinders: 4 in-line
Bore and stroke: 65mm x 67.70mm
Compression ratio: 8.8:1
Power: 39hp at 5500rpm
Transmission: Five-speed and front-wheel drive

Final drive: 14/57
Suspension: Front – MacPherson strut with transverse arm and coil spring. Rear – trailing arm and coil spring
Tyres: 145/70 x 13in
Steering: Rack and pinion
Brakes: Front discs and rear drums
Top speed: 87mph (140km/h)
Fuel consumption: 55mpg (5.8L/100km)
Wheelbase: 2200mm
Track: Front – 1270mm. Rear – 1276mm
Length: 3227mm
Width: 1487mm
Height: 1435mm
Weight: 710kg

CINQUECENTO SPORTING
1994-1998
Engine: Type 176 B2. 000
Location: Front transverse
Capacity: 1108cc
Valves: 8 valves and a single overhead camshaft
Cylinders: 4 in-line
Bore and stroke: 70mm x 72mm
Compression ratio: 9.6:1
Power: 54hp at 5500rpm
Transmission: Five-speed and front-wheel drive
Final drive: 15/58
Suspension: Front – MacPherson strut with transverse arm, coil spring and anti-roll bar. Rear – trailing arm and coil spring
Tyres: 155/65 x 13in (165/55 x 13in from 1995)
Steering: Rack and pinion
Brakes: Front discs and rear drums
Top speed: 150km/h
Fuel consumption: 55mpg (5.13L/100km)
Wheelbase: 2200mm
Track: Front – 1270mm. Rear – 1276mm
Length: 3227mm
Width: 1487mm
Height: 1435mm
Weight: 735kg

SEICENTO
1998-2003
Engine: Type 1170 A1. 046
Location: Front transverse
Capacity: 899cc
Valves: 8 overhead valves

Cylinders: 4 in-line
Bore and stroke: 65mm x 67.70mm
Compression ratio: 8.8:1
Power: 39hp at 5500rpm
Transmission: Five-speed and front-wheel drive
Final drive: 14/57
Suspension: Front – MacPherson strut with transverse arm and coil spring. Rear – trailing arm and coil spring
Tyres: 155/65 x 13in
Steering: Rack and pinion (Power: Steering: optional)
Brakes: Front discs and rear drums
Top speed: 87mph (140km/h)
Fuel consumption: 55mpg (5.8L/100km) ??
Wheelbase: 2200mm
Track: Front – 1268mm. Rear – 1260mm.
Length: 3319mm
Width: 1508mm
Height: 1445mm
Weight: 730kg

SEICENTO SPORTING
1998-2003
Engine: Type 176 B2. 000
Location: Front transverse
Capacity: 1108cc
Valves: 8 valves, sohc
Cylinders: 4 in-line
Bore and stroke: 70mm x 72mm
Compression ratio: 9.6:1
Power: 54hp at 5500rpm
Transmission: Five-speed and front-wheel drive
Final drive: 16/57
Suspension: Front – MacPherson strut with transverse arm and coil spring. Rear – trailing arm and coil spring
Tyres: 155/65 x 13in
Steering: Rack and pinion (Power: Steering: optional)
Brakes: Front discs and rear drums
Top speed: 150km/h
Fuel consumption: 55mpg (5.13L/100km)
Wheelbase: 2200mm
Track: Front – 1268mm. Rear – 1260mm
Length: 3319mm
Width: 1508mm
Height: 1440mm
Weight: 750kg

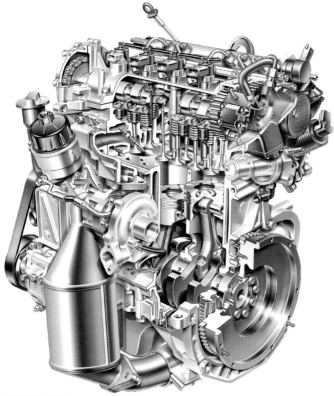

SEICENTO
1998-2001*
Engine: Type 1170 A1. 046
Location: Front transverse
Capacity: 899cc
Valves: 8 overhead valves
Cylinders: 4 in-line
Bore and stroke: 65mm x 67.70mm
Compression ratio: 8.8:1
Power: 39hp at 5500rpm
Transmission: Five-speed and front-wheel drive
Final drive: 14/57
Suspension: Front – MacPherson strut with transverse arm and coil spring. Rear – trailing arm and coil spring
Tyres: 155/65 x 13in
Steering: Rack and pinion (Power: Steering: optional)
Brakes: Front discs and rear drums
Top speed: 87mph (140km/h)
Fuel consumption: 55mpg (5.13L/100km)
Wheelbase: 2200mm
Track: Front – 1268mm. Rear – 1260mm
Length: 3319mm
Width: 1508mm
Height: 1445mm
Weight: 730kg

*A new base model was introduced in 2001 called the Seicento S, fitted with the 1108cc engine.

SEICENTO SPORTING
1998-2003
Engine: Type 176 B2. 000
Location: Front transverse

Cylinders: 4 in-line
Capacity: 1108cc
Valves: 8 valves and sohc
Bore and stroke: 70mm x 72mm
Compression ratio: 9.6:1
Power: 54hp at 5500rpm
Transmission: Five-speed and front-wheel drive
Final drive: 16/57
Suspension: Front – MacPherson strut with transverse arm and coil spring. Rear – trailing arm and coil spring
Tyres: 155/65 x 13in
Steering: Rack and pinion (Power: Steering: optional)
Brakes: Front discs and rear drums
Top speed: 94mph (150km/h)
Fuel consumption: 55mpg (5.13L/100km)
Wheelbase: 2200mm
Track: Front – 1268mm. Rear – 1260mm
Length: 3319mm
Width: 1508mm
Height: 1440mm
Weight: 750kg

NUOVA PANDA 1.1 Fire
2004-
Engine: Type 187 A.1000
Location: Front transverse
Cylinders: 4 in-line
Capacity: 1108cc
Valves: 8 valves and a single overhead camshaft
Bore and stroke: 70mm x 72mm
Compression ratio: 9.6:1
Power: 54hp at 5000rpm
Transmission: Five-speed manual ('Dualogic' optional) and front-wheel drive
Final drive: 3.562
Suspension: Front – MacPherson strut, telescopic shock absorbers, coil springs and anti-roll bar. Rear – torsion beam
Tyres: 155/80 x 13in
Steering: Rack and pinion with optional power steering
Brakes: Discs front and rear
Top speed: 94mph (150km/h)
Fuel consumption: 50mpg (5.7L/100km)
Wheelbase: 2299mm
Track: Front – 1366mm. Rear – 1357mm
Length: 3540mm
Width: 1578mm
Height: 1540mm
Weight: 840kg

NUOVA PANDA 1.2 Fire
As above except for:
Engine: Type 188 A.4000
Capacity: 1242cc

Bore and stroke: 70.8mm x 78.86mm
Compression ratio: 9.6:1
Power: 60hp at 5000rpm
Final drive: 3.438
Tyres: 155/80 x 13in
Top speed: 97mph (155km/h)
Fuel consumption: 50mpg (5.6L/100km)
Weight: 860kg

NUOVA PANDA 1.3 Multijet
As above except for:
Engine: Type 188 A.8000
Capacity: 1251cc
Valves: 16 valves and a double overhead camshaft
Bore and stroke: 69.6mm x 82mm
Compression ratio: 18:1
Power: 70hp at 4000rpm
Tyres: 155/80 x 13in or 165/65 x 14in
Top speed: 100mph (160km/h)
Fuel consumption: 65.7mpg (4.3L/100km)
Weight: 935kg

NUOVA PANDA 100 HP
As above except for:
Engine: Type 169 A.3000
Capacity: 1368cc
Bore and stroke: 72mm x 84mm
Compression ratio: 11:1
Power: 100hp at 6000rpm
Final drive: 4.077
Tyres: 195/45 R15
Top speed: 115mph (185km/h)
Fuel consumption: 43mpg (6.5L/100km)
Weight: 975kg

NUOVA PANDA 4 x 4*
As the Panda 1.2 except for:
Engine: Type 188 A.4000
Capacity: 1242cc
Compression ratio: 9.8:1
Power: 60hp at 5000rpm
Final drive: 4.929 and four-wheel drive
Brakes: Discs front and rear
Tyres: 185/65 x 14in
Top speed: 91mph (145km/h)
Fuel consumption: 42.8mpg (6.6L/100km)
Weight: 980kg
* 1.3 Multijet versions are available in some markets.

AUTOBIANCHI A112 SPECIFICATIONS*
Typical A112 engines as used throughout the range between 1969 and 1985. Dates shown are when the engine type first appeared.
A112 Base E
1969-1973
Engine: Type A112 A. 000

Capacity: 903cc
Bore and stroke: 65mm x 68mm
Compression ratio: 9.0:1
Power: 44bhp at 5800rpm
Max. torque: 6.45kgm at 3600rpm

A112 Abarth S1-S3
1971-1976
Engine: Type A112 A1. 000
Capacity: 982cc
Bore and stroke: 65mm x 74mm
Compression ratio: 10.0:1
Power: 58bhp at 6600rpm
Max. torque: 7.5kgm at 3800rpm

A112 Base E S2-S3
1973-1975
Engine: Type A112 A. 000
Capacity: 903cc
Bore and stroke: 65mm x 68mm
Compression ratio: 9.0:1
Power: 47bhp at 5600rpm
Max. torque: 7.1kgm at 3600rpm

A112 Base S3
1975-1977
Engine: Type A112 A. 000
Capacity: 903cc
Bore and stroke: 65mm x 68mm
Compression ratio: 9.0:1
Power: 42bhp at 5400rpm
Max. torque: 7.0kgm at 2800rpm

A112 Abarth S3
1973-1975
Engine: Type A112 A2. 000
Capacity: 1050cc
Bore and stroke: 67.2mm x 74mm
Compression ratio: 10.4:1
Power: 70bhp at 6600rpm
Max. torque: 8.7kgm at 4100rpm

A112 E S4
1977-1979
Engine: Type A112 B1. 000
Capacity: 965cc
Bore and stroke: 67.2mm x 68mm
Compression ratio: 9.2:1
Power: 48bhp at 5600rpm
Max. torque: 7.3kgm at 3300rpm

*Because Autobianchi is a peripheral topic in this book, full technical specifications are not shown. Comprehensive details are published by Editoriale Domus in *Tutte Le Lancia*.

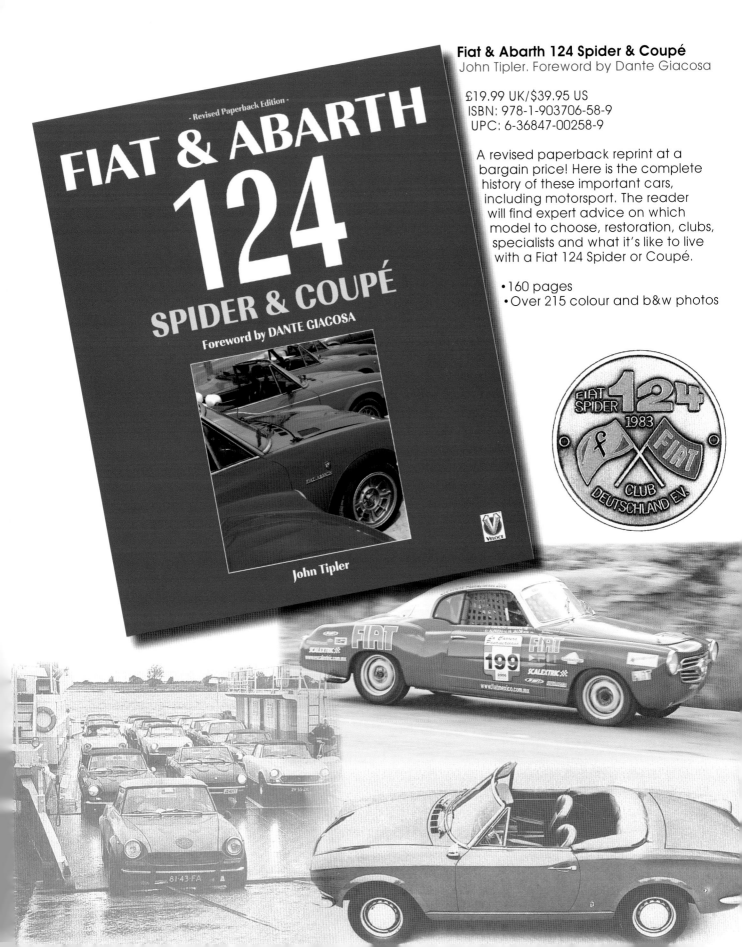

Fiat & Abarth 124 Spider & Coupé
John Tipler. Foreword by Dante Giacosa

£19.99 UK/$39.95 US
ISBN: 978-1-903706-58-9
UPC: 6-36847-00258-9

A revised paperback reprint at a bargain price! Here is the complete history of these important cars, including motorsport. The reader will find expert advice on which model to choose, restoration, clubs, specialists and what it's like to live with a Fiat 124 Spider or Coupé.

- 160 pages
- Over 215 colour and b&w photos

INDEX

- Updated & Enlarged Second Edition -

FIAT & ABARTH

500, 600 & Seicento

- Malcolm Bobbitt -

Fiat & Abarth 500, 600 & Seicento Updated & Enlarged 2nd Edition
Malcom Bobbitt

£29.99
ISBN: 978-1-903706-69-5
UPC: 6-36847-00269-5

From the famous Topolino to the award-winning Cinquecento and the modern Seicento, here's the definitive story of the baby Fiats, with particular emphasis on the Nuova 500. Read, too, about the motorsport success of Abarth versions.

- 192 pages
- Over 200 colour & b&w photos

structure and mechanical parts of the car

1.375
4' 6"

1.345
4' 4³/₄"

3.345
10' 11½"

3.215
10' 6½"

500 C
2 - seater

600
4 - seater

The A-Z of popular scooters & microcars – cruising in style!
Michael Dan

£29.99 UK/$59.95 US
ISBN: 978-1-845840-88-4
UPC: 6-36847-04088-8

An extensively illustrated reference guide to classic scooters and microcars with specification data presented in A-Z order. Nostalgic recollections by the author based on ownership and personal experience bring to life these facinating vehicles.

• 256 pages
• Over 440 colour photographs

Microcars at Large!
Adam Quellin

£14.99 UK/$29.95 US
ISBN: 978-1-845840-92-1
UPC: 6-36847-04092-5

Full of original colour illustrations, this volume charts the history and development of bubblecars and microcars from the middle of the twentieth century to the present day. This is a lavishly illustrated guide to the weird and wonderful world of microcars, from the basic bubblecars of the 1950s to the sophisticated models of today.

• 112 pages
• Over 110 colour illustrations

Building an Emergency Plan

A Guide for Museums and Other Cultural Institutions

Compiled by
Valerie Dorge and Sharon L. Jones

THE GETTY CONSERVATION INSTITUTE   LOS ANGELES

The Getty Conservation Institute
1200 Getty Center Drive
Suite 700
Los Angeles, California 90049-1684

Dinah Berland, *Managing Editor*
Nomi Kleinmuntz, *Manuscript Editor*
Anita Keys, *Production Coordinator*
Jeffrey Cohen, *Designer*

Printed in the United States
of America

10 9 8 7 6 5 4 3 2 1

Library of Congress
Cataloging-in-Publication Data

Building an emergency plan : a guide for
museums and other cultural institutions /
compiled by Valerie Dorge and Sharon L. Jones.

    p.   cm.
    Includes bibliographical references and index.
    ISBN 0-89236-529-3 (alk. paper)
    1. Museums—Management—Planning—
Handbooks, manuals, etc.   2. Emergency
management—Handbooks, manuals, etc.
3. Cultural property—Protection—Handbooks,
manuals, etc.   I. Dorge, Valerie, 1946–   .
II. Jones, Sharon L., 1961–   . III. Getty
Conservation Institute.
AM121.B85   1999   98-55487
0699.2—dc21   CIP
                                  r99

The Getty Conservation Institute works
internationally to further the appreciation
and preservation of the world's cultural heritage
for the enrichment and use of present and
future generations. The Institute is an operating
program of the J. Paul Getty Trust.

Contents

Appendixes

Foreword

Hardly a week goes by without a story in the news about the destruction and havoc caused by a natural disaster striking some populated area of the world. If we also take into account the destructive events caused by human beings—war, terrorism, arson—disasters become an almost daily item in newspapers and on television. What is often omitted from reports detailing loss of life and property, however, is the all-too-frequent fact that cultural institutions and sites are affected and valuable cultural heritage damaged or destroyed.

Perhaps because Los Angeles is an area that is always "between two earthquakes," and every year we also run the risk of fires and mud slides, preparation for emergencies is taken very seriously at the Getty. The emergency plan of the J. Paul Getty Museum has served as a model for many other museums in the United States. The Getty Conservation Institute has also been involved in training and education of museum professionals on this topic.

It is impossible to eliminate natural disasters, and no one can reasonably expect that all damage can be avoided. Much can be done, however, to mitigate the effects of destructive natural events and to reduce the risk of damage or loss in other types of emergency situations.

This book is a complete guide to developing an emergency preparedness and response plan tailored to the specific needs of your institution. Its aim is to help you to become better prepared and to respond appropriately to protect your staff, visitors, and collections in the event of an emergency. Although you may assume that such a planning process will be formidable and complicated—and therefore expensive—this need not be the case. The success of the emergency planning process requires a strong commitment from the director and the participation of all staff, but the process is not complicated. Once undertaken, it can be a very positive learning and team-building experience for the institution. Many of the steps suggested here require minimal or no financial resources, while the return on time invested is immediate.

Thankfully, the majority of institutions will never have to face a major disaster. What a price to pay, however, if the unthinkable happens and you are not prepared! Years of conservation, care, and investment can be reversed in a few hours or even a few minutes. It is on those occasions that the time spent developing a preparedness and response plan will be fully rewarded.

The Getty Conservation Institute is grateful to the many individuals and institutions that contributed their expertise and experiences to this publication. I would like to especially acknowledge the work of Valerie Dorge, whose commitment to this effort has resulted in a publication that we hope will be a valuable guide in the development of your emergency plan.

Timothy P. Whalen
Director
The Getty Conservation Institute

Preface

December 1999 will bring to an end the International Decade for Natural Disaster Reduction. This designation was made by the United Nations General Assembly to raise global awareness about the need for preventing, or at least mitigating, the destruction that natural disasters—such as floods and earthquakes—can cause to cultural heritage. During this decade, great advances have been made at the regional, national, and international levels to protect cultural heritage not only against natural disasters but against disasters that are caused by human activity—including wars, bomb threats, and fires, the last of which often occur during building renovations.

Since the mid-1980s, the Getty Conservation Institute (GCI) has worked actively as an advocate for the protection of cultural property and toward the development of practical solutions to technical problems faced in protecting collections and buildings in emergency situations. Many of the GCI activities in this area have been carried out in collaboration with our colleagues at the J. Paul Getty Museum. Director John Walsh and his staff have long been committed to emergency preparedness and response planning, and to sharing this knowledge through participation in research, conferences, and emergency missions. The Museum's "Emergency Planning Handbook" has been the model for the emergency plans of many cultural institutions in the United States.

One such collaboration with the Museum took place in January 1992, when we jointly organized a workshop, "Emergency Planning in Museums," for museum directors and their senior staff. Its objective was to communicate the importance of emergency planning and to emphasize the need for involvement at the highest level of the institution's organization in order to facilitate the development and implementation of successful emergency plans.

Building an Emergency Plan is the result of a GCI project that began in 1995 as a proposed series of training workshops to follow the 1992 workshop. However, in the process of identifying written material to support these activities, we recognized the lack of a clear, step-by-step guide to developing emergency plans tailored to meet the specific needs of museums and other cultural institutions. With that realization, we focused our efforts on creating a publication that would fill this need.

The publication started as a draft document compiled by Elisabeth Cornu, head of objects conservation at the Fine Arts Museums of San Francisco, and myself, with input from our colleagues at the J. Paul Getty Museum: Jerry Podany, head of antiquities conservation; and Brian Considine, conservator of decorative arts and sculpture. Wilbur Faulk, the director of Getty Center Security, provided advice at specific stages of manuscript development.

The original material was transformed into a working tool for professionals by Sharon Jones, an education technologist and a professional writer. The final publication is a practical guide that walks the users, step-by-step, through their respec-tive responsibilities in the planning process. Jones also gathered additional information through interviews with five colleagues in the cultural community who had experience in emergency preparedness and/or response. The following is a brief summary of the relevant experience of these advisers.

Barbara Roberts was head of decorative arts conservation at the J. Paul Getty Museum during the early stages of the Museum's emergency preparedness and response process. Since 1988, as a hazard mitigation consultant, she has participated at an international level in advocacy, training, and response activities, as well as in emergency missions.

Gail Joice is senior deputy director and registrar of the Seattle Art Museum. She was instrumental in developing and implementing the Museum's emergency plan. She chaired the American Association of Museums' Risk Management and Insurance committee from 1990 to 1995, and authored the committee document, "Questions to Ask Yourself When Preparing a Disaster Plan," a reference source for the "Questions to Consider" sections of this publication.

As director of the Barbados Museum and Historical Society, Alissandra Cummins guided her staff through the process of developing a written emergency plan that is regularly practiced, reviewed, and updated. Cummins also contributes to the efforts of the Museums Association of the Caribbean and other organizations to create a regional preparedness network to address the many hazards faced by cultural institutions in the Caribbean.

Conservator Johanna Maria Theile Bruhns participated in the salvage and recovery of collection items from the Museo de Arte Popular Americano in Santiago, Chile, damaged in the 1985 earthquake that destroyed the museum building. She also participated in the subsequent development of the museum's emergency plan, which aimed at avoiding a potential repeat of the 1985 devastation.

David Mathieson is supervisor of conservation at the Mystic Seaport Museum. He plays an important role in the regular review and practice of the emergency plan, and he promotes the importance of emergency preparedness through conference presentations, articles, and now this publication.

The emergency plans from each of the institutions represented in this project were used as background information; Figure 1 and the appendixes at the back of this book provide examples of format and content of specific sections of these emergency plans. You will note extensive differences (as evident in the tables of contents in appendix B). You will also see the similarities (for example, the job descriptions of the Seattle Art Museum emergency plan clearly are similar to those of the 1997 Getty Center "Emergency Planning Handbook"—a slightly revised version of the J. Paul Getty Museum's 1988 handbook, which was used as a guide). While it is very useful to benefit from the experience of colleagues who have been through the lengthy and somewhat complex emergency preparedness and response process, all the advisers stress the importance of developing a plan to meet the specific needs of the institution.

Publications that were consulted for additional information include *Steal This Handbook! A Template for Creating a Museum's Emergency Preparedness Plan*, by Allyn Lord, Carolyn Reno, and Marie Demeroukas, published in 1994 by the Southeastern Registrars Association; *Maritime Museum Emergency and Disaster Preparedness and Recovery Manual*, published in 1995 by the Council of American Maritime Museums; and two publications through the International Council of Museums (ICOM) and the International Committee on Museum Security, *A Manual of Basic Security*—by Robert B. Burke and Sam Adeloye, 1986—and *Museum Security Survey*, published in 1981.

Building an Emergency Plan is unique in a number of ways. First, it has a user-friendly format, which includes such tools as "Questions to Consider" and "Suggested Exercises" to help you address your institution's specific needs during the process. Second, the material has been organized into three parts that reflect the three main staff responsibilities in the emergency preparedness and response planning process: the director, the emergency preparedness manager, and the leaders of the departmental teams. Third, the responsibilities for preparedness and response activities have been assigned to different teams. This organizational structure is based on the experience of the advisers.

Acknowledgments

This publication is the culmination of the work of many people. In addition to the individuals already named, other contributors include John DiFrancesca, who assisted Sharon Jones in developing the first draft of chapters 1–3; Canadian Conservation Institute colleagues Deborah Stewart, David Tremain, and Paul Baril; Ann Blaschke and Tom Osborn of Getty Center Security; Peggy Tate Smith of rights and reproductions at the Mystic Seaport Museum; Shelley Bennet and Joe Shuster of the Huntington Library; and GCI colleagues Sheri Saperstein and Lorena Barros, who provided project assistance.

The publication would not exist without then-Director Miguel Angel Corzo's commitment to GCI's advocacy for the protection of cultural property, and without the commitment of Marta de la Torre, director of the Agora program and former director of the training program, who patiently guided this project through its winding evolution from course to publication.

Grateful acknowledgment is also extended to Dinah Berland, who ably managed the editorial production of this publication at the Getty Conservation Institute with the valuable assistance of editorial consultants Dianne Woo, developmental editor; Nomi Kleinmuntz, copy editor; and Scott Patrick Wagner, reference editor and electronic file manager. Thanks are due also to GCI staff members Valerie Greathouse for bibliographic verification, and Fiona Klonarides, who served as permissions editor. Special thanks to Jeffrey Cohen of Trust Publication Services for his very clear and useful design, and to Anita Keys, production coordinator, who shepherded the book into print.

Valerie Dorge

Introduction

*Unfortunately, most people in the world view natural disasters with fatalism.
They think that nothing can be done about them. This attitude is understandable but wrong. We have to try to change it. There is, in fact, a great
deal that can be done to save lives and limit the damage.*

—Olavi Elo
Director secretariat
International Decade for Natural Disaster Reduction

On March 3, 1985, an earthquake measuring 7.8 on the Richter scale struck
Santiago, Chile. At least 146 people were killed, and more than one million
others were injured. The quake destroyed the museum building belonging to
the Museo de Arte Popular Americano in Santiago, along with many of the
artifacts, including a major collection of Chilean folklore ceramics. The collection
had to be moved to another museum so that a new facility could be built.

Earthquakes, fires, floods, hurricanes, and other displays of nature's
wrath present a common and continual threat to cultural institutions all over
the globe, which house a majority of the world's invaluable artifacts, historical
documentation, and works of art, including sculptures, paintings, books, and
ethnographic objects. Threats also can be a result of human activity, such as
vandalism and terrorist bombings. Whereas many of these disasters remain out
of our control, the ability to prepare and respond to them properly and effectively is *within* our control.

Table 1 is a sampling of emergency situations and the cultural property
that was either destroyed or seriously affected. Few institutions are willing to
make public the damage caused by disasters, particularly those caused by electrical fires or other internal problems that might have been the result of neglect.

The importance of emergency preparedness and planning cannot be
emphasized enough, not only to the population at large, but to an institution's
staff, administration, and board of trustees. *Building an Emergency Plan* is
designed to guide the director and staff of any cultural institution through the
long but essential process of creating an emergency plan. In addition to
describing the team approach in the planning process—from the emergency

Table 1   **Some Recent Disasters Affecting Cultural Institutions Around the World**

Earthquake	1997	Basilica of St. Francis	Assisi, Italy
	1995	Kobe City Museum, Museum of Modern Art	Kobe, Japan
	1989	Asian Art Museum	San Francisco, California
		Cooper House, other historic buildings	Santa Cruz, California
	1985	Museo de Arte Popular Americano	Santiago, Chile
Terrorist Bombing	1994	Argentine Israeli Mutual Association, Archives	Buenos Aires, Argentina
	1993	Galleria degli Uffizi	Florence, Italy
Flood	1997	Numerous museums, libraries, archives, historic buildings	Southern Poland
	1995	Museu Nacional	Rio de Janeiro, Brazil
	1995	Santa Barbara Museum of Art	Santa Barbara, California
	1993	Casa de la Cultura	Portoviejo City, Ecuador
	1988	Carillo Gil Museum	Mexico City, Mexico
	1986	Museo Colchagua	Colchagua Province, Chile
Fire	1997	Thomas Wolfe Historic Site	Asheville, North Carolina
	1996	La Compañía de Jesús	Quito, Ecuador
	1993	Yuma Arizona Art Center	Yuma, Arizona
	1992	Windsor Castle	Berkshire, England
	1988	The Cabildo, Louisian State Museum	New Orleans, Louisiana
	1988	Library of the Russian Academy of Sciences	Leningrad, USSR
	1986	Hampton Court Apartments	London, England
	1985	Huntington Library/Gallery	San Marino, California
	1985	York Minster	York, England
	1981	Stanford Library	Stanford, California
Hurricane	1989	City Hall, other historic buildings	Charleston, South Carolina
	1989	More than 200 historic buildings	Charlotte, North Carolina
War	1993	National Museum of Afghanistan	Kabul, Afganistan
	1991–93	Zemaljski Muzej	Sarajevo, Bosnia
		Numerous other historic buildings	Bosnia
	1991–93	Gradski Muzej	Vukovar, Croatia
		Numerous other historic buildings	Croatia
	1990	Kuwait National Museum	Safat, Kuwait
Volcanic Eruption	1995	Montserrat National Trust Museum	Richmond Hill, Montserrat

preparedness manager to the departmental teams—this book provides useful tips to help in assessing your institution's vulnerabilities, developing strategies for evacuating people and collections, and organizing a response and recovery plan that returns operations to normal. Ways to generate and maintain enthusiasm and to change fatalistic attitudes toward emergency preparedness are also addressed.

How to Use This Book

Building an Emergency Plan is designed to guide an institution and its staff through the process of developing a team-based emergency preparedness and response program, which results in the creation of an emergency preparedness and response plan. The book is organized into three parts.

Part I (chapters 1–2) is designed as a resource for the director of the institution. It provides an introduction to the emergency planning process and describes the director's responsibilities, which include setting a policy, establishing a budget, and communicating with the board of trustees.

Part II (chapters 3–5) is intended as a resource for the emergency preparedness manager (EPM). The EPM is designated by the institution's director to oversee the development and implementation of the emergency preparedness and response program and to head the emergency preparedness committee (EPC).

Part III (chapters 6–9) is to be used as a resource for four departmental preparedness teams—safety and security, collections, buildings and maintenance, and administration and records—that work in conjunction with the EPC. A copy of each chapter should be distributed to the appropriate departmental team leaders and representatives of those departments who are on the EPC. Chapter 6 is for the safety and security team, chapter 7 for the collections team, and so forth. Each chapter outlines what team members need to consider in researching issues related to the emergency plan. If your institution does not have all these departments, staff members should divide the duties and responsibilities among themselves.

Located throughout this book are a series of "Suggested Exercises" and a series of "Questions to Consider." These elements provide brainstorming ideas and data-gathering tips to assist you in relating the information to your specific institution.

Emergency preparedness materials from other institutions, including evacuation procedures, supply and equipment lists, and action checklists, are provided in appendixes at the end of the book. The following "Terms to Know" section defines and clarifies the various terms used throughout. Variations of these terms can be found in related literature.

Terms to Know

Communications coordinator: Works closely with the director and the emergency response coordinator during an emergency situation.

Departmental preparedness team: Assists the emergency preparedness manager and the emergency preparedness committee in the emergency preparedness and response process. Each team provides input as appropriate for the function, or department, each represents.

Disaster: An event that results in significant loss, damage, or destruction. An emergency can become a disaster if immediate action is not taken to protect staff, visitors, and the collection.

Emergency: An unanticipated event or series of events that requires immediate action.

Emergency plan handbook: Describes staff response for all potential emergencies, chains of command during an emergency, and recovery procedures. Contains fact sheets, supply lists, and contact lists. The handbook is distributed to all staff.

Emergency preparedness and response plan (a.k.a. the emergency plan or "the plan"): Identifies an institution's vulnerabilities to emergency situations; indicates how to prevent or mitigate potential effects; describes staff response; and provides a blueprint toward recovery. The plan eventually should be condensed into an emergency plan handbook.

Emergency preparedness and response process: A structured, ongoing effort to build an emergency preparedness and response program that includes creation and maintenance of a written plan, as well as an emergency plan handbook.

Emergency preparedness and response program: A systematic, multidepartmental program that guides staff through the emergency preparedness process and leads to the development and maintenance of a comprehensive emergency plan.

Emergency preparedness committee (EPC): Oversees the development and implementation of the emergency preparedness and response program. Led by the emergency preparedness manager, the committee should include senior administrators and representatives—appointed by the director—from each of the institution's key functions.

Emergency preparedness manager (EPM): Leads the emergency preparedness committee through the preparedness and response program. The director may assume this responsibility or assign it to a senior staff member. In either case, alternates should be selected.

Emergency response coordinator (ERC): Coordinates all response and recovery activities during an emergency.

Hazard: A natural or human-caused phenomenon that may occur in or near the institution and may threaten human life and well-being or cause physical damage and economic loss.

Preparedness: Activities that prepare and equip personnel to handle an emergency, such as training staff in evacuation procedures, compiling and maintaining up-to-date contact information, and stockpiling supplies.

Prevention: Activities, such as eliminating hazards, that focus on preventing an emergency from occurring and on reducing harm to people, collections, and property in the event of unavoidable emergencies.

Recovery: Actions taken following an emergency in order to return operations to normal. Depending on the type and extent of the emergency, this can be a long-term process.

Recovery plan: Part of the overall emergency plan, the recovery plan outlines what steps to take to restore normal operations.

Response: Activities that provide temporary care and relief for victims of emergencies and prevent avoidable casualties and property damage.

Response plan: Part of the overall emergency plan, the response plan includes procedures to be taken in response to any emergency.

Risk: The possible injury or loss of life, or damage to property from the identified hazard or hazards.

Staff emergency procedures: Concise, step-by-step descriptions of what should be the staff's first response in the event of an emergency—usually published as a handout.

Threat: An indication of imminent danger.

Vulnerability: The extent to which geographic region, community, services, collections, and structure(s) are likely to be damaged or disrupted by the impact of a hazard.

We found that the process of planning for disasters has some surprising side benefits. The working groups who develop the plan learn a lot about each other's work. You get real solidarity out of the process. There's the important subliminal message for the staff that the museum is making a conscientious effort to care for its visitors, its collection—and them.

— John Walsh
Director
The J. Paul Getty Museum

Part I

For the Director

Overview

The two chapters that follow are designed to serve as a resource for you, the director, in developing and guiding the emergency preparedness and response program for your institution.

Chapter 1 introduces the general requirements of an emergency plan, lists the benefits of an emergency preparedness and response program, and explores four case histories of museums that have developed plans and refined them following either a real emergency or a practice drill. This chapter also discusses the reality of emergencies and the threat they pose not only to your institution, but also to you, your staff, and those who visit your institution. Advice is provided from administrators who have experienced emergencies firsthand and have initiated preparedness and response programs as a result, or who have recognized a need for and developed such a program, perhaps based on the experience of others.

Chapter 2 provides an overview of the director's responsibilities in the program. Also covered are the roles of the emergency preparedness manager (EPM), the emergency preparedness committee (EPC), the emergency response coordinator (ERC), and the departmental planning teams; the tasks that your staff will need to perform to build an effective emergency preparedness and response program; and what can be done without spending an excessive amount of money to reduce immediately the risk faced by your institution. Depending on the size of your institution, you may wish to become more involved in the planning process beyond the tasks outlined in this chapter. In this case, you should also read the chapters in Part II, which are designed for use by the EPM and the EPC.

CHAPTER ONE

An Introduction to Emergency Preparedness and Response Planning

It is Thursday night, and you are alone in your office, working late. Deep in thought, you sit at your desk, surrounded by documents concerning next year's budget. Most of the staff has left for the day. The maintenance crew is working in another wing of the museum. The silence is broken by a muffled popping noise, but you do not think anything of it. Unbeknownst to you, an electrical wire has shorted out inside a wall near the main exhibit hall. As you continue preparing the budget report, sparks lead to flames. One wall is soon engulfed. The collections—and your life—are at risk.

Your institution is equipped with smoke alarms, of course. But have the batteries been checked and replaced recently? How long will it take before smoke from the fire triggers an alarm? If flames block a hallway or stairway near your office, how will you escape? Do you have a mask to wear to protect your lungs from the smoke? Is a flashlight at hand? Where are the emergency telephone numbers? Does the maintenance crew know what to do or whom to call? Do local firefighters know what special techniques to use to protect the collection? Are up-to-date copies of institution records stored off-site? Who is going to handle the news media?

You know what the answers to these questions should be, but are they in fact true for your facility? In recent years, there has been much discussion of emergency preparedness and response. The 1990s have been designated the International Decade for Natural Disaster Reduction (IDNDR) by the United Nations General Assembly. Has all this talk, though, made a difference to you, the director, and your institution? How much planning have you and your staff actually done?

Unfortunately, the answer from most directors is very little. Too much competition for staff time, energy, and resources is a common explanation given. Emergency preparedness often is not at the top of the list of priorities—until it is too late. The threat to an institution can be drastically reduced by launching and maintaining an effective preparedness and response program. Doing so is easier than you think, and more valuable than you realize.

Table 2   **Twenty-four Years of Museum Fires Resulting in Losses of More Than US$1 Million**

August 9, 1993	Museum	Oakland Museum, Oakland, California
	Cause	defective exhibit motor in storage room
	Protection system	smoke detectors, but no sprinklers
	Loss	gallery and some loaned items, estimated at $1 million
June 2, 1993	Museum	Oshkosh Public Museum, Oshkosh, Wisconsin
	Cause	welding ignited interior roof space during renovations
	Protection system	smoke detectors in the museum, but none in the area, no sprinklers
	Loss	10% of the collection and collection records, estimated at $2 million
April 19, 1993	Museum	Yuma Arizona Art Center, Yuma, Arizona
	Cause	electrical (suspected)
	Protection system	smoke detectors, but no sprinklers
	Loss	historic building and 39 objects, with some smoke and water damage, estimated at $1.5 million
November 20, 1992	Museum	Windsor Castle, Berkshire, England
	Cause	blow torch used during renovations (suspected)
	Protection system	no smoke detectors or sprinklers
	Loss	tower, several rooms, tapestries, and minor paintings, estimated at $90 million
May 11, 1988	Museum	The Cabildo, Louisiana State Museum, New Orleans, Louisiana
	Cause	spark from welding equipment during renovations
	Protection system	smoke detectors, but none in the area, no sprinklers
	Loss	furniture collections in the attic, roof, structural damage, estimated at $5 million
February 14, 1988	Museum	Library of the Russian Academy of Sciences, Leningrad, USSR
	Cause	electrical (suspected)
	Protection system	no smoke detectors or sprinklers
	Loss	building, 400,000 volumes, water damage to 3.6 million volumes , no loss value given
March 31, 1986	Museum	Hampton Court Apartments, London, England
	Cause	candle in private apartment
	Protection system	no smoke detectors or sprinklers
	Loss	one life (a resident), upper floors, roof, two paintings, and period furniture, estimated at $6 million
October 17, 1985	Museum	Huntington Gallery, San Marino, California
	Cause	electrical, in the elevator
	Protection system	smoke detectors in the gallery, but none in the elevator or elevator shaft, no sprinklers
	Loss	elevator and elevator shaft, one minor painting, extensive smoke damage, estimated at $1.5 million

Facing the Facts

The reasons for preparedness are self-evident, but resistance to emergency plans in museums—including drills, practice sessions, and staff training—has remained. It's that familiar combination of avoidance and denial. Nevertheless, emergency planning is a matter of common sense and responsibility.

— John Walsh
   Director
   The J. Paul Getty Museum

An emergency may come in the form of a natural disaster, such as an earthquake, a hurricane, a forest fire, a volcanic eruption, or a flood. It is more

Table 2, *continued*

April 29, 1985	Museum	Los Angeles Public Library, Los Angeles, California
	Cause	arson (an employee)
	Protection system	smoke detectors, but no sprinklers in the open stacks
	Loss	building interior, roof, and 70% of the collection, estimated at $24 million
December 31, 1984	Museum	Byer Museum of Art, Evanston, Illinois
	Cause	electrical (suspected)
	Protection system	smoke detectors, but no sprinklers
	Loss	upper two floors and roof, with extensive water damage, estimated at $3 million
January 23, 1982	Museum	Franklin D. Roosevelt National Historic Site, Hyde Park, New York
	Cause	faulty electrical wiring
	Protection system	smoke detection system, but not in the attic
	Loss	attic, 30% of the furnishings in three rooms, major smoke and water damage to the central portion of the house, estimated at over $2 million
July 8, 1978	Museum	Museum of Modern Art, Rio de Janeiro, Brazil
	Cause	smoking or defective wiring (suspected)
	Protection system	no smoke dectectors or sprinklers
	Loss	most of the interior, the roof, and 90% of the collection, estimated at $50 million
February 22, 1978	Museum	San Diego Aerospace Museum, San Diego, California
	Cause	arson
	Protection system	no smoke detectors or sprinklers
	Loss	building and entire collection, including 40 planes and library, estimated at $16 million
September 30, 1970	Museum	National Museum of American History (Smithsonian Institution), Washington, D.C.
	Cause	electrical short in an exhibit
	Protection system	smoke detectors, but no sprinklers
	Loss	two galleries with their exhibits, some water damage, estimated at $1 million
August 9, 1970	Museum	The Henry Ford Museum, Dearborn, Michigan
	Cause	electrical
	Protection system	smoke detectors, but no sprinklers in the area
	Loss	several historic displays of shops and equipment, estimated at $2 million

All monetary values shown are in U.S. dollars.

likely, however, that the threat will be localized and caused by human activity. Fire is the most common cause of damage to cultural property. Table 2 shows a sampling of institutions that have suffered fire-related losses of more than US$1 million between 1970 and 1993.[1]

Each day, television news broadcasts show graphic images of floods, fires, civil disturbances, and other emergencies around the world. In the last thirty years, economic losses from natural disasters have tripled, rising to more than US$120 billion during the 1980s. That figure does not include the losses from human-caused disasters, such as civil unrest, military coups or invasions, arson fires, and burst dams.

Awareness of these and other threats to our cultural heritage is growing rapidly. In addition to the declaration of IDNDR by the United Nations, many countries have ratified the 1972 United Nations Convention for the Protection of the World Cultural and Natural Heritage. Furthermore, many nations have signed the 1954 United Nations Convention for the Protection of Cultural Property in the Event of Armed Conflict.

The expanding global and regional interest in emergency preparedness and response can work to your advantage. You can capitalize on this concern as you solicit support for your emergency preparedness and response efforts.

"If a disaster happens, it happens," you may say to yourself. "There's little I can do to prevent it." That is a common belief. True, you cannot *prevent* a natural disaster, but you can drastically *reduce* its effect on human life and property. You also can take on a major role in safety and prevention efforts to eliminate the more common threats of fire caused by poor wiring or old plumbing and damage caused through lack of supervision during renovation work.

Or you may say, "I don't have the time to make emergency preparedness and response a priority." Consider the implications of that attitude. What would you say to the community after a fire ravages the collection? Would you speak of the wiring that needed to be replaced, or the roof that you knew was not fire-resistant?

You may be thinking, "We cannot afford emergency preparedness. We are a small museum, and I am pushing my staff and budget as hard as I can." In reality, considering the value of the collection and/or your building, what you *cannot* afford is to ignore the need for an emergency preparedness and response program. Staff members will understand that they have a personal stake in this effort, and they will appreciate your concern about their safety and that of visitors and the collection.

In 1985, at the Huntington Library Art Collections and Botanical Gardens in San Marino, California (in the Los Angeles area), fire broke out at night in the electrical wiring of a gallery elevator. The 1777 *Portrait of Mrs. Edwin Lascelles* by Sir Joshua Reynolds, which hung on a gallery wall on the ground floor opposite the elevator, was destroyed when the heat caused the elevator doors to burst open. At the time, the institution did not have an emergency plan. Today it does, and it has been put to the test more often than Shelley Bennett, curator of British and Continental art at the Huntington, cares to recall. "We have had every disaster you can think of," she says, referring to earthquakes, flooding, and other emergencies that have plagued Los Angeles in recent years. "The only thing I do not have to talk about are locusts!"[2]

By outlining what employees should do, what their priorities for action should be, and where to turn for help, the Huntington Library's emergency preparedness and response plan has made a tremendous difference in the institution's ability to cope with a crisis. "In the immediate response to a disaster, you are often frozen," adds Bennett.[3] A well-thought-out emergency plan quickly remedies that.

As the director, you may be confident that you will not "freeze" in a crisis. Bear in mind, however, that in all likelihood you will not be there when an emergency strikes your institution. Nevertheless, having an emergency preparedness and response plan in place will enable those who are present to act responsibly.

Suggested Exercise

At your next management meeting, take a moment to discuss a scenario in which a fire breaks out in your most highly valued gallery. Indicate where the fire begins and at what time. Brainstorm who might be present and how long it might take before the fire is discovered. What kind of damage would be caused by flames or by smoke? What emergency procedures should be followed? Is your facility both equipped and prepared to follow such procedures? Identify your institution's strengths and weaknesses.

The Emergency Preparedness and Response Planning Process

> *One of the secret ingredients that will contribute toward your being able to sustain the energy and attention needed to devise one of these plans— and it is not glamorous work—is the understanding that, yes, the final report is significant, but the process is equally important. The remarkable things that one learns about the institution's strengths, to some extent, but about its weaknesses, more so, are as valuable as the final plan.*[4]

— Robert Bergman
  Director
  Walters Art Gallery, Baltimore, Maryland

In setting up an emergency preparedness and response program, the goal is to make the process of planning, assessment, and review of the emergency plan part of a regular routine. Launch the program by announcing an institutionwide emergency preparedness policy and appointing an emergency preparedness manager (EPM). This notifies the staff, from the beginning, of the importance of emergency preparedness and response. From there, the program produces a written emergency plan that is tested regularly and adjusted as needed.

A successful program requires commitment, patience, teamwork, and an annual budget. The most time-consuming and costly requirement is staff participation. The benefits of staff involvement, however, are numerous and extend far beyond the main goal of saving lives and collections in the event of a crisis. "Staff bonding is one of the great benefits," remarks Gail Joice, senior deputy director and registrar of the Seattle Art Museum, Seattle, Washington. "We joke about it because of our preparation work; if an earthquake is going to hit, we'd like it to be while we are at the museum. There is a sense of well-being in that."

"We've learned the power of acting as a group," Alissandra Cummins, director of the Barbados Museum and Historical Society, says. "We've learned the importance of continual dialogue and working together on general issues such as preparedness."

Other benefits that have been identified through the emergency preparedness and response process are

- greater potential for protecting human lives and property;
- greater safety awareness and preservation of assets;
- education and heightened staff awareness on professional and personal levels, leading to employee empowerment and higher staff morale;
- heightened security;
- higher ratings for risk management/insurance, which can lower premium costs;
- increased community recognition and outreach, including increased volunteer participation;

- greater community support, such as fund-raising, for capital improvements;
- collaboration and stronger relationships with peers at other institutions;
- two-way exchange of information with the media, resulting in more accurate reporting; and
- fulfillment of fiduciary responsibilities for board members, director, and staff.

Table 3 shows a breakdown of the responsibilities involved in the emergency preparedness and response program.

Table 3   **Individual Duties and Responsibilities in the Emergency Preparedness and Response Program**

Director	• Sets emergency program policy • Appoints EPM, EPC, ERC • Appoints communications coordinator, if necessary • With EPC, does initial vulnerability assessment • Presents assessment to board to secure board's commitment • Establishes budget for program • Continues to act as liaison between EPM and board • Oversees development of list of resources (agencies, organizations, local police/fire departments, other cultural institutions) • Oversees and guides involvement of community and media in the planning process
Emergency preparedness manager (EPM)	• Works with director to appoint EPC, ERC, and communications coordinator • Heads EPC • Works with EPC to appoint departmental teams and team leaders • Organizes and conducts staff drills • Keeps director up to date on progress • After disaster occurs, holds postmortem review meetings
Emergency preparedness committee (EPC)	• Oversees departmental teams and team leaders • Works with EPM, ERC, and team leaders to select response teams • Develops list of resources (agencies, oragnizations, local police/fire departments, other cultural institutions); establishes relations with such resources • Involves and establishes contacts with community and media • Uses initial vulnerability assessment to identify potential hazards • Distributes hazard data to departmental teams for development of detailed vulnerability and asset assessment report • Keeps EPM up to date on teams' progress • Implements preventive/preparedness measures as recommended by departmental teams • Develops response plan and recovery plan based on information from departmental teams • Writes and distributes the emergency plan
Emergency response coordinator (ERC)	• Works with EPM, EPC, and team leaders to select response teams • Implements preventive/preparedness measures as recommended by departmental teams • During a disaster, sets up and runs emergency command center
Departmental preparedness teams	• Four teams: safety/security, collections, buildings/maintenance, administration/records • Each consists of 2 teams: preparedness team and response team • Each preparedness team submits 2 reports to EPC: (1) vulnerability/asset assessment and (2) outline of response procedures • Response teams contribute to the departmental preventive-preparedness measures, response plan, and recovery plan • All information and data are submitted to EPC for inclusion in the emergency plan

Devising the Emergency Plan

Once the process of planning for an emergency has begun, it builds its own momentum. You will probably finish a considerable distance from where you thought you might end up, but you will be there to tell a fine story and to be justifiably proud that life, safety, and the cultural property with which you spend your daily life is right there with you.

— Barbara Roberts
Conservator and hazard mitigation consultant

From the emergency preparedness and response program, the emergency plan is formed and kept up to date. The plan's chain of command, contact information, and response and recovery procedures are then published in an emergency plan handbook, which is made available to all employees.

The emergency plan should cover four protection measures:

1. **Prevention.** Eliminate hazards or reduce their potential effects on staff and visitors, on the collection, and on other assets. For example, clearing away debris from around the outside of the building helps eliminate the potential for a fire that could endanger lives and damage property.
2. **Preparedness.** Prepare and equip personnel to handle an emergency. For example, create emergency telephone lists, stockpile supplies, and train staff and volunteers how to use them.
3. **Response.** Prevent injury and limit losses after the event. For example, train staff and volunteers to evacuate visitors, colleagues, collections, and records safely.
4. **Recovery.** Prepare and train staff to carry out the process that returns operations to normal. For example, following a disaster, staff and volunteers may spend months sorting through the gift store inventory and discarding damaged items, or sorting through the collection and carrying out basic washing or surface-cleaning tasks.

The emergency plan should also include a description of when to activate response procedures and to what degree they should be carried out. Steps on how to communicate to staff that the institution is operating in "emergency mode" and when to declare that an emergency is over should also be addressed. The plan should explain duties and procedures in the following areas:

Organization
- The roles of the response team or teams in an emergency
- How to set up a central base of operations following an evacuation
- How to set up a communications and public relations post

People
- When to evacuate staff and visitors, and who should make the decision
- How to establish an emergency shelter
- How to provide medical assistance if necessary
- How to contact staff and volunteers and their families via an emergency telephone and address list that includes trustee officers and volunteers
- How to contact external experts for support or assistance

Collections, buildings, and other assets
- When to relocate or evacuate the collection, and who should make the decision
- How to contact the insurance agent(s)
- How to perform damage assessments
- How to protect the building and grounds
- What supplies are needed and where they are stored

To be effective, the emergency plan needs to be

- actively supported by the director, governing body, and all levels of staff;
- simple, focusing mainly on situations that are most likely to occur;
- flexible enough to accommodate unanticipated situations;
- realistic in its assessment of museum resources; and
- tested regularly, and at least annually, with an emergency drill and debriefing.

In devising the emergency plan, staff must work together to gather information regarding the institution, the collection, and the potential threats, as well as to implement preventive measures and develop emergency response procedures. For example, one of the first steps is to do a vulnerability analysis. Employees may be motivated to suggest equipment or construction projects that require substantial funding resources: for example, new electrical wiring; a fire sprinkler system; or a stronger, more hurricane-resistant roof. These suggestions probably will not come as a surprise to you and, in many cases, may involve maintenance problems that have not been addressed due to lack of funds. A dilapidated plumbing system, an antiquated furnace, or a leaky roof naturally put a collection at risk.

A comprehensive emergency preparedness and response program requires a substantial commitment of staff time and financial resources. Once the vulnerability analysis is done, the data gathered can support a public emergency preparedness development campaign. Bring these financial priorities to the attention of board members, the institution's supporters, and the local community. Encourage the local media to work with you to improve awareness of your facility. Some institutions have successfully used the media to alert the community to their needs and to solicit donations for their emergency preparedness and response program.

The questions in Table 4 at the beginning of chapter 2 (page 28) will serve as a quick assessment of your institution's need for an emergency plan. Many steps can be taken immediately to remedy certain problems, even if the institution is on a restricted budget. In general, these steps include

- identifying potential natural and human-caused disasters specific to the area and assessing the vulnerability of the museum to these threats;
- identifying assets (including staff resources, collections, and buildings) and prioritizing them in order of importance;
- developing and implementing measures designed to mitigate the effects of potential disasters, such as training staff in the use of fire extinguishers and installing smoke detectors and fire suppression systems;
- determining steps to be taken in response to an emergency, including evacuation of staff and the public, and evacuation or relocation procedures for the collection; and
- creating plans for recovering from disasters, communicating with the public, and resuming normal operations.

If employees are involved in the planning and reviewing process and have been trained in their individual roles and general procedures, they and the institution as a whole will be able to

- anticipate, mitigate, and work to avoid the effects of disasters, particularly those that are the result of a human-caused emergency situation;
- be prepared so as to avoid panic when an emergency or a disaster occurs;
- respond and recover as quickly as possible, with minimal ill effects on life, resources, and services; and
- maintain staff morale during an extremely stressful time period.

Taking a Cue from Other Institutions

In preparing your facility's emergency plan, it is helpful to examine the plans established by other institutions. The following case histories present the stories of four museums that currently have emergency preparedness and response programs: the Barbados Museum and Historical Society, the Museo de Arte Popular Americano, the Mystic Seaport Museum, and the Seattle Art Museum. For some of these museums, it took an emergency, or several, before their administrators decided to develop a plan. They explain here how they did it— and why.

Case 1   Barbados Museum and Historical Society

The Barbados Museum and Historical Society, St. Ann's Garrison, St. Michael, Barbados. Courtesy of the Barbados Museum and Historical Society.

Location: St. Michael, Barbados, British West Indies

Director: Alissandra Cummins

Area: 20,000 square feet (1,860 square meters), including 10,000 square feet (930 square meters) in galleries

Employees: 26

Collection: Archaeology, natural history, militaria, fine art, decorative art, social and industrial history, toys and dolls, textiles, ethnographic artifacts, photographs, and other ephemera

Impetus for emergency plan: Devastation of the Caribbean islands in 1988 by Hurricane Gilbert

---

Information for this case was provided by Alissandra Cummins, director of the Barbados Museum and Historical Society and an adviser in the development of this book.

Sources consulted: U.S. National Trust for Historic Preservation, the Caribbean Conservation Association, and the Island Resources Foundation workshop, 1991; and the emergency preparedness initiatives of the Museums Association of the Caribbean, launched in 1954[5]

Potential natural hazards faced: Hurricanes, floods, fires

Emergency plan highlights: Staff telephone numbers; site maps of the museum showing exits, galleries, and so forth; location of fire alarms and smoke detectors; step-by-step instructions for equipment and procedures, including shutting off utilities; evacuation procedures for staff, visitors, and collections; guidelines for handling objects; and a list of who has copies of the plan. The plan lists addresses, telephone numbers, and contacts for companies and institutions that have agreed to provide emergency equipment if needed. The response effort is led by six core teams of four members each that are assigned to specific areas, such as galleries or administration. The plan includes instructions for each team. The plan is revised after each annual drill and subsequent evaluation. The current plan is the seventh draft.

Annual budget for emergency planning and implementation: US$2,500–$5,000

Lessons learned in the process of developing an emergency plan:

- The response plan must be launched at least forty-eight hours before a hurricane hits.
- At least two physically strong people must make up part of each team.

- In the event of a national disaster, do not assume there will be immediate access to mainland resources.
- Institutions must lobby for priority status in community response plans. Collaboration with other cultural institutions helps build lobbying power.
- The police or fire department cannot always be relied on during the response phase of a national disaster.
- The media are interested in emergency preparedness efforts. Share information with them to encourage prompt, accurate coverage in the event of an emergency.
- Permanent internal protective shutters should be installed before a disaster strikes, such as in storage locations and on library cases. This eliminates time needed to install temporary shutters during emergencies.
- Archival, fine art, and other vulnerable objects should be stored in impermeable cartons to reduce packing time in an emergency. Keep extra cartons on hand in the administrative offices for packing files in the event of an emergency.
- Local companies will donate needed emergency supplies if asked.
- Share your plan with officials of local or national civil emergency response organizations, such as the fire department and civil defense.
- Check and change batteries regularly in smoke alarms, radios, flashlights, and cameras (which also should be loaded with film).
- Ask local insurance companies to supply risk management material.

Building the team: National emergency response planners in Barbados had published a booklet outlining what residents should do to protect themselves and their families in the event of a hurricane, but two-thirds of the Barbados Museum staff had never seen this booklet. Those responsible for the museum's emergency response plan reminded staff of the available resources, posted lists of shelters, and created a buddy system in which employees with cars were assigned to pick up those without cars.

How the plan stood up to the test: Museum emergency preparedness planners initially believed they would need to activate response efforts twenty-four hours before a hurricane was expected to hit. After testing the plan, however, they realized that staff would be more concerned about the safety of their own families at that time than with protecting the museum. Consequently, the planners decided that efforts would begin more than forty-eight hours beforehand. "That was a major decision," says Alissandra Cummins. "It required recognizing the psychological effects that such a plan would have upon the staff."

Words of advice: According to Cummins, the hardest part of the emergency preparedness and response process comes at the beginning: convincing yourself as director that engaging in the process is the right thing to do. "Once you start, it is not so scary in its immensity or complexity," she explains.

Case 2   Museo de Arte Popular Americano, Facultad de Arte, Universidad de Chile

Front view of the newly constructed building of the Museo de Arte Popular Americano, Facultad de Arte, Universidad de Chile, Santiago, Chile. Courtesy of the Museo de Arte Popular Americano.

Information for this case was provided by conservator Johanna Maria Theile Bruhns, coordinator of the restoration program of the Facultad de Arte, Universidad de Chile, Santiago. She was also an adviser in the development of this book.

Location: Santiago, Chile

Director: Silvia Rios

Area: 7,449 square feet (692 square meters)

Employees: 12, plus students from the Facultad de Arte restoration program

Collection: Textiles, wood, sculpture, prints, ceramic, ethnographic and folklore artifacts

Impetus for emergency plan: A devastating earthquake measuring 7.8 on the Richter scale that hit Santiago in March 1985. The earthquake killed at least 146 people, injured more than one million others, and destroyed the museum building and much of the collection. The undamaged and salvaged items in the collection were moved to another museum until a new building opened in 1997.

Sources consulted: *Emergency Measures and Damage Assessment After an Earthquake* by Pierre Pichard.[6] Also, S. A. S. Enrique Strahenberg, then-director of the Schloss Eferding in Eferding, Austria, who happened to be in Chile during the March 1985 earthquake, shared his institution's emergency preparedness materials.

Potential hazards faced: Earthquakes, fires, floods, political demonstrations

Emergency plan highlights: The plan is divided into two major areas: people and collections. It describes the evacuation procedures, designates employee tasks, and describes where emergency supplies are stored. It contains maps of the museum and phone numbers of all employees and of police and fire officials. Security guards are expected to guide people out of exhibit areas and the library, whereas specific staff members have been assigned that task for nonpublic office areas.

Annual budget for emergency planning and implementation: US$1,000 for first year of implementation

Lessons learned in the process of developing an emergency plan:

- Regular meetings with fire officials can be useful.
- Regular drills allow gradual refinement of the emergency plan.
- Employees should carry identification cards to avoid being mistaken for demonstrators during political protests or for spectators during emergencies.
- Emergency preparedness and response materials developed by other museums should be consulted for ideas.
- Multiple copies of damage assessment forms must be available in case electricity goes out during an emergency, rendering photocopiers inoperable.
- A systematic evacuation procedure allows employees to pack priority objects, documents, and so on, quickly and to locate them afterward.
- Security officers must have access to a list of high-priority objects in case an emergency occurs when no institution administrators are available.
- Plastic sheets and stones, for use as weights, should be stored in offices in case the roof leaks or is damaged.
- The institution should have an alarm system so staff can alert police during a robbery.

Building the team: Memories of the 1985 earthquake proved to be an effective inspiration and motivation for the museum to launch its emergency preparedness and response program. With the passage of time, the daily challenge of running the museum has taken precedence, causing some team members to lose their enthusiasm and drive in maintaining the program. Consequently, emergency planning leaders have had to find ways to restimulate that interest and concern. "After the earthquake, it was very easy to convince the museum staff to participate in emergency planning," says conservator Johanna Maria Theile Bruhns. "The difficulty now is continuing emergency planning day by day. When you don't have problems, it seems everybody starts to relax a little too much. It is difficult to make them realize that you have to think about emergencies even when nothing is happening."

How the plan stood up to the test: "We learned from the earthquake in 1985 that it is important to have a good and easy-to-follow emergency plan ahead of time, one that everyone understands," explains Theile Bruhns. "By the time a disaster happens, it is too late to come up with a plan, not only because the building can collapse but also because you lose the ability to think clearly." The museum conducts regular emergency drills, which has helped familiarize staff with the process. "At first, the staff didn't feel secure about what they needed to do and whether they were doing it well, but now that we are having drills regularly, we don't have any problems at all," Theile Bruhns adds.

Words of advice: As Theile Bruhns points out, "In working with other museums, we realize that collaboration is important, as we are small, with very little money. Together, we wield more power and can obtain assistance more easily."

Case 3   Mystic Seaport Museum

View of some of Mystic Seaport Museum's buildings and one of the ships in its collection, showing the museum's location on the waterfront in Mystic, Connecticut, which makes it susceptible to seaborne hazards. Courtesy of the Mystic Seaport Museum. Photo: Judy Beisler.

Location: Mystic, Connecticut

President and director: J. Revell Carr

Area: 40 acres (16.2 hectares)

Employees: 445 regular full- and part-time, 200 seasonal

Collection: More than two million objects, including art, tools, books, photographs, film and video footage, sound recordings, ship plans, maps and charts, plus the world's largest collection (480-plus) of historic ships and small craft, as well as historic buildings

---

Information for this case was provided by David Mathieson, supervisor of conservation at the Mystic Seaport Museum in Mystic, Connecticut, and an adviser in the development of this book.

Impetus for emergency plan: In 1938, eight years after its founding, the Marine Historical Society—now called the Mystic Seaport Museum—was hit by a hurricane. The library collection suffered US$1,000 in losses. The threats from Hurricanes Carol and Edna in 1954 prompted museum administrators to take preventive action. Plans already developed were put into written form. In the process, it was discovered that a hurricane or tropical storm threatened the region about every five years. Between 1890 and 1991, thirteen hurricanes and ten storms had struck the region. Late fall and winter storms are another potential threat.

Sources consulted: None, since few cultural institutions were engaged in emergency planning at the time

Potential natural hazards faced: Floods, fires, and storms, ranging from summer hurricanes to severe blizzards

Emergency plan highlights: The museum's plan consists of 100-plus pages on preparedness and approximately 75 pages on recovery procedures. It outlines categories of hurricane strength and defines hurricane, severe weather, and tornado warnings. It describes the five-stage alert process (condition alert: possible development of severe weather; condition watch: storm due within forty-eight hours; condition 1: thirty-six hours to a storm; condition 2: twelve to eighteen hours to a storm; and condition 3: storm is imminent) and outlines duties of the fifteen department and response teams during those stages. AM and FM radio and television stations are listed, as are Internet addresses that provide weather information; staff who have received first-aid training; elevations of all buildings above mean low water (MLW); and town, state, and federal authorities.

Comprehensive plans and procedures have been developed for the museum's various departments, and responsibilities have been divided among teams. For example, in the curatorial, exhibition, and interpretive departments, Team A handles formal exhibits, the registrar's office, and all storage areas; Team B is responsible for village exhibits; Team C is in charge of communication among the departments; and Team D is responsible for the interpretive and program areas. The shipyard department handles all ships, small craft, and related areas of concern.

Annual budget for emergency planning and implementation: It is difficult to separate the costs of emergency planning from the US$23-million annual budget. After more than forty years of honing the emergency plan, restocking of emergency supplies and materials, housekeeping, and maintenance are considered the responsibility of individual departments.

Lessons learned in the process of developing an emergency plan:

- Expect emergencies to happen at the most inopportune time.
- Recruit graduate students to analyze and evaluate your emergency plan for academic credit.
- Document all preparedness and response steps with a simple-to-use automatic camera.
- Make emergency planning part of administrators' and employees' job descriptions.
- Do not adopt another institution's emergency plan without doing an analysis of the needs specific to your institution.
- Develop an emergency plan for temporary exhibits as well as for the permanent collection.
- Before an emergency happens, research what should be done to recover various artifacts and put the steps into writing.
- Prepare advance press releases describing your emergency plan.
- Check with your local civil defense officer, or the authority who would be in charge of local recovery, to see how your plan for recovery fits into their plans. The civil authorities are most concerned with safety of lives and property. The materials you have stored for your recovery may be required for use for the public good.
- Encourage input from employees who have lived in hurricane- or tsunami-prone areas and who most likely understand the need to prepare for such disasters.

Building the team: Often the biggest challenge to the team is people's difficulty in relinquishing authority. This is especially true for conservators. At Mystic Seaport Museum, many employees are directly responsible for important components of the collection. Preservation shipyard workers may have labored for years restoring the vessels, yet under extreme emergency conditions, as part of the response procedure, they may be instructed to swamp or scuttle some of the vessels in order to protect them.

How the plan stood up to the test: In 1976, following Hurricane Belle, museum officials realized that they needed to do a much better job detailing what should be done during the recovery phase of any crisis. The museum arranged for two graduate students from the University of Delaware Art Conservation Department to review the emergency research suggestions for the recovery manual. In the process, administrators learned that some of the basic underlying assumptions made in their previous emergency plan had been incorrect. The National Hurricane Center predicted that a category 4 hurricane could hit the New England area within the next five years. The U.S. Army Corps of Engineers and the Federal Emergency Management Agency (FEMA) also predicted that a category 4 hurricane could produce a flood level in the Mystic River estuary of 18.7 feet (5.7 meters). Previously, it had been assumed that a flood would submerge only the first floor of the buildings on the museum property. An 18.7-foot rise in the river would put most two-story buildings entirely underwater. The museum's response plan for floods called for relocating items from the first to second floors in many buildings, which obviously would not have safeguarded them during a major flood. Since then, the plan has been through, and is still going through, many changes.

Words of advice: As flood waters subside and the devastation of a severe disaster confronts staff and the volunteer corps, will the institution's collection be at the forefront of their thoughts? Doubtful. "Their concerns will run in order of family, then maybe their own property, and then possibly the institution's collection," says David Mathieson, supervisor of conservation. "Disasters happen to communities. It is the people within this community whom we work with. If we do not take into consideration the needs of the people around us while creating our plan, our plan will fail."

Case 4   Seattle Art Museum

The Seattle Art Museum, Seattle, Washington, showing Jonathan Borofsky's sculpture, *The Hammering Man*. Courtesy of the Seattle Art Museum. Photo: Susan Dirk.

Information for this case was provided by Gail Joice, senior deputy director and registrar of the Seattle Art Museum and an adviser in the development of this book.

Location: Seattle, Washington

Director: Mimi Gardner Gates

Area: 144,000 square feet (13,392 square meters) downtown; 33,800 square feet (3,143.4 square meters) in Volunteer Park

Employees: 120 full-time

Collection: Approximately 22,000 objects, including paintings, sculpture, decorative arts, ethnographic material, prints, photographs, and textiles

Impetus for emergency plan: Loma Prieta earthquake in San Francisco Bay Area, California, October 1989

Sources consulted: Barbara Roberts, hazard mitigation consultant; Jerry Podany, head of antiquities conservation at the J. Paul Getty Museum; and the J. Paul Getty Museum "Emergency Planning Handbook" [7]

Potential natural hazards faced: Earthquakes, volcanic eruptions, windstorms, blizzards

Emergency plan highlights: The ninety-eight-page plan follows the J. Paul Getty Museum model. In addition, it contains sections on emergency procedures for the library and how to deal with volcanic ash. (The Seattle Art Museum's job description for an emergency plan coordinator is shown in Fig. 1, page 34.)

Annual budget for emergency planning and implementation: US$5,300, including first-aid and CPR classes

Lessons learned in the process of developing an emergency plan:

- Use another cultural institution's plan as a model, but do not automatically adopt it without evaluating it according to your institution's needs.
- Appoint several "true believers"—staff members who feel strongly about having an emergency plan—to the planning committee.
- Involve the board of trustees.
- Make sure someone else on staff (other than the director) has access to cash and credit in case of emergency.
- Resource lists also can be used in nonemergencies and should be made available.
- Help employees overcome their fears of a disaster by holding practice response drills so they know how to respond in a real emergency situation.
- Help employees prepare their own homes for an emergency.

Building the team: The museum's emergency planners provided staff with hard hats and on-site earthquake kits and arranged for discounts on first-aid kits. One emergency drill focused on the safety of employees' families. The museum sent two of its emergency planning leaders to San Francisco to visit museums following the devastating 1989 earthquake. The leaders returned home "with the fear of God in them" and the realization that they had to design their plan to be effective, reports Gail Joice, senior deputy director and registrar for the museum.

How the plan stood up to the test: Drills revealed that the museum's public announcement system was not sufficiently audible in all rooms. The emergency plan outlines a "buddy system" in which each employee is responsible for making sure others in his or her working area are safe. In their twice-annual drills, the organizers often test the buddy system by "hiding" a staff member. For one drill, the museum photographer was instructed to stay in his studio during the evacuation. No one checked the studio to make sure it was empty. "Colleagues were feeling sheepish that they hadn't checked for who had been left behind," Joice says. "In the rush to get out, you must stop and think. This drill experience gives us the confidence that this will not happen again."

A real emergency revealed a financial oversight in the plan. In November 1994, the downtown Seattle area experienced a major power outage, which could have placed museum artifacts in need of temperature control at risk. Diesel was low in the emergency generator, and the museum was in danger of running out of fuel. Staff had to arrange emergency delivery of fuel early on a Saturday morning, then realized they did not have cash or access to a company credit card to pay for it. Joice used her personal American Express card. "We've since made arrangements with the diesel company, and they'll accept our charges on company credit," she says. "Now, as senior deputy director, I have a company credit card." The museum also has the emergency generator refueled immediately following routine testing.

Words of advice: Use other museum emergency plans as a starting point. "It is too overwhelming to think about how to do it from scratch," comments Joice.

Notes

1. Adapted from David Liston, Securma Web site report (1997), by permission of site owner Ton Cremers (Web site address: >http://museum-security.org/listtext2.html<).

2. Shelley Bennett, from a telephone conversation with Sharon Jones, 1997.

3. Ibid.

4. Robert Bergman, "Developing a Disaster Plan: The Director's Perspective," in *Emergency Preparedness and Response: Materials Developed from the NIC Seminar, October 17, 1990, Washington, D.C.* (Washington D.C.: National Institute for the Conservation of Cultural Property, 1991), 17. Reprinted with the permission of Heritage Preservation (formerly National Institute for the Conservation of Cultural Property).

5. Since the 1991 workshop, members of the Museums Association of the Caribbean (MAC), including the Barbados Museum and Historical Society, have organized a number of area emergency preparedness and response workshops, and in 1996 signed an agreement with the Caribbean Disaster Emergency Relief Agency (CDERA), whereby MAC coordinates CDERA's activities for regional cultural organizations from its Barbados headquarters.

6. Pierre Pichard, *Emergency Measures and Damage Assessment After an Earthquake* (Paris: Unesco, 1984).

7. J. Paul Getty Museum, "Emergency Planning Handbook" (J. Paul Getty Museum, Malibu, Calif., 1988, photocopy).

Chapter Summary

This chapter

- **reminded you of the potential threats of natural and human-caused disasters;**

- **introduced the emergency preparedness and response process;**

- **outlined the general requirements of the emergency plan; and**

- **presented four case examples of museums that have gone through the planning and testing process.**

In review, an emergency preparedness and response program

- **requires commitment from the director and an investment in staff time and costs;**

- **has benefits that far outweigh the costs; and**

- **will save money in the long run.**

CHAPTER TWO

The Role of the Director

As the director of your institution, you are the guiding force behind the emergency preparedness and response process. Certain duties may be delegated to qualified staff members, but you are ultimately responsible for the development and implementation of the emergency preparedness program and the creation of the emergency plan. You must generate enthusiasm for the program among staff and your institution's board of trustees, motivate staff and maintain their interest in and focus on the effort, provide support to individual departments where needed, collaborate with your counterparts at other institutions and with experts in emergency planning, and guide community outreach efforts.

But where do you start? You can gauge the current level of your institution's emergency preparedness by taking a simple test. The questions shown in Table 4 on the following page address key issues in developing an emergency planning program. The questions are not in any particular order. Administer the test to a few staff members, as well. If you or a member of your staff cannot answer even three of the questions in the affirmative, your institution is not as prepared for an emergency as it should be.

Table 4   **Is Your Institution Adequately Prepared for an Emergency?**

	YES	NO	UNSURE
Are up-to-date emergency telephone numbers and/or addresses posted in central locations?			
Is staff prepared to handle an emergency, including sounding an alarm and using fire extinguishers?			
Is there an emergency supply inventory, and is it up to date?			
Has the backup power supply been tested recently, and does it have adequate fuel? Are flashlights and batteries readily available?			
Have alarm and fire suppression systems been tested recently?			
Are emergency exits accessible? Do all locks have keys nearby?			
Are fire extinguishers fully charged and accessible?			
Is a nonsmoking policy enforced?			
Is electrical wiring in good condition?			
Does a general institutionwide cleanup take place on a semiannual basis, with the entire staff participating?			
Are floors clear of wood shavings, paper, cloth, packing, and other flammable materials?			
Are walkways clear of debris?			
Are drains and gutters clear?			
Are heating and electrical system motors free of dust and clutter?			
Are special precautions put in place during construction, renovation, and repair activities?			
Are up-to-date copies of important documents and records stored off-site?			
Is the insurance provider aware of the emergency plan and of the institution's probable maximum loss?			
Are important collections stored away from windows and pipes?			
Have elevators and automatic door closures been tested regularly in fire-response drills? Are doors clear of obstructions?			
Are pipes and plumbing regularly checked for leaks?			
Has the fire department visited the site lately (i.e., within the last six months)?			
Are your building and grounds up to local safety codes?			
Are you prepared to handle a medical emergency?			
Has staff been given any advice or training in home safety?			
Are overhanging trees cut away from the building?			
Do local police, fire, and security services have copies of your institution's site plan, indicating location of utility mains and various kinds of extinguishers?			
Have arrangements been made for use of off-site storage, deep-freeze facilities, dehumidifiers, and so on, if necessary during an emergency?			

Creating an Emergency Plan

We found that the process of planning for disasters has some surprising side benefits. The working groups who develop the plan learn a lot about each other's work. You get real solidarity out of the process. There's the important subliminal message for the staff that the museum is making a conscientious effort to care for its visitors, its collections—and them.

— John Walsh
Director
The J. Paul Getty Museum

Each institution is unique not only by the nature of its collections but also by its facility, its geographical location, its community resources, and its employees and volunteers. In developing your institution's emergency plan, a great deal of time can be saved by examining plans other institutions have implemented (see chapter 1, particularly the case histories). Keep in mind, however, that although such input is valuable, your plan must address your institution's own needs.

An effective emergency preparedness and response program requires the completion of a number of information-gathering and decision-making tasks to be carried out by staff participants. Table 5 on the following page summarizes the major tasks and indicates which staff member or members are involved. The first six tasks are covered in this chapter; cross-references to tasks covered in other chapters are also indicated. Some of the tasks may be shared by more than one person.

Depending on the size of your institution, you may delegate to others most of the planning and implementing duties of the emergency plan. Do not, however, delegate the leadership. You must set the tone and maintain impetus for the process, because many employees prefer to ignore the unpleasant task of thinking about disasters. It is also your responsibility to bring the issue of emergency preparedness to the attention of the institution's trustees and supporters and to local government officials. When necessary, you should be the one to collaborate with your peers at other institutions in order to share ideas and resources.

As director, your six most important tasks are as follows (each is described more fully in this chapter):

Task 1: Set an institutionwide emergency preparedness policy.

Task 2: Designate responsibility and provide support.

Task 3: Involve the institution's trustees.

Task 4: Establish a budget.

Task 5: Contact others for advice and support.

Task 6: Involve the community and the news media.

Table 5   **Principal Tasks in Developing an Emergency Preparedness and Response Plan**

	Action	• Responsible position / body ✳ Relevant chapter(s)
Goals / priorities / scope	Set a policy that identifies the goals and priorities of the planning process and defines its scope.	• Director ✳ Chapter 2
EPM / EPC responsibilities	Appoint an emergency preparedness manager (EPM) and create an emergency preparedness committee (EPC) that includes representatives from key departments.	• Director/EPM ✳ Chapters 2–3
Trustees' commitment	Develop the initial assessment of risks and vulnerablilities. Present it to the board of trustees. Secure the board's commitment to the process.	• Director ✳ Chapter 2
Budget	Establish a budget for developing and implementing the preparedness and prevention activitites.	• Director ✳ Chapter 2
Staff involvement	Involve all staff in the emergency preparedness program.	• Director/EPC/preparedness teams ✳ Chapters 4–5
Agency/institution involvement	Contact local, regional, and national emergency agencies and other cultural institutions or organizations that may be of assisstance.	• Director/EPC/preparedness teams ✳ Chapters 2–4, 6–9
Community involvement	Involve the community, including the institution's neighbors, local firefighters, and the news media.	• Director/EPC/preparedness teams ✳ Chapters 2–9
Team / leader responsibilities	Appoint departmental preparedness teams and team leaders and equip them with the necessary tools and information.	• EPM/EPC ✳ Chapters 3, 6–9
Hazards	Identify the potential natural and human-caused hazards specific to the area.	• EPC ✳ Chapters 3, 6–9
Assets / vulnerabilities	Identify assets and the vulnerability of the institution, including collections, people, infrastructure, and administrative records.	• EPC/preparedness teams ✳ Chapters 3, 6–9
Coordinator responsibilities	Appoint and emergency response coordinator (ERC) and a communications coordinator if necessary.	• Director/EPM ✳ Chapters 2–3
Chain of command	Identify the chain of command and response teams, with a contingency list of successors.	• EPM/EPC preparedness teams ✳ Chapters 2–3, 6–9
Prevention / preparedness	Implement preventive and preparedness measures for staff, the public, the collections, and other assets.	• EPC/ERC/preparedness teams ✳ Chapters 3, 6–9
Response	Develop response measures, such as evacuation procedures, notification of chain of command, and setting up a temporary base of operation.	• EPC/ERC/preparedness teams ✳ Chapters 3, 6–9
Facts/maps/supplies and equipment	Compile fact sheets, maps, and lists of contacts, and stock emergency supplies and equipment.	• EPC/ preparedness teams ✳ Chapters 6–9
Recovery	Develop a plan for recovering from the emergency and restoring normal operations.	• EPC/preparedness teams ✳ Chapters 3, 6–9
Emergency plan	Develop the emergency plan and write the emergency plan handbook. Review and update all procedures on a regular basis.	• EPC ✳ Chapters 3, 5
Drills / training	Establish routines to keep the plan viable. Train staff in emergency response activities. Conduct drills annually. Evaluate results.	• EPC/preparedness teams ✳ Chapters 5, 6–9

Task 1

Set an institutionwide emergency preparedness policy

Our director has taken emergency planning very seriously. He has made staff time and resources available and provided direction to the entire staff. He has made it clear that while we may get a laugh out of our annual emergency drills, this is serious business.

— Brian Considine
Conservator of decorative arts and sculpture
The J. Paul Getty Museum

No one wants to think about the possibility that he or she may be caught in a dangerous situation. People become uncomfortable and wish to change the subject whenever it comes up. Your employees are no different.

For their own safety and for the well-being of the institution, your staff must be motivated to take emergency preparedness seriously. To do this, you should put into writing the institution's commitment to emergency preparedness and describe the extent to which the plan will be developed. This commitment must start with you and be impressed upon all levels of staff, including part-time employees and volunteers. The policy should identify the goals of the process and establish priorities. The policy should also

- explain why emergency preparedness and response planning is important to the institution;
- state that the safety of visitors and staff is the primary goal;
- state that the process will address the buildings, preservation of the collections and equipment, security of vital records, and restoration of normal activity;
- identify the position or group responsible for implementing the emergency response plan; and
- encourage staff members to familiarize themselves with the emergency plan, to become involved in the process, and to participate in training and drilling exercises.

The policy should be posted for employees to read and be published as the introduction to the emergency plan handbook, a written compilation of procedures, contact telephone numbers, and other information that is distributed to all staff and placed in strategic locations for quick reference during a disaster.

Questions to Consider

- **Is the collection more important than the building?**

- **Can the collection itself be prioritized?**

- **What are the institution's moral and legal obligations toward the safety of staff, visitors, and the collections?**

- **Keeping in mind the types of emergencies that can be expected and the size of your institution, what type of emergency response plan is best?**

- **How serious must an emergency be to activate the plan, and who will make that decision—for example, you or the emergency response coordinator (or ERC alternate in the chain of command at that time)?**

Task 2

Designate responsibility and provide support

The challenge for the director is going to be delegating to the right person or groups of people the job of organizing the staff in this coordinated effort to address the problem. Once the director is sold on it, he or she has to sell the entire staff and has to maintain a certain level of interest in the plan. Everything else can be delegated.

— Jerry Podany
  Head of antiquities conservation
  The J. Paul Getty Museum

Every staff member will be affected by an emergency. Therefore, all staff must be involved at some level in the emergency preparedness and response planning process and must work together, sharing information, collaborating on projects, and identifying risks and priorities. This team approach is crucial. Collaboration and cooperation speed up the process and promote a synergy that enhances the overall emergency planning effort, as well as staff morale.

You will need to appoint a broad-based emergency preparedness committee (EPC) to oversee the development and implementation of the emergency preparedness and response program and report its findings and assessments to you. This committee should include senior administrators and representatives from every key department. Depending on the size and focus of your institution, these departments can include some or all of the following: administration, computer systems, collections, conservation, security, buildings and maintenance, public relations, library, and volunteer resources.

Experts in corporate team building recommend selecting members based on skill and potential, not personality. Three categories of skills are key to the success of the committee: technical and functional, problem solving, and interpersonal. Include at least a few "true believers"—employees who believe strongly in emergency preparedness—and, whenever possible, employees who have previous experience in emergency preparedness or related areas.

To remain focused on its goals, the committee needs an emergency preparedness manager (EPM). If you wish, you may serve in this capacity. A strong leader, the EPM must have the tenacity to guide the committee through the long and sometimes tedious process of creating an emergency plan. The EPM should have solid administrative skills, be familiar with the institution's various departments and collections, and have knowledge of all potential threats and disasters. She or he also should keep you up to date on the committee's progress and oversee much of the community outreach effort (see chapter 3, pages 47–52, for more information).

Next, an emergency response coordinator (ERC) should be selected. The ERC would take charge in an actual emergency, coordinating all response and recovery activities. This position requires calmness in the face of calamity and a thorough understanding of the emergency plan. The ERC should be given broad authority in the event of a disaster, such as the ability to dispense petty cash or authorize expenditures.

It is preferable to appoint one person who has the skills to serve as both EPM and ERC. After you designate an EPM, determine whether he or she also qualifies as an ERC. If he or she does not qualify or does not wish to take on both responsibilities, you and the EPM can work together to appoint an ERC, or you can delegate that task to the emergency preparedness committee.

You should also appoint and train at least one backup person for the EPM and ERC roles. In fact, any staff member may find himself or herself in the position of being the first person on-site to handle an emergency and thus should know what is expected; that is why involvement of all staff in the planning process is crucial.

The job description of the response coordination position (in this case, called the emergency plan coordinator) at the Seattle Art Museum, shown in Figure 1 on the following page, provides an example of the duties of this very important position.

A Team Effort

The EPC may delegate certain phases of the plan—such as recovery efforts or certain planning tasks—to departmental teams. For example, during the planning stages, one team may focus on the needs, priorities, vulnerabilities, and assets of the museum's collections, while another focuses on the building and equipment. The teams gather information and make assessments that are submitted to the EPC, which in turn submits a report to you, the director.

This book has been designed to support a departmental team approach to emergency preparedness and response. Chapters 6–9 contain information specific to safety and security, collections, buildings and maintenance, and administration and records, respectively. These chapters are distributed to each department, but all the information should be integrated into the emergency plan, because the emergency response and recovery teams will have to perform many of the procedures simultaneously.

EMERGENCY PLAN COORDINATOR

RESPONSIBILITIES: Assesses the need for the Emergency Plan and declares it to be operational when necessary; directs all operations while museum is in emergency status; continues to assess the emergency accurately--its progress, potential damage, and responses--and commands the staff based on these assessments; determines cessation of state of emergency.

LINE OF SUCCESSION

1. Director
2. Associate Director/Museum Services
3. Associate Director/Curatorial
4. Chief of Security

ACTION CHECKLIST:

____ Assesses incident and declares Emergency Plan is in effect; must evaluate any incident which may become a serious emergency.

____ Quickly gathers information and develops initial strategy based on personnel available and the nature of the emergency.

____ Takes immediate steps to assign appropriate staff to reduce or eliminate risk (for example: stop the flow of water, unclog the drain, etc.).

____ Immediately appoints Collections, Protective Services, Personnel and Media Managers, using attached work sheet and Emergency Plan Organizational Chart.

____ Receives the Emergency Plan Coordinator's Supply Kit and a portable radio from Protective Services.

____ Establishes a command post and clearly announces its location and who is in charge.

____ Arranges for chronological documentation of significant events, using an assistant if possible.

____ Receives and evaluates reports from all subordinates.

____ When practical, informs Chairman and President of the Board of Trustees.

____ Ensures the protection of personnel and assets during the emergency.

____ Authorizes mutual aid efforts when appropriate. (See Fact Sheet on Local Museums)

____ Continually reevaluates state of emergency and priorities.

____ Thoroughly briefs his/her replacement.

____ Declares emergency over.

Fact Sheets: Emergency Plan Coordinator

1. Portable Radios
2. Assignment Work Sheet
3. Organizational Chart
4. Personnel List (with phone numbers)
5. Local Museums

Figure 1 Job description of the emergency plan coordinator from the Seattle Art Museum's *Emergency Planning Handbook.*

Each departmental team consists of a preparedness team and a response team (some members may belong to both). The preparedness team will thoroughly assess the safety and security procedures currently in place in its respective department, identify where the institution is vulnerable, and produce two reports for the committee summarizing its findings:

Report 1 is a vulnerability and asset analysis that also recommends preparedness and protection measures—for example, what should be done to prevent damage to institution property, structures, collections, and functions and to reduce injury to staff or visitors in the event of an emergency.

Report 2 outlines the role of the departmental response teams during an emergency. For example, the safety and security team leader may be responsible for evacuating people, while a member of the collections response team is assigned to document object damage. The report should include a list of necessary equipment and supplies needed and a list of hazardous materials stored on-site.

Questions to Consider

- Do you have a staff member qualified to serve as both EPM and ERC?
- Do you have a staff large enough to justify two people overseeing the process?
- What level of support should you and the trustees offer the EPM and the ERC?
- What will be the chain of command if the primary appointees are unable to serve during an emergency?
- How much authority should you give the EPM and the ERC to address conflicts between existing policy and the emergency plan?
- Should you set a time line for the planning process?
- Who are the most qualified members of your staff to oversee the survey of collections, records, equipment, and other assets?
- Who among your staff are enthusiastic about emergency preparedness?
- Who are unenthusiastic but must be nurtured and brought into the process as key players? How can you motivate and include them?
- Who are knowledgeable about first aid, security, or emergency procedures?
- Who among your staff are good team players?

Task 3

Involve the institution's trustees

Early in the planning process, it is helpful to involve your board of trustees, which holds fiduciary responsibilities for the institution. As community leaders, they can assist in obtaining permission for the use of additional resources, such as people, equipment, and funds, at the time of a disaster. When the EPC has provided you with an initial risk-and-vulnerability assessment, present it to the trustees. It is important to make them aware of potential threats to staff and visitors and to the institution's assets, and to make sure they are committed to the prevention and preparedness efforts.

In making your presentation to the trustees, articulate clearly what you wish to achieve from the emergency preparedness and response program. Ask the trustees to discuss how much the institution is willing to compromise. Ask them also to take a role in the emergency preparedness and response program. Perhaps one of the trustees is a board member for another public or private institution that has an emergency plan. Trustees could also take a leadership role in any fund-raising efforts to support the program. Remind them of the institution's moral obligations to prevent or mitigate the effects of potential threats that the emergency preparedness committee identifies. You might point out that the major cause of loss to cultural institutions is from human impact—occurring during renovations or reconstruction—and therefore can be prevented. Refer to Table 2 (pages 10–11) to quote figures.

Questions to Consider

- Would the board of trustees want to take on emergency preparedness in their next development campaign?

- Should they be involved in the annual drills and other preparedness training exercises?

- How will the trustees and the community react if you do not bring the potential threats to their attention before disaster strikes? Would they feel differently if a relative were visiting the institution when an emergency occurred?

- How can the trustees personally assist in any response or recovery process?

Task 4

Establish a budget

Initially we spent very little money. We were more concerned with recognizing the resources that we had on hand. The crucial thing we needed to put into the budget was a line item for the emergency drill each year.

— Alissandra Cummins
   Director
   Barbados Museum and Historical Society

As stated in chapter 1, a successful preparedness and response program requires a substantial commitment of staff time and financial resources. The extent of the latter obviously will depend on many factors, including the size and type of the institution, its financial resources, the potential hazards, and so on. No major financial considerations should be made until the EPC completes its assessment of the institution's vulnerabilities. The vulnerability analysis will identify the potential hazards and therefore the priorities in terms of prevention and preparedness efforts. This analysis should reflect the fact that very few institutions are not at risk from the major cause of loss and destruction in cultural institutions—that of fire during renovations or construction activities.

One of the EPC's first steps in the preparedness and response process should be to develop a draft budget that will be revised according to the hazards identified and again as the preparedness and preventive measures are implemented. Prevention will be the most cost-effective phase of the preparedness process. Again, implementation steps will be based on the identified hazards, and the available funds allocated accordingly. Budget allocation in this area is a very important and very difficult task; decisions made at this point may have enormous implications in the event of an emergency. An example is the decision not to install fire detectors in the attic of the Franklin D. Roosevelt Historic House in Hyde Park, New York, during installation of a fire detection system, thus saving US$2,500. A subsequent fire, caused by faulty wiring, resulted in more than US$2 million in restoration costs.

Once the plan is in place, annual budget costs should be minimal—these range from US$2,500 to $5,300 in the case histories in chapter 1. The major cost is for staff time—for example, to maintain first-aid and CPR certification, and for the annual drill. Gail Joice, senior deputy director and registrar of the Seattle Art Museum, advises that it is important to also include maintenance of the emergency preparedness plan in the institution's five- or ten-year budget projection. One of the major staff costs for the Seattle Art Museum is the inclusion of all security staff in training activities, including the overtime costs for those members on weekend shifts to participate in weekday training sessions and the costs of repeat sessions to accommodate various shifts.

The annual budget should include maintaining response equipment and supplies. At the Mystic Seaport Museum, each department is responsible for including these costs in their annual department budget. However, unless an emergency situation occurs during the year to deplete supplies, maintenance costs should be minimal. In the initial process of developing preparedness and response supplies and equipment, it may be surprising how much of these already are on hand in the various departments of the institution.

The one other major financial consideration is that of recovery in the event of a major disaster. As Carl Nelson warns, "A natural disaster may create a financial one. If possible, build up reserves in every budget. Disruption of business in subsequent months—and years—can cause major financial damage."[1]

Remember that many significant steps in the prevention and preparedness process can be done at minimal cost (see "Immediate Steps to Take," pages 40–41). Remember also the board of trustees, local businesses, and the community, in terms of fund-raising for your institution's emergency preparedness and response program.

Questions to Consider

- What will be your institutional liability for expensive traveling exhibits if an emergency plan is not in place?

- Are grants available to support your emergency preparedness efforts?

- Are major philanthropists willing to donate funds to purchase necessary equipment or to underwrite a needed capital expense?

Task 5

Contact others for advice and support

You and your staff do not, and should not, have to embark on this journey to emergency preparedness alone. During the 1990s—the decade of natural disaster reduction, as designated by the United Nations—most countries have established committees to create national emergency response plans. These plans, however, may not affect individual institutions, but the committees themselves can be a tremendous resource. An important development during this decade is the founding in 1996 of the International Committee of the Blue Shield (ICBS) by four nongovernmental organizations: the International Council of Archives (ICA), the International Council of Museums (ICOM), the International Council on Monuments and Sites (ICOMOS), and the International Federation of Library Associations and Institutions (IFLA). The ICBS members are working together to organize risk preparedness internationally and to provide a network of expertise for disaster response. Many countries are forming national committees of ICBS. Furthermore, the committees may have passed along advice, materials, and other information to local organizations and other knowledgeable sources. These contacts can save you time and money.

Take the time to locate and get in touch with experts in your community, nationally and internationally.

- Ask local emergency officials for referrals.
- Talk to colleagues at nearby museums, art galleries, and libraries.
- Contact earthquake, flood, or other disaster researchers at local universities.
- Talk to authors of emergency plans for local schools, libraries, and government buildings.
- Contact national and international organizations of museum professionals, such as directors, curators, security, and conservators, and associations of other related professionals, such as architects and engineers.
- Consider using local fire protection agencies as a resource.

If no conservator is on your staff, the EPC should consult conservators at other cultural institutions, in private practice, or at regional or national conservation centers regarding preventive and response procedures for your institution's collection.

The "Directory of Selected Organizations" at the end of this book contains a number of contacts that may be of help. This is only a sampling of what is available. Many of the organizations listed have Web sites that provide links to numerous other relevant organizations.

Task 6

Involve the community and the news media

The EPM will do most of the community outreach, but, as director, you are the public figure representing your institution. You have access to the more influential members of the community. You may want to establish a personal rapport with the local fire and police chiefs, for example. Include them on the guest list for special events, and invite them to tour the facility and advise on preparedness and response issues. If you are seen as publicly pushing the emergency preparedness process, community leaders are more likely to get behind the effort.

You also will need to decide in advance of an emergency what role you and the board of trustees will play during and after an emergency. A spokesperson should be designated to handle the media. Depending on the size of your institution, there may be a need to appoint a communications coordinator, who can deal with the media and take on a number of other responsibilities. Discuss this with the EPM. See chapter 3, task 4 (page 52), and chapter 4 for details on the role and responsibilities of a communications coordinator.

Questions to Consider

- **Have you met community leaders in the neighborhood? Do you cultivate their interest in your institution?**

- **Have you met the regional and state disaster officials? Have they toured the institution? Do they know what is in the collection? Are they aware of your interest in emergency preparedness?**

- **Are there any relevant regional, state, or national boards, task forces, or committees that you should join?**

- **Can you realistically handle media inquiries during an emergency? During the recovery phase? In what situations would the media outreach be more effective with your name and face attached to the message?**

Immediate Steps to Take

A comprehensive emergency preparedness and response program can seem like a daunting process; however, there are plenty of tasks you and your staff can complete as first steps in the process that will take no more than a month and will greatly reduce the risks without greatly increasing the budget. Some of these activities—for example, moving flammable materials away from heat sources inside the building and clearing dry brush away from outside the building—can prevent a disaster. The following are some important steps to take.[2]

Establish a chain of command. Assign basic responsibilities among staff—for instance, who is in charge of evacuation, who is in charge of acquiring emergency supplies. Prepare a list of these positions, the designated persons, and their home telephone numbers and addresses. Reproduce the list on laminated cards and distribute to staff.

Practice good housekeeping. Make sure all areas (hallways, offices, storage closets) are free of clutter that might fuel a fire. Use common sense; keep collections off the floor in storage areas and breakable objects away from edges of shelves.

Lead a cleanup effort. Remove all unnecessary detritus from around the building, clean gutters and drains, and so forth.

Collect emergency numbers and addresses. Post emergency telephone numbers and, with their permission, home addresses of staff, as well as telephone numbers of fire and police departments.

Gather supplies. Identify available supplies that can be used in emergencies, such as fire extinguishers, first-aid kits, food supplies, flashlights, paper goods, hand carts, battery-powered radios, cameras, shovels, mops, brooms, polyethylene bags, crowbars, lumber, and buckets.

Prepare records. Make a duplicate set of important documents (building plans, personnel and administration records, collections inventories, etc.) and store this set off-site. Remember that access may be needed on a twenty-four-hour basis.

Make contact lists. Compile a list of local sources of supplies and services that might be needed in an emergency, such as storage for the collection if it must be relocated. Include names, addresses, and telephone numbers of building contractors your institution has used recently.

Compile fact sheets. Create step-by-step outlines of specific emergency-related duties, such as turning on the emergency generator or shutting off the gas, water, and electricity.

Duplicate keys. Make copies of necessary keys and store them in a safe and separate location.

Investigate free services. Contact the Red Cross, the local fire department, and your insurance agent; they may provide training in first aid and emergency response and/or inspections and advice services.

Network. Develop a relationship with emergency preparedness organizations within your community and with peers at other cultural institutions.

Make money accessible. Set up a credit card account with key staff members as cardholders for emergency purchases. Keep a resource of petty cash on hand for emergencies.

Notes

1. Carl L. Nelson, *Protecting the Past from Natural Disasters* (Washington, D.C.: Preservation Press, National Trust for Historic Preservation, 1991), 78.

2. Adapted from Wilbur Faulk, "Organizing, Preparing, Testing, and Revising an Emergency Planning Program" (J. Paul Getty Trust, Santa Monica, Calif., February 1993, typescript).

Chapter Summary

This chapter explained the emergency preparedness and response program and focused on the six areas where you, as director, must take leadership.

In review, the director must

- set a policy on emergency preparedness and response planning;

- designate an emergency preparedness manager and emergency response coordinator to coordinate the team effort, and select alternates for these positions;

- convince the board of trustees to support the emergency preparedness and response process and program;

- establish a budget to support the program;

- network with experts and colleagues at other cultural institutions; and

- involve the community and news media.

Continue to Part II if you are also serving as the EPM. If you are not, give the designated EPM a copy of this book and schedule a meeting to discuss its contents and your expectations.

The disaster contingency planner must transcend the comfortable world of the office and situate him or herself in the frenzied, panic-stricken environment that prevails when disaster strikes. This person must think the unthinkable, foresee the unforeseen, and expect the unexpected.

— John P. Barton
and Johanna G. Wellheiser
An Ounce of Prevention

Part II

For the Emergency Preparedness Manager

Overview

This part, which consists of chapters 3–5, is designed to serve as a resource for the emergency preparedness manager (EPM). The EPM is designated by the director to head the emergency preparedness committee (EPC) and oversee development and implementation of the emergency preparedness and response program.

The EPM's primary responsibility is guiding the committee through the information-gathering process that leads to the development of a written emergency plan. The EPM also may be expected to assume the role of emergency response coordinator (ERC), who is in charge of response efforts during an emergency. At least one backup EPM and ERC (or more if desired) should be appointed and trained in case the designated EPM/ERC cannot perform his or her duties or is unavailable.

Although Part II refers throughout to one primary designated EPM, those in the chain of command for the position should be thoroughly familiar with the role of the EPM.

Chapter 3 presents an overview of the emergency preparedness and response program. This chapter also explains the role of the EPM and the EPC in the emergency preparedness and response program; outlines what the EPM must do to get the committee to work as effectively as possible; emphasizes the importance of teamwork and gives strategies for building an effective team; and guides the EPC through the tasks needed to compile an emergency plan and produce the emergency plan handbook.

Chapter 4 discusses the role of communications—internal and external—both during the planning process and in actual emergencies. It includes information on team communications, working with the media, and equipment considerations. Intended as a resource for the EPM, the EPC, and the communications coordinator, the chapter also explains the role of communication in the emergency preparedness and response process; suggests ways to ensure good communication, internally as well as externally; explains the role of the communications coordinator during an emergency; and suggests ways of dealing with the media, including how to write news releases.

Chapter 5 helps the EPM, the EPC, and the departmental preparedness teams develop a training program and organize emergency drills. It outlines a variety of activities that prepare staff for emergencies. The chapter also lists training exercises that build skills and generate interest and enthusiasm; suggests a variety of protection- or response-related training activities; suggests guidelines for building effective teams and effective emergency preparedness and response training exercises; and helps the EPC plan meaningful, institution-wide drills.

The "Suggested Exercises" and "Questions to Consider" that appear throughout will help you apply the material presented in these chapters to the specific requirements of your institution.

CHAPTER THREE

The Role of the Emergency Preparedness Manager and the Emergency Preparedness Committee

Making Emergency Preparedness Happen

The disaster contingency planner must transcend the comfortable world of the office and situate him or herself in the frenzied, panic-stricken environment that prevails when disaster strikes. This person must think the unthinkable, foresee the unforeseen, and expect the unexpected. In addition, the planner must take into account the foibles of human nature, particularly the foolhardiness of those who rely on fail-safe systems that can, and do, go wrong. Finally, he or she must be able to select people who will be able, in the event of a disaster, to quickly and efficiently put the plan into operation. Unfortunately, it takes a disaster to reveal those very people who perform well under adverse conditions. [1]

— John P. Barton and Johanna G. Wellheiser
  An Ounce of Prevention

The director of your institution has just informed you that he or she wants to launch an emergency preparedness and response program, and you have been asked to lead a cross-departmental effort to develop a comprehensive emergency plan. Now what? If you have never been involved in emergency planning, you may not know where to start. This chapter is designed to help you lead the emergency preparedness committee (EPC) through the emergency preparedness and response planning process and gather the information needed to develop a written emergency plan.

Bear in mind, however, that emergency preparedness does not happen overnight; it is an evolutionary process. Eighteen months to two years is not an unreasonable time frame for development and implementation of an effective program.

As you address issues related to emergency preparedness and response, you may have a change in attitude. You may confront your deep-seated fears of being caught in an earthquake or a tornado, or you may realize that you can make a difference in the safety and protection of historic objects. Changes in others may be seen as well. You and your colleagues may bond together as a team, and staff members may feel more empowered. Eventually, everyone will feel safer at work and may begin applying this newly gained expertise to ensure the safety of family members at home.

Review chapters 1 and 2 before proceeding. Be sure to review Table 3 in chapter 1 and complete the test in chapter 2 (Table 4).

The Role of the Emergency Preparedness Manager

As EPM, you are the hands-on motivator. The director should help create an environment in which emergency preparedness and response are taken seriously, but you are the person who will make it happen. To do so, you need to

- lead the EPC through the process of gathering information needed to write an emergency plan;
- work with the director to designate an emergency response coordinator (ERC)—which could be yourself—and alternates for the position (the ERC is responsible for overseeing the response efforts for your institution in the event of an emergency);
- work with the EPC to launch a training program that helps staff members address fears associated with emergency preparedness and provides them with the skills they need in a crisis;
- keep the director and board of trustees up to date on the committee's progress; and
- involve outside service agencies, such as the Red Cross, local police and fire departments, and the civil defense department.

You probably will be handling your duties as EPM in addition to your regular job responsibilities. Make your role as EPM a priority: Human lives, as well as irreplaceable cultural property, are at stake.

As chair of the EPC, you are in charge of the following four tasks (these tasks and the steps involved in each—when applicable—are described in the following pages):

Task 1: Contact others for advice and support.

Task 2: Designate responsibility and provide support.

Task 3: Appoint departmental preparedness teams.

Task 4: Appoint a communications coordinator.

Task 1

Contact others for advice and support

Local emergency service agencies can help you build an emergency plan that complements other plans already in place in the community. You need to know realistically how much assistance your institution could receive in the event of a wide-scale emergency. Information and support provided by these agencies can significantly reduce the amount of time and resources necessary for developing the emergency plan. In addition, local agencies should be aware of the institution's needs and planning efforts so they can provide the most efficient support in a crisis. Remember that hospitals, schools, and general population needs will be met first by city, state, and national agencies in an emergency situation. The following emergency service agencies may be consulted:

- civil defense department
- emergency management agency
- local fire department
- hospital/ambulance authorities
- military
- police department
- Red Cross and other relief agencies

Once established, contact should be maintained throughout the planning process and after the emergency plan is in effect, so the plan can be kept up to date.

Questions to Consider

- Do other institutions in the region have emergency plans? Are they willing to share them with you?

- Who in the community is knowledgeable about emergency preparedness and could serve as a resource?

- What state, regional, and local emergency agencies should be contacted before, during, and after a disaster, and how can a solid relationship be developed beforehand with these agencies?

- Should outside emergency agencies have access to your institution's floor plans?

<table>
<tr><td>

Task 2

Designate responsibility and provide support

</td><td>

Step 1

Build an effective committee

As explained in chapter 2, the EPC should include senior administrators and representatives of most, if not all, departments. These departments may include any or all of the following, depending on the size of the institution: administration, collections, conservation, security, buildings and maintenance, public relations, library, and volunteer resources. The director will appoint the members. As emergency preparedness manager, you will act as committee chair. To create an effective committee, keep the following steps in mind:

- Set a regular schedule for meetings; anticipate obstacles, such as the demands of the EPC members' regular job responsiblities; and set realistic goals, objectives, and deadlines. Be careful not to try to take on too many of these tasks at once, particularly in the early stages of the preparedness process.
- Start with a few immediate performance-oriented tasks and goals to unite the group; for example, compile a list of department staff home telephone numbers and addresses.
- Set clear rules for EPC members regarding such policies as attendance, confidentiality, and constructive confrontation.
- Give committee members specific deadlines for assignments, and record the deadlines in the agenda minutes.
- Develop a system of publicizing internally the progress of the emergency preparedness and response program. For example, photos of a drill might be displayed on an employee bulletin board. Discuss this system at a full staff meeting.
- Exploit the power of positive feedback, recognition, and reward.[2]

See chapter 5, "Training," for more team-building strategies.

</td></tr>
</table>

Suggested Exercise

Begin one meeting with an emergency scenario. Describe a situation—for example: a group of schoolchildren are in a second-story exhibit gallery when a fire breaks out and blocks the stairwell; or, a water main breaks under the floor of the storage room. Solicit and discuss responses.

Six months later, present the same scenario again, and assess whether committee members' responses have improved.

Step 2

Generate the essential documents

As a basic tool, the committee should produce the following documents in the early stages of the emergency preparedness and response program:

- A statement of purpose, including goals and objectives, of the emergency preparedness and response program. A copy of the institution's emergency preparedness policy developed by the director is later given to the departmental preparedness teams.
- A contact list of key staff, including job titles, roles in the emergency plan, and office and home phone numbers and addresses. This list

should be arranged in the order in which the persons are to be contacted.
- An organizational chart that contains descriptions of the duties and responsibilities of the committee members and the staff.
- A draft budget for the emergency preparedness and response program. This can be revised as the planning progresses and vulnerabilities are identified.

Task 3

Appoint departmental preparedness teams

All staff, from custodians to top administrators, must be included in the process at some point. You never know who might be in the building during a crisis; therefore, as many people as possible should be trained. Many institutions have created teams to carry out preparedness measures and to lead emergency response and recovery activities, such as relocation and/or salvage of objects. The team approach also helps maximize the use of specialized skills.

In this book, the EPC is the central coordinating team. At certain stages of the planning process, you will probably want departmental teams to investigate issues related to specific sections of the institution, such as collections or records. For example, during the planning stages, one team may focus on the protection of staff and the public; another on the needs, priorities, vulnerabilities, and assets of the collections; and a third on the building and equipment.

This book has been designed to support a departmental team approach to emergency preparedness and response. Chapters 6–9 contain information specific to safety and security, collections, buildings and maintenance, and administration and records. The number and type of teams depend on the organization of your institution. Though each department team generates and presents its information independently, all information collected needs to be integrated into the emergency plan.

As detailed in chapters 6–9, each departmental preparedness team will produce two reports for the EPC:

Report 1 is a vulnerability and asset analysis that also recommends preparedness and protection measures—for example, what should be done to prevent damage to institution property, structures, and collections, and impairment to services and to reduce injury to staff or visitors in the event of an emergency.

Report 2 outlines the role of the departmental response teams during an emergency. For example, the administration and records team will be responsible for providing access to temporary funds. The response team may include some or all of the preparedness team members. The report should include a list of relevant contacts, equipment and supplies needed, and a list of any hazardous materials stored on-site.

Figure 2 depicts the team approach to creating the institution's emergency plan. The diagram shows the chain of command, from the director to the EPM to the EPC to the departmental teams. Each departmental team consists of a preparedness team and a response team, each of which gathers data on

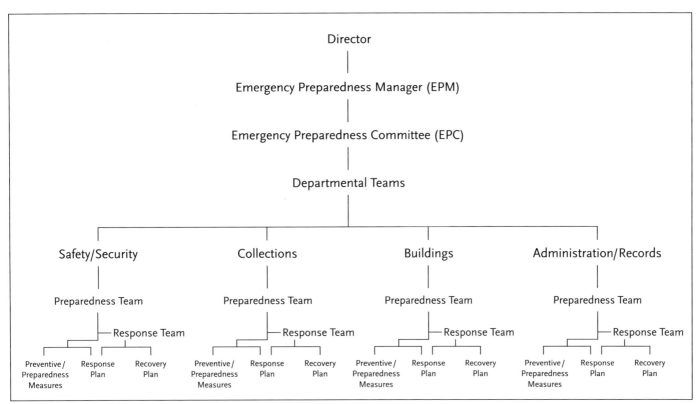

Figure 2   Organizational chart showing chain of command and division of departmental teams with their respective duties.

preventive/preparedness measures, response procedures, and recovery procedures. This information is given to the EPC to be incorporated into the emergency plan.

In smaller institutions, a departmental team may consist of only a few people. Appendix A shows how the Barbados Museum and Historical Society, with a staff of twenty-six, organized their teams for response and recovery situations. When putting together teams, keep these guidelines in mind:

- Each team should have a leader and at least one backup leader. Five is the optimum number of members for each team; communications may break down in a larger group.
- Each team member should be assigned responsibilities and be capable of carrying out those responsibilities.
- Special emphasis should be placed on training members to handle their designated responsibilities.

Do not overlook other personnel who are on hand regularly, such as guides, volunteers, contract security officers, and contract laborers. These individuals may be able to provide support in any emergency response operation. By becoming involved, they will also be better informed in the event of an emergency. Neighbors may also be a resource, if willing and trained.

Task 4

Appoint a communications coordinator

Most institutions will appoint a communications coordinator—and, as with the other key positions, a number of alternates—to answer all questions, formal and casual; to offer information to the public; and to obtain external information as needed during an emergency. Having a communications coordinator significantly reduces the confusion that often arises during and after emergencies and improves the consistency and accuracy of released information. The first choice for this position is usually the public relations director, who is familiar with all aspects of the institution's functions and is accustomed to dealing with the media. Smaller institutions might delegate communication responsibilities to the EPM, the director, or a media-savvy member of the board of trustees.

The communications coordinator works closely with the director during an emergency, reporting directly to the ERC. The plan should instruct employees to refer all media questions to the communications coordinator or designated spokesperson. At the same time, a high priority should be placed on keeping the coordinator fully informed and up to date on events.

In an emergency, the key responsibilities of the communications coordinator are to perform or supervise the following:

- Gather and coordinate information for dissemination through the media.
- Gather and disseminate information from external sources, such as the extent of the emergency that is not localized to the institution.
- Assess accuracy of information.
- Coordinate news releases with investigating agencies, such as fire and police departments and civil defense.
- Keep staff, visitors, and the community informed.
- Be accessible to the media and maintain control of their activities on-site following an emergency.
- Keep a log of all media information that has been released (what was released, when, and to whom).
- Refrain from making decisions or stating opinions on controversial or questionable topics unless these have been previously discussed with the director.
- Solicit public support.

See chapter 4 for more details about communications-related issues.

The Role of the Emergency Preparedness Committee

The responsibilities of the EPC include the following:

Task 1: Assess the hazards.

Task 2: Identify assets and vulnerabilities.

Task 3: Implement preventive measures.

Task 4: Implement preparedness measures.

Task 5: Develop the response plan.

Task 6: Develop recovery procedures.

Task 7: Write the emergency plan.

Task 1

Assess the hazards

Step 1

Identify potential emergencies

The committee's first step is to prepare a report identifying what natural or human-caused emergencies may threaten the institution. The characteristics of the region and the institution's property should be considered in order to determine the likelihood of emergencies and their potential severity. Relevant state and local authorities can provide long-term records regarding natural hazards pertinent to the area, such as major floods, seasons of severe storms and high tides, and so forth. Secondary and tertiary effects that might accompany a hazard also must be taken into account; for instance, earthquakes can cause structural damage, but may also cause fire, as well as sewage, water, and gas leaks. Each of these effects can, in turn, initiate further hazards. (See "Questions to Consider," on the next page.)

The variety of emergencies the EPC identifies include, but are not limited to, the following:

Natural disasters
- flash flood
- slow-rising flood
- electrical, range, brush, or forest fire
- earthquake
- hurricane, tornado, windstorm
- blizzard, heavy snow
- volcanic eruption, lava flow
- mud slide
- tidal wave

Industrial disasters

- electrical power failure
- fuel supply failure
- water supply failure
- sewer failure or backup
- explosion
- chemical spill
- structural collapse
- structural fire (internal)
- exposure fire (external)
- nuclear power plant accident

Accidents

- broken fuel pipelines
- broken water or sewer pipes
- downed electrical or phone lines
- construction equipment
- motor vehicles
- transport of chemicals or fuels
- transport of nuclear materials
- weapons

Human impact

- vandalism, careless handling of collection
- armed robbery, theft
- arson
- bombing, bomb threat
- conventional or nuclear warfare
- riots, civil disturbance
- terrorist attack (other than bomb)

Questions to Consider

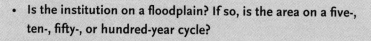

- Is the institution on a floodplain? If so, is the area on a five-, ten-, fifty-, or hundred-year cycle?

- Is an old dam located upriver?

- Is the institution in a seismic zone?

- Is the institution's plumbing in disrepair?

- Where are the drains? Are drains and gutters cleaned on a seasonal basis?

- Is the institution dependent on a local utility for power?

- Is the region prone to fires?

- Has the institution been a target of criminal activity?

Step 2

Identify potential damage from emergencies

Architectural features. Roof type, foundation age, window size, and dozens of other factors make your institution unique, often in ways that render it vulnerable in an emergency. Committee members should consider how the hazards they have identified would affect the building, staff, visitors, collection, and emergency response procedures. The following types of damage should be considered.

Fire and other heat-related damage. This can result from rapid oxidation of most types of cultural objects and can potentially destroy them. Smoke from fires can coat walls, floors, and all such objects with soot in seconds.

Water damage. This can occur as a consequence of rainstorms, hurricanes, floods, burst pipes, fires, and other emergency situations. Water may warp, split, and rot wooden and other organic materials or lead to rust, mold, corrosion, or general deterioration of objects containing metal. Water also dissolves pigments and may deposit fuels and chemicals onto works of art, causing secondary damage.

Structural failure. Water, sewer, power, and fuel lines can break when structural failure occurs, leading to water and chemical damage or fires. Cultural property may be damaged or even destroyed if the building is damaged.

Chemical damage. This type of damage can result from smoke, chemical spills, burst fuel lines and storage containers, and a host of related events generally known as industrial or hazardous materials accidents. Chemicals may corrode, dissolve, weaken, or stain objects. Secondary damage can also occur as a result of a natural disaster, such as an earthquake.

Human impact. Handling of wet, soot-covered, or damaged works of art can cause further problems. Evacuation should be undertaken only as a last resort, and should not be undertaken without due consideration of how the objects will be carried and stored. Workers must be trained in proper handling of objects. The possibility of injury to staff members during an emergency must be taken into account. If a staff member is injured, he or she will be unable to participate in the response plan and will require assistance from others. This will reduce the number of people able to care for the collection. As EPM, you should build flexibility into the emergency plan and make sure assistance will be available both to injured individuals and for the handling of the collection.

Questions to Consider

- How will fire and smoke affect evacuation or relocation procedures?

- In what situations is evacuation truly necessary? Who decides? Where is the closest safe repository for cultural objects?

- When and how can objects be moved to the neighboring gallery, another floor, another building, another town, or out of the country?

- How could the presence of a chemical hazard interfere with emergency procedures?

- Should evacuation or relocation plans anticipate the possibility of probable structural damage and provide alternative routes?

Step 3

Distribute the hazard assessment report

Once the EPC has drafted the hazard assessment report, the committee distributes it to members of the departmental teams. The report gives the teams a clearer understanding of the nature of the potential threats, which in turn encourages them to take the emergency preparedness and response program more seriously. Using the report as a guide, the teams assess the institution's vulnerability in terms of their respective departments—collections, administrative processes, infrastructure, or security systems.

Task 2

Identify assets and vulnerabilities

Step 1

Assign department preparedness teams to survey the institution's assets and vulnerabilities

After the potential risks and hazards have been identified, the next step is to set priorities in terms of who is vulnerable to injury and what assets are susceptible to damage; consider this in relation to each potential hazard or a series of disaster scenarios. The safety and lives of visitors and staff are first priority. Assets include buildings, collections, administrative records, equipment, and furnishings.

The EPC can delegate this assignment to the departmental preparedness teams, which should include individuals with particular expertise. For example, one team member may need to research the structural integrity of different parts of the building, the stipulations of insurance policies, or the preservation and conservation needs of the collection. A structural engineer could contribute the structural information; an administrator or a registrar could contribute the insurance requirements; and a curator or conservator could describe the needs of the collection. A preparator may know how best to handle or pack the collection.

If team members do not have the appropriate expertise, they should work with external consultants. If no conservators are on staff, conservators from museums, regional or national conservation centers, or national or international conservation organizations can be contacted. An architect, a structural engineer, and a mechanical or electrical engineer are important specialists to utilize.

Questions to Consider

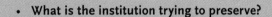

- **What is the institution trying to preserve?**

- **What is the institution prepared to lose, and what is vital to save?**

- **Are the risks serious enough to warrant immediate action to protect lives and vulnerable property?**

- **Who will review the prioritization lists before they are submitted to the director for approval?**

- **What degree of confidentiality should be maintained for these decisions, and how will this be done?**

Step 2

Give the preparedness teams a clear mandate of their role

As EPM, make sure members of the preparedness teams have copies of the institution's emergency preparedness policy, the committee's statement of purpose, and the hazard assessment report. In addition to submitting two written reports, the teams are expected to contribute verbally to the emergency plan as well. In carrying out their research assignments, team members will find appropriate help and recommendations in chapters 6–9. The following is an outline of their assignments.

Safety and security. Specific directions for assessing safety and security are given in chapter 6. This team should receive the assistance of both the collections and the buildings and maintenance researchers in preparing the following reports:

Report 1 provides suggestions for protecting visitors and staff and for preventing damage to the security aspect of the institution's activities.

Report 2 gives recommendations for security functions during an emergency. This report should include lists of equipment and supplies needed and any hazardous materials that are stored on-site, job descriptions for the response team, and recommended recovery procedures.

Collections. Specific directions for assessing the vulnerability of the collections are provided in chapter 7. This team should work with the safety and security and the buildings and maintenance researchers in preparing the following reports:

Report 1 provides suggestions for preventing or mitigating damage to the collections.

Report 2 gives recommendations for the role of collections teams during an emergency. This report includes lists of objects to be protected or relocated in the event of certain emergencies; recommended techniques for moving, protecting, or salvaging the collection; a list of the tools and materials needed for those procedures; job descriptions for the response team; and recommended recovery procedures.

Buildings and maintenance. Specific directions for assessing the building and its infrastructure are indicated in chapter 8. This team should consult with the collections and the safety and security researchers in preparing the following reports:

Report 1 provides suggestions for preventing or reducing damage to the building and its infrastructure.

Report 2 gives recommendations for the role of buildings and maintenance teams during an emergency. This report should include copies of such documents as floor plans and electrical and mechanical installation schematics; location of emergency exits, shut-off valves, evacuation routes, and shelters; lists of emergency tools and materials; contact lists of emergency organizations, such as fire marshal, police, and city engineers; recommended procedures for assessing safe reentry; job descriptions for the response team; and recommended recovery procedures.

Administration and records. Specific directions for assessing administration and records are provided in chapter 9. This research requires the participation of the institution's risk manager, controller, staff counsel, insurance agent, and safety and security team in preparing the following reports:

Report 1 provides suggestions for preventing damage to important administrative records.

Report 2 gives recommendations for the role of administration and records teams during an emergency. This report should include lists and location of important documents, disaster-related requirements of the insurance policy, a list of equipment and procedures to provide visual documentation for supporting insurance claims, job descriptions for the response team, and recommended recovery procedures.

Task 3

Implement preventive measures

Step 1

Consider and address additional suggestions and measures

As identified in "Terms to Know" in the introduction to this book, prevention involves activities that focus on preventing emergencies from occurring (particularly potential human-caused emergencies) and on reducing harm to people or damage to property in emergency situations that cannot be avoided.

Working with the EPC, compile the suggestions provided by the preparedness teams, then edit and prioritize them. Have a brainstorming session to come up with any opportunities not already suggested for reducing damage during all of the potential threats identified in the vulnerability and assets analysis. The following may help generate ideas:

- If the institution is in a seismic zone, position the collection out of the path of potential falling furnishings, pipes, and so forth, and ensure that objects will not block entrances and exits if they move or fall.
- If the institution is in a coastal area or on a floodplain, research flood, high tide, and hurricane records over the last century to establish known high-water levels, and ensure that, where possible, buildings are above the critical level. Make sure that collections are displayed and stored above the level or can be moved quickly to a safe area if necessary.
- Bring gas, electricity, sewage, and water systems up to reliable operational standards. Make sure they can be turned on or off quickly. Eliminate leakage. Ensure that fuel sources are available for emergency power.

Refer to chapters 6–9 for more ideas.

Step 2

Implement the preventive measures

The EPC has submitted its final vulnerability assessment and preventive measures report to you, the EPM. Depending on your institution's budget and policy changes, which may be necessary for implementation, you may need to prepare formal proposals for the director and the board of trustees to implement the preventive measures. If budgetary constraints are an issue, implement the preventive measures in the order of their designated priorities (life and safety issues first). Measures that have little or no financial implications also can be implemented.

Task 4

Implement preparedness measures

Step 1

Consider and address additional suggestions and measures

Preparedness measures enable the institution to respond quickly and effectively in an emergency situation and potentially mitigate its damaging effects. Preparedness can actually prevent some emergencies. For example, a well-trained security officer using a nearby fire extinguisher can prevent a wastebasket fire from destroying the building. All staff, not just those who have been assigned specific responsibilities in an emergency, should be trained in emergency procedures. Preparedness measures can be taken before a disaster strikes, such as posting and distributing up-to-date staff contact lists. Others are put in place when an emergency situation is imminent; for example, the staff at the Barbados Museum and Historical Society installed shutters on all windows immediately after a hurricane warning was issued.

Working with the EPC, compile the suggestions provided by the preparedness teams, then edit and prioritize them. Have a brainstorming session to determine any opportunities not already suggested for improving preparedness. The following may help generate ideas:

- Make sure the collection has been fully inventoried and, if possible, catalogued with both written and photographic documentation. This is particularly necessary to support any insurance claim.
- Make duplicates of all important documents and store them off-site.
- Consider installing quick-release mount systems so that objects can be moved efficiently if necessary.
- Ensure that realistic quantities of emergency supplies are on hand or readily available—again, prioritize according to the threats identified in the vulnerability analysis.

Step 2

Implement the preparedness measures on a priority basis

As with preventive measures, depending on the budget and policy changes that may be necessary for implementation, you may need to prepare formal proposals for the director and the board of trustees to implement the measures. Similarly, you will find that many preparedness measures also can be implemented with little or no financial implications; simply copying all important institution documents and storing the duplicate set off-site can make a major difference in any recovery procedure.

Task 5

Develop the response plan

Step 1

Appoint the response teams

The ERC should work with you, the EPC, and the leaders of the departmental preparedness teams to identify the chain of command in the event of an emergency and to determine appropriate response teams. The structure of these teams depends on the types of threats faced and on the contents of the collection. The preparedness teams may recommend who should participate on the response teams and can develop job descriptions. Once identified, the response teams should participate in the planning process to become familiar with the reasoning that supports every aspect of the emergency plan. The response teams should receive appropriate training (see chapter 5).

Appoint backups for each position, and alternates for the backups. Recognize that the only person present when a disaster occurs may be a night security officer. The only function he or she may need to fulfill is to notify the appropriate staff member and let that person know how best to enter the building. The director and ERC should know staff capabilities *in advance* so that impossible requests and expectations are not made. It is also critical to ensure that, during and after an emergency, team members work sensible shifts and have a chance to rest and eat.

As already discussed, in an emergency the ERC leads the response teams, and you (if you are not also the ERC) and the EPC must be willing to delegate to the ERC the reporting structure for the entire staff during an emergency. Cooperation between the response teams is important. For example, the buildings and maintenance response team must be able to obtain the help it needs to make the building safe enough for people, then to address the needs of the collections.

See chapters 6–9 for more details regarding the roles and responsibilities of departmental response teams.

Questions to Consider

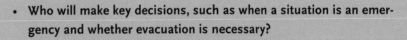

- Who will make key decisions, such as when a situation is an emergency and whether evacuation is necessary?

- Who will be responsible for which functions?

- How will emergency response team members communicate during a crisis? Via bullhorns? Walkie-talkies? Messengers? Where are communication devices stored in the building? Have staff members been trained to use two-way radios?

- Who is responsible for contacting staff members' families?

- Do employees need identification badges so they can be identified quickly by fire officials in an emergency?

Step 2

Compile an emergency procedures handout

What should a receptionist do if she or he receives a bomb threat? What should a security officer do immediately following an earthquake? What should a maintenance worker do if he or she detects a suspicious odor? These are the types of questions that should be answered in a concise document that clearly describes procedures staff should follow in specific emergency situations. The safety and security team will develop a draft of emergency procedures as part of Report 1—it can then be made into a handout and distributed to staff. The handout should give step-by-step instructions on what to do in the event of likely emergencies, including medical emergencies; flooding and water damage; power outages; suspicious behavior and personal safety; chemical spills, gas leaks, and suspicious odors; earthquakes; fires; phone threats, mail threats, and suspicious objects; explosions; and civil disturbances.

Step 3

Compile and write the response plan

Once the departmental preparedness teams have developed the response procedures relevant to their sections and established their response teams as indicated in Report 2 (see page 50), the EPC can then compile the institution's response plan.

The response plan, to be included in the emergency plan handbook, should contain

- a description of the roles of the response teams and the chain of command;
- information on assisting the ERC in setting up a central base of operations—the emergency command center—following a staff evacuation, and establishing who should implement evacuation;
- procedures to be followed for specific emergencies;
- instructions for establishing emergency shelters;
- instructions for providing medical assistance;
- a list of supplies that will be needed, and where these are to be stored;
- information on relocating, evacuating, and/or salvaging objects and important documents;
- contact information for staff and volunteers;
- instructions for setting up a communications and public relations post;
- a directory of external experts to be contacted for support or assistance;
- contact information for the institution's insurance agent;
- instructions for performing damage assessments; and
- information on protecting the building and grounds.

Task 6

Develop recovery procedures

Step 1

Compile information from departmental preparedness teams

Once an emergency situation has stabilized, the recovery process begins. Recovery procedures do not prevent damage that has already occurred; instead, they are intended to guide staff through the cleanup process and minimize further damage to objects. These procedures are to be developed by the preparedness teams.

Recovery procedures fall into four main areas:

Collections recovery. Staff should be given step-by-step instructions on what to do to take the institution from the stabilization of collections damaged in an emergency through their long-term recovery and availability to visitors, scholars, and others. These procedures are developed by the collections team. The team should name leaders and alternates for each aspect of recovery (such as salvage, stabilization, and supplies). Collections recovery procedures should identify a process for determining priorities and offer details on how various objects should be checked for damage from dirt, debris, fire, mold, volcanic ash, water, and so forth.

Data and telecommunications systems recovery. These procedures should guide staff through the reestablishment of full telecommunications services, including recovery of critical automation systems, and the return to normal business operations. These procedures are developed by the safety and security, buildings and maintenance, and administration and records teams.

Financial systems recovery. These procedures should guide staff through the recovery of financial and payroll systems, the reestablishment of historical and current data, and the return to normal activities. These procedures are developed by the administration and records team.

Buildings recovery. Staff should be guided through the stabilization of structural elements and the return to normal operations, including whether outside experts need to be consulted before the buildings are declared safe to reenter. The procedures should detail how buildings should be inspected for damage from fire, dirt, debris, mold, water, and so forth. The procedures also should describe how to clean the air, glass, masonry/concrete/brick, mechanical and electrical systems, metal, plaster and dry wall, tile, porcelain, and woodwork. Conservators may be required to devise cleaning systems for those structural details. These procedures are developed by the buildings and maintenance team.

Step 2
Write the recovery plan

After the departmental preparedness teams have identified the recovery procedures that will move the institution from a state of emergency back to normal operations, this information is turned over to the EPM and EPC and formulated into a recovery plan. The recovery plan, along with the response plan, is incorporated into the emergency plan.

The recovery plan should

- outline the responsibilities of the recovery team and identify team leaders and the chain of command;
- identify how to document damaged areas, objects in the collection, and other assets with photography, video, and written reports;
- identify specialists to be consulted regarding damage to objects or buildings;
- mandate breaks every ninety minutes during recovery procedures, with refreshments provided if possible;
- identify who should handle objects and when handling might be necessary, and provide handling procedures;
- describe the inventory process for all objects processed; and
- describe how volunteers should be signed on and supervised, and provide task sheets for the functions they will perform.

See chapters 6–9 for more information regarding recovery procedures specific to the individual departmental teams.

Task 7
Write the emergency plan

Step 1
Compile the emergency plan

Once all information on preventive measures, preparedness measures, response procedures, and recovery procedures has been gathered from the departmental teams, the emergency plan is written. (Review Fig. 2, page 51.) The emergency plan also should include a description of when to activate response procedures and how to communicate to staff that the institution is operating in emergency mode, as well as when to declare an emergency over.

To be effective, an emergency plan needs

- to have the active support of the director, governing body, and all levels of staff;
- to be simple, focusing mainly on situations most likely to occur;
- to be flexible enough so that it can be effective in unanticipated or unavoidable situations;
- to be realistic in its assessment of museum resources; and
- to be tested at least annually with an emergency drill.

To develop the plan, the EPC must have identified the hazards facing the institution, as well as its assets and vulnerabilities. The plan should incorporate all issues identified by committee members and departmental teams. Ensure that as many staff members as possible have participated in the process. This level of involvement not only educates and motivates staff, but, more important, also taps into all relevant and available knowledge and skills.

The plan should include the following protection measures:

Prevention. Eliminate hazards or reduce their potential harm to people and potential damage to buildings and the collection. For example, if the facility is in a seismic zone, secure objects on display to prevent movement or damage.

Preparedness. Prepare and equip personnel to handle an emergency. For instance, create emergency telephone lists, stockpile supplies, and train staff and volunteers in how to use them.

Response. Prevent injury and limit loss. For example, train staff and volunteers to evacuate visitors, colleagues, collections, and records safely. Response activities are those that can be carried out in the first forty-eight hours after an emergency.

Recovery. In returning operations to normal, make sure that participants are properly trained and guided in making the recovery process as efficient as possible. For example, reestablish telecommunications and financial systems, and inspect buildings for water, fire, and other damage.

The plan must also address the following areas:

Evacuating/relocating staff and the public. Design exit routes for every conceivable location in each building. Be sure to consider the vulnerability of those routes to the identified hazards. Develop procedures for determining if the building is empty, and design a system of checking in so that all staff and visitors can be accounted for. Evacuation or relocation procedures should specify a destination, which may change depending on the emergency. Prescribe protocols for distributing these responsibilities among members of the response teams. Specify the criteria team leaders should use to make decisions. (For additional information, see chapter 6, task 3, pages 124–25.)

Evacuating/relocating objects and records. Develop protocols by which a curator, registrar, preparator or conservator, or the ERC will have the authority to approve the movement of objects and administrative documents. This should include the criteria for making such a decision, as well as for the techniques to be utilized. Procedures for protecting or salvaging various objects, in terms of type and extent of damage, also should be carefully described. Determine who should be trained in these techniques. The plan should identify secure relocation areas. (See chapter 7 for information on evacuating objects, and chapter 9 on evacuating records.)

Ensuring staff and visitor safety. In the emergency plan, provide directions for fast, safe evacuation, and for administering first aid, documenting injuries, securing professional medical assistance, providing follow-up counseling for staff, and so on. Will a first-aid area be set up? With what medical supplies and equipment? Make sure there are sufficient emergency provisions of food, water, blankets, and medical supplies. (See chapter 6 for more information.)

Taking security measures. Design a set of procedures by which your response team and/or security staff will protect personnel and visitors and the collections. You may want to prescribe rules for what people can and cannot do, as well as what areas of the institution should be cordoned off. Plan for every contingency, such as evacuation or relocation, power loss, and even terrified visitors. (See chapter 6 for further information.)

Taking protective measures. Give instructions in the plan for turning off the utilities—such as gas, electricity, and water. Include descriptions of how to prevent or mitigate the effect of an impending threat—for example, how to organize a sandbag effort or board up windows before a storm. Materials that must be on hand should be identified. (See chapter 8 for more information.)

Involving administration. Administrative personnel will be instrumental in protecting or relocating administrative records. Factor their role into the plan, such as gaining access to cash if banks are not open. During certain emergencies, it may be necessary to have a telephone bank set up to enable staff to dispense information. (Further information can be found in chapter 9.)

Assessing the damage. It is likely that your institution's insurance policy stipulates the damage assessment procedures that should be taken. Who should carry out the assessment? Does an insurance agent have to see a damaged object before it is moved? What forms of documentation are required for a claim? Preparedness measures include keeping preprinted damage assessment forms and documentation equipment, such as Polaroid cameras, in an accessible location. (Refer to chapter 9 to learn more.) If the buildings have incurred damage, an assessment (perhaps by an outside agency) is also necessary before staff can be allowed back into the building.

Step 2
Write the emergency plan handbook

Once the EPC has completed a draft of the emergency plan, it should be circulated among staff for comments or discussed at a staff meeting. Feedback from staff at all levels should be considered, as should any fears or expectations, and appropriate revisions should be made as soon as possible. The next step is to use the information in the emergency plan to compile the emergency plan handbook.

The Getty Center's "Emergency Planning Handbook"[3] includes the following:

- policy statement from Stephen D. Rountree, vice president of the J. Paul Getty Trust
- introduction by Wilbur Faulk, director of Getty Center Security
- staff emergency procedures
- summary of the organizational emergency response
- evacuation procedures
- emergency communications
- organizational chart showing the chain of command
- checklists
- fact sheets
- on-site supplies
- off-site resources
- training information

The complexity of an institution's emergency plan depends on a number of factors, including size of the institution, types of hazards identified, number of buildings, and variety of the collections (for example, Mystic Seaport Museum in Mystic, Connecticut, has a collection of ships).

Appendix B contains contents pages from existing emergency plan manuals. One is from a large institution, the Getty Center; the second from a medium-size museum, the Seattle Art Museum; the third from a smaller museum, the Barbados Museum and Historical Society; and the fourth from the Mystic Seaport Museum, which has very specialized needs. The 36 pages of the Barbados Museum and Historical Society's emergency plan serves that institution's purposes well. The Mystic Seaport Museum's "Severe Weather Manual" contains approximately 180 pages and is devoted to the museum's main hazard—potential seaborne disasters.

Notes

1. John P. Barton and Johanna G. Wellheiser, eds., *An Ounce of Prevention: A Handbook on Disaster Contingency Planning for Archives, Libraries, and Record Centers* (Toronto: Toronto Area Archivists Group Education Foundation, 1985), 1. Used by permission.

2. Adapted from Jon. R. Katzenbach and Douglas K. Smith, *The Wisdom of Teams: Creating the High-Performance Organization* (New York: HarperBusiness, 1993).

3. Getty Center, "Emergency Planning Handbook" (J. Paul Getty Trust, Los Angeles, 1997, photocopy).

Chapter Summary

This chapter outlined how to launch an emergency preparedness and response program and lead the emergency preparedness committee through the process of developing an emergency plan. It emphasized the importance of building a cohesive team and working with outside experts such as fire officials. This chapter

- explained the role of the emergency preparedness manager and the emergency preparedness committee in the planning process;

- outlined what the EPM must do to get the EPC working as effectively as possible;

- outlined the role of the departmental preparedness teams and types of information the teams should gather; and

- guided the EPC through the tasks needed to compile the emergency plan and produce the emergency plan handbook.

CHAPTER FOUR

Communications

CHAPTER FOUR

Why Communication Is Important

Communication is not just about devices—it has to do with how you convey information, whether in writing, visually, or orally. It is also about the subliminal messages conveyed "between the lines." And it is about the communications climate you create, as in "no concern is too small" or "the door is always open."

— Barbara Roberts
Conservator and hazard mitigation consultant

An effective communications system is a natural consideration when preparing for emergencies or disasters (Fig. 3). Working closely with the director and emergency response coordinator (ERC), a communications team must be prepared to

- oversee all external communications during an emergency;
- ensure that a clear internal communications system is in place;
- gather, compile, and coordinate information for dissemination through the media;
- gather, compile, and disseminate incoming information regarding the state of the emergency in the area;
- serve as liaison with outside agencies and the community;
- serve as liaison to families of employees and visitors;
- inform donors and/or other institutions of the status of their gifts or loaned objects; and
- manage all outside telephone communications.

Communication can also encompass

- communicating clearly and early on with insurance agents, lawyers, trustees, police departments, emergency agencies, and the media;

Figure 3 A floor warden, holding a megaphone for communicating with her team, as she checks list to verify that all staff members have arrived at the designated location during an evacuation drill at the Getty Center. Photo: Joe Alarcon.

- keeping the emergency plan simple so that it conveys the essentials in a straightforward manner;
- listening to the fears and concerns of staff and remaining open to discussions of sensitive issues or conflicts;
- suggesting ways to help staff members protect their own homes and families;
- providing accurate and adequate information to those involved in developing the emergency plan;
- keeping staff and trustees up to date on the preparedness process;
- informing staff members of their roles during an emergency and providing them with regular training sessions;
- maintaining thorough records of all that happens during drills and actual incidents;
- obtaining honest and thorough feedback on the execution of the plan; and
- providing evacuation maps and instructions in other languages.

The most obvious communications questions may include, How will we transmit internal and incoming information to one another? How can we keep the public informed? What happens if the phones do not work? Who will be in charge of talking to the media?

The emergency plan must address these issues, which are discussed later in this chapter. The bottom line is that good communications before, during, and after a disaster—as well as during the planning process itself—create the potential for full recovery.

A breakdown in communications is not always obvious. Say, for example, that at institution XYZ, the leaders of every department—collections, security, buildings, and administration—all agree that the facility is prepared to respond properly to a disaster. "We have a plan," each of them says. Actually, the institution has four separate plans, and each leader is not familiar with the other three plans. Furthermore, no staff member besides these four people is aware that any plan exists at all.

Unfortunately, all too often one or a few individuals toil in isolation on the emergency plan. Except for a binder that might one day magically appear on desks throughout the institution, nothing else is done to make others aware of the process.

As emergency preparedness manager (EPM), the tone you set during the planning process affects the entire emergency plan and its execution. An effective plan benefits immensely from broad and effective communication during the planning process—internally as well as with outside institutions, such as emergency agencies and the media. Likewise, an effective response to a disaster requires that all persons know the institution's plan and their role in it.

Many emergency planning experts recommend beginning at the personal level. While the emergency preparedness committee (EPC), of which you will be in charge, is convening, create awareness among staff by scheduling presentations or handing out pamphlets from the Red Cross and other agencies that give advice on how to protect home and family during a disaster. Or buy first-aid kits in bulk and sell them to employees at a discount. Doing so can engender goodwill and cooperation for the forthcoming planning process. Barbara Roberts, conservator and hazard mitigation consultant, and Gail Joice, senior deputy director and registrar of the Seattle Art Museum, stress the importance of sending the message that an institution puts staff members and their families first.

The following tasks will help you establish effective communication during the emergency planning process (these are described in detail on the following pages):

Task 1: Focus on building team communications.

Task 2: Equip the preparedness teams with the proper tools and information.

Task 3: Update staff on the progress.

Task 4: Cultivate contacts with outside agencies.

Task 5: Utilize the media.

Task 1

Focus on building team communications

Take the human element into account, encouraging imagination, leadership, cooperation and level-headedness. A lack of any of those qualities will be just as serious as any shortage of blotting paper, plastic sheeting, plywood or rubber boots.[1]

— John E. Hunter
Supervisory staff curator
National Park Service, U.S. Department of the Interior

Having a broad spectrum of participation from all staff ensures that your planning efforts will reflect a wide range of views. Teamwork is essential to a good emergency response program. The following methods help team members communicate and function effectively during the planning process:

Encourage an open, supportive environment. Group members must feel free to contribute ideas and feelings and must believe others will listen. An informal, comfortable, and relaxed atmosphere tends to work best. Encourage frank, constructive criticism devoid of personal attack. Allow members to express their fears and anxieties at the beginning.

Establish a cooperative climate. Members must work to demonstrate mutual trust and respect. The key is coordination, not domination or manipulation. Encourage all team members to participate, keeping discussion pertinent to the group's task. Carefully consider disagreements and seek to resolve them rather than to dominate the dissenter. Seek to reach decisions by consensus.

Make clear assignments and set clear expectations. This makes it harder to drop the ball or pass the buck at meetings. If the team's rules and assignments are not focused, neither will the team's work be. Some rules you may want to consider involve[2]

- attendance (e.g., interruptions to take phone calls are not allowed);
- discussion (e.g., forbidden topics are not allowed);
- constructive confrontation (e.g., helpful criticism and views, not personal attacks, are encouraged); and
- contributions (e.g., everyone does real work).

Schedule debriefing time. Encourage team members to talk with one another in a casual, more personal way after each meeting or presentation. This is the time to stop thinking about emergency or disaster scenarios. It is a time for members to relax, a time to express fears or concerns.

Suggested Exercise

It is important to evaluate all ideas. Rushing to judgment on a suggestion can discourage members from sharing potentially valuable ideas. Ask your group to come up with ten or fifteen deflating statements that people should avoid making during the initial development phase. Here are some examples:

"We tried it before, and it didn't work."

"It's too expensive."

"We could never do that."

"We've never done it that way before."

Task 2

Equip the preparedness teams with the proper tools and information

You cannot expect everybody who is going to take on the responsibility of formulating a disaster response plan to have been through a disaster. You can provide them with a better understanding of the reality through the available resources, such as publications and presentations by people whose entire profession revolves around preparing for disasters.

— Jerry Podany
  Head of antiquities conservation
  The J. Paul Getty Museum

How do you provide the information the preparedness teams need? What information-gathering suggestions can you give to team leaders? Do not let the committee or departmental teams assume that all the information needed exists in their collective experience and knowledge. Here are ways to add to the contributions that team members make:

- Schedule presentations by outside experts, such as representatives from a national emergency organization—for example the Federal Emergency Management Agency (FEMA) in the United States, local fire department officials, and preparedness experts. Staff members are more likely to respect the advice of an authority in the field than that of a colleague. As an added benefit, such presentations provide the most current information. Some public agency personnel will make presentations at no charge.

- Arrange for presentations by local individuals who have actually been through a disaster. These people could be business owners, newspaper reporters, the first person on the scene at a museum emergency, volunteers who helped in recovery efforts, or a National Guard or military officer who assisted in evacuating objects. The details and perspectives they provide are invaluable.

- Screen videos simulating actual disasters. For example, the Seattle Art Museum used the Los Angeles Fire Department's earthquake video to great effect. "It really makes you realize what it is like to be there," says Gail Joice.

- Supply names and telephone numbers of officials in cultural institutions throughout the world that have experienced high-profile disasters, such as the 1993 bombing of Uffizi Gallery in Florence, Italy, or the 1988 fire at the Louisiana State Museum. Depending on your budget, it may be helpful to have team members interview some of these individuals.

- Copy and distribute papers on such topics as the latest earthquake protection measures or dispelling myths on how people act in disasters.

- Provide written accounts of disasters, whether from newspaper archives or museum publications. Photographic documentation is especially effective.

Task 3
Update staff on the progress

Providing regular updates on the progress of planning efforts helps educate staff about preparedness and keeps it fresh in their minds. Updates also help build confidence in the institution. "There is the important subliminal message for the staff that the museum is making a conscientious effort to care for its visitors, its collections—and them," remarks John Walsh, director of the J. Paul Getty Museum.[3]

To maintain staff interest, alternate standard memos with more creative means of disseminating information. A few examples:

- Display in the staff room a pictorial exhibit of protective measures the institution is implementing.
- Prop a poster-size disaster picture on an easel, accompanied by a bulleted list titled, "What We Are Doing to Prevent This." List important preparedness measures the museum is implementing.
- Videotape protection efforts throughout the building, from building new storage-room shelving to installing quick-release mounts to filling emergency supply crates. Screen the video for the entire museum staff. Keep the presentation short, and conduct a question-and-answer period afterward. The tape can also be used in workshops with other institutions.

Input from staff can be solicited by setting up an emergency suggestion box. You can also gather feedback and input by circulating a questionnaire among staff. Informed workers who feel their opinions count make more-eager participants. Also be sure to keep the board of trustees up to date. Make preparedness updates a regular agenda item for the board and/or invite trustees to presentations, or make emergency preparedness the focus of the next board retreat.

Task 4
Cultivate contacts with outside agencies

Making contact with external businesses, institutions, and individuals *before* something happens is an integral part of emergency preparedness. Doing so leads to faster response time during incidents and can help streamline the recovery process. For example, do local fire department officials know where the chemical storage areas are and where *not* to spray water through the windows? Can you schedule informal meetings with these officials for the exchange of such information?

Similarly, establish a relationship with local hardware and other supply stores ahead of time. Decide who should be authorized to make purchases there in the event of an emergency, and whether cash, credit cards, or a line of credit should be used.

If your institution does not have a conservator on staff, contact the nearest conservation facility or private laboratory and make sure its staff knows what type of collection you have. Does the conservator or facility have the expertise the collection requires, or will you have to make contact with a specialized conservation consultant?

Any tool that reduces the chaos of the moment improves the chances of recovering precious objects and stabilizing the buildings after disaster strikes. One useful tool is *The Emergency Response and Salvage Wheel* produced by the National Institute for the Conservation of Cultural Property.[4]

Questions to Consider

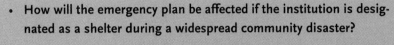

- How will the emergency plan be affected if the institution is designated as a shelter during a widespread community disaster?

- Have you discussed with local authorities whether the institution is listed as a priority for assistance? (Remember to mention that the institution is host to school groups and other public tours.)

- Is there a complete, easy-to-read list of emergency telephone numbers for local authorities, and are copies posted in areas that would enable immediate access?

- Are all lists of phone numbers, including temporary storage locations, current?

- Is the local utility company aware of the institution's urgent need to have power restored immediately after an emergency?

Task 5

Utilize the media

Contrary to public opinion, the media can be a helpful resource rather than the source of problems. In fact, you can use the media to your benefit throughout a disaster and its aftermath. Take advantage of the opportunity *during* the planning process to publicize your efforts. Doing so lets the public know the institution cares about the safety of its visitors, increases public awareness about emergency preparedness, and helps raise money to pay for protective measures. Here are a few ideas:

- Invite the media to one of your drills, either to cover the drill or to participate and act out their part, or both.
- Suggest a story to the local newspapers or television stations about the unique aspects of emergency preparedness in regard to the institution's collection.
- Send out regular press releases to publicize unique aspects of the plan, photo opportunities, preparedness speakers scheduled to appear at the institution, upcoming staff drills, or volunteer training sessions. Though you may never see an article out of the releases, this "drip system" approach keeps your institution in the minds of reporters and editors.
- Publicize a fund-raising event to benefit emergency preparedness efforts.

Be prepared for the media. Have background materials on your institution, its collections, and the emergency plan written in advance. Make it your responsibility to ensure that reporters get accurate information. Also, know and respect reporters' deadlines. Make it easy, not hard, for them to do a story.

Developing an Effective Communications Program

It is much easier to respond positively in a difficult situation if you are aware of what is happening. The goal of any effective emergency plan is to keep the lines of communication open in both directions so that information and instructions can reach all staff. It is also essential that communications remain rapid and accurate. The absence of these attributes can result in inappropriate or inefficient responses to subsequent problems.

The following tasks will help you and the EPC develop a simple, flexible, and effective communications program for the overall emergency plan (each task is discussed more fully on the following pages):

Task 1: Evaluate equipment needs.

Task 2: Establish emergency communications procedures.

Task 3: Set guidelines for dealing with the media.

Task 4: Plan for the unexpected.

Task 5: Establish communications procedures for recovery.

Task 1

Evaluate equipment needs

Suggested Exercise

How many alternatives to standard, in-house telephone service can you name in one minute?

There is no denying that communications in the event of a disaster—particularly a regional disaster—will be difficult. Telephone lines, if they are working at all, will probably be jammed, and if lines are down, even power backup systems may be useless. You need an alternate means to stay in touch. As technology surges ahead, more and more alternatives to regular telephone service have been developed that could be employed in a disaster.

What answers did you come up with—cellular phones, walkie-talkies, handheld radios? Pay phones are often the first to be restored in a disaster. What about e-mail? And what if none of the above works or is available? One solution is to rely on one of the oldest forms of communication known to humans: runners. Staff members can set out on bicycle or on foot.

Start by determining what the institution has on hand now. You may want to identify which staff members have personal cellular phones. What is the best backup, given the particular risks associated with the location and based on your budget? The publication *A Manual of Basic Museum Security*[5] identifies the following emergency communication options:

- voice communications
- hand signals
- written reports
- signs and graphics with rules and regulations
- whistle signals
- flashlight signals
- bell signals

- electric light signals
- telephone signals
- sirens and horns (fire)
- radio communication
- coded announcements
- intercoms

Questions to Consider

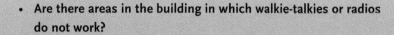

- Are there areas in the building in which walkie-talkies or radios do not work?

- Do all staff members know how to use the communications equipment?

- Does any equipment require batteries or chargers? Are the batteries installed? Are replacements on hand? What is the source of power for battery chargers? Are they regularly tested? Whose responsibility is this?

- Are alternative devices stored throughout the building, including in storage areas?

- Does anyone on staff have a ham radio license? Is there an association you can connect with during an emergency, such as the Amateur Radio Emergency Association (AREA)?

- Should runners obtain signatures to document that the messages they carry were delivered to their intended destination?

- Is the telephone list of emergency numbers located near each emergency telephone? Do staff members have a copy at their desks?

- If the institution has a public announcement system, is it sufficiently audible in all rooms? If not, how will you get evacuation and other emergency information to everyone in the building?

- Are telephones installed in the elevators?

Regardless of the alternative methods you choose, make sure that the emergency command center, established by the ERC, is able to communicate with any unit of your operation. If the emergency is confined to the building, you may be able to have the telephone company restore service quickly or install new phones to handle the increased volume of calls.

Task 2
Establish emergency communications procedures

You and the communications coordinator (or designated institution spokesperson if no coordinator has been appointed) are to establish the procedures to follow during an actual emergency. Both internal procedures (how information is communicated within the organization) and procedures pertaining to people and agencies outside the institution need to be addressed. As with every emergency response team member's role, the specific procedural responsibilities of the communications coordinator should be rehearsed during drills to identify any weak links in communications. Don't wait until an actual emergency to discover and resolve these problems. See chapter 5 for more training-related activities.

Step 1
Address internal communications

Emergency communications procedures begin the moment the response plan goes into effect, but because communication can be greatly reduced for a considerable period of time during an emergency, how will staff and visitors know that the plan has been activated? Will an announcement be broadcast over a public address system? Will workers use the "buddy system" to make sure staff and visitors are safe and accounted for?

Emergencies and disasters often seem to happen at the worst possible time and under the worst possible conditions. In other words, bad wiring could start a fire at 2 A.M. in a locked corner office during a rare blizzard, when only a substitute security officer is on duty. Although this is not a highly likely scenario, it emphasizes the possibility that staff will be at home when disaster strikes, which brings up various concerns your planning should address.

If disaster strikes during work hours, predesignated people can step in and fill the emergency team roles to which they were appointed. These individuals, however, may be preoccupied with the safety of their families and homes. An effective solution is to have one person—most likely the human resources director—be in charge of contacting families. The Seattle Art Museum's solution is to allow small groups of people to go to the communications center to call loved ones. "If the situation allows for it, that is the more humane approach," explains Gail Joice. Your institution probably has pay phones on-site, which generally are the most reliable after a disaster.

Suggested Exercise

As you prepare this section of the emergency plan, it is helpful to imagine various worst-case scenarios and what kind of response is best in each. Be specific. The more details you include, the more realistic the exercise and the more useful the results. Envision the water rising in your office or hear the wind snapping telephone poles. Imagine the worst that can happen, from a communications standpoint, then imagine you had two days to prepare for the disaster. What would you do? How would it be different if you had no time to prepare? What could you do now to prepare for such a scenario?

This exercise helps guide you toward an effective response plan.

Questions to Consider

- How will staff members communicate with the institution if the emergency happens when they are at home?

- Under what circumstances should staff stay at home?

- Are there key people who should get to the institution even if they have to walk miles?

- Do you have an up-to-date telephone list of emergency staff phone numbers? Have you distributed copies of the list to all staff for both office and home reference?

- Are emergency team roles clear for those who can make it to the site?

- Do staff members keep an out-of-state emergency contact number on hand in case phone system breakdowns prevent them from reaching their families directly?

Here are a few good rules of thumb for communicating during an emergency:

- Keep each communication to a minimum.
- Never give more than three instructions (two are ideal) at a time, and keep them short.
- Give instructions in writing. This practice results in more efficient communications.

Many preparedness experts recommend thoroughly and meticulously recording the entire response, salvage, and recovery phases—both for insurance purposes and to benefit the institution in evaluating the effectiveness of the plan. Neither you nor any of your colleagues will remember the myriad details of the operation a month later. Assign one person to be the recorder—ideally, a member of a response team. Document all actions in writing or with images. If photographic or video equipment is unavailable, it may be possible to roughly sketch an object or a scene. Tape-recording observations is also a quick method.

Step 2
Address external communications

The appendixes to the emergency plan should contain instructions for contacting outside agencies and individuals (i.e., police and fire departments, utilities, hospitals, insurance agents, technical experts, etc.), along with notes about services offered. Always date the list and update it periodically. Consider contingency plans for contacting these agencies if normal communications are down or overloaded.

If the institution closes, the communications coordinator will need to inform not only the media but also such entities as the local convention and visitors bureau, scheduled group tour organizers, paid tour guides, and volunteers. It is essential to contact your board officers, or at least the chair/president of the board, to notify them of the emergency and the institution's status. Also consider contacting key local officials (mayor, governor, etc.), trustees, and others to appeal for assistance.

Other considerations need to be made for visitors during a crisis. For example, if walkie-talkies or public address systems are used, establish code names for certain emergency situations so that you can notify staff without causing undue panic among visitors. Avoid alarmist terms such as *code red*. Have staff practice using radios and following rules of essential communication to avoid blocking the channels with useless talk.

You may also wish to acquire maps and evacuation instructions in other languages. What are the predominant languages spoken by visitors to the institution? The J. Paul Getty Museum identified nineteen languages among and now publishes maps in a multitude of languages.

Step 3
Set guidelines for working with volunteer emergency workers

It is not unlikely, especially during a regional disaster, that in the aftermath the institution will be inundated with well-meaning volunteers eager to help. Develop in advance a system that helps you effectively use the skills and energy of these volunteers. The effectiveness of their assistance depends on the effectiveness of your communication with them. *Protecting the Past from Natural Disasters*[6] offers the following suggestions for working with volunteers:

- Clarify expectations on each side.
- Define jobs to be done.
- Set specific goals, weighing costs against benefits.
- Persuade volunteers to do needed work that they may not have envisioned, such as answering telephones.
- Provide recognition for the volunteers' contributions, from public thanks to free lunches, if the budget permits.
- Say no to volunteers if you cannot adequately direct them.

Task 3

Set guidelines for dealing with the media

Dealing with the media is one of the most critical tasks in an emergency. How your institution responds to a crisis within the first twenty-four hours can have a lasting impact on its public image and relationship with the media. Working with the media both before and after an emergency can turn them into a resource rather than a problem source.

The following basic steps will help you, your communications coordinator, and your staff deal wisely with the media. The publications *Steal This Handbook! A Template for Creating a Museum's Emergency Preparedness Plan*[7] and *Maritime Museum Emergency and Disaster Preparedness and Recovery Manual*[8] have been used as references.

Step 1

Establish rules for handling reporters

The basic rule for staff to know regarding interacting with reporters is that staff members should *not* interact with them. Advise employees not to start rumors or gossip about the emergency situation and to avoid making casual remarks that could be picked up and disseminated. Such remarks could be embarrassing or inaccurate or could cause a public relations problem. Every staff member should be trained in how to use communications equipment and in how to conduct himself or herself with the media. Role-playing is a particularly good way to practice the latter (see chapter 5 for more information).

Urge all staff to follow these additional rules:

- Never say "No comment." Explain that the communications coordinator will provide the information when and if it becomes available. Do not hesitate to say "I don't know."
- Avoid all speculation of cause or blame, especially if authorities are investigating the event.
- Keep information that might be damaging to the institution or to an individual confidential.
- Do not release the names of injured individuals or fatalities until family members have been notified.

Step 2

Know how to create a good news release

Remember, the media will report an emergency whether you like it or not. This is the opportunity to influence what the media will say. The following are general rules governing news releases for emergency events. These rules can be adapted for other types of releases, such as an appeal for volunteer assistance. The communications coordinator should use this opportunity to influence what will be reported; in other words, provide sufficient, accurate information while maintaining control of how much information is disseminated.

- Date the news release and use the words "For immediate release" at the top. Provide information on the person to be contacted for more details—usually the communications coordinator.
- Answer these questions in the first few sentences: What happened? Why and how did it happen (if known)? When and where did it take place? Who was involved?
- State all the facts clearly and concisely. You may, however, need to omit certain details if they interfere with an investigation or compromise a policy of donor confidentiality. Reassure the public, if possible, that the majority of the most valued holdings are safe.
- Never divulge the value of damaged or destroyed objects. Instead, indicate that they are irreplaceable and/or have research value, or report, "We have considerable loss and are trying to substantiate the dollar damage." One museum lost credibility in the eyes of its community after initially estimating its losses at US$1 million, then revising that amount to US$700,000 the following day and, two years later, increasing it to US$8 million, and counting.
- Assure the public that the institution is aware of what happened, is cooperating with the authorities, and has initiated its emergency response plan, and that a team of trained personnel is at the site working as quickly as possible to resume normal operations. Say that you will continue to provide all appropriate information to the media.
- Indicate what steps have been taken to correct the situation and to prevent or minimize its recurrence.
- Avoid placing or taking blame.

Use news releases to give the "hard news," the basic facts about the incident. A photograph with a short caption can add visual impact and improve the chances of getting coverage. It is also helpful to provide background information so that a reporter can fill out the story. For example, summarize the institution's history or give a biographical sketch of the artist of a damaged painting. Prepare whatever information you can in advance and store it with the emergency supply kits. The director should approve all releases, with a copy going to the trustees when possible.

Step 3
Learn how to handle interviews

When giving an interview, whether for print or electronic media, follow the guidelines in step 2 for creating a good news release. Before the interview, review the key points you want to emphasize. Rehearse, if necessary. Here are some additional suggestions:

- As in step 1, say "I don't know" rather than "No comment," adding that you will attempt to find the answer. Focus on facts rather than on opinions. Do not speculate.
- Use simple, descriptive language, and do not ramble.
- Make your message clear. Repeat it if necessary.
- Be consistent with each reporter.
- Relax and be as positive as possible.
- Listen carefully to a question before answering it.
- For a print interview, prepare written materials to support your statements and have them on hand.
- State that monetary donations will be gratefully received and will be put to good use to preserve the collections.

For television interviews:

- Choose an appropriate location; do not let cameras impede the recovery process.
- Give the reporter your undivided attention.
- Ignore accompanying cameras, microphones, and technicians.
- Keep your answers short and clear. Correct any inaccurate information contained in the questions.
- Again, state that donations of money will be gratefully received and will be put to good use to preserve the collections.
- After the interview, ask when the tape will air. Obtain a tape later to complement your documentation of the event.

Task 4
Plan for the unexpected

Before cellular phones were available, a major storm made its way onto Connecticut's shoreline the very day the telephone system at Mystic Seaport Museum was being changed. Putting the communications portion of its comprehensive and well-rehearsed emergency plan into action required a great many quarters for use at the pay phones. (At least someone had thought to have quarters on hand!) Planning for the unexpected is essential; it is like having a backup plan for the backup plan.

When the unexpected happens, on-the-spot ingenuity is called for, which can be fostered during the planning process. During the 1994 power outage at the Seattle Art Museum (see pages 24–25), the museum's spokesperson quickly got word to the media that the museum would be closed. Despite this effort, the museum still had crowds of people knocking on its doors, wondering why it was closed and when it would reopen. Admissions staff volunteered to take turns standing outside in the frosty, biting wind to inform people. Meanwhile, the museum had a graphic design employee make signs to put on the doors. Senior staff members communicated their appreciation to the museum workers by joining them on-site and bringing them hot coffee and pastries.

Task 5

Establish communications procedures for recovery

The tone and timing of postdisaster communications affect the entire recovery operation, from how workers are accommodated to how effectively the media are handled. In building the plan, consider the following steps.

Step 1

Make information a priority

The smallest historical societies could have collections that mean more to their particular communities than anything at the Metropolitan Museum in New York City does.

— Barbara Roberts
Conservator and hazard mitigation consultant

The more information staff members have about a disaster and about the institution's status and problems, the better they are able to cope and assist in the event of an emergency. When that information is accurate and direct, it leaves less room for rumors and untruths to disrupt the recovery process. In the aftermath of a disaster, consider scheduling sessions with the entire staff or in smaller groups. Tell employees what happened, what has been done about it, what is in progress, how the institutution is doing, and so forth.

You may be in a situation in which the community cares deeply about the institution and its heritage. There may be people outside weeping. Look for the positive side in the situation and communicate it to the community. For example, name some of the precious works of art or artifacts that are safe.

If you need to communicate with large groups of people, consider using flyers. For example, following Hurricane Hugo in 1989, the Preservation Society of Charleston quickly produced and circulated a flyer suggesting that owners of historic buildings install temporary roofing until proper materials and help could be obtained. Similarly, preservation officials in California found themselves fighting the unwarranted rush to demolish historic buildings that had been red-tagged after the Loma Prieta earthquake in 1989. Several preservation organizations launched a "second opinion" campaign by distributing information packages detailing alternatives to demolition. This information went to government administrators and officials, preservation groups, architects, and others, and succeeded in saving hundreds of houses. The packages included lists of essential information, such as qualified structural engineers, loan sources, and suggested preservation strategies.

This type of education can consitute a major part of the communications responsibilities after an event. If the community or region looks to the institution for expertise, consider offering any of the following:

- standard conservation and/or recovery literature
- technical consultation or services
- seminars for contractors or other recovery-related workers

- workshops on specific topics, such as general salvage techniques for heirlooms
- access to your institution's list of suppliers

Step 2

Build debriefing and counseling sessions into the plan

Taking care of yourself and your workers will help you better care for the collections after disaster strikes. Depending on the size of the institution, this is an important and time-consuming responsibility that cannot be assumed by the communications coordinator, the ERC, or the EPM. A human resources coordinator should be assigned to this role.

Debriefing for all workers participating in the response and recovery effort should take place every day from the beginning of an incident. A debriefing is a specific, focused intervention to help employees deal with the intense emotions that are common at such a time.[9] Encourage staff members to voice their concerns and feelings. A local community mental health center can help set up the debriefing and assist in incorporating crisis counseling into the plan. It is normal to feel depressed to some degree after a disaster. Discuss this and other stress reactions with staff. You may want to arrange for a mental health professional to address the debriefing. People may have strong and conflicting emotions to deal with, particularly if there is death or widespread destruction.

Staff members who feel the need to stop working must be allowed to freely communicate this to officials. Look for signs of stress among workers (e.g., fatigue, anger, and fear). Early identification and intervention are key to preventing worker burnout. Breaks should be mandatory, particularly when it becomes evident that worker effectiveness is diminishing. Bathroom facilities—even if they are improvised—must be provided, as well as food and beverages, shelter, and a place to sit or lie down. Paying attention to—and planning ahead for—the mental well-being of workers conserves a precious resource that is necessary for the months or years it may take for the institution to fully recover.

Step 3

Be on the lookout for media opportunities

Though they bring destruction and damage, disasters also bring opportunities to repair, replace, and rehabilitate buildings and collections, raising them to standards higher than those that existed before. This is made possible through the fund-raising and promotional campaigns generated after a disaster. Knowing how to work with the press, especially if good relations with key media personalities have been established beforehand, can affect how well the museum survives—and even thrives—in a postdisaster climate.

For the next four to six months following an emergency event, public awareness of the need for emergency preparedness will be at an all-time high. There is no better time to launch a fund-raising effort to help pay for recovery, to build a new facility, or to put mitigation and preparedness measures into effect. A well-prepared museum director has a ready "wish list" to capitalize on the opportunity. As EPM, discuss this with the director.

This is also the time to promote crucial public relations efforts, such as the "second opinion" campaign that saved hundreds of historic California houses from demolition after the Loma Prieta earthquake (see step 1, page 84). Or, once the city or town has been made safe, organize a community campaign to let tourists know that business is back to normal. This fosters good relations with emergency organizations and other individuals to publicly acknowledge a job well done. For instance, if the fire department provided extraordinary service, acknowledge it in a news release.

Look for the human-interest stories that would attract the media and cast a positive light on the institution. Twenty-four hours after a devastating hurricane struck in 1996, the Museum of Antigua and Barbuda reopened its doors to become a sanctuary for displaced schoolchildren while anxious parents worked to put their lives back together again.

Step 4
Evaluate the plan and its execution

After a disaster—even after every training drill—it is essential to hold a "post-mortem" discussion of the emergency plan to evaluate what was learned from the experience.[10] First, thank all who contributed, acknowledging each staff member individually for her or his role in the response effort. The discussion must be as free and open as possible to determine what went wrong, what went right, and why. Stay focused on the topic. Too often, this process turns into a potpourri of after-the-fact justifications and defenses of what people did, rather than a candid assessment of problems encountered or improvements needed.

Avoid finding fault (except in extreme cases) and indicate the institution's desire to learn from the entire experience. Encourage an atmosphere of honest self-assessment by starting with yourself. What could you have done differently? What would have worked better? How could you improve next time? What was learned that could be applied to the next emergency?

Questions to Consider

- Have you maintained good records of what happened during the event, and have you asked for thorough feedback from all involved persons?

- Have you followed up with local authorities to ask for their input on how to make the plan work better in the future?

- Did backup equipment (cellular phones, radios, backup generators, portable systems, off-site computer networks) work as planned?

- Were the communications systems within the site and with external agencies effective?

- Was there a network in place to check on, protect, and attend to staff and visitors throughout the entire site?[11]

Notes

1. John E. Hunter, "Preparing a Museum Disaster Plan," in *Southeastern Museums Conference, 1991 Disaster Preparedness Seminar Proceedings*, ed. Martha E. Battle and Pamela Meister (Baton Rouge, La.: Southeastern Museums Conference, 1991), 53–66.

2. Jon R. Katzenbach and Douglas K. Smith, *The Wisdom of Teams: Creating the High-Performance Organization* (New York: HarperBusiness, 1993), 119–27.

3. Getty Conservation Institute, "Emergency Preparedness and Response," *Conservation: The GCI Newsletter* 7 (winter 1992), 11–12.

4. *The Emergency Response and Salvage Wheel* (Washington, D.C.: National Institute for the Conservation of Cultural Property, 1997) is a rotating slide chart that provides information on emergency response steps and salvage procedures. It was developed in cooperation with the National Task Force on Emergency Response, an initiative that also involved FEMA and the Getty Conservation Institute. It can be purchased by contacting the National Task Force, 3299 K St. NW, Washington, DC 20007.

5. Robert B. Burke and Sam Adeloye, *A Manual of Basic Museum Security* (Leicester, Great Britain: International Council of Museums and the International Committee on Museum Security, 1986), 77. Reproduced by permission of the ICOM Committee for Conservation.

6. Carl L. Nelson, *Protecting the Past from Natural Disasters* (Washington, D.C.: Preservation Press, National Trust for Historic Preservation, 1991), 111.

7. Adapted from Allyn Lord, Carolyn Reno, and Marie Demeroukas, *Steal This Handbook! A Template for Creating a Museum's Emergency Preparedness Plan* (Columbia, S.C.: Southeastern Registrars Association, 1994), 193–94. Used by permission.

8. Adapted from Council of American Maritime Museums, chap. 9 in *Maritime Museum Emergency and Disaster Preparedness and Recovery Manual* (Manitowoc, Wisc.: Council of American Maritime Museums, 1995), 10–12. Used by permission.

9. Mary H. Lystad, "People in Emergencies," in *Perspectives on Natural Disaster Mitigation: Papers Presented at 1991 AIC Workshop* (Washington, D.C.: Foundation of the American Institute for Conservation of Historic and Artistic Works, 1991), 24.

10. D. Allatt, "Preventive Maintenance in a Museum Facility" (proceedings of the Canadian Museums Association Security Special Interest Group Emergency Planning Workshop, Victoria Memorial Museum Building, Ottawa, Canada, March 25–26, 1986).

11. Gail Joice, "Questions to Ask Yourself When Preparing a Disaster Plan" (AAM Risk Management and Insurance Committee, American Association of Museums, Washington, D.C., April 1994, typescript).

Chapter Summary

This chapter described the importance of communications to the overall effectiveness of the emergency response plan and, ultimately, to the success of your recovery efforts. As EPM, you must look at communications broadly—not solely as a matter of devices but as a way to convey essential information so that it is heard and understood, both during the planning process and in actual emergency situations.

The chapter also

- identified tasks to help establish communications in an emergency preparedness and response program;

- described how to evaluate communications equipment needs;

- described the responsibilities of the communications coordinator;

- explained how to establish communications procedures for emergency situations and during the recovery; and

- described guidelines for dealing with the media.

CHAPTER FIVE

Training

No emergency plan will be successful if staff and other relevant personnel—such as volunteers—are not properly trained. As emergency preparedness manager (EPM), you must provide guidance and support in making sure employees and volunteers have the knowledge and skills to respond effectively, efficiently, and appropriately in an emergency situation. Drills, debriefings, and training sessions must be conducted regularly. In addition, the psychological impact on employees of emergency preparedness training—as well as that of the emergency itself—must be addressed. As EPM, you must also foster teamwork and team-building skills.

Where do you start? The questions in Table 6 are designed to help you assess the current level of your staff's readiness in the event of an emergency. If you cannot answer at least three of the questions in the affirmative, your employees—and your institution—are not as prepared as they should be.

A year after your institution's emergency plan has been formulated and published, take the test again. It will provide a measure of the progress that has been made. You may be quite encouraged by the results.

Why Training Is Important

According to Red Cross information, people normally operate at about 20 percent of their ability to make decisions during an emergency. Therefore, you need to be able to do things in an emergency almost by rote. With training, you can professionally accomplish what needs to be done even if a great deal of your brain is essentially shut down from disbelief, shock, and fear. The first training priority is to involve everybody. This is not just something done by the top administrators or a few people down the ladder who handle security. It is not something that can be done by a person with a megaphone. We need to do this as a team.

— Barbara Roberts
Conservator and hazard mitigation consultant

Table 6   **Is Your Staff Prepared?**

	YES	NO	UNSURE
Do all staff members know how to use a fire extinguisher, turn off water and power, and activate alarms?			
Do staff members have enough opportunities to practice the tasks they are expected to perform quickly in a crisis?			
Are staff members encouraged to volunteer for response teams at other institutions that are experiencing emergencies so they can obtain real-life experience?			
Have personnel been taught how to carry fragile objects, and trained to assess when to move collections and when to wait for conservators or art handlers?			
Are volunteers included in emergency drills, playing the roles of injured persons or put in positions where they might have to report on or respond to a crisis?			
Does the emergency plan include lists of staff and volunteers who have gone through first-aid and CPR training?			
Do nonconservators know which objects in the collection are most sensitive to extreme fluctuations in relative humidity?			
Have local police and fire officials been consulted about the institution's special needs? Have they been asked to help with training?			
Are step-by-step directions posted near all emergency equipment, and are staff members aware of their existence?			
Do appropriate persons know where the water shut-off valves are located? What about the electrical switch, fuse panels, or controls for heating and air-conditioning units? Do these individuals know how to safely turn these off?			
Have staff members been assigned responsibility for handling media inquiries during a crisis and received appropriate training?			
Has a team been trained to conduct an initial site survey after the building is determined safe?			
Has this team been trained to document damage to artifacts, equipment, and the building with videotape, photographs, and written observations?			
As a training procedure, have you included a telephone/messenger exercise to locate and notify staff members of an emergency?			
Have staff members been trained in how to handle a bomb threat?			

Why train? The answer is simple: Training can prevent some disasters by preparing you and other staff members to function as efficiently as possible, despite the ensuing chaos. Training also helps cultivate teamwork, a crucial factor in an emergency situation. When people feel they have a stake in the institution, they are more likely to take their responsibilities in an emergency seriously. Being included in the process also allows people at all levels to provide valuable suggestions necessary to the development of a first-rate emergency plan that is tailor-made for the institution.

The message of placing people first must be emphasized, no matter how the training program is structured. In an emergency, saving lives must be the first priority.

Basic training methods include

- group discussions
- simulations/role-plays
- supplementary handouts
- instructional brochures or signs
- videos
- review sessions
- self-assessment exercises
- hands-on workshops
- presentations by experts
- field trips
- mental drills
- full drills

Who Should Be Trained?

Everyone on the staff—administrators, curators, docents, security officers, and custodians—should be prepared for worst-case scenarios. The importance of involving all staff in emergency training can manifest itself in large and small ways. At the Barbados Museum and Historical Society, a new, untrained custodial worker failed to realize the significance of the mold that was forming around an air-conditioning unit in a room containing historical maps. Only when a trained person saw the mold a day or two later was the problem reported to senior management and addressed. "Training helps make people more comfortable with a potentially dangerous situation and psychologically prepared and better organized," says Alissandra Cummins, director of the Barbados Museum.

Most staff members need to practice evacuation procedures, basic object handling, and salvage techniques. At some museums, administrators encourage employees to take training efforts seriously by informing them that emergency preparedness is a priority that cannot be ignored, and that employees who do so could suffer the consequences. That is the approach taken at the Mystic Seaport Museum, which has been battered by numerous blizzards and severe storms and which seems to be hit by a major hurricane every five years or so. "With bad weather always a threat, no one can afford to shirk his or her responsibilities," emphasizes David Mathieson, the museum's supervisor of conservation.

Each spring, the Mystic Seaport Museum's emergency plan is updated. All staff members must update and revise their section of the plan. If the new material does not meet the museum's standards, it is sent back to the appropriate personnel. "If an acceptable draft is not finished by the deadline, the person responsible cannot go on vacation—and this has happened," Mathieson continues. "We take this very seriously." For administrators who favor this approach, he adds, the deadlines for completing the emergency plan could be set to coincide with annual salary evaluations.

As staff members develop skills, keep in mind that a major emergency will bring outsiders to the institution's door with offers of untrained assistance. These volunteers may be community members, military personnel, or other emergency workers eager to help protect, evacuate, or salvage objects. Decide in advance how you are going to use these untrained volunteers. Consider training a portion of the staff to give on-the-spot training.

"Whatever cannot be done in advance has to be done by instructional word-of-mouth by a group of people who were trained beforehand," explains Jerry Podany, head of antiquities conservation at the J. Paul Getty Museum. Basic training can include the following:

- emergency procedures, including fire drills
- employee identification procedures
- last-person-out responsibilities
- security and building procedures during open and closed hours
- responsibilities when issued keys
- locking of safes and high-security vaults
- special-access responsibilities with alarmed areas, key cards, vault or safe combinations, and access lists
- emergency and general information numbers to use
- first aid and CPR
- security/fire/safety inspections and responsibilities
- occupational safety
- reporting procedures for observed safety hazards
- object handling and protection procedures

Where to Start?

One of the most effective things we can do to prepare for emergencies is to provide ourselves with training and an increased awareness of disaster response.[1]

— The Getty Center
   "Emergency Planning Handbook"

To many, fire drills are a joke. Ever since we were young, we have participated in emergency evacuation exercises without really thinking about what would happen in an actual emergency. This passive attitude has become a habit that must be broken. Many people are apathetic toward emergency preparedness and response training. That is what the administrators at the Seattle Art Museum discovered when they launched an ambitious training program. "At the start, we had trouble getting people to take this seriously," says Gail Joice, the museum's senior deputy director and registrar. "There is an initial resistance, a fear of the unknown, and some people are in denial."

Therefore, the first task you, as emergency preparedness manager (EPM), face in training is to engage staff members. You may wish to start your effort on the anniversary of an emergency, just to give staff and the community more reasons to take the emergency preparedness and response training seriously. Take care, however, to dispel the fears that will naturally occur when you ask people to contemplate the worst. The following activities will cost little or no money, while making those who participate feel they are part of a team:

Task 1: Carry out a general cleanup.

Task 2: Teach staff to be keen observers.

Task 3: Bring in other experts to teach certain skills.

Task 4: Conduct a basic fire extinguisher lesson.

Task 5: Expand the fire drills.

Task 6: Test the notification system.

Task 7: Encourage staff to bring emergency preparedness home.

Task 8: Teach staff members how and when to handle objects.

Task 9: Make emergency-related mental drills a common occurrence.

Task 10: Conduct planned drills.

Task 11: Anticipate psychological impact.

Task 12: Build the team.

Task 13: Record and critique.

Task 14: Evaluate the training program.

Task 1

Carry out a general cleanup

As a team project, get staff members involved in throwing out rubbish. This exercise serves as a morale booster and also reduces the hazards every cultural institution faces. In fact, most museum emergencies are caused or worsened by inferior housekeeping, poorly maintained equipment, or improper use of the building. Once the debris is gone, people can put the empty spaces to better use. The cleanup also helps people become more acquainted with the layout of the institution, including escape routes that might be needed someday.

Recommend that staff members wear jeans or old clothing for the cleaning. The casual atmosphere will make them more receptive to listening to basic safety precautions. The following is a sampling of the safety tips you can impress on staff during this exercise:

- Do not store anything near heating vents or boiler rooms.
- Store heavy objects on lower shelves.
- Avoid placing items directly underneath water pipes.
- Store paints, chemicals, and cleaners in well-ventilated, fireproof cabinets.
- Keep motors free of dust buildup, and make sure appliance cords are in good shape.

- Check trash receptacles at the end of the day for smoldering materials. Empty them every night.
- Store works of art and artifacts in closed containers or protective bags made of chemically inert materials, which provide air circulation and filter out particulates.
- If the institution is in a seismic area, secure or strap down computers, fax machines, computer scanners, bookcases, and other office equipment to the walls or furniture. If securing to a wall, make sure to drive the attachment into a stud.
- Unplug electrical equipment, such as dry-mount machines, tacking irons, and portable electric heaters after use, and be careful as to where heat-producing equipment is stored.
- Unplug computers during thunderstorms or if a storm is forecast for that night, and change surge protectors every three to four years.

Task 2
Teach staff to be keen observers

A clerk in the gift shop spots a dark stain on the ceiling, indicative of a water leak. An information desk volunteer notices a visitor acting strangely in the entryway or waiting area. A maintenance worker discovers a pile of trash left by construction workers near a heat vent. Each person noticed something unusual that had the potential to become an emergency situation.

Staff members must be empowered to report their observations and be made to understand that this is considered part of their job duties. Provide training in observation techniques. Volunteers also must be instructed in basic security measures, as they can provide a vital link in the security chain. Consult members of the safety and security team for more training ideas.

Task 3
Bring in other experts to teach certain skills

An easy way to reduce some of the training burden for an institution is to turn to organizations that specialize in emergency preparedness.

Other cultural institutions. There is no sense in reinventing the wheel. Take advantage of the expertise of other institutions that already have developed training programs. Keep in mind that every emergency plan will be unique, and not everything one institution does will be applicable to yours. Consult directors of other cultural institutions that have suffered emergencies. Find out what worked and what did not work for them.

The Red Cross and local ambulance services. These groups can provide training in CPR and first aid.

Fire department. Firefighters can teach staff how to use fire extinguishers and to make sure extinguishers are regularly serviced and in working order. Fire inspectors also can identify potential fire hazards in the buildings and on the grounds and explain how these hazards could be diminished. In addition, fire personnel can test the available water pressure.

U.S. Army Corps of Engineers (or a comparable government agency). The Corps will know if the museum is on a floodplain. It also can calculate the level the water is likely to reach. If the museum is in a flood-prone area, ask how staff should be trained in filling and using sandbags properly.

Police department. Talk with authorities about how you should train personnel on handling bomb threats or acts of vandalism. Provide police with the security plan, location maps, and, possibly, keys.

Local businesses. Training and emergency preparation requires money and supplies. Do not be afraid to solicit donations from local businesses and corporations. A computer company donated Styrofoam packing materials to the Barbados Museum and Historical Society. In addition, a lumber company provided free wood and cut it to specification to make protective shutters, and another source donated heavy-duty boxes for moving the collection. "Usually people are happy to give. They'd rather give for emergency preparedness than wait to hear from us when we are totally devastated and needing tens of thousands of dollars," says Alissandra Cummins, director of the Barbados Museum.

Weather bureaus. Keeping in touch with weather forecasters is essential during seasons of inclement weather. A member of one of the preparedness teams should be assigned to develop direct contacts with bureau staff and learn the routine for weather-related warnings and alerts.

Ham radio operators. Find out whether any employees are ham radio operators. If not, train interested staff members how to contact sources of help by radio.

Insurance carriers. Insurers can provide free inspections and advice. Arrange for committee members and other relevant staff to be present during an inspection.

Task 4

Conduct a basic fire extinguisher lesson

Like the general cleanup activity in task 1, this exercise will call for another "blue jeans" day. Ask staff members to meet in the parking lot or another appropriately paved area at designated times. Arrange for firefighters to teach them the proper way to use a fire extinguisher (Fig. 4). You may be amazed by the number of people who do not know how to perform this simple technique. Any lesson on using a fire extinguisher or other equipment should follow these guidelines:

- Provide a step-by-step description of the procedure, using illustrations where appropriate.
- Provide a follow-along demonstration.
- Provide periodic opportunities to practice.
- Teach the thirty-second rule: If the fire cannot be put out in thirty seconds with a fire extinguisher, stop trying, and evacuate as quickly as possible.

Ask people to describe the locations of fire extinguishers throughout the building. Perhaps give a prize to the person who can name the highest number

Figure 4   Staff of the J. Paul Getty Museum participating in a fire-extinguisher training session. Photo: Brian Considine.

of locations. This exercise could inspire a constructive debate over whether extinguishers are located in the most convenient, accessible spots. Have the building's interior and gallery spaces been modified since the extinguishers were first hung? Be sure that fire extinguishers and fire blankets are kept at strategic locations throughout the building, such as on every floor and near doors and exits.

Also, discuss who will be responsible for ensuring that the rechargeable fire extinguishers and smoke detection equipment are maintained and tested on a regular basis, as mandated by the local fire department. This person or committee should determine the appropriate type of rechargeable fire extinguishers to have on hand, such as water-based, carbon dioxide, Class A, or Class B. This responsibility should be included in staff job descriptions.

Fires are categorized in three ways: Class A fires are fueled by ordinary combustibles, such as wood, paper, and textiles. Class B fires feed on flammable materials, such as oil-based paint and solvents. Class C fires are triggered by energized electrical equipment, including appliances, wiring, and fuse boxes. High-pressure water extinguishers will put out Class A fires but can cause water damage. Extinguishers using a very fine water mist are now available. Carbon dioxide extinguishers put out Classes B and C fires; they are recommended when fragile materials are involved, but the gas can damage glass. Dry chemical extinguishers (ABC), which leave a powdery residue, can be used on all three classes of fires.

The employees responsible for the fire extinguishers also may be the ones who periodically inventory and reorder emergency supplies. Dry-cell batteries, for instance, need to be periodically replaced.

Consult the safety and security and the buildings and maintenance teams for more suggestions on emergency equipment that staff should learn to use.

Task 5
Expand the fire drills

Fire drills can be mundane and fail to leave an impression, as all of us can recall from our school days. When training staff, it is helpful to turn a routine drill into a more challenging exercise. Before the drill begins, block a stairway that people ordinarily would use; this will force them to determine, on the spot, the next best way to flee the building. Have a staff member feign injury—perhaps a broken leg—and encourage colleagues to figure out how to evacuate that person. Finally, arrange for an employee to hide inside the building. When the rest of the staff members have assembled outside, see if anyone notices the person's absense.

Exercises like these help build quick-thinking skills and emphasize the need for preparedness. It will become clear, for example, how important it is to store first-aid kits in visible or easily accessible areas, and to implement a system to help determine whether all staff members have been evacuated.

Task 6
Test the notification system

On a weeknight, ask a few staff members to stay after hours. They are to phone every employee and volunteer and say, "This is an exercise. If there were an emergency at the museum right now, would you be willing to come down here to assist? How long would it take you to arrive?"

The first time that staff members at the J. Paul Getty Museum tried this exercise, they discovered that 10 percent of the employee home telephone numbers were wrong. The exercise not only gave administrators a more accurate idea of how far people lived from the museum and who would be able to assist in an emergency, but also indicated the need to keep the list of staff addresses and phone numbers up to date.

For staff members who do not have telephones at home, the exercise would have to be modified. Several employees could be dispatched to the homes of these colleagues. During the drive, they could note how long it would take to reach the museum during an emergency.

Task 7
Encourage staff to bring emergency preparedness home

Even if staff are unable to leave due to impassible roads or the like, being prepared at home will provide some peace of mind so that they may be able to concentrate on the task at hand.[2]

— Wilbur Faulk
   Director of Getty Center Security
   The J. Paul Getty Trust

One of the most powerful ways to motivate personnel to fully participate in crisis planning is to assist them in being prepared for an emergency at home. Focusing on staff members and their families makes employees feel that the institution genuinely cares about them. It also forces them to face the reality that the lives of people very dear to them could be endangered by a failure to be prepared.

The Seattle Art Museum conducted earthquake workshops that provided practical advice on how to prepare for an earthquake. The museum also bought first-aid kits in bulk, along with food-grade water barrels, which staff in turn could buy quite cheaply for use at home. "We found the whole training process less daunting by implementing this effective way to get the staff engaged," Gail Joice points out.

If staff members are prepared in their own homes, they will be more likely to be devote extra attention to the institution's needs during a crisis. "When we started the process of emergency planning, we asked each staff member: Do you have the emergency booklet issued by the national committee for emergency preparedness? Do you know where your emergency shelter is? About two-thirds weren't aware of either. One of the things we put in place was to remind staff of these resources," says Alissandra Cummins.

Task 8

Teach staff members how and when to handle objects

Not every employee knows the proper way to handle damaged items in a museum collection. During an emergency, the impulse to save valuable objects will be strong, and staff members should understand that their untrained actions could actually harm these objects. Coordinate collections-related training issues with the collections team, in accordance with the guidelines developed as part of their contribution to Report 2 (see chapter 7, task 3, pages 158–60).

Collections staff should instruct colleagues in what to do on the scene of an emergency, including handling procedures and basic salvage techniques.

Task 9

Make emergency-related mental drills a common occurrence

You gradually come to realize that this whole process of emergency preparedness is almost like another operation. The only way to deal with it is on a daily basis.

— Alissandra Cummins
  Director
  Barbados Museum and Historical Society

Are you ready to make tough choices? A good way to prepare is through mental drills. Mental drills are simple to do and cost nothing but are an important part of the training process. While setting the scene of an emergency, these drills can reveal gaps in the best-laid contingency plans. They also can prompt you to find answers to problems that might never have occurred to you, to the emergency preparedness committee, or to your team colleagues.

By conducting a mental triage drill, followed by roundtable discussions, a priority list of action items emerges through consensus. This list should be posted in each department and given to appropriate personnel. A copy should be stored in a safe, secure location. At some institutions, every object and collection is ranked and labeled according to importance; this helps to ensure that the most valuable items will be saved should persons unfamiliar with the collections arrive on the scene. Some experts recommend that the objects most threatened by such hazards as water, fire, or chemicals be saved first. The collections team is responsible for establishing this procedure in advance.

In a mental drill, an unlimited number of scenarios can be visualized. Following are five ideas:

Scenario 1: An earthquake hits while the museum is holding an indoor concert. Should all guests be escorted out, or should some be enlisted to help? What are the first priorities?

Scenario 2: During a hurricane, a collections storage room fills with water. The electricity is still on, and the electrical sockets are submerged in water. Will you get electrocuted if you enter? What should you and your colleagues do?

Scenario 3: It is 6 P.M., and you are one of the last people to leave the building. You smell smoke but hear no smoke alarm. Has the alarm malfunctioned? As you investigate, the smell of smoke becomes stronger as you approach a gallery. What do you do?

Scenario 4: Fire has broken out. The lights go out, four exits are blocked by fire, and someone has fallen and sustained a back injury while running down the stairs. What should happen next?

Scenario 5: A crazed person shouting obscenities begins slashing paintings and splashing works of art with an unknown liquid. How should you react?

Task 10
Conduct planned drills

Conduct your first drill after staff members have been given an opportunity to develop an understanding of the program and to adequately rehearse any new skills related to the emergency plan. For greater impact, try to schedule the drill near the anniversary of an emergency that is well known in your community.[3]

— Wilbur Faulk
Director of Getty Center Security
The J. Paul Getty Trust

Planned drills do not come in a one-size-fits-all format, and there is no single correct way to hold one. Keep your first drill short and simple. The drills can increase in length and complexity as staff members become more sophisticated in emergency preparedness and response activities. Tailor the drills to the types of emergencies common to the institution's geographic area.

The following are guidelines for planned drills:[4]

- Do not wait until the plan is completely written before holding the first drill. Stay up to date on the progress of the EPC and the departmental teams. One priority of the drill is to help you find the holes in the plan as it is being developed.
- The drill should teach success, not failure; build confidence, not apprehension.

- Use the EPC's vulnerability assessment report to identify the most likely emergency scenario and build a drill around that. If your facility is in a hurricane zone, do a hurricane drill. If brush fires are a major threat, do a brush-fire drill.
- Hold drills during the appropriate time of year. For instance, an ideal time to hold a tornado drill is in the late winter or early spring.
- Focus on life safety. Use triage to create realistic injuries and deaths in order to test first-aid and CPR skills. Enlist a few department heads to play roles of injured visitors so that subordinates become accustomed to the idea of making decisions on their own.
- Include opportunities to test fire extinguisher training, movement in emergency situations, use of special tools and equipment, and ability to shut off utilities.
- Keep the details of a planned drill secret. This will ensure an element of surprise that normally would be found during an emergency.
- At each drill, assign a few staff members to observe and evaluate the exercise.
- Have the appropriate response team member(s) document the drill with photos and video, which you can use later as training tools or in emergency preparedness grant proposals or fund-raising campaigns.
- Create public awareness. Pass out flyers about the drill to visitors and include a free pass for another day's visit to the museum or institution.
- During a post-drill debriefing, allow the team members to evaluate the drill, identify what worked well, and find any flaws in the emergency plan. Have them also identify any additional needs for training. Discuss any psychological impact the drill had on participants.
- Do not expect the first drill to go well, but expect to learn from it.

Drills should be built on the problems and solutions identified during mental drills. Do not be surprised if the tidy solutions suggested during brainstorming sessions do not work during a real drill. That, after all, is one of the purposes of the exercise.

Full drills not only help keep staff alert, but also can assist an institution in detecting holes in its emergency plan. At the Barbados Museum and Historical Society, for instance, the staff had mentally gone over the steps needed to protect glass cabinets containing rare historical papers in a hurricane. But during a drill, the staff discovered that attaching the pine shutters to the cabinets took far too long after a hurricane warning. Consequently, the museum now keeps the shutters in place during hurricane season. "The cases look unattractive, but who cares?" Alissandra Cummins says.

Use of props during a full drill adds a sense of reality to the exercise. For instance, put a dozen soaked books in the library, a sopping rug in a gallery, or chipped ceramics in a display case. If these items were real objects from the collection, how should people handle them?

Make sure each employee has the opportunity to play a key role. People need to be trained to know what their jobs are during an emergency, as well as what other's jobs are, since emergencies will not always happen when all key members of the emergency response team are at the facility. An institution needs backup people for every important job. The best way to become familiar with a task is to act it out. According to a U.S. government publication, *Organizational Behavior in Disasters and Implications for Disaster Planning:*

> A frequent error in emergency planning is that planners forget that they will have to orient, train or educate others (e.g., people and groups) relative to their respective roles under disastrous circumstances. Knowing the role/responsibilities of a few key officials and planners, or the organization, is not enough. The counterpart roles of others must be clear to facilitate coordination and an integrated emergency response. Of necessity, this requires teaching others what is or will be expected of them.[5]

Drills can help identify which staff members perform best under pressure. It is not necessarily the people one normally would expect. Some people may panic and be unable to carry out their responsibilities. When assigning jobs in anticipation of a real emergency, utilize those who have stood out during drills. Some examples of planned drill scenarios are as follows:

Scenario 1: A demonstration of college students has turned violent in the streets a block away from the museum. Sirens and explosions can be heard. A group of schoolchildren is in the museum at the time, and neither the school bus driver nor the bus is to be found. A small group of benefactors, many of them senior citizens, are meeting in the library. Ask staff: When would you close the museum? What would you do with the visitors? Who will take care of them? What should be done to protect the building and the collection?

Scenario 2: Due to rainfall in the mountains, a nearby river is slowly rising. Experts say it could rise to levels not seen in a hundred years. Within two days, the first floor of the main building may be under water. Ask staff: What should you move? Who will do the moving? Where will you store objects in the collection? What supplies are needed to treat water damage?

Scenario 3: An earthquake causes a power outage. The museum director, a conservator, and three visitors are trapped in an elevator. The facility is dark, and the backup generator is not working. A small fire, caused by a broken gas main, is threatening a gallery. Ask: Do you know how to activate the alarms and automatic fire suppression devices? How will fire officials be notified? Will phones work without power? How will you rescue the people in the elevator?

Scenario 4: During a hurricane, gale-force winds have shattered windows in the galleries, and three people have been badly cut by the flying glass. Who will care for the injured people? Where will first aid be performed? In the meantime, the collections are getting wet from the incoming rain and the electricity is out. What should be done first? Should the windows be covered? With what? What objects should be moved? How will you move them? Who will move them?

Scenario 5: Smoke or, if applicable, volcanic ash is seeping into the building. Should vents be closed or opened? Who knows how to close them or shut off the gas and electricity? What else should be done?

Do not worry about creating a drill scenario that is too outlandish. As Vance McDougall of the National Museums of Canada pointed out at a 1986 emergency planning workshop:

> Remember, emergencies occur at the worst possible time, in the worst possible place, under the worst possible conditions. . . . Always critique your drills against all possible situations regardless of how remote their occurrences may seem. Never permit yourself to become complacent. When everything seems to be going well, that should be regarded as the first danger signal. BEWARE![6]

At the Mystic Seaport Museum, administrators arranged to have their communication system upgraded on a weekend when no bad weather was expected. Sure enough, Hurricane Bob hit while the museum had no phone service. Staff grabbed fistfuls of quarters from the admission proceeds and made calls at pay phones across the street. "When the storm calls, your director will be on the West Coast, and your plant manager will be in the hospital undergoing surgery. Then the hurricane will hit. I will guarantee it," notes David Mathieson.

Task 11

Anticipate psychological impact

Employees, volunteers, and others may experience secondary injuries— emotional injuries—following a disaster.[7]

— The Getty Center
"Emergency Planning Handbook"

The Getty Center "Emergency Planning Handbook" discusses the progression of responses that may be experienced by individuals after an emergency. Six stages are identified:

1. Impact of the event (at the time of the event)
2. Shock (24–48 hours after the event)
3. Suggestibility (1–3 days after the event)
4. Euphoria (1–2 weeks after the event, during the initial response phase)
5. Ambivalence (when the critical response phase passes)
6. Reintegration (2–9 months after the event, when the routine returns to normal and the environment is stable)

Several types of follow-up steps are suggested to help staff members deal with the psychological impact. These include providing outside counseling, being aware of changes in staff responses, setting up support groups, providing a debriefing within forty-eight hours after an emergency—which all staff members are required to attend—reorganizing work schedules as necessary, and reestablishing normal operations as soon as possible.

The psychological impact of emergencies and disasters should be addressed in training exercises. Set aside debriefing time after a full drill or a real emergency for staff members to talk about their experiences. Ask people how they are feeling. Drills can become total mayhem and will inevitably agitate and worry some people. In addition to holding roundtable debriefings, consider installing a suggestion box so that the more reticent staff members can share their feelings, comments, and observations.

Task 12
Build the team

Over time, each person has recognized that his or her individual experience has had an impact on the museum's experience. The staff is empowered. They have become more confident of themselves and their skills.

— Alissandra Cummins
Director
Barbados Museum and Historical Society

By conducting full drills and doing the exercises suggested in this chapter, you will be giving staff members the opportunity to work together and hone their teamwork skills. Cross-departmental training is another method of building the team. For example, the maintenance staff can teach conservators how to turn off the water and power. Preparators and conservators can teach janitors how to carry works of art and artifacts. Registrars can share information about accession numbers and the proper marking of boxes.

Building a successful team means taking risks involving conflict, trust, interdependence, and hard work. The following guidelines, adapted from Katzenbach and Smith,[8] will help:

Select members based on skills, knowledge, and attitudes. Recruit people on the basis of three categories of relevant skills: technical and functional, problem solving, and interpersonal. All efforts at team building should focus on the process and on accomplishing the intended tasks. One way to foster commitment is to involve as many people as possible in the emergency preparedness and response program. Identifying "true believers" in emergency preparedness and inviting them onto the team helps craft the proper atmosphere.

Emphasize urgency, direction, and clear rules. The more urgent and meaningful a team's purpose, the easier it is to evolve into a well-functioning team. Emergency preparedness certainly carries the element of urgency, but you may face some heavily entrenched disbelief, which is often based on fear of the unknown. Emphasize urgency without scaring people.

Be clear about your expectations of the team. If your goals and rules are not focused, neither will be the team's work. Enforcing the rules lends credibility to the team. Consider putting into place rules involving the following:

- attendance (e.g., no interruptions to take phone calls)
- discussion (e.g., no forbidden topics)
- confidentiality (e.g., what we discuss here stays within the group unless another option is agreed on)
- analytic approach (e.g., facts are friendly)
- end-product orientation (e.g., everyone gets assignments and does them)
- constructive confrontation (e.g., conflicting views build strength)
- contributions (e.g., everyone does real work)

Be aware of your actions. Leaders set the tone. Convey to team leaders the seriousness of your commitment by devoting time to the process and freeing up time for team members to do their work. Team leaders will pick up on your patience and persistence and pass it along to their respective team members.

Set immediately achievable goals and tasks. Establishing a few challenging *yet achievable* goals that can be reached early on can bring a team together and instill a sense of early accomplishment that sets the pace. Be sure to include in the performance goals a clear "stretch" component, or challenges that your team may initially regard as "virtually impossible, if not crazy."

Inject fresh facts and information. Do not let the teams assume that all the information needed exists in their collective experience and knowledge. You can enrich their approach, even startle them into action, with new information. For example, you might bring in a research paper that shatters myths about how people act in emergencies, or a list of new protection techniques.

Schedule debriefing time. Encourage team members to talk with each other in a more casual, personal way after every session. This is the time for members to relax, reflect, and express their fears or concerns. Debriefing allows teams to bond and helps individuals move on without fear.

Exploit the power of positive feedback, recognition, and reward. Positive reinforcement works as well in a team context as it does elsewhere. Even the strongest egos respond to positive feedback, as long as it is genuine. Although satisfaction in the team's performance ultimately becomes the most cherished reward, teams appreciate sincere recognition.

Task 13
Record and critique

Keep thorough written and photographic records of what happens during full drills and any executions of emergency procedures. Then subject the emergency plan and performance of all participants in emergency operations to a candid critique as soon as possible after operations have returned to a semblance of normalcy. Encourage feedback from all involved persons through written reports, interviews, and group meetings. What went well? What did not work?

Task 14
Evaluate the training program

All training activities should include some form of evaluation. Did participants enjoy the training program? Did they think they learned anything? What did they like or dislike? Do their supervisors believe they obtained new skills? Through surveys, questionnaires, focus groups, and roundtable discussions regarding the training activities, you will gather information that will help you make improvements. Be sure to measure *reactions* and *learning*.[9]

Reactions. Measure trainee reactions to training activities. "The more favorable the reactions to a program, the more likely trainees are to pay attention and learn the principles, facts and techniques discussed."[10] Make the comment sheet anonymous to encourage honest reactions and allow trainees to make additional comments not covered by the questions.

Learning. Measure the knowledge acquired, skills improved, or attitudes changed due to training. Build evaluation into the training by setting up before-and-after situations in which trainees demonstrate whether they understand the principles or techniques being taught. If facts are being taught, conduct a paper-and-pencil test.

Questions to Consider

- Who will carry out the initial training?

- Once trained, can staff train colleagues or new employees?

- How often should training be repeated?

- Who is responsible for keeping training updated?

- Are staff members trained in what to do in situations requiring actions beyond their routine or their level of skill?

- How will you keep track of which staff members have learned first aid, know how to use emergency equipment, or know how to handle cultural objects during an evacuation?

- How will the training efforts be evaluated?

- Are trustees included in the training exercises? Neighbors? Friends of the institution? Volunteers? Other sections of the local community?

- If there are no conservators on staff, have you talked to employees about what immediate measures to protect the collection will be allowed at the disaster site before a conservator arrives?

- Is there a forum through which employees may comment and voice their reactions during and after the training process?

Emergency Preparedness and Response Training Suggestions

Table 7 lists guidelines for emergency preparedness and response training activities. Consider these guidelines when you plan and when you evaluate training exercises. They will help staff members personally identify with the emergency preparedness and response program.

Table 7   **Guidelines for Training Activities**

Guideline	Example
Engage the staff and volunteers in discussions and situations in which they confront dilemmas regarding emergency response and emergencies in general.	"Let's talk about hurricanes. Does anyone have a particularly powerful memory of a hurricane? Why is it so memorable? Were you prepared for it? Did you have the supplies and equipment you needed? Did you lose anything of value? What did you not expect?"
Allow active participation, such as role-playing opportunities. Create situations in which staff can reflect on the challenges and advantages of being a part of a team.	"We are going to do a role-playing exercise in which we take turns playing the role of the reporter and the spokesperson. Here is a data sheet with the facts about a late-night fire that the institution just experienced, and a fact sheet on the institution's emergency plan. Who would like to go first?"
Anticipate adversity in emergency preparedness.	"As you go about your regular job, what obstacles do you encounter as you try to complete tasks related to the emergency preparedness process? Do you have the time? The resources needed? Has anyone figured out a clever way to build these tasks into their day?"
Show the connection between emergency preparedness and participants' jobs.	"As you know, emergency planning is being built into each of your job descriptions. It is a priority identified by the director. I know the idea of emergencies makes some of you uncomfortable, but it is a reality that we need to deal with. We want to protect lives and the collection."
Provide instructional materials, ongoing learning opportunities, and performance support.	"Here is a handout that walks you through the operation of the new walkie-talkies. Read through it first, and then we will practice using them. The handouts will be stored with the walkie-talkies. In the future, we will sometimes start our meetings using walkie-talkies to communicate, just for practice."
Give employees plenty of opportunities to practice the skills they are expected to perform in the frenzy of a crisis.	"Next Monday we will do our annual fire-extinguisher exercise. All of you have done this before, right? If you have not, please see me after this meeting. The rest of you, please review the fire-extinguisher operation instructions between now and the exercise."
Help employees acquire new skills and knowledge by creating situations in which learning can occur within realistic contexts.	"John is going to walk you through our procedures for treating wet books and tapestries. In our emergency drill next month, some of you will need these skills."
Provide feedback so trainees know what they are doing well and where they need to improve.	"Judy, you played the role of the spokesperson very well in that exercise. You answered Jim's questions when you could and deferred to emergency officials when appropriate. Remember that you do not have to rely on memory when explaining the emergency plan. You have a fact sheet to hand out."
Provide incentives—rewards, recognition, or remuneration—to elicit, improve, and maintain emergency planning efforts.	"Phil, who put the collections team in touch with a conservator who specializes in salvaging water-damaged books, has won the emergency preparedness employee-of-the-month award. Congratulations!"

Notes

1. Getty Center, "Emergency Planning Handbook" (J. Paul Getty Trust, Los Angeles, 1997, photocopy).

2. Wilbur Faulk, "Organizing, Preparing, Testing, and Revising an Emergency Planning Program" (J. Paul Getty Trust, Santa Monica, Calif., Feb. 1993, typescript).

3. Wilbur Faulk, "Are You Ready When Disaster Strikes?" *History News* 48 (Jan./Feb. 1993), 9. Used by permission of the American Association for State and Local History.

4. Adapted from interviews with the experts who advised on the compilation of this book, and from Faulk, "Organizing, Preparing, Testing."

5. Enrico Quarantelli, *Organizational Behavior in Disasters and Implications for Disaster Planning*, Monograph Series, vol. 1, no. 2 (Emmitsburgh, Md.: National Emergency Training Center, 1984), 29.

6. Adapted from Vance McDougall, "Museum Security, Fire, and Safety Emergency Plans" (paper presented at the Security Special Interest Group Emergency Planning Workshop, Canadian Museum Association, Ottawa, Ontario, Canada, March 25–26, 1986), 6–7. Used by permission.

7. Getty Center, "Emergency Planning Handbook."

8. Jon R. Katzenbach and Douglas K. Smith, *The Wisdom of Teams: Creating the High-Performance Organization* (New York: HarperBusiness, 1993), 119–27.

9. Donald Kirkpatrick, "Great Ideas Revisited: Techniques for Evaluating Training Programs," *Training and Development* (Jan. 1996), 54. Used by permission.

10. Ibid., 56. Used by permission.

Chapter Summary

This chapter

- explained why training is crucial to the emergency preparedness and response effort;

- recommended training topics and suggested who should present these topics and who should receive specific training;

- provided suggestions for emergency response drills; and

- described mental drills and explained their importance in emergency preparedness.

Over time, each person has recognized that his or her individual experience has had an impact on the museum's experience. The staff is empowered. They have become more confident of themselves and their skills.

— Alissandra Cummins
Director
Barbados Museum and
Historical Society

Part III

For the Departmental Team Leaders

Overview

This part, which consists of chapters 6–9, is a resource for the four departmental teams—safety and security, collections, buildings and maintenance, and administration and records—that work with the emergency preparedness committee to develop a comprehensive emergency preparedness and response program. Part III is designed to help team leaders create an organizational and procedural structure in which the process of planning, assessment, and review of the emergency plan becomes part of the regular routine.

Each chapter that follows is to be distributed to the appropriate team. As the teams work through their chapters, they may refer to Table 5 (chapter 2, page 30) for a breakdown of the planning process. The questions in the test in Table 4 (chapter 2, page 28) provide a guideline for assessing the institution's level of preparedness. Figure 2 (chapter 3, page 51) diagrams the organizational structure of the program.

Although each of the following chapters is addressed to the departmental team leader, those in support positions also must be fully familiar with the leader's role in the process. If your institution does not have the four specific departments listed, the emergency preparedness committee should divide the responsibilities accordingly.

Chapters 6–9 explain the role of each departmental team in the emergency preparedness and response program; explain how to assess the needs of the program; suggest what leaders need to think about and ask to determine appropriate prevention, preparedness, and response measures; identify the content of the two reports each team will develop for the emergency preparedness committee; and explain the role of each departmental response team in an emergency.

Each chapter includes "Questions to Consider" to assist in the planning process and "Suggested Exercises" to help you relate the material to your institution.

For an overview of the emergency preparedness and response program, please consult chapters 1–3. For training ideas, see chapter 5.

CHAPTER SIX

The Safety and Security Team

As the institution builds an emergency plan, safety- and security-related issues must be addressed. This chapter is designed to serve as a resource for you, the leader of the safety and security team.

Your Role in the Process

Of all the departmental teams, safety and security has the most important responsibility: to save lives and prevent or reduce injury. You and your team will do this by putting into place—if not in place already—a system of rules and practices that make the museum less vulnerable to accidents and better equipped to respond to an emergency.

Saving the collection is not this team's top priority, and you may have some difficulty convincing other staff members of this. Remind them that by working to make the institution safer for people, a system and structure will be developed that makes the collection less vulnerable to theft and other threats.

The team's job is to thoroughly evaluate the safety and security procedures currently in place, identify where the institution is vulnerable, and produce two reports to the emergency preparedness committee (EPC) that summarize its findings:

Report 1 is a vulnerability and asset analysis that recommends preparedness and protection measures; that is, what should be done to prevent the loss of human life in the event of an emergency and to reduce damage to the security aspect of the institution's functions. (See pages 114–20.)

Report 2 is an outline of response procedures and techniques, including the role of the safety and security response team during an emergency. It should include a list of equipment and supplies needed, as well as a list of any hazardous materials stored on-site. (See pages 120–37.)

Two tasks are necessary to begin the process of compiling this information and developing your team's portion of the emergency preparedness and response plan.

Task 1: Assemble the preparedness team.

Task 2: Interact with other teams and with the EPC.

Task 1

Assemble the preparedness team

Security staff regularly review the plan, pointing out the gaps and deficiencies. They have helped us develop realistic scenarios based on their experience. They are part of a general consultative process developed to empower all staff in their particular roles. They are of considerable importance in determining what preventive measures should be put in place, through their observations on the status of the buildings, equipment, and so forth. One member also is appointed to each of the six core response teams.

— Alissandra Cummins
  Director
  Barbados Museum and Historical Society

Suggested Exercise

To get team members thinking about how familiar they are with their surroundings, blindfold them and take them to any part of the institution. Tell them there has been an earthquake or a hurricane, the power is out, and they cannot see and cannot use the elevators (or a similar scenario). Remove the blindfolds. Rope or block off a stairwell or door beforehand so they will have to figure out an alternate escape route. In addition, one person has an injured leg and will need to be carried out. After the exercise, hold a debriefing session. Support and reassure those who were shaken by the experience.

You are in charge of appointing the safety and security team and of guiding team members in gathering accurate, efficient information and in organizing a well-coordinated response to any emergency. Building a successful team means taking risks that involve resolving conflict, establishing trust, and encouraging interdependence. Refer to chapter 5 on training for information on assembling and building effective teams.

Select team members on the basis of three categories of skills: technical and functional, problem solving, and interpersonal. All efforts at team building should focus on the process and on accomplishing the intended tasks. Communication skills are important, as your team will be interacting with nearly every department in the institution. Involve other members of the department in the planning process so they will more readily support the recommended changes in policy and procedures. Identifying and appointing "true believers" in emergency preparedness will help generate enthusiasm and create the proper atmosphere. Include "nonbelievers" as well, to forge a well-balanced, cohesive unit that enables all members to do the best they can.

As part of the recommendations in Report 2, you and your team will describe the roles and responsibilities of the safety and security response team, which may or may not include all members of the preparedness team. This team, along with a team from each of the other three departments, will respond in an actual emergency situation.

Interact with other teams and with the EPC

To produce the two reports for the EPC, you and your team must work closely with the three other departmental teams in certain areas, as indicated below.

Collections
- Setting guidelines for relocating or evacuating objects
- Identifying emergency shelters

Buildings and maintenance
- Establishing evacuation routes for people
- Establishing evacuation routes for collections
- Determining preventive building maintenance
- Identifying and preparing emergency shelters
- Housekeeping in collaboration with the collections team

Administration and records
- Setting guidelines for relocation or evacuation
- Resolving administrative and legal issues regarding relocating and evacuating people and property
- Documenting activities

In collaborating with other teams, work through the EPC to set up meetings between your team and the others. This hierarchical method helps avoid territorial disputes that can occur during the process. It becomes a top-down mandate rather than a lateral agreement. You may want to include a member from the EPC during these meetings.

When needed, include a member of the other departmental teams, as applicable. This works well as long as the team is discussing matters that pertain to this person's area of expertise. If discussions cover areas specific only to safety and security, it can be a waste of time for the person from the other team.

This collaboration is required for the overall success of the emergency preparedness and response program and may require a shift in attitudes on the part of colleagues. According to *A Manual of Basic Museum Security*:

> Too often the importance of the guard in the total scheme of the museum has been overlooked, and no effort to train guards or to upgrade their quality and status is undertaken. Guards have been recruited from the ranks of the unskilled, unemployed, and retired; or the museum simply contracts with the security agency. In both cases, the guards are often poorly paid and they have enjoyed little esteem and few opportunities for career advancement.[1]

The emergency preparedness and response process and program are likely to give security officers a higher profile, in terms both of image and responsibilities. Administrators often discover during emergency drills that security officers know the institution better than anyone else does. The security staff is also the front line of defense against many emergencies, since security officers regularly inspect windows, doors, skylights, and other openings; look for leakages in roofs and windows; identify fire hazards; and secure locks. The most common emergencies—fire and water pipe breaks—usually occur when only security officers are present at the institution.

The role of security officers at the Barbados Museum and Historical Society expanded as a result of emergency planning. "This is particularly the case when the plan was revised and, for the first time, we developed alternate plans for off-hour periods at the museum, with only one security officer in place," says Alissandra Cummins. "Security staff have received further training in making a judgment and taking the initiative."

As the emergency program develops, the value of a trained, efficient security force will become clear to everyone involved. This realization helps break down any existing hierarchical barriers.

Preparing Report 1:
Vulnerability and Asset Analysis

How vulnerable is your institution—its staff and its collection—to fire, theft, flood, or any other emergency or hazard? The safety and security team's job is to work with the emergency preparedness manager (EPM) and the EPC to assess this aspect.

The accuracy and thoroughness of the assessment will greatly affect the success of the institution's efforts to protect people and to prevent or minimize damage to the collection. Some examples of potential vulnerabilities are listed below. You and your department colleagues already may be aware of some of these weaknesses; others may become apparent only in the analysis process. All of them, however, ultimately affect the institution's preparedness and response capabilities.

- Security personnel do not have a list outlining the chain of command if a problem arises.
- Security staff do not know first aid or CPR, or where first-aid kits are stored.
- First-aid kits are not regularly restocked.
- Staff members do not have identification cards, so law enforcement may not allow them onto the property during a crisis.
- There is no log-in system that could easily identify who was in a particular building when a fire broke out.
- Few staff members know how to use fire extinguishers.
- Master keys may be inaccessible if only the security chief has the combination to the safe.

The following tasks will lead you and your team through the process of information gathering in order to prepare Report 1:

Task 1: Conduct a security survey.

Task 2: Evaluate the security force.

Task 3: Evaluate the inventory systems.

Task 4: Evaluate the monitoring of people.

Task 5: Evaluate equipment needs.

Task 6: Invite local agencies and individuals to participate.

Task 7: Recommend security-related protective measures.

Task 1

Conduct a security survey

The first task is to survey the current safety and security system and evaluate its efficiency. Encourage the team to look at the institution with a fresh eye to jump-start their imagination in this search for vulnerabilities. Before you begin, review with your team the hazard assessment prepared by the EPC, which ranks the likely and/or potential risks to the institution. With these in mind, the team's job is to assess systematically the risk of specific types of damage to safety and security. For example, if the EPC identifies a significant risk of earthquake, you must assess what effect a quake might have on staff and visitors and on the institution as a whole.

The following issues, excerpted from *A Manual of Basic Museum Security*, should be considered when determining security priorities and vulnerabilities:[2]

Building
- Size of the institution
- Type of facility—museum, archaeological site, and so on
- Number of visitors and visitor flow experience
- Available alarm protection
- Environmental conditions and monitoring controls
- Lighting
- Number of public entrances
- Exterior and interior wall openings: entrances, exits, and windows

Staffing
- Need for nighttime staffing

Collection
- Public image of objects on exhibit
- Type of collection and threats to the collection
- Size, location, support, and shape of objects on exhibit
- Ownership of objects
- Value (intrinsic, administrative, and research)
- Display techniques used
- Location in the museum
- Construction and design of the exhibit area: fire, safety, and ability to patrol
- Construction security of display cases

Administration

- Exhibition hours and schedule of operations
- Insurance coverage of objects
- Crime experience and exposure in the museum (from a crime and incident analysis)
- Funds available for protection, training, and additional staff or consultants
- Police and fire response reliability, response time, and support on arrival

Task 2

Evaluate the security force

For financial reasons, the institution may not be able to have twenty-four-hour protection of the collection or an elaborate electronic system of alarms and detectors. This is probably a mistake. Not only is the institution more vulnerable to theft when no one is present, but should a fire break out in a storage room, how far would it spread before someone notices and activates a response?

Many institutions organize the security force around "states of security." The following states have been excerpted from Burke and Adeloye:[3]

> **State 1:** The museum or site is closed to public and staff. . . . In this state there is minimal use of staff and the greatest use of alarm systems and physical security.
>
> **State 2:** The museum is closed to the public, but staff is at work. . . . Moderate to no use of security personnel is combined with moderate use of alarm systems. Staff screens all entry and maintains an entry and departure register.
>
> **State 3:** The museum is opened to the public while staff is at work. . . . In this state there must be a higher staff awareness in nonpublic areas, a maximum use of security personnel in public areas, and moderate use of alarm systems, primarily for the protection of exhibits.
>
> **State 4:** The museum is opened to the public but staff is not working. . . . During these hours, the museum's security program relies most heavily on the staff or security personnel and its alarm system and access control systems to protect nonpublic areas.

If a contract security force is used, you may want to talk to the EPC about renegotiating the contract. The portion of the contract that defines acceptable standards of performance of security officers can be adjusted to include emergency preparedness, mitigation, and response duties. You may also wish to discuss bringing the security staff onto the regular payroll.

Some institutions do not have sufficient resources to pay for the security force's expanded role, but the value of bringing security in-house may compel senior administrators to locate the funds. The U.S. Holocaust Memorial Museum in Washington, D.C., is a case in point.[4] The museum's protection services administrators wanted to replace contract security officers with federal employees because they believed the latter would "demonstrate greater initiative in monitoring security systems, recommending changes, and improving operations." Senior management supported the idea and downsized in other areas in order to hire ten full-time officers.

Questions to Consider

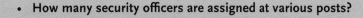

- **How many security officers are assigned at various posts?**

- **Is there a backup force in the event of an emergency?**

- **Do security officers receive training in how to recognize damage to objects on display? Are they trained in the art of observation?**

- **Do supervising officers receive any special emergency response training?**

- **Do officers feel they have an important role in protecting visitors and staff and in protecting and preserving the collections?**

Task 3

Evaluate the inventory systems

As you conduct the security survey, you will need to work with the collections team and the administration and records team to review the institution's inventory systems. For instance, do the identifying marks contain a number or code, and are the marks resistant to deletion or alteration so that they can be used to identify a stolen object?

Important categories of information are identified in *Protecting Cultural Objects in the Global Information Society*:[5]

- photograph
- Object ID[6] number
- type of object
- object name
- title
- materials and techniques
- measurements
- inscriptions and markings
- distinguishing features
- subject
- date or period
- maker
- description

Although these categories are intended for the collections, they can be used as a guide for the inventory of furnishings and other assets. For a detailed list of inventory considerations, refer to the *Museum Security Survey*.[7]

Task 4
Evaluate the monitoring of people

If an earthquake struck right now, would you know who is in the exhibit galleries, offices, and laboratories and could be at risk? Whether they are staff members or visitors, the people who travel through the institution's doorways are your responsibility once crisis strikes. A system should be in place to monitor who is in the buildings at all times. This system can be as simple as a log or a visitor count, but it must be maintained.

In addition, evaluate screening procedures for staff and volunteers. Are staff and volunteers fingerprinted? Is fingerprinting necessary? Are security screening devices needed for sensitive areas?

Questions to Consider

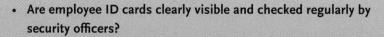

- Are employee ID cards clearly visible and checked regularly by security officers?

- Who has keys to the buildings? Are they taken home? What is the procedure if keys are lost or missing?

- Are temporary and unsalaried personnel supervised during working hours?

- Do the buildings have different entrances and exits for staff, contractors, personnel, and visitors?

- Are security officers stationed at all staff exits to check contents of briefcases, parcels, and so forth?

- Is access to different areas of the institution controlled or restricted based on the nature of the collections therein?

- Are visitors in nonpublic areas registered in and out, and do they wear temporary badges or other means of identification?[8]

Task 5

Evaluate equipment needs

You cannot ask for additional security equipment such as walkie-talkies or fire extinguishers unless you have a realistic idea of what the department has. Determine what the institution has on hand now. Based on the budget, and given the particular risks associated with the institution's location, what equipment is needed most? The following are security-related types of equipment:

- communications system
- detectors, alarms, and sensors (to monitor heat, smoke, water, and the entry to the institution or museum)
- fire detection systems
- fire extinguishers
- fire suppression systems
- people-monitoring system
- closed-circuit television cameras
- defense equipment and firearms
- emergency power supply

Suggested Exercise

Describe the following scenario to your team members: Weather forecasters say a storm is headed toward an area that includes your institution, bringing with it gale-force winds and heavy rainfall. The storm is expected to hit tomorrow night. What is the security force's role during emergency preparations? Should you close the museum? When? Who will check and stock supplies? If power fails, will the alarm system or telephones work? Will any objects be at risk if the temperature control devices fail? What else should be considered?

Questions to Consider

- If the institution has a public announcement system, is it sufficiently audible in all rooms? If not, how will you communicate emergency and evacuation information to everyone in the building?

- Does the sprinkler system have an automatic cutoff after a fire is extinguished?

- Is the detection/alarm/extinguishing system appropriate to the objects and the area covered in each case?

- What kind of exterior alarm is in operation?

- Are alarm buttons located near entrances?

- Are tape recorders connected to telephones to record bomb threats and extortion messages?

Task 6

Invite local agencies
and individuals
to participate

Staff members immersed in the emergency planning process often make the mistake of overlooking local or regional services and resources. Fire departments, for example, can provide beneficial information and sound advice. The information flow works both ways: You learn from fire officials, who in turn learn about your institution and its special needs. Consider also inviting any or all of the following agencies or services, either to make presentations to the team or to walk through the institution. Coordinate your presentations with the EPC, other teams, or all staff, since everyone may benefit.

- police
- military (can be problematic in some countries)
- local chapter of the U.S. National Guard
- staff members or former staff members from institutions that have experienced an emergency situation or the preparedness process
- staff of state or national government emergency agencies
- Red Cross search and rescue

Task 7

Recommend
security-related
protective measures

Protective measures are steps taken to reduce or eliminate hazards that threaten people or the collections. They may be as simple as posting a chain-of-command telephone list near telephones throughout the museum or as complicated as installing an automatic fire detection or suppression system.

Protection is a long process and one that never ends. Remind team members from time to time that it is a priority. You also may need to remind museum administrators of their commitment to emergency preparedness if you find yourself lobbying for funding to purchase a more costly protection device.

Preparing Report 2:
Outline of Response Procedures and Techniques

In Report 2, you and your team will detail safety and security procedures and techniques for responding to any type of emergency. Instructions must be included for ensuring the safety of people and objects. This includes how to activate the chain of command, handle emergency equipment, and relocate people and/or collections. The report must include lists of items, such as emergency supplies and equipment available, on-site as well as off-site. Job descriptions for the safety and security response team must also be provided.

There are plenty of emergency plan templates from other institutions to help you get started, but you must not simply copy sections from someone else's plan. It is not the written plan that prepares a museum for an emergency, but the *process* of planning. The fact that you and your team are grappling with these issues now, in the comfort of a conference room, means you will be better prepared to respond to a crisis.

The following tasks will help you contribute to an emergency response plan that is simple, detailed, and flexible:

Task 1: Identify potential temporary bases of operations.

Task 2: Identify potential safe rooms and/or outside shelters.

Task 3: Determine emergency evacuation routes.

Task 4: Develop the safety and security response team.

Task 5: Develop emergency procedures.

Task 6: Detail recovery procedures.

Task 7: Create lists of staff and resource contact information.

Task 8: Create fact sheets and maps.

Task 9: Stock emergency supplies and equipment.

Task 10: Establish routines to keep the plan viable.

Task 11: Identify and implement appropriate training.

In preparing your report, you and your team will have to address a number of important issues. Some will be general to all the departmental team reports; others will be specifically on safety and security issues. The following questions will help you address some issues and prompt you to identify others.

Questions to Consider

- Who decides when the emergency procedures should be put in place? The director? The emergency response coordinator (ERC)? The chief of security? What is the line of succession?

- How will the command system work if the emergency happens on a weekend or after hours (as emergencies have a tendency to do)?

- How will the contact system work if telephone lines are down? Walkie-talkies? Bicycles? Cellular phones? Beepers?

- Will the chain of command fit into, and take into account, those from emergency agencies such as the civil defense or the fire department, which will override the institution's procedures?

- Who will be in charge of keeping your part of the plan current? (Remember, people change jobs, telephone numbers change, new equipment is purchased and old equipment is discarded, companies go out of business, and agency responsibilities change.)

- To whom does your team report during an emergency?

- Who will coordinate with emergency organizations, such as the U.S. Federal Emergency Management Agency (FEMA), and with the insurance company?

Task 1

Identify potential
temporary bases
of operations

During an emergency, a central base of operations, or emergency command center, must be established, from which the response and recovery teams can operate following an evacuation. The location of this command post varies depending on the nature of the disaster; a hurricane requires a different location than an earthquake does. In some cases, it may be the security office. In others, the command post could be set up on or near the property.

When identifying potential sites for the command center, consider the various threats facing the institution. If flood is a potential hazard, make sure the post is on the highest point in the surrounding area. If wildfires are a possibility, make sure heavy brush and trees do not surround the command post.

Work with the ERC and leaders of other departmental teams to identify criteria for the base of operations. Once established, the command post should be manned by the ERC and leaders of the departmental response teams. You may want to consider limiting access to the command post to minimize interference to critical decision making.

In general, command post locations should be based on

- access to relevant emergency information and communication (on and off the property) and communication equipment that will assist those handling command operations;
- location with minimal safety risk;
- central location for easy access of staff and easy access to emergency equipment; and
- location near a road to allow for ready access by a radio-equipped vehicle for use if other systems fail or extra communication facilities are needed.[9]

Questions to Consider

- **Is the security office owned and operated by institution personnel?**

- **Are the walls of the security office of solid construction?**

- **What is needed to set up an outdoor base of operations? In what cases would this be advisable?**

Task 2
Identify potential safe rooms and/or outside shelters

In some emergencies, safe rooms and/or outside shelters will be needed to house staff members, visitors, and the collection. As with the temporary emergency command center, the ideal shelter location will vary depending on the type of threat. Work with the buildings and maintenance team to identify and evaluate potential sites. Consult with the collections team to determine shelter needs for objects. Solicit the administration and records team's input in identifying shelter needs for equipment and documents, and in considering the legal issues involved in moving people and property.

The following recommendations for emergency shelters have been been adapted from *Steal This Handbook!* [10] with input from advisers to this book:

Size. Ensure that the shelter is large enough to fit the maximum number of staff and visitors likely to be at the institution at any one time. Allow 5–6 square feet (0.47–0.56 square meters) per adult and 3 square feet (0.28 square meters) per child. It also should be large enough to accommodate emergency supplies and priority objects.

Accessibility. Take into account the route necessary to reach the shelter and the size of the openings through which objects must pass.

Security. The shelter must offer the highest level of security. This means a minimum number of openings so the shelter can be sealed and access controlled completely.

Physical safety. The shelter should be isolated from the exterior by adjacent rooms or corridors. Walls and ceilings should be free of plumbing, pipes, and so forth.

Environmental stability. Make sure the shelter is environmentally stable. Add materials such as carpets and curtains to buffer the relative humidity, and have humidifiers or dehumidifiers on hand.

Lighting. Make sure adequate lighting is provided. There should be no windows or skylights if the institution is in a seismic area or subject to tornados, to avoid the danger of broken glass.

An ideal shelter should *not* have any of the following:

- exterior walls that are likely to be partially or completely destroyed
- roofs with windward edges (usually south and west), long spans, overhangs, or load-bearing wall supports
- corridors and ends of corridors that have exit doors facing directly to the outside
- spaces with windows facing the direction from which a storm or hurricane is likely to approach
- interior locations containing glass (display cases, glass doors, skylights)

Questions to Consider

- From which direction do potential natural hazards (e.g., hurricanes, windstorms, brush fires, flash floods, volcanic ash) come in your institution's area?

- How does the local emergency management agency's plan for placement of civil shelters affect your plan?

- In a general-area emergency, the institution itself may become a shelter. How will you protect the collections in such a situation?

- Does anyone other than the maintenance staff know where the toilet paper, plastic bags, and disinfectant are?

Task 3

Determine emergency evacuation routes

Work with the buildings and maintenance team to determine evacuation routes for emergency situations. The evacuation plan should include

- two separate means of exit from each floor, including basements;
- an exit plan for every location in each building;
- routes that provide speedy exit, simplicity, access (including disability access), and safety (lighting, no possible obstructions);
- designation of a safe area where people can gather once they are evacuated;
- a procedure for what to do with staff and visitors once they are gathered in the safe area, bearing in mind that considerable time may pass before reentry is possible or, potentially, proves to be no longer possible at all;
- a system that verifies whether everyone has evacuated the building and reached the designated safe area;
- maps showing evacuation routes and exits posted in all public and staff areas on each floor;
- first-aid kits, flashlights, fire extinguishers, keys to shelter/supply sites, and a copy of the emergency plan handbook and staff emergency procedures posted by every exit; and
- wheelchairs at a variety of locations.

In planning an evacuation, keep the following in mind:

- People are the first priority. Special care and consideration should be made for the well-being of staff during and following response activities.
- Some natural emergencies allow time for the implementation of stages of response activities. There may be two days' warning for hurricanes and floods, but only a few hours for tornadoes and brushfires and no warning at all for earthquakes.

- Provide staff members with badges so they can be identified quickly by police or fire department officials.

See appendix C for sample evacuation plans from the Getty Center and the Barbados Museum and Historical Society.

Questions to Consider

- **Are emergency exits equipped with emergency lighting?**
- **Are stairwells adequately lighted?**
- **Are all ramps and stairways equipped with guard rails?**
- **Are first-aid kits well stocked and in appropriate places?**
- **Do elevators return to the ground floor when the alarm is activated?**
- **Where are the "safe areas" or "areas of refuge" for disabled staff and visitors who are unable to use the stairs?**

Task 4
Develop the safety and security response team

The security staff, in the case of fire or earthquake, has to take the public out of the building. The guards also have a list of the twenty most important objects in the museum. In the case of a bomb threat, they call in the special police. Also, every afternoon they check the exhibits and bathrooms for bombs after we close the museum.

— Johanna Maria Theile Bruhns
  Coordinator, restoration program
  Facultad de Arte, Universidad de Chile, Santiago

Step 1
Compile a list of necessary actions

The role of the safety and security team will vary depending on the institution and the emergency. One team member probably will need to

- make decisions to relocate or evacuate people and objects, if necessary (the collections response team must be consulted, but the safety and security team must know when they may take action in regard to the collection—for example, at night, if no collections staff are present);
- activate the chain of command;
- contact emergency organizations;
- attend to injuries;

Figure 5   Security officers setting up an emergency shelter and supplies during an evacuation drill at the Getty Center. Photo: Valerie Dorge.

- restrict movement of nonemergency personnel; and
- secure the buildings and grounds.

The Getty Center's safety and security team has the following responsibilities during an emergency:[11]

- Establish priorities for staff and visitor safety and physical security.
- Oversee the safety and welfare of all people on the site, the security of the site and buildings, emergency communications, and the allocation and distribution of all emergency equipment, supplies, and transportation.
- Conduct search-and-rescue operations, direct first-aid teams, and coordinate food, shelter, and sanitation.
- Allocate and deliver all emergency supplies, equipment, and vehicles during emergency operations, and distribute communications tools (cellular phones, radios, walkie-talkies).
- Ensure effective operation of all technical security, fire, and emergency communication systems; oversee notification of evacuation and relocation of building occupants (Fig. 5).

At the Barbados Museum and Historical Society, museum security officers are expected to contact management if an emergency threatens or occurs. The safety and security team oversees evacuations of staff and visitors. A disaster team, which includes the director, the curators, the administrator, a special events manager, a structural engineer, and an architect, takes over after an emergency. Members of the disaster team enter the buildings to ascertain the physical condition of the buildings and the collections. Disaster team members determine if and how the recovery team begins its work.

At the Mystic Seaport Museum, every department, including security, undertakes a series of procedures as a storm approaches. Forty-eight hours before a storm is due, security personnel meet with the chief protection officer to review plans, adjust schedules, and implement storm watch procedures. Thirty-six hours before the storm, security personnel prepare emergency supplies for movement from storage to the central control station. At eighteen hours, security personnel clear the museum and parking lot of visitors, transfer emergency supplies to the central control station, and assume posts at the property gates, at a first-aid station, at the central control station, and in patrol vehicles. Just before the storm hits, security personnel return to the central control station and remain there until authorized to return to their posts.

Step 2

Develop response team job descriptions

We have paid much more attention to the ability of security staff to communicate clearly and effectively, whether in written or verbal form. Meticulous observation and reporting are crucial. One senior security officer now joins the management staff in interviewing and evaluating new officers.

— Alissandra Cummins
   Director
   Barbados Museum and Historical Society

Now that the necessary actions have been designated, they must be assigned to team member positions. Give each job a title that accurately reflects the chief function of the job. For instance, you may want to assign team leaders to certain areas or functions, such as conducting the evacuation, setting up the command center, or administering first aid. Next, list that position's duties and responsibilities. Pay particular attention to the types and number of duties. Match similar duties (e.g., leadership duties, assistance duties, and physical duties) so that one person is not expected to fulfill completely different tasks.

Following that, list the staff position assigned to the role, along with at least two alternates in a line of succession. The number of alternates you designate depends on how important certain skills are to the position. The administration and records team, which is experienced in writing job descriptions as part of its human resources function, can coordinate the writing of job descriptions in each of the four departmental response teams.

The response team job description for responsibility in safety and welfare of employees and visitors (appendix D) is from the Seattle Art Museum's *Emergency Planning Handbook*.[12] Note that in addition to simple and clear responsibilities, the description also designates which staff position should fulfill the role. If the person in that position is unavailable, the first alternate takes on these responsibilities. The description also states whom this team member reports to and provides a checklist of actions expected of the position. In short, nearly anyone could fill the position if necessary.

Suggested Exercise

Propose the following scenario to team members: It's a hot summer night. At 7 P.M., a passerby tells the security officer that he believes he saw smoke coming from the attic window of the main building. A group, mostly senior citizens, is meeting in that building.

List the steps that must be taken over the next twenty-four hours to save those in the building, put out the fire, and protect and salvage objects. Who does what? If a key person is not around, who takes his or her place?

Committing to paper the responsibilities of each position helps to define roles. In addition to familiarizing the persons in the primary and backup positions with their role and that of colleagues, putting it in writing makes it easier for an alternate to run down the "checklist" of work to be carried out. This will help keep the emergency recovery on track.

Questions to Consider

- Who is responsible for summoning help? What is the best way to reach local authorities if the phones are not working?
- Who will have the authority to allow staff back into the buildings?
- Who documents all significant activities and events?
- Who announces the location of the emergency command center?
- Who calls in off-duty security personnel, if necessary?
- Who coordinates the deployment of arriving staff, ensuring that all needs are met according to priority?
- Who patrols the perimeter to prevent trespassing, theft, and looting? Use the buddy system here, particularly at night.

Task 5

Develop emergency procedures

What should a receptionist do if he or she receives a bomb threat? What should a security officer do immediately following an earthquake? What should a maintenance worker do if he or she detects a suspicious odor? These are the types of questions that should be answered in a staff emergency procedures handout, which your team will submit to the EPC as part of Report 2. The handout should

- give prominent placement to the telephone numbers for security staff;
- include the operating hours of the security office;
- include a telephone number to call if security is unreachable;
- describe available emergency supplies;
- explain how long emergency generators will operate;
- describe locations of first-aid kits;
- give step-by-step instructions on what to do in the event of any likely emergencies (including medical emergencies; flooding and water damage; power outage; suspicious behavior and personal safety; chemical spills, gas leaks, and suspicious odors; earthquakes; fire; telephone mail threats; suspicious objects; explosion; civil disturbance; and elevator entrapment; and
- describe employee evacuation procedures.

The staff emergency procedures handout should be concise, should address all relevant emergencies, and should be printed in bright, readily identifiable colors so it can be quickly found in a crisis. Give all employees a copy and have them sign a checklist indicating that they have read it. Remind them that they should read the handout on a regular basis and update it whenever necessary.

Task 6

Detail recovery procedures

Recovery measures occur after an event has happened. They are designed to enable the museum—and its collection—to return to normalcy in an orderly, phased, reasoned and methodical fashion. Recovery measures begin when the disaster situation has stabilized and professionals have evaluated the damage and suggested further, long-term actions. Recovery can be a long process, taking years in some cases.[13]

— John E. Hunter
Supervisory staff curator
National Park Service, U.S. Department of the Interior

Step 1

Consider damage assessment issues

Working with the three other departmental preparedness teams, you and your team will build damage assessment procedures into the response plan. Determine what role safety and security will play in the damage assessment process. Once an area of the institution has been identified as a hazard, how will it be marked? In what cases will a security officer be posted at a hazard site?

Documentation of physical damage is critical not only for salvage and conservation of historic buildings, but also for insurance claim purposes. Claim forms and documentation equipment, such as still cameras or video cameras, should be safely stored and easily accessible. If visual documentation equipment is unavailable, do the documentation in writing.

Step 2

Determine recovery procedures

You and your team should coordinate efforts with the three other teams to identify recovery procedures that move the museum from a state of emergency into the state of normal operations. In the aftermath of an emergency, these recovery procedures can be used as a guide in developing a recovery plan.

Security-related recovery procedures include the following:

- Secure the building and grounds with extra security, if necessary.
- Work with the buildings and maintenance team to ensure a safe work environment for staff and volunteers.
- Work with the collections team to secure the collection.
- Help develop and implement the recovery plan.

Step 3

Address issues of mental and physical well-being

*We recognize that many of you will want to go home as quickly as possible
following an emergency. We understand and support that desire. If you
do leave the property, please proceed carefully. If you find you are unable to
get to your destination, we welcome you to return to the Getty Center.*[14]

— The Getty Center
"Emergency Planning Handbook"

The above statement reflects the conflict staff members will have in the event
of an emergency—such as flood, forest fire, or major seismic activity—that
threatens their families and homes as well as the institution. If the disaster
occurs while they are at work, their first concern will be for their families and
homes; if they are at home, no matter how committed those employees are
to their institution, they will be hesitant to leave until they are confident that
everything is under control at home.

If the emergency takes place during work hours, the ERC and response
team leaders must put the well-being of staff first during response, salvage,
and recovery operations. Jerry Podany, head of antiquities conservation at the
J. Paul Getty Museum, recalls how workers assisting in recovery efforts after
an earthquake in Japan were highly organized and worked at a high energy level
for extended hours. In the end their extreme fatigue negatively affected their
work. As team leader, be sure to schedule regular breaks, as well as provide food,
a place to eat and rest, and bathroom facilities.

"You have to respond in a reasonable way and work that into the plan,"
Podany says. "If you do not have a plan in place, you respond emotionally."
In Japan, Podany witnessed one recovery group patching one painting amid a
rubble of pottery shards. "I thought it was silly to patch a painting when
there was so much devastation around them," he recalls. "But it made a huge
difference to that group. It really energized them."

Step 4

Require frank after-action reports

Every encounter with a disaster or an emergency is an opportunity for learning.
That is the purpose of after-action reports that detail the actions taken
and the results observed. First, it is important to emphasize and praise what
went right, then examine problems encountered or mistakes made. Do
not allow these reports to be after-the-fact justifications and defenses of what
the response team did; they must be candid assessments of what occurred—
problems and all.

Indicate to team members your desire to learn from mistakes, not to punish people for them. Encourage an atmosphere of honest self-assessment, starting with yourself. What could you have done differently? What would have worked better? How could you improve your response next time? What did you learn that could be applied to the next emergency?

Task 7

Create lists of staff and resource contact information

Once you have the list, do not rest on your laurels, thinking, Well, we have a list so we're done! Lists go out of date quickly, so it is important to update them at least once a year.

— Gail Joice
Senior deputy director and registrar
Seattle Art Museum

Furnish the EPC with the names of all staff members, along with their work and home telephone numbers and home addresses. This information makes it easier to notify staff during an emergency, and the institution also can check whether staff members are OK if they have not reported to work following a large-scale emergency. Develop other means of contact in the event of a widespread emergency in which the telephone system may not be functioning. Make sure employees have contact numbers for out-of-state family members in the event that all local telephone services are jammed. Make a list of special skills available from among the staff; for example, is someone a former nurse, search-and-rescue team member, or National Guard member? It is also important to establish relations with individuals and organizations that the team might have contact with during an emergency. With help from the other departmental preparedness teams, produce lists with names, telephone and fax numbers, street and e-mail addresses, and contact persons.

Update all lists and check the contacts regularly. Are the listed companies still in business? Are the contact persons still at the company? Have phone numbers or e-mail addresses changed? Use significant dates to help you remember to update the contact lists. For example, if the institution is in an earthquake-prone area in the United States, do the updating on April 1 (April is National Earthquake Preparedness Month).

Here are some external resources you may wish to include:

- sources of additional security officers
- health and water-testing authorities
- doctors and hospitals
- mental health advisers
- emergency equipment rental resources
- sources for supplies and materials (include name of staff person authorized to purchase)

Questions to Consider

- **Have you posted a list of emergency numbers in strategic places in the buildings for staff emergency reference?**

- **Who is responsible for updating the lists?**

- **Does the central security control station have the list permanently posted for immediate response?**

- **Is there a copy of the list outside the buildings for use after an evacuation?**

Task 8
Create fact sheets and maps

The safety and security team is responsible for developing the following fact sheets:

- a flow chart of chain of command in emergencies
- operating instructions for emergency equipment, such as generators, radios, walkie-talkies
- step-by-step instructions for turning off valves for gas, electricity, water, and so forth
- basic first-aid recommendations

The safety and security team also is responsible for creating maps that identify emergency exits, describe evacuation routes, and alert staff members to where they can find the following:

- emergency shelter, supplies, and first-aid locations
- emergency equipment, such as extinguishers
- communications devices
- keys to such areas as supplies and storage

Task 9
Stock emergency supplies and equipment

Emergency supplies should be stored in two locations: inside the institution, in case it becomes a shelter itself, and outside the institution, for situations that require evacuation or if the building is not occupied when the emergency occurs. Large quantities of expensive items or perishable materials need not be stockpiled. Instead, identify suppliers and make arrangements for emergency delivery as needed.

Security personnel often are responsible for checking and replenishing emergency supplies. Keep lists readily available, and make sure all staff members know where the supply caches are and who has access, including keys. Emergency supplies should include the following:

- water (three days' supply: one gallon [4.5 liters] per person per day, as recommended by the American Red Cross)
- food
- blankets
- first-aid kits
- battery-powered radio and/or walkie-talkies
- flashlights
- spares of each type of battery
- sanitary supplies

Other supplies:

- cash and/or traveler's checks to purchase supplies not on hand
- camera, flash unit, batteries, and rolls of film
- suitable clothing—hard hats, gloves, eye protection, fire-retardant overalls
- carts and dollies
- boxes, buckets, and other containers for carrying smaller objects
- waterproof labels, tape, and pencils
- emergency generator and fuel (operate only in proper ventilation)
- fire extinguishers
- breathing equipment, such as respirators and dust masks
- small backpacks or carrying bags for tools and supplies needed for the initial response

Note: Candles are *not* recommended because of their potential for causing fire and/or an explosion if there are any gas leaks. Other supplies should be based on the types of potential emergency situations identified in the risk assessment. For example, if the institution is in a floodplain, clothing such as rubber boots and raincoats, as well as plastic sheeting and bags of sand, should be kept on hand. For fire, store buckets, shovels, rakes, and hoes.

See appendix E for a list of supplies and equipment needed for a mobile/portable first-aid box, an emergency response cart, and a disaster supply box.

Suggested Exercise

During a meeting of the security staff, conduct a mental exercise. Ask staff members to close their eyes, then give them an emergency scenario. Say the sprinkler system accidentally discharges, or a fire breaks out in a workroom. Ask a volunteer to describe, step by step, how he or she would respond. Ask detailed questions: What do you do first? Whom do you call? What phone do you use? Where are the keys? Where are the necessary tools, supplies, maps, and lists? Encourage others to make recommendations.

Questions to Consider

- Have you determined what supplies and equipment are likely to be needed?

- Have you provided sufficient protection for the supplies so they will be available and undamaged in the event of a disaster?

- Are supplies and equipment available to remove water and debris from affected objects or institution areas?

- What are the nearby sources for the replacement of damaged or inaccessible materials previously assembled? Where is the "shopping list"? Who can purchase the materials? [15]

Note: Remember, credit cards may not be usable in a disaster if telephone lines are down; a cash economy will be in effect.

Task 10

Establish routines to keep the plan viable

The following are a few examples of possible daily and periodic checklist activities for the safety and security team. You may be inspired to think of others. Compare lists with the other departmental preparedness teams.

Daily checklist activities:

- Exhibit gallery cases remain secure and all display objects are accounted for.
- All external doors and windows and appropriate internal doors are locked, and the keys are in their designated locations.
- After closing time, no visitors are in public areas, such as washrooms.
- Computer files and systems are backed up.
- Staff members who have not signed out are accounted for in the building.

Periodic checklist activities:

- Update the contact information lists.
- Reorder emergency supplies if necessary.
- Replace batteries in emergency equipment, such as flashlights and radios.
- Ensure that fire extinguishers are inspected and recharged if necessary.
- Test all alarms and protection systems after closing to the public and when most staff members are not in the building (after notifying staff, as appropriate).
- Provide the emergency preparedness manager (EPM) with updated documents that are part of the emergency plan, including fire exits, changes in visitor flow, and operating instructions for new equipment.
- Review collection inventory documents, including loan forms.

- Update the duty roster to reflect staff and other institutional changes.
- Verify that outside experts and/or resource information is up to date.

In addition, make sure that evacuation drills are conducted regularly.

Task 11
Identify and implement appropriate training

What skills and knowledge do security personnel need? Training and support are available from many sources, including international and national security organizations, such as the International Committee on Museum Security of the International Council of Museums. Local police, fire, and military are the most immediately available resources. Extensive literature is available for each particular security need, including security officer training, emergency planning, alarms, and access control. Major museums and museum associations, such as the American Association of Museums (AAM) security committee, may be willing to share their training procedures for security managers and officers.

Members of the security force should be trained not only to perform guarding tasks, but also to recognize material damage and deterioration and to be familiar with the museum, its collections, and its history. *A Manual of Basic Museum Security*[16] suggests the following training skills related specifically to responding to emergencies:

- Exemplify leadership, calm, and authority in handling persons in any emergency.
- State the four fire response steps of reporting, annunciating, evacuating, and fighting the fire, in that priority order.
- State each individual's role and responsibility in evacuating the area, only as instructed by security supervisors.
- Recognize major life-threatening medical emergencies, and respond by calling immediately for emergency assistance.
- Take commonsense measures in a medical emergency to support breathing and prevent excessive bleeding, keeping ill or injured persons comfortable and out of public sight as much as possible.
- Recognize general crimes against persons, property, and the museum, and report them immediately.
- Protect people over property and collections in criminal or violent situations.
- Respond to bomb threat signals by searching the assigned area without touching anything, and report any unusual condition or suspected objects immediately by phone.

Practice evacuation procedures

Security personnel are responsible for carrying out evacuations. Security officers need practice in conducting an evacuation, as does the rest of the staff.

Does everyone on staff know what immediate action to take when the emergency alarm sounds? After seeing to the personal safety of staff and visitors, thoughts turn to the collection. Do employees know which objects in the collection to evacuate first? If not, can they find the priority list quickly? Do they know where supply kits of packaging materials are, and do they have access to that location? Do they know the routes to internal or external shelters? Do they know who is in charge and to whom they need to report?

Teach observation techniques

Year-round, emergency-response training for your security or other designated staff is imperative and should include basic fire fighting, first aid, cardiopulmonary resuscitation, utility shutoffs, and emergency collections movement.[17]

— Wilbur Faulk
   Director of Getty Center Security
   The J. Paul Getty Trust

Security officers are trained to watch for suspicious behavior and threats to security. Every staff member must understand that security is of prime consideration within his or her delegated duties. Staff should receive training in security and fire protection, including good observation techniques.

Talk with the EPC about including security- and safety-related duties in job descriptions for every employee and allowing security personnel to train other staff members. Sales clerks in the gift shop and receptionists at the entrance can act as security officers, not only for their immediate area but also for adjacent areas. Volunteers also can be instructed in security; in some museums they provide a vital link in the security chain.

Following are a few basic training methods. You may choose to employ several, either independently or simultaneously. (See chapter 5 for more information on training.)

- group discussions
- simulations/role-playing
- supplementary handouts
- videos
- review sessions
- self-assessment exercises
- hands-on workshops
- presentations by colleagues or consultants who have hands-on knowledge of the scenarios the institution might face

Questions to Consider

- Do officers and key staff members know how to operate electrical and water supply systems or other important building systems?

- Are officers trained in what to do in unusual situations or those situations requiring special skills or instructions beyond their routine or beyond their level of skill?

- Does anyone check to make sure that visitors and staff members sign in and use their real names when they enter the buildings?

- Can security staff conduct fire extinguisher training for other staff?

- Do all staff members know how to get to the roof of the building, and how to direct others to the roof?

- Does everyone know the location, both off-site and on-site, of emergency keys, hard hats, flashlights, fresh batteries, hoses, and fire hydrants?

- Is any staff member trained to use a fire hose? Should any employees be trained?

Notes

1. Robert B. Burke and Sam Adeloye, *A Manual of Basic Museum Security* (Leicester, Great Britain: International Council of Museums and the International Committee on Museum Security, 1986), 12. Reproduced by permission of the ICOM Committee for Conservation.

2. Ibid., 10. Reproduced by permission of the ICOM Committee for Conservation.

3. Ibid., 6–7. Reproduced by permission of the ICOM Committee for Conservation.

4. Suzanne Ashford, "A Contract Guard Force Versus a Proprietary Force" (presentation to the National Conference on Cultural Property Protection, Arlington, Virginia, Feb. 20–24, 1995), 31–33.

5. Robin Thornes, *Protecting Cultural Objects in the Global Information Society: The Making of Object ID*, ed. Marilyn Schmitt and Nancy Bryan (Los Angeles: J. Paul Getty Trust, 1997), 25.

6. Object ID is a standard system, developed by the Getty and its partners, for identification of works of art and artifacts. For free copies of an eight-minute video on Object ID, a one-page checklist, or the Getty publication *Protecting Cultural Objects in the Global Information Society*, write to the Getty Information Institute, 1200 Getty Center Drive, Los Angeles, CA 90049 USA; or send a request by e-mail to objectid@getty.edu.

7. International Committee on Museum Security, *Museum Security Survey*, ed. Diana Menkes, trans. Marthe de Moltke, based on the document by George H. H. Schröder (Paris: International Council of Museums, 1981), 24–25.

8. Adapted from International Committee on Museum Security, *Museum Security Survey*, 26–28, with input from advisers on the compilation of this book.

9. Adapted from "Command Post: Establishing" in Getty Center, "Emergency Planning Handbook" (J. Paul Getty Trust, Los Angeles, 1997, photocopy), Fact Sheets section.

10. Adapted from Allyn Lord, Carolyn Reno, and Marie Demeroukas, *Steal This Handbook! A Template for Creating a Museum's Emergency Preparedness Plan* (Columbia, S.C.: Southeastern Registrars Association, 1994), 177–79. Used by permission.

11. Adapted from "Summary of Emergency Response Roles" in Getty Center, "Emergency Planning Handbook," Checklist section.

12. Seattle Art Museum, *Emergency Planning Handbook*, rev. ed. (Seattle: Seattle Art Museum, 1994).

13. John E. Hunter, "Preparing a Museum Disaster Plan," in *Southeastern Museums Conference, 1991 Disaster Preparedness Seminar Proceedings*, ed. Martha E. Battle and Pamela Meister (Baton Rouge, La.: Southeastern Museums Conference, 1991), 53–66.

14. Getty Center, "Emergency Planning Handbook," Evacuation section.

15. Taken from Gail Joice, "Questions to Ask Yourself When Preparing a Disaster Plan" (AAM Risk Management and Insurance Committee, American Association of Museums, Washington, D.C., April 1994, typescript).

16. Burke and Adeloye, *Basic Museum Security*, 95. Reproduced by permission of the ICOM Committee for Conservation.

17. Wilbur Faulk, "Are You Ready When Disaster Strikes?" *History News* 48 (Jan./Feb. 1993), 9. Used by permission of the American Association for State and Local History.

Chapter Summary

This chapter

- outlined the role of the safety and security team in the emergency preparedness process;

- described the information required in the two reports prepared by the safety and security team for the emergency preparedness committee;

- guided you, the team leader, through the process of assessing the vulnerability of your institution's safety and security program;

- helped define the roles and responsibilities of the safety and security response team; and

- identified tasks to guide your team through the process of designing a response and recovery plan that is simple, detailed, and flexible.

In review, the emergency preparedness process is a long-term commitment on the part of staff, teams, and committees. You cannot, and should not, expect changes to come quickly or easily. Interdisciplinary teamwork is difficult and requires a change in attitude that may be slow in coming at first. The payoff—in peace of mind, in the safety of people, and in the protection of cultural objects and irreplaceable records—will be great.

CHAPTER SEVEN

The Collections Team

As the institution's emergency plan is developed, several collections-related issues must be addressed. This chapter is designed to be a resource for you, the leader of the collections team. For an overview of the emergency preparedness and response planning process, please consult chapters 1–3. For training ideas, see chapter 5.

Your Role in the Process

It is a wet and windy day. A huge fire has broken out in the west wing of the museum, threatening the entire building but leaving enough time to evacuate a few items from the collection. As you watch in horror, a well-meaning volunteer attempts to save a prized painting. In his hurry, he grabs the painting and accidentally damages the frame while rushing out the door. Or, instead, the volunteer bypasses that valuable painting to save a bronze, one of several identical ones owned by the museum.

Now, picture the same scenario, only this time a staff member trained in emergency art-handling removes the painting, taking care not to touch its surface, bypasses the replaceable bronze cast, and walks quickly but calmly to the evacuation door.

Effective emergency planning can make a difference when it comes to your institution's collections. This is why you and your team's contribution to the overall emergency preparedness and response program is so important. Emergency planning can be no better than the information on which it is based, and no other department of the institution has more knowledge of the collections than you and your staff.

The job of the collections preparedness team is to evaluate the collection thoroughly to determine where the institution is vulnerable and what to do during an emergency. The team produces two reports for the emergency planning committee that summarize its findings:

Report 1 is a vulnerability and asset analysis that identifies the collection's vulnerability to damage and recommends measures for preventing damage. (See pages 142–53.)

Report 2 is an outline of recommended procedures and techniques for evacuating, salvaging, and recovering prioritized objects, and the role of the collections response team. (See pages 154–71.)

With the information you provide, the institution will be able to

- set priorities in the institution's efforts to prevent damage to the collection;
- know which objects to evacuate first, if necessary, and how to handle them properly; and
- recover and preserve as much of the collection as possible and as quickly as possible in the event of a disaster.

As you begin the process of compiling this information and developing your portion of the response plan, as team leader you will need to perform the following tasks:

Task 1: Assemble the preparedness team.

Task 2: Interact with other departmental teams and with the emergency planning committee (EPC).

You and your department colleagues may have spent much of your adult lives tending to the objects in the collection—so much time, in fact, that they may feel like family. As a result, the process of deciding which objects should be saved first can be painful. Similarly, the notion that people not accustomed or trained in handling collections may handle them in an emergency is near blasphemy to many collections managers and staff. An important role of the collections preparedness leader is to address this issue with all collections staff members and prepare them for such an event.

"The collections people need to recognize that everyone on staff will want to help them," says conservator and hazard mitigation consultant Barbara Roberts. "They can manage it quite well and with joy on their faces if they have trained every member of the museum staff in how to carry a tapestry or a table or whatever."

At the same time, it is important to keep the collections in perspective. Though they are the heart of the institution, they are not the sole focus of emergency planning. People take precedence. No object is worth a human life.

Task 1

Assemble the preparedness team

Personnel functioning as one well-oiled machine during emergencies produce dramatically better results than scattered, chaotic responses by individuals. That is why team building is such a critical component of true emergency preparedness. Building a successful team means taking risks that involve resolving conflict, establishing trust, and encouraging interdependence. Refer to chapter 5 on training for information on assembling and building effective teams.

You are in charge of appointing the collections preparedness team and of guiding team members in gathering accurate, efficient information and in organizing a well-developed preparedness and response plan. Select team members on the basis of three categories of skills: technical and functional, problem solving, and interpersonal. All efforts at team building should focus on the process and on accomplishing the intended tasks. Communication skills are important, as your team will be interacting with nearly every department in the institution. Involve your department colleagues in the planning process so they will more readily support the recommended changes in policy and procedures. Identifying and appointing "true believers" in emergency preparedness will help generate enthusiasm and create the proper atmosphere. Be sure to include "nonbelievers" as well; this will forge a well-balanced, cohesive unit that enables all members to do the best they can.

As part of the recommendations in Report 2, you and your team will describe the roles and responsibilities of the collections response team, which may or may not include all members of the preparedness team. This team, along with a team from each of the other three departments, will respond in an actual emergency situation.

Task 2

Interact with other teams and with the EPC

Before you begin your vulnerability and asset assessment, you will need to obtain from the EPC the overall hazard analysis. This identifies what emergencies may threaten the institution and characterizes the types of damage associated with each. It will help focus your team's efforts.

During your planning, work closely with the other three departmental teams on certain areas, as indicated below:

Safety and security
- Security of emergency shelters
- Screening of volunteers to help in evacuation/emergency salvage
- Security of the building if there is structural damage
- Security of the collection in the event of relocation or evacuation

Buildings and maintenance
- Places to store cultural objects
- Preventive building maintenance
- Housekeeping practices
- Secondary storage sites
- Evacuation routes for collections

Administration and records
- Collections insurance issues
- Inventory and intellectual control
- Documentation of activities

In collaborating with other teams, work through the EPC to set up meetings between your team and the others. This hierarchical method helps avoid territorial disputes that can occur during the process. It becomes a top-down mandate, rather than a lateral arrangement. You may want to include a member from the EPC during these meetings. When needed, include a member of the other departmental teams, as applicable. This works well as long as your team is discussing matters that pertain to this person's area of expertise. If discussions cover areas specific only to collections, it can be a waste of time for the other person.

This collaboration is required for the overall success of the emergency preparedness program. The planning process is likely to give buildings, maintenance, and security staff a higher profile, in terms of both image and responsibilities. It may also require—or cause—a shift in attitudes on the part of other professional staff.

Preparing Report 1: Vulnerability and Asset Analysis

To the collections team, vulnerability means how much loss or damage the collections will sustain in an emergency or a disaster, or from exposure to a hazard.[1] When assessing the collections' vulnerability, look for weaknesses, checking every area of the collections to determine how susceptible the objects are to damage from potential risks. The accuracy and thoroughness of the assessment greatly affects the success of efforts to protect against or minimize damage to the collections, so it is not an effort to be taken lightly.

Some examples of potential vulnerabilities are listed below. No doubt you and your colleagues are aware of some, if not all, of these weaknesses. Some may become apparent only during the analysis process. All, however, may ultimately affect the institution's potential preparedness and response capabilities. Discuss with your team the ramifications of

- objects stacked on the storage room floor;
- sloppy housekeeping practices;
- unreliable inventory and documentation of the collections;
- display objects not appropriately secured; and
- the institution's low priority in an energy crisis.

In Report 1, you will suggest protective measures to reduce the identified vulnerabilities. The next section of this chapter contains a more in-depth discussion of those measures.

The vulnerability and asset analysis also involves determining which items or groups in the collections should receive priority in protection (before an event) and in handling and moving and/or salvage (during/after an event). When you set priorities in advance, you gain time and do not try to protect or save objects of lesser importance or risk at the expense of those that truly deserve attention.

The following tasks will help your team complete the assessment:

Task 1: Look at the collections with a fresh eye.

Task 2: Assess risks of damage.

Task 3: Evaluate your documentation and inventory systems.

Task 4: Invite local agencies and individuals to participate.

Task 5: Set priorities for the collections.

Task 6: Recommend preventive measures.

Task 1

Look at the collections with a fresh eye

Suggested Exercise

With your team, take a "worst-case stroll" through a small area of the museum. Decide on an emergency scenario, such as a hurricane that slams ashore just fifteen miles from your location. Be specific. How strong is the wind? What time of day is it? Imagining details makes the exercise more real and the end results more useful. Now list all the possibilities of damage that can occur to collections in that area. How long would it take to remove and package each of the objects, if you could do so before the emergency strikes? What are the top twelve items that three people could move to a safer environment? How long would that take?

I myself feel stress in having to set priorities for what should be saved in an emergency situation. My entire career is built on caring for art, and so to think that I might have to leave something behind is very difficult. These are hard choices.

— Gail Joice
Senior deputy director and registrar
Seattle Art Museum

It is not unusual in cultural institutions, large or small, to find people who have worked with the collections for many years. These individuals find it especially difficult to look at the same objects in a new way.

Guide your team in regarding the collection objectively, engaging their imagination in the search for vulnerabilities. A painting by Monet, for example, becomes, for a moment, only a piece of fabric with oil paint on its surface and four pieces of wood around it, hanging on a wall. What happens to canvas and wood when soot lands on it? What does intense heat do to oils on canvas? Can one person remove and package the painting? These are the kinds of observations your team should make. Remind them that imagining and planning for the worst will help protect the collection during an emergency.

The type of exercise described here, which is used by many institutions engaged in emergency planning, requires a "stop, think, listen, talk it out" routine that is immensely helpful in facing the reality of an emergency. Experts recommend doing these scene-setting exercises often, with a different scenario each time.

Task 2
Assess risks of damage

How vulnerable is the institution—its people and the collection—to the threats of fire, flood, and any other emergency or hazard? Your team's job is to work with the emergency preparedness manager (EPM), the EPC, and other departmental preparedness teams to assess this vulnerability from a collections point of view.

You and your team need to assess systematically the risk of specific types of damage to the collections. In other words, you will focus on the myriad *effects* that the hazards can cause for the collections. If the EPC identifies a significant risk of flooding, what effect will water and/or mud have on the collections? Since water can swell, warp, split, rot, corrode, dissolve, and contaminate, how would it specifically affect items in the collections? The obvious answer is that water would affect different objects differently.

The following steps will ease the assessment process.

Step 1
Group objects that would be affected in similar ways

Place the collection items into categories of potential damage by asking questions such as

- What are the most likely hazards identified by the EPC?
- Which items (ceramics, unreactive metal, etc.) will be minimally affected by muddy water?
- Which items (leather, paper, wool-based textiles, etc.) are susceptible to bacterial or mold contamination?
- What could shatter in an earthquake (large sculptures, glass specimen jars, ceramics, etc.)?

Remember that fire is the leading cause of damage to cultural institutions and their collections. No institution is immune to this hazard and the damage it can bring from water, mold, smoke, and structural collapse.

Step 2
Separate categories into components for further study

Once you set up the categories, separate each into components and study these in more detail. Would you handle wet textiles differently from wet paper? Can a stone ax head remain in water longer than a glass bowl without potential damage?

These kinds of exercises not only are critical to the preparedness process, but also can inspire your team to view the collection in new and creative ways. If the institution's staff is small or does not include a conservator, there is much conservation literature available to assist in setting priorities. An outside conservator, conservation center, or conservation training program also may be consulted. Another useful tool is the *Emergency Response and Salvage Wheel.*[2]

Task 3

Evaluate your documentation and inventory systems

> *Unfortunately, very few objects have been documented to a level that can materially assist in their recovery in the event of theft. Even for objects that have been so documented, the information collected is extremely variable.*[3]
>
> — Robin Thornes
> *Protecting Cultural Objects in the Global Information Society*

As you conduct the survey, make sure you evaluate your inventory system. Work with the safety and security team in this regard. All objects brought into a collection should be identified immediately. Do the identifying marks contain a number or code, and are these marks resistant to deletion or alteration so that they can be used to identify a stolen object? Consider that a lack of preparedness and/or prevention could be an invitation to a robbery.

Important categories of information are identified in Thornes:[4]

- photograph
- Object ID[5] number
- type of object
- object name
- title
- materials and techniques
- measurements
- inscriptions and markings
- distinguishing features
- subject
- date or period
- maker
- description

Several levels of documentation are relevant:

Object identification. Collection records ideally include a written description and image (sketch, photograph, video) of each object or group of holdings, kept in a safe storage location. Store duplicate records off-site, along with duplicate photographic records, if the budget permits. If possible, consider digitized storage of images.

Object condition assessment. Keep this written assessment with the object records, and store duplicates off-site.

Basic inventories. These are a generalized accounting of the types of objects in the collection. "If, during an emergency, you can account for only 420 sculptures and the institution has 450, you know you have a problem," explains Barbara Roberts. "Keep in mind that wet books, for example, swell and will take up more shelf space than when dry." This basic inventory is the minimum form of object-tracking recommended; however, most institutions have no workable inventories. For a detailed list of inventory considerations, refer to *Museum Security Survey*.[6]

Questions to Consider

- **If there is an electronic inventory, have you stored a hard-copy printout of the contents of each storage area inside the room, as well as off-site? (If electricity is out, a computer cannot generate an inventory list.)**

- **Who has access to copies of the collection inventory?**

- **Are the registration and conservation records up to date?**

- **Has each object been photographed and have duplicate copies been made?**

- **Have copies of the inventory been included with the off-site duplicate records?**

- **Is there an updated loan list with contact information?**

Task 4
Invite local agencies and individuals to participate

Institutions often make the mistake of overlooking local or regional services and resources. Fire departments, for example, are reservoirs of valuable information and practical assistance. The information flow works both ways: You learn from the fire officials, who in turn learn about the institution and its special needs. Consider inviting any or all of the following to make presentations to the team, and coordinating such presentations through the EPC. Other teams or all staff also may benefit by participating.

- police
- military (can be problematic in some countries)
- local chapter of the U.S. National Guard
- newspaper reporter who has covered disasters
- retired or current staff of institutions that have experienced emergencies (be sure to keep track of current phone numbers and addresses)

As a visual aid, ask presenters to bring along news clippings, videotapes, and photographs of emergencies and the damage they cause. Acquire more advice and information by talking with staff of institutions or emergency response organizations that have been through the emergencies you are studying. This kind of research is worth the effort.

"I find that it is so easy for people to abstractly talk about a flood," reports Jerry Podany, head of antiquities conservation at the J. Paul Getty Museum. "But it is a whole other thing when they have seen photos and talked to people who were there, wading through the muck. There is so much that does not get recorded but should have been."

Questions to Consider

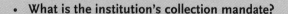

- **What is the institution's collection mandate?**
- **What is the institution prepared to lose, and what is vital to save?**
- **What are the criteria for setting priorities, and who establishes it?**
- **Would standard forms be helpful in the process?**
- **What procedures will be established for protecting these and all objects in an emergency?**
- **Who will review the prioritization lists before they go to the EPC? Who has final approval?**

Task 5

Set priorities for the collections

Setting priorities helps determine how important each asset is to the institution, thereby indicating which assets should be protected before others. It also enables staff to concentrate on saving the most important assets during salvage and recovery operations following an emergency. Each institution's priorities will be different. If your institution does not already have a priority list, consider the questions above before beginning the process. If a priority list does exist, have these questions been considered? Your team might want to reevaluate the list.

Step 1

Determine how value is to be assessed

There are various ways to assess the importance of an object to the institution. You may want to consider a combination of the following options:

- historical/cultural/religious value
- economic value
- vulnerability of certain object to specific hazards (e.g., remove photographs, paper, and textiles first in a flood)
- your institution's mandate
- rarity or replacement possibilities (e.g., classify as "irreplaceable," "replaceable at a high cost," or "easily replaceable")

- loan status
- condition of and/or damage to objects (e.g., rescue all objects not yet damaged)

Step 2

Set priorities for handling and possible evacuation and/or salvage

Based on the criteria chosen in step 1, which items would you take if you had only thirty minutes to evacuate? If you had sixty minutes? If you had three hours? What items would you move first in a flood? Which would you move after an earthquake?

You may know the answers, but what if you are not present at the institution when an emergency strikes? Even if you are, how will others know which pieces are the most important to the institution? That is why a list is needed that indicates, in descending order, what objects are most important to save. A "top ten" list could be compiled for every section (which could amount to as many as 300 to 400 objects), or a ranking could be done of every single item in the collection. Remember, the criteria may be different for each type of hazard.

If conservators are on staff, have them discuss the list with the curators, collections managers, and/or preparators from the point of view of objects vulnerability for their areas of expertise. If no conservators are on staff, you may need to consult conservation literature or an outside conservator. See the list of conservation organizations at the end of the book (pages 261–62). Also, curators should assist in reviewing the priority list. The finalized list will become part of the overall emergency plan.

Questions to Consider

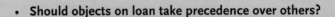

- **Should objects on loan take precedence over others?**

- **Do you have written permission from lenders to handle the objects they own in an emergency?**

- **Are the items on the priority list covered under the institution's insurance policy?**

- **Who has copies of the priority list? Where are copies stored? What are the security considerations for this list?**

- **When and how often will you update the priority list? Every time a new exhibit is installed? Who will update it?**

- **How and to whom will you distribute updates? (Be sure to include dates.)**

Task 6

Recommend preventive measures

Perhaps it is human nature to deny what we cannot predict, but as conservators who are continually fighting nature—human or otherwise— preparation for the unseen is, or should be, a daily activity.

— Jerry Podany
  Head of antiquities conservation
  The J. Paul Getty Museum

The vulnerability analysis indicates ways to eliminate hazards that threaten the collection and ways to reduce the potential effects of those hazards. These measures must be implemented immediately, for a plan without execution is like having no plan at all.

Implementing protection measures can be as easy as having an institutionwide cleanup day or as complex as installing an automatic fire detection/ suppression system. Often, however, protection efforts advance only as far as the cheapest and easiest solutions, leaving the more complex and expensive issues until later—which often means never.

"It is like moving paintings away from leaky pipes because you spotted vulnerability, but never fixing the pipes," says Jerry Podany. "Eventually the paintings will find their way back to the same dangerous situation, and nothing has been achieved."

Instill a prevention state of mind in your team members. Protecting the collections is an ongoing process that never truly ends, and you may have to remind your team of this from time to time. You will know you are in the right frame of mind when you make it a regular practice to walk through the galleries, looking for ways to improve protection. To foster this type of thinking among your team members, consider the following:

- a weekly team trip to a different section of the institution to look specifically at prevention options
- a "protection suggestion" list posted in a central location, on which any staff member may offer ideas either by name or anonymously; a "prevention suggestion of the week" award could be given to the employee who comes up with the most effective or innovative measure; incentives could range from tickets to a local cultural event to a half day off
- a one-time "detect, protect, and collect" contest to see who can come up with the most protection measures in a specified amount of time

Resources for measures to help protect the collections can be found far and wide—and as close as the local fire department, your institution's insurance agent, and other museums or institutions in your area. Colleagues, particularly those who have helped develop their institution's plan or have participated in an emergency, may offer useful tips you may not have thought of.

Which measures should you implement first? This will vary from institution to institution, depending on budget and ability. A recommended approach is to focus first on the collections as a whole, then on storage areas, and finally on display objects.

Step 1

Protect the collections as a whole

A simple and inexpensive prevention measure is to use a day normally closed to the public and devote it to a thorough cleanup. This simple step alone can significantly lower the fire hazard. Cleaning up in itself makes everyone feel good and costs nothing except possibly the rental of a large trash container. It is advisable to consult local authorities on hazardous waste disposal for paint or chemicals prior to this process.

— Barbara Roberts
Conservator and hazard mitigation consultant

You will need to work closely with the buildings and maintenance team—because the structure and the physical plant play a leading role—and with the safety and security team. Consider all factors and elements that affect the entire collection, such as poor electrical wiring and leaky roofs.

A look at common factors in library fires is telling. According to the National Fire Protection Association, factors common to the most destructive fires in libraries without automatic fire protection systems are arson, delayed discovery, delayed reporting, and the absence of any automatic suppression or detection capability.[7] All are factors that libraries and museums can protect against.

Simple smoke detection systems could aid in quicker discovery, and automatic suppression systems help provide a quicker response. (Consider ways to avoid water damage as a result of sprinkler systems, as in installing water deflectors.) Guidelines regarding when to call emergency services versus when to attempt to put out a fire by yourself are helpful in avoiding delayed reporting; developing close relations with the local fire department is also helpful.

Although it is impossible to eliminate the threat of arson, taking precautions can greatly minimize the likelihood of a serious fire. Precautions include increased security measures, perimeters around objects, and fire extinguishers installed throughout the institution. In some cases, simply taking an inventory of the collection can be the most effective protection measure. How can you begin to protect what you do not know you have?

An incident at the Huntington Library Art Collection and Botanical Gardens in San Marino, California, indicates that tidiness goes a long way. Rare, leather-bound books on the desks of scholars were soaked and nearly ruined during a "sprinkler flood" set off by a fire alarm in the building. Had the books been returned to their proper cases or otherwise protected on the desks, they would not have become wet.

The following are ideas for protecting the collection as a whole:

- Keep collections out of areas that contain physical hazards (water pipes, boilers, steam lines, etc.).

Suggested Exercise

Look around your office. What personal items can you take home? What books can be returned to the institution library or the public library? What paperwork can you file, and how much clutter can you eliminate? Be brutal in your effort to clear away as much as possible. While you are at it, look for signs of insect pests and rodents. Imagine how high the pile of unnecessary boxes and papers would be if all staff members cleared their offices as well.

- If applicable in your country, have the institution listed as a cultural institution instead of as an industrial user. This may exempt it from energy cutbacks, which can cause humidity crises.
- If you are part of a large institution, such as a university, make sure you have (or attempt to gain) control over the temperature and humidity in the collections areas (i.e., exhibit galleries, storage).
- Work with the buildings and maintenance team to ensure the soundness of the building and its systems and to establish strict construction rules to prevent fires.
- Work with the safety and security team to adopt adequate security screening procedures and to establish no-smoking rules and restrictions on food and drink in all areas that contain collections.
- With the buildings and maintenance team, consider methods to increase insulation in historic buildings to protect against weather or loss of heat during a power outage.

As you implement protection procedures, document as many as possible. Documentation is a powerful tool for communicating progress in emergency preparedness and provides evidence of the measures taken for insurance purposes. The best documentation is photographs with captions, such as "Item before/after being tied down" and "Shop before/after cleanup." Video-taped records also work well.

Display photos on walls or bulletin boards in staff areas so employees can see the progress being made toward preparedness, or distribute an emergency preparedness bulletin to all staff. This builds not only confidence in the emergency preparedness and response program but also morale on your team. Be sure to credit those on (or off) your team whose suggestions resulted in measures undertaken.

| Step 2 |

Protect storage areas

It is common for a full two-thirds or more of a collection to be in storage (Fig. 6). Securing this space and making it as safe as possible in advance enables you during an actual emergency to turn your attention to the display objects. Of course, if most of the collection is on display rather than in storage, then the display objects would take priority over storage protection.

Work with your colleagues in buildings and maintenance on some of these activities. Ask collections staff members at other institutions for innovative and practical ideas for protecting stored collections. Considerable literature on this topic also is available.

Figure 6   Sculpture and decorative arts storage area at the Seattle Art Museum, showing preventive measures implemented to protect against earthquake—the museum's main hazard. Courtesy Seattle Art Museum. Photo: Paul Macapia.

Questions to Consider

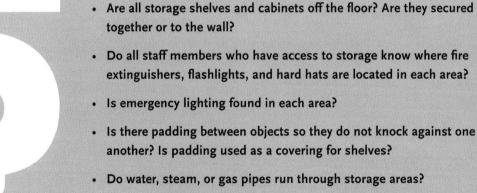

- Are all storage shelves and cabinets off the floor? Are they secured together or to the wall?

- Do all staff members who have access to storage know where fire extinguishers, flashlights, and hard hats are located in each area?

- Is emergency lighting found in each area?

- Is there padding between objects so they do not knock against one another? Is padding used as a covering for shelves?

- Do water, steam, or gas pipes run through storage areas?

- Are water detector alarms located on storage room floors? Do they connect to a central station?

- Are hard copies of all computer collection inventories available in case computers are inoperable? Where are the printouts stored?

Step 3
Protect objects on display

Once storage areas are protected, attention can shift toward protecting the exhibits. Commonsense measures play a significant role in this area.

An important factor in protecting the collections is to minimize fluctuations in relative humidity and temperature, excessive light levels, and long periods of display for the various objects in the collection. Work with buildings and maintenance colleagues on these activities. If no one on staff has expertise on recommended environmental conditions for collections and historical buildings, consult with experts. Considerable literature also exists on these topics.

Questions to Consider

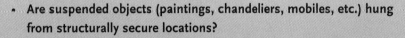

- Are suspended objects (paintings, chandeliers, mobiles, etc.) hung from structurally secure locations?

- Are objects displayed beneath suspended items (i.e., a table below a chandelier in a room setting)? If so, is the chandelier securely held in position?

- How well attached are light tracks and security cameras?

- Are barriers in place to prevent visitors from touching objects on open display?

- Are small objects in open-room settings out of reach of visitors? Are they secured to an immovable support?

Step 4
Budget for preventive measures

The planning phase not only gives you an emergency plan, but also builds the budget to carry out these activities ahead of time so that the institution's vulnerability is reduced.

— Barbara Roberts
Conservator and hazard mitigation consultant

Prevention is the most cost-effective phase of developing preparedness plans. Time and money spent in this area pays enormous dividends. The priorities for protection that you set will determine the budget for resolving these problems. It is easier to request funding or to raise money within the community for specific, concrete projects than for the amorphous goal of achieving emergency preparedness.

The problem in "selling" prevention lies in measuring intangibles. In other words, you may never know how many emergencies your prevention efforts actually eliminated.

Preparing Report 2:
Outline of Response Procedure and Techniques

The second report you and your collections team will prepare for the EPC contains the recommended procedures and techniques for responding to an emergency *from a collections point of view*. It should include instructions for handling, evacuating, salvaging, and recovering prioritized objects. The report should also contain lists, such as telephone numbers of emergency storage contacts, and emergency supplies and equipment. Job descriptions for the collections response team are provided as well.

Do not kid yourself or your team: The process is a long one. The 300-word job description for the J. Paul Getty Museum emergency response collections manager—one position among many—took hours and hours of deliberations to develop.

Of course, there are plenty of emergency plan templates to help you get started. Remember, however, that your work is not done simply by copying applicable sections verbatim from another manual. The institution's greatest resource is a well-trained staff that is accustomed to thinking through emergencies. This is what the *process* of preparedness and response planning provides.

Establish an effective response system

The following tasks will help you craft a simple, detailed, and flexible response plan:

Task 1: Identify potential safe rooms and/or outside shelters.

Task 2: Develop the collections response team.

Task 3: Set guidelines for moving objects.

Task 4: Detail recovery procedures.

Task 5: Create lists of staff and resource contact information.

Task 6: Create fact sheets and maps.

Task 7: Stock emergency supplies and equipment.

Task 8: Establish routines to keep the plan viable.

Task 9: Identify and implement appropriate training.

In preparing your report, you and your team will have to address a number of important issues. Some will be general to all the team reports; others will be issues specific to collections. The questions on page 155 will help you address some issues and may prompt you to identify others.

Questions to Consider

- Who will be in charge of keeping your part of the plan current? (People change jobs, telephone numbers change, new equipment is purchased and old equipment is discarded, companies go out of business, and agency responsibilities change.)

- To whom does your team report during an emergency?

- What will be the effect on the collections of a long-term disruption of services? A short-term disruption?

Task 1

Identify potential safe rooms and/or outside shelters

In some emergencies, safe rooms and/or outside shelters will be necessary to house staff members, visitors, and objects. Consult with the safety and security and the buildings and maintenance teams to determine the best locations for these safe rooms and to coordinate their preparation. You may want to have storage options outside the institution as well. For example, you may want to freeze water-damaged books and papers and store them in the appropriate facility, such as a local icehouse or meat locker. After a major fire in 1988 at the Soviet Academy of Science Library in Leningrad, millions of books were safely dried by citizens using home refrigerators and returned without loss.

The following recommendations for an effective safe area have been been adapted from *Steal This Handbook!*[8] with input from advisers to this book:

Size. Ensure that the shelter is large enough to fit the maximum number of staff and visitors likely to be at the institution at any one time. Allow 5–6 square feet (0.47–0.56 square meters) per adult and 3 square feet (0.28 square meters) per child. It also should be large enough to accommodate emergency supplies and priority objects.

Accessibility. Take into account the route necessary to reach the shelter and the size of the openings through which objects must pass.

Security. The shelter must offer the highest level of security. This means a minimum number of openings so the shelter can be sealed and access controlled completely.

Physical safety. The shelter should be isolated from the exterior by adjacent rooms or corridors. Walls and ceilings should be free of plumbing, pipes, and so forth.

Environmental stability. Make sure the shelter is environmentally stable. Add materials such as carpets and curtains to buffer the relative humidity, and have humidifiers or dehumidifiers on hand.

Lighting. Make sure adequate lighting is provided. There should be no windows or skylights if the institution is in a seismic area or subject to tornadoes, to avoid the danger of broken glass.

Coordinate efforts with the safety and security team on questions such as

- Who has authorized access to the safe rooms? (Color-coded badges could visually indicate authorization.)
- How will the museum maintain security for the safe rooms or outside storage/shelters?

Task 2
Develop the collections response team

This is one of the most critical tasks in all of emergency preparedness and response planning. It is the crux of the plan: Who does what? It is not a case of assigning an individual name to a function, but rather determining which functions are necessary and then incorporating those into job descriptions. A number of alternates in a line of succession should be designated to fill each role should the primary appointee be unavailable. This flexibility is crucial, since no one knows when an emergency will strike or who will be in the building at the time.

Step 1
Compile a list of necessary actions

> *Remember that there may seem to be a lot to do. Take problems one step at a time, and slowly but surely it will all come together.*
>
> — Barbara Roberts
> Conservator and hazard mitigation consultant

What should happen when an emergency occurs at the institution? The following are but a few of the many activities that may be required from the collections response team, depending on the nature and/or seriousness of the situation:

- Develop the initial response strategy, based on the specific emergency.
- Attempt to isolate the affected area.
- Retrieve emergency supplies.
- Contact emergency organizations, area support institutions, and so forth.
- Assess damage.
- Initiate relocation, evacuation, and possibly salvage measures for the collection.
- Document all response activities (a crucial function).

Looking at other emergency response plans can inspire other activities that may not have occurred to you or your colleagues. One of the most productive ways to assemble this kind of information specific to the institution is to create scenarios such as the "worst-case stroll" exercise described on page 143.

Step 2

Develop response team job descriptions

In this step, the responsibilities of team members must be designated. Give each job a title that accurately describes the chief function of the job. For instance, you may want to assign teams and team leaders to the areas of salvage, stabilization, and supplies. Next, list each team member's duties and responsibilities. Pay special attention to the type and number of duties. Match similar duties (e.g., leadership duties, assistance duties, and physical duties) so that one person is not expected to fulfill completely different tasks.

Following that, list the staff position assigned to the responsibility, along with at least two alternates. The number of alternates you designate depends on how important certain skills are to the position. For example, if it is critical to have a person with conservation experience directing the collections response team, the team leader job description should list a number of backup people for the position. For the movement of objects, a preparator or other departmental person could serve as a backup. Remember that "appropriate training" is the operative phrase. More damage can occur as a result of careless handling than of the emergency event itself. The administration and records team, which is experienced in writing job descriptions as part of its human resources function, can coordinate the writing of job descriptions in each of the four departmental response teams.

The job description for the collection safety manager (appendix F) is from the Seattle Art Museum's *Emergency Planning Handbook*.[9] Note that in addition to simple and clear responsibilities, the description also lists five other positions in a line of succession to fill the role. The description also states to whom this team member reports and provides a checklist of actions expected of the position. The museum's plan also lists positions for conservation supervisor, art registration supervisor, and art relocation supervisor, with the appropriate checklists of responsibilities.

In a smaller institution, these responsibilities would be allocated accordingly (see a sample response plan in appendix G—guidelines for evacuating the collections from the Barbados Museum and Historical Society).[10] Checklists and guidelines help staff stay focused in their positions and follow the most efficient course of action, without missing details due to fear and confusion. They also reflect the "big picture" for the EPM and the institution. If only the first two priority tasks are completed, other teams can consult the checklist to find out what is happening and how to coordinate their actions accordingly. This procedure enhances communication and saves time.

Questions to Consider

- Who decides when and how to remove water from a flooded gallery? Who carries this out?

- Who authorizes the relocation or evacuation of collections?

- Who is authorized to operate fork lifts and freight elevators?

- Who is responsible for bringing materials to the designated salvage area?

- Who is responsible for maintaining supply levels?

- Who will drive the vehicles to transport objects to a new site (and where are the keys)? Who will load and unload?

Task 3

Set guidelines for moving objects

Resist the urge to move anything in the first steps. Even with a well-trained team, damage can occur during a relocation or evacuation process; therefore, nothing should be moved without a compelling reason to do so.

— Brian Considine
  Conservator of decorative arts and sculpture
  The J. Paul Getty Museum

Step 1

Establish authority for deciding if, and at what point, objects should be moved

Generally, the person designated as the collections response team leader will give the go-ahead to move objects, if conditions require. But who may move them and under what circumstances? At the Seattle Art Museum, staff members who are authorized to move objects wear blue photo identification badges during work hours. If the emergency happens after hours, the collections leader will authorize blue-badge access to those in charge of evacuating objects.

You will have to decide what to do if an object or sections of the collection are in imminent risk of damage or further damage, and no qualified staff members are available to assist in removal. Should you authorize an inexperienced person to remove the objects?

Questions to Consider

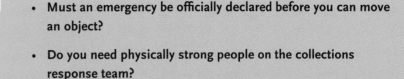

- Must an emergency be officially declared before you can move an object?

- Do you need physically strong people on the collections response team?

- Should teams be designated for moving large objects?

- What are insurance policy guidelines regarding moving objects?

- Is it better to train people to put out a small fire rather than to move objects?

Step 2

Coordinate with the safety and security team and the administration and records team to screen volunteers

Depending on the magnitude of the emergency, strangers may offer to help. Together with members of the safety and security team and the administration and records team, you will have to decide the following:

- Should strangers be allowed to handle objects? (Most institutions recommend that you find work for them other than working with the collections.)
- What sort of security screening and sign-in and -out procedures would be required of those volunteering to work with the collections?
- What kind of supervision would be needed? What kind of training would be needed and is practical on short notice? A golden rule is: Stop! Think! Organize! Have no more than five persons on a team, including the team leader.

Step 3

Provide guidelines for handling objects

As team leader, you need to decide how to provide special instructions for handling priority objects. Some institutions print the instructions directly on the priority list or an attachment. Often it will depend on your specific collection.

Ideally, every staff member and daily volunteer should be trained in the basics of emergency art handling. Some of those personnel should be trained in how to train others. For example, during a large-scale disaster, the military or National Guard may be assigned to guard and/or assist in evacuation and will need to be trained on the spot. "[These individuals] are going to be part of the response effort—good or bad—and they are likely to trudge through your building and collection," cautions Jerry Podany. "With a little training, they could be a great resource."

See task 9 (pages 167–71) for further discussion of training in emergency art handling.

Task 4

Detail recovery procedures

Recovery measures occur after an event has happened. They are designed to enable the museum—and its collection—to return to normalcy in an orderly, phased, reasoned and methodical fashion. Recovery measures begin when the disaster situation has stabilized and professionals have evaluated the damage and suggested further, long-term actions. Recovery can be a long process, taking years in some cases.[11]

— John E. Hunter
Supervisory staff curator
National Park Service, U.S. Department of the Interior

Step 1

Consider damage assessment issues

Who will carry out the damage assessment? A staff conservator? A curator? A registrar? An outside conservator? This must be incorporated into the response team job descriptions, unless outside conservators will be called in. If your institution is small, you may have to assess the damage yourself. You may need to answer the following questions at that time:

- Who will give authorization that a building is safe to reenter?
- What objects are damaged?
- What is the type and extent of the damage?
- What are the priorities (depending on the criteria—e.g., damage type, object value, etc.)?
- What can be safely moved elsewhere?
- How will damage and salvage operations be documented?
- What equipment and supplies are needed?

Remember, never enter a damaged structure until it is designated as safe to do so by the authorized person (which may be the fire department official). Use the "buddy system," have a means of communication with those outside, and report out regularly.

Documentation of the damage is critical not only for salvage and conservation, but also for insurance purposes, possible legal action, fund-raising, and controlled media coverage. Documentation equipment, such as cameras or video cameras, should be safely stored and easily accessible, along with insurance damage claim forms. If a photographic or video camera is unavailable, do the documentation in writing. Prepared checklists can make written documentation more effective.

In the United States, federal conservation money is available when a federally declared disaster has taken place and museum objects have been damaged. *However, documentation of damage, along with photographs of objects before they were damaged, is required.* Additional funding for temporary relocation of objects, equipment purchases, and so forth, also may be available through the Institute of Museum and Library Services and the National Endowment for the Humanities in Washington, D.C.

Step 2

Determine salvage and stabilization priorities

Salvaging involves retrieving collections, objects, or fragments of objects from damaged areas. Stabilizing means minimizing the damage done or damage that could occur soon. Together, the two constitute "first aid" for the collection, covering everything from completely wetting a partially wet textile (to avoid water stains) to freezing water-soaked books to applying a facing paper onto lifting paint layers.

What is salvaged and stabilized first depends on the nature of the emergency situation and on what was damaged and how. In a flood, for example, you may choose to turn your attention to a number of soaked rare books, whereas after an earthquake you may decide to focus on the shattered sculpture in the gallery entrance. Do not forget to refer to your collections priority list established during the planning phase.

Any salvage and stabilization procedures must be accompanied by the precaution that before such activities take place, consideration should be given to whether further damage would occur if the objects were (a) left in their present location and (b) simply protected for the time being until a clearer idea can be obtained of the situation and, if no conservator is on staff, a conservator can be consulted.

Questions to Consider

- What requirements does your insurance carrier have regarding salvage/stabilization priorities and procedures?

- What priority do on-loan objects receive in salvage operations? Does your loan agreement address the issue? Who communicates with lenders? How?

- Who will document all the stabilization procedures? How will this be done? Do the emergency kits contain a supply of standard forms?

- Who establishes the procedures? Who will carry them out? When? Where?

Step 3

Determine recovery procedures

You and your collections team should work with the three other departmental teams to identify recovery procedures that move the institution from a state of emergency to the state of normal operations. These recovery procedures can be used as a guide in developing a recovery plan in the aftermath of an emergency.

Collections-related recovery procedures may include some or all of the following, depending on the emergency:

- Secure the collection.
- Determine specific recovery needs and goals.
- Determine what resources are needed and mobilize them. Resources could include the department recovery team, external specialists, and supply or storage vendors.
- Gather supplies and equipment.
- Arrange for conservation assistance if objects have been damaged and the institution does not have a conservation department.
- Relocate or evacuate objects, if necessary.
- Begin object stabilization.
- Document procedures with photographs, videotape, and written records.
- Work with the administration and records team to review and coordinate claims and conservation work with insurance agents.
- Begin long-term conservation.
- Return objects to galleries or storage.

Step 4

Address issues of mental and physical well-being

> *An important part of preparedness is planning for the potentially long period of time before the building or buildings can be reoccupied. It could be hours. It could be weeks. It can be a difficult period—a time when something happens followed by another long waiting period. How do you take care of all the people in the meantime? This needs a lot of organization.*
>
> — Jerry Podany
> Head of antiquities conservation
> The J. Paul Getty Museum

During salvage and recovery, team leaders need to pay attention to pacing and motivation. Jerry Podany recalls how workers assisting in recovery efforts after an earthquake in Japan were highly organized and worked at a high energy level for extended hours. In the end, their extreme fatigue negatively affected their work. As team leader, be sure to schedule regular breaks, as well as provide food, a place to eat and rest, and bathroom facilities.

"You have to respond in a reasonable way and work that into the plan," Podany says. "If you do not have a plan in place, you respond emotionally." In Japan, Podany witnessed one recovery group patching one painting amid a rubble of pottery shards. "I thought it was silly to patch a painting when there was so much devastation around them," he recalls. "But it made a huge difference to that group. It really energized them."

Step 5

Require frank after-action reports

Every encounter with a disaster or emergency is an opportunity for learning. That is the purpose of after-action reports that detail the actions taken and the results observed. First, it is important to emphasize and praise what went right, then examine problems encountered or mistakes made. Do not allow these reports to be after-the-fact justifications and defenses of what the response team did instead of a candid assessment of what occurred—problems and all.

Indicate to team members your desire to learn from mistakes, not to punish people for them. Encourage an atmosphere of honest self-assessment, starting with yourself. What could you have done differently? What would have worked better? How could you improve your response next time? What did you learn that could be applied to the next emergency?

Task 5

Create lists of staff and resource contact information

Once you have the list, do not rest on your laurels, thinking, Well, we have a list, so we're done! Lists go out of date quickly, so it is important to update them at least once a year.

— Gail Joice
Senior deputy director and registrar
Seattle Art Museum

Furnish the EPC with the names of all your staff members, along with their work and home telephone numbers and home addresses. This way, staff can be reached at home during an emergency. If the event happens during work hours, one person can be delegated the task of telephoning each person's home to avoid jamming the phone lines. Also, develop other means of contact in the event of a widespread emergency in which the telephone systems may not be functioning. Make a list of special skills—for example, is any employee a former nurse, search-and-rescue team member, or National Guard member?

It is also important to establish communication with individuals and organizations that your team may need to contact during an emergency. For instance, if your team determines that it might need to use refrigerated trucks to move objects to a commercial freezer off the premises, you must make the arrangements now, not during the emergency. Now is also the time to create lists of names, street and e-mail addresses, and telephone and fax numbers so they are easily accessible during an emergency.

Update the lists regularly, and check the contacts at the same time. Are the listed companies still in business? Are the contact individuals still at the company? Have telephone or fax numbers or e-mail addresses changed? Use significant dates to help you remember to update the contact lists. For example, if the institution is in an earthquake-prone area in the United States, do this on April 1 (April is National Earthquake Preparedness Month).

Here are some external resources you may wish to include on the lists:

- conservators/conservation centers
- insurance agents
- warehouses/commercial freezers
- moving trucks/refrigerated trucks
- volunteers trained in emergency response and handling procedures
- emergency organization contacts (e.g., a fire chief who is familiar with the sensitivities of the collection)
- emergency equipment rental resources such as freeze-drying companies
- construction contractors
- sources for supplies and materials (including the name of the staff member authorized to make purchases)

Task 6
Create fact sheets and maps

These lists are developed in collaboration with the other preparedness teams, particularly safety and security. You will have to balance security concerns with the need for fast access in an emergency. Deposit duplicates of all these items in a safe but accessible place both inside and outside the building. Coordinate this effort with the administration and records team.

Collections department fact sheets should include the following:

- object priority list
- guidelines for protecting and handling objects
- operating instructions for special equipment
- protective measures for scientific equipment
- object relocation form
- object damage assessment report
- hazardous materials lists (work with the buildings and maintenance team to produce this list, which must be available to fire departments)

Maps that your department should produce or areas that should be included in general maps:

- gallery and collection storage areas, including location of priority objects
- chemical storage cabinets
- interior and exterior emergency supplies and equipment
- emergency shelter and storage areas
- access and keys to such areas as supplies, storage, electrical circuit boxes (carefully discuss who is authorized to hold keys for emergency situations and how to override automatic closing devices or obtain access to areas with card key entry)

See appendix H for the fact sheet list from the Getty Center's emergency planning handbook; see appendix B.2 for a page from the Seattle Art Museum plan's table of contents.

Task 7
Stock emergency supplies and equipment

An up-to-date and adequate supply of materials and appropriate equipment can mean the difference between minimal or no damage to the collections and complete disaster. You may want to coordinate supply stocking with other teams. Large quantities of expensive items or perishable materials need not be stockpiled. Instead, identify suppliers and make arrangements for emergency delivery, as needed.

Depending on your specific collections, these supplies and equipment may include (but are not limited to) these essentials:

- containers and packing material for relocating objects (pads, tape, scissors, boxes, markers, paper, etc.)
- a backup generator *and* extra fuel
- wet/dry vacuums

- fire extinguishers
- floor fans
- plastic covering sheets
- trolleys and carts
- freezers
- flashlights and batteries
- water and high-energy food (Power Bars, trail mix, etc.) for staff
- cameras, film, pens, paper, and other items for documentation

More extensive lists are included in appendix E.

The first rule of thumb regarding supplies and equipment is to store separate caches of them internally and externally so that staff members have access to undamaged supplies. Post maps of supply locations.

Some people recommend including instruction sheets for recovery methods in supply kits. Jerry Podany says handouts of that nature are an excellent backup to training and can be distributed *before* an emergency occurs. Doing so *during* an emergency is ineffective and only adds paper clutter to the disaster site.

Questions to Consider

- Who is in charge of ensuring that supplies are kept current (e.g., batteries) and full (e.g., fuel)? How often should supplies be checked? (Annually? After drills?)

- Do all staff members know where supplies are located? Are maps showing these locations posted?

- Are supplies labeled clearly? (The Seattle Art Museum keeps supplies in large crates painted bright yellow to visually orient staff to the supply caches.)

- Do supplies include operating manuals and instructions for equipment?

Task 8
Establish routines to keep the plan viable

The following are a few examples of possible daily and periodic checklist activities for the collections team. You may be inspired to think of others. Compare lists with the other department preparedness teams.

Daily checklist activities:

- Confirm with the security department that exhibit gallery cases remain secure and that all display objects are accounted for.
- Collection storage areas are locked, and the keys are in their designated locations.

- Electrical equipment, such as hot plates in the conservation laboratory, is turned off.
- Hazardous materials are safely stored, and waste materials containers are ready for disposal, as appropriate.
- Computer files and systems are backed up.

Periodic checklist activities:

- Maintain scientific equipment according to manufacturers' specifications.
- Reorder emergency supplies, if necessary.
- Duplicate new inventory documents and store them off-site with other duplicates.
- Provide the EPM with updated documents that are part of the emergency plan, including operating instructions for new equipment and a list of hazardous supplies.
- Review collection inventory documents, including loan forms.
- Update the duty roster to reflect changes in staff and other institutional changes.
- Verify that outside experts and/or resource information is up to date.

Task 9

Identify and implement appropriate training

You will need to train staff members in relocation or evacuation procedures, but more important, you will need to instruct them when to move collection items and when *not* to do so. Training in general salvage techniques also is required. Consider teaching your staff how to train volunteers for collections-related activities that you have identified as an added resource in an actual emergency.

Training is only the first step. You also must practice and conduct drills repeatedly to help determine the plan's weaknesses and to refine procedures. Work with the EPC in coordinating all training and drill exercises.

Who should be trained?

Collections are the heart of an institition. Therefore, most experts recommend that all staff members be trained in basic procedures that can save or minimize damage to these cherished objects. If a fire starts early one morning, the receptionist and three volunteers may be the only ones in the building. An earthquake late at night may find only a night security officer and a janitor on the premises. *Everyone on staff should practice being the first person on the scene of an emergency.* Your collection will be that much better off.

Training others connected to the museum, such as volunteers, trustees, and docents, can provide an additional layer of support in an emergency. Publicizing such efforts can raise community awareness and help in fundraising for prevention efforts.

What skills and knowledge are needed?

Evacuation procedures. Does everyone on staff know the immediate action to take when the emergency alarm sounds? Jerry Podany likes to test his staff's readiness with impromptu drills. He walks in, announces a scenario, and listens to employees call out their actions. If the scenario is an earthquake, a number of people will inevitably discover that they do not fit under their desks because of all the material they have accumulated in that space.

In a disaster, after the personal safety of staff and visitors is ensured, staff should turn their attention to the collections. Like lines in a play, response actions must be rehearsed regularly, but with different scenarios each time.

Questions to Consider

- **Do staff members know which objects to evacuate first? If not, can they find the priority list quickly?**

- **Do staff members know where supply kits of packaging materials are, and do they have access to that location?**

- **Do staff members know the routes to internal or external shelters? Do supplies include operating manuals and instructions for equipment?**

- **Do staff members know who is in charge and to whom they should report?**

Good intentions have ruined many an artifact. A well-meaning staff member from another department may think he or she is helping by gathering a few precious artifacts for evacuation, when in fact he or she may be doing more harm than good. You have to make sure that the urge to be a Good Samaritan does not supersede appropriate precautions for art handling.

— Gail Joice
Senior deputy director and registrar
Seattle Art Museum

Basic art handling. The following information regarding art handling, adapted from the Seattle Art Museum's *Emergency Planning Handbook*, emphasizes the importance of having only trained personnel handle art objects, except in extreme circumstances.

What if an emergency occurs and no staff members specially trained in handling works of art are on the scene? Who will protect the art? Will they know what to do without causing further damage?

All staff members must be trained in the basic procedures to protect the collections during an emergency. All art should be moved *only* by trained personnel, unless it is threatened by imminent destruction. Because most objects require special handling, it is preferable to await the instructions of the appropriate collections staff. There are, however, situations where clear and present danger to a collection will require those who are in the area to act swiftly. It is thus crucial that all staff members receive at least minimal training.[12]

Here are some basic rules to follow:

- Do not move an object unless and/or until it is absolutely necessary to do so.
- Never pick up an object until you have identified a safe place to put it down.
- Never leave objects on the floor.
- Never attempt to carry more weight than is comfortable for you.
- Recruit the help of several people if the object is heavy or awkward.
- Never handle or lift a sculpture by a projecting member, such as an arm or head, and use both hands to support the sculpture.
- Walk slowly and carefully. Do not walk backward.
- Do not smoke while handling objects or while you are in the same room with them.
- Report all object damage immediately to the appropriate staff member.

Questions to Consider

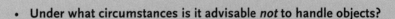

- **Under what circumstances is it advisable *not* to handle objects?**

- **What is the process by which a staff member decides what to handle and what not to handle? Who makes these decisions?**

- **What happens when no staff member trained in art handling is available and there is no alternative but to move an object?**

The guidelines you and your team develop will be specific to the collections. As examples, see appendix I for art-handling fact sheets from the Seattle Art Museum and the Barbados Museum and Historical Society.

Salvage techniques. The first thing to remember about salvage efforts is that managing the situation is more important than the salvage itself. Once the situation is under control, efforts should focus on deciding if and when objects have to be moved, whether to follow the priority lists, or if the objects require salvage treatment.

Many variables come into play during salvage efforts. If enough staff members are present and there is minimal damage, collections staff with salvage expertise can handle the situation. But there may be times when staff members with no salvage expertise must assist. If, in your team's vulnerability assessment, potential damage effects were categorized, those can now be used to develop training activities on salvage techniques for specific types of damage. (See steps 1 and 2 under task 2, "Assess risks of damage," pages 144–45.) For example, in the case of water-damaged fabric, it may be appropriate to wet the fabric completely before it dries to avoid water stains. You can demonstrate and/or practice this with staff using noncollection textiles.

If no conservators are on staff, contact the conservation department of other institutions in the area, or local, state, or national professional conservation organizations for assistance.

Remember that caution must be used in appling any general guidelines to salvage steps, as there are a variety of determining factors in the preservation of individual objects or groups of objects. It is better to concentrate efforts on collections care and mitigation of potential damage to the collections.

The following are a few basic emergency "first aid" principles for salvage, if immediate action is absolutely necessary. They do not address all problems that will arise, but they can minimize the damage that may occur until help arrives. *The Emergency Response and Salvage Wheel* is an ideal resource for further basic guidelines.[13]

- Do not move objects unless absolutely necessary.
- Protect objects from further damage (this may or may not require moving them).
- When secure space is available, separate the damaged objects from the undamaged objects and try to maintain pre-emergency environmental conditions for both groups.
- Bag or lightly wrap damp objects made of organic materials (other than paper) in plastic and store them in a cool, well-ventilated space away from undamaged objects. Examine daily for mold growth. If any is found, open the bag to allow air drying and increase air movement.
- Lay wet or otherwise damaged paintings horizontally, face up, supported at the corners to ensure air circulation beneath them. Allow to air-dry.
- Wrap wet books or interleave wet documents with waxed paper or freezer paper as soon as possible and freeze them, or air-dry them in an adequate airflow.
- Quickly air-dry wet metal, glass, or ceramic objects. If necessary, gently mop with clean, dry, lint-free cloths.
- Keep objects that have dried in a cool, well-ventilated place, away from those that never got wet.
- Inspect partially damp objects daily for mold. Wipe off any mold with a dry cloth and increase air circulation. Isolate the objects from other objects to prevent spread of mold.

- Handle smoke-damaged, scorched, charred, or dirt-caked objects as little as possible. Do not try to clean them at this point. If they are dry, treat as dry; if wet, treat as wet.

Training methods. The following are basic methods that can be used in training activities. You may choose to employ several, either independently or simultaneously. See chapter 5 for more information on training.

- group discussions
- simulations/role playing
- supplementary handouts
- videos
- review sessions
- self-assessment exercises
- hands-on workshops
- presentations by colleagues or consultants who have hands-on knowledge of the scenarios the institution might face

Questions to Consider

Does everyone on your staff know

- **how to direct firefighters and others through local streets to the institution;**

- **how to get to the roof of the building or direct others to the roof;**

- **where emergency alarms and fire extinguishers are;**

- **the location, both off-site and on-site, of hard hats, flashlights, fresh batteries, hoses, fire hydrants;**

- **where supply kits for packaging the office equipment are (do staff members have access to that location?);**

- **the routes to internal or external shelters;**

- **who is in charge and to whom to report; and**

- **how to evacuate computer files?**

Notes

1. John E. Hunter, "Preparing a Museum Disaster Plan," in *Southeastern Museums Conference, 1991 Disaster Preparedness Seminar Proceedings*, ed. Martha E. Battle and Pamela Meister (Baton Rouge, La.: Southeastern Museums Conference, 1991), 56.

2. *The Emergency Response and Salvage Wheel* (Washington, D.C.: National Institute for the Conservation of Cultural Property, 1997) was published in cooperation with the National Task Force on Emergency Response, an initiative that also involved FEMA and the Getty Conservation Institute. It can be purchased by contacting the National Task Force, 3299 K St. NW, Washington, DC 20007.

3. Robin Thornes, *Protecting Cultural Objects in the Global Information Society: The Making of Object ID*, ed. Marilyn Schmitt and Nancy Bryan (Los Angeles: J. Paul Getty Trust, 1997), 1.

4. Ibid., 25.

5. See page 137, note 6.

6. International Committee on Museum Security, *Museum Security Survey*, ed. Diana Menkes, trans. Marthe de Moltke, based on the document by George H. H. Schröder (Paris: International Council of Museums, 1981), 24–25.

7. National Fire Protection Association, *NFPA 910 Protection of Museums and Museum Collections* (Quincy, Mass.: National Fire Protection Association, 1991), 8.

8. Adapted from Allyn Lord, Carolyn Reno, and Marie Demeroukas, *Steal This Handbook! A Template for Creating a Museum's Emergency Preparedness Plan* (Columbia, S.C.: Southeastern Registrars Association, 1994), 177–79. Used by permission.

9. Seattle Art Museum, *Emergency Planning Handbook*, rev. ed. (Seattle: Seattle Art Museum, 1994).

10. Barbados Museum and Historical Society, "Emergency Plan" (Barbados Museum and Historical Society, St. Michael, 1994, photocopy), 28–29.

11. Hunter, "Preparing a Museum Disaster Plan," 58.

12. Seattle Art Museum, *Emergency Planning Handbook*, 67–69.

13. *Emergency Response and Salvage Wheel*.

Chapter Summary

This chapter

- outlined the role of the collections preparedness team in the emergency preparedness process;

- described information required in the two reports to be delivered to the emergency preparedness committee;

- provided guidance through the process of assessing the vulnerability of the collection;

- helped define the roles and responsibilities of the collections response team; and

- identified tasks to guide you and your team through the process of designing a response plan that is simple, detailed, and flexible.

In review, the emergency preparedness process is a long-term commitment on the part of the institution's staff, teams, and committees. You cannot and should not expect changes quickly or easily. Interdisciplinary teamwork is difficult and requires a change in attitude that may be slow in coming. The payoff—in peace of mind, in the safety of staff and visitors, and in the protection of objects and irreplaceable records—will be great.

CHAPTER EIGHT

The Buildings and Maintenance Team

This chapter addresses the issues involving the buildings, the systems, and their maintenance that must be dealt with as the emergency plan is developed. It is designed to be a resource for you, the leader of the buildings and maintenance team.

For an overview of the emergency preparedness and response program, please consult chapters 1–3. For training ideas, see chapter 5.

> *If the building withstands the wind, holds back the water or retains structural integrity during an earthquake; if sufficient safety precautions have been installed such as fire sprinklers, alarmed water and fire sensors, flood drains, and structural supports, then complete loss can be avoided. Because of this, where your building is located, what condition it is in, how the contents are distributed, what protection it offers and receives, and how often it is maintained are just as important as defining the threats from without. If the building fails during an event, there is little, if anything, to protect the people and collection.*
>
> — Jerry Podany
>   Head of antiquities conservation
>   The J. Paul Getty Museum

Your Role in the Process

Because a building shelters the institution's most important priorities—people first, and collections second—it can be the first and strongest line of defense in an emergency or disaster. At the same time, poorly maintained buildings and equipment can cause or worsen emergency situations.

As head of the buildings and maintenance team, you probably are intimately familiar with your institution's structure and systems. You and other members of the buildings and maintenance staff know its structural shortcomings, its strengths and weaknesses, and its vulnerabilities. You nurse along old and outdated systems on a daily basis, and you are aware that emergencies are a very real possibility.

If you are not the head of the buildings and maintenance department, you will have to depend heavily on the head to provide advice and guidance in emergency planning. If the institution is small, or one in which buildings and maintenance workers come from city or university work crews, you may not have building engineers or supervisors on staff; in these cases, you will have to rely on outside expertise.

The job of the buildings and maintenance preparedness team is to thoroughly evaluate the building and its systems to determine where the vulnerabilities are and what to do during an emergency. The team produces two reports for the emergency planning committee (EPC) that summarize its findings:

Report 1 is a vulnerabilities and assets analysis that recommends preparedness and protective measures: what to do to prevent damage to the building and, by extension, to people and collections, in an emergency.

Report 2 outlines the role of the buildings and maintenance response team during an emergency. It also should include lists of repair and service vendors and their contact information, as well as equipment and supplies needed, and it should address training issues pertinent to the team's expertise.

As you begin the process of compiling this information and developing your portion of the response plan, you, as team leader, will accomplish two tasks:

Task 1: Assemble the preparedness team.

Task 2: Interact with other teams and with the EPC.

Task 1

Assemble the preparedness team

Personnel functioning as one efficient, well-oiled machine during emergencies produce dramatically better results than scattered, chaotic responses by individuals. That is why team building is such a critical component of true emergency preparedness. Building a successful team means making decisions and discussing and taking risks that involve resolving conflict, establishing trust, and encouraging interdependence. Refer to chapter 5 on training for information on assembling and building effective teams.

You are in charge of appointing the buildings and maintenance preparedness team and of guiding team members in gathering accurate, efficient information and in organizing a well-coordinated response to any emergency.

Select team members on the basis of three categories of skills: technical and functional, problem solving, and interpersonal. All efforts at team building should focus on the process and on accomplishing the intended tasks. Communication skills are important, as your team will be interacting with nearly every department in the institution. Involve your department colleagues in the planning process so they will more readily support the recommended changes in policy and procedures. Identifying and appointing "true believers" in emergency preparedness will help generate enthusiasm and create the proper atmosphere. Be sure to include "nonbelievers" as well—this will forge a well-balanced, cohesive unit that enables all members to do the best they can.

As part of the recommendations in Report 2, you and your team will describe the roles and responsibilities of the buildings and maintenance response team, which may or may not include all members of the preparedness team. This team, along with a response team from each of the other three departments, will respond in an actual emergency situation.

Task 2

Interact with other teams and with the EPC

There often is an adversarial relationship between collections and the buildings and maintenance staff. Collections people ask the impossible of buildings and maintenance people. Many do not understand the extent to which they have to make do with second-rate machinery, second-rate systems, and second-rate help in some cases. These people know the problems. They can tell you stories that will make your hair go white overnight if you listen to them. They must be given credence and they must be heard during the planning process and in training.

— Barbara Roberts
Conservator and hazard mitigation consultant

To produce workable recommendations for the emergency plan, you and your team must work closely with the other three departmental teams in the following areas:

Safety and security
- Evacuation routes for people
- Evacuation routes for collections
- Safety of emergency shelters
- Safety of buildings, if there is structural damage

Collections
- Location of and requirements for emergency shelters
- Additional storage requirements
- Guidelines for relocating and evacuating objects
- Housekeeping practices

Administration and records
- Building-insurance issues
- Repair and maintenance record keeping
- Utilities and environmental systems documentation
- Documentation of activities

In collaboration with other teams, work through the EPC to set up meetings between teams. This hierarchical method helps avoid territorial disputes that

Figure 7   Buildings and maintenance staff of the Barbados Museum and Historical Society installing shutters on the museum's windows to protect against an advancing hurricane. Courtesy of the Barbados Museum and Historical Society. Photo: Alissandra Cummins.

can occur during the process. It becomes a top-down mandate, rather than a lateral agreement. You may want to include a member of the EPC during these meetings. When needed, include a member of the other departmental teams, as applicable. This works well as long as your team is discussing matters that pertain to this person's area of expertise. If discussions cover areas specific only to buildings and maintenance, it can be a waste of time for the other person.

This collaboration is required for the overall success of the emergency preparedness program. The planning process is likely to give buildings, maintenance, and security staff a higher profile, in terms of both image and responsibilities. It also may require—or cause—a shift in attitudes on the part of other professional staff.

At the Barbados Museum and Historical Society, emergency planning has given the so-called white-collar staff members a greater appreciation for the abilities and input of building maintenance staff (Fig. 7). "Emergency planning has helped to break down a lot of barriers and misconceptions among various types of staff," says director Alissandra Cummins.

Preparing Report 1:
Vulnerability and Asset Analysis

In cultural institutions, the consequences of physical damage to the building are often more crucial than the actual damage itself. For example, shingles torn from the roof during a hurricane cost little in time and money to repair, but the damage from wind and rain to precious collections, interior furnishings, collections records, and so forth, can be devastating.

How vulnerable is the building (or buildings) and its systems to fire, flood, hurricane, earthquake, and other hazards? Your team's job is to work with the emergency preparedness manager (EPM) and the EPC to assess this vulnerability from a buildings and maintenance point of view.

The accuracy and thoroughness of your analysis will greatly affect the success of the efforts to protect against or minimize loss of human life and damage to the collections. Report 1 should suggest protective measures to reduce the identified vulnerabilities. Examples of potential vulnerabilities are listed below. You and your colleagues are already aware of some or all of these weaknesses; others may become apparent only in the analysis process. All, however, ultimately may affect the institution's preparedness and response capabilities.

- The building is not secured to foundation.
- The machine room is kept spotless, but access corridors are jammed with crates, catalogues, and cafeteria/special events equipment and supplies (sloppy housekeeping practices that could increase the fire hazard, block exits, etc.).
- The institution has low priority in an energy crisis and no independent means of generating backup electricity (this could ruin objects sensitive to heat or low humidity).
- There is neither time nor equipment to keep gutters and drains clear.
- No regulations are in place regarding construction work crews (such as no supervision during construction activities).
- Fire, smoke, or water detection and/or suppression alarm systems are inadequate.
- Few employees know how to use fire extinguishers.
- Electrical chain saws are on hand for landscape maintenance and emergency use, but no hard hats, work boots, or hand tools are on hand.
- Outdoor landscaping material, furniture, or other items that could become airborne in a hurricane or tornado are not secured.
- Storage areas are infested with insects or rodents. (Should your team or the collections team address this problem?)
- Attics have no fire doors.
- Cafeteria food deliveries use the collections freight elevator.
- Requests are repeatedly made for money to upgrade systems but fall on deaf ears.
- Electrical wiring does not meet code standards. There are few power outlets, and extension cords are in constant use.

The following tasks will help you complete the vulnerability and asset analysis:

Task 1: Survey the buildings, surroundings, and systems, and identify priorities.

Task 2: Evaluate buildings and maintenance staff.

Task 3: Evaluate equipment needs.

Task 4: Invite local agencies and individuals to participate.

Task 5: Recommend building-related protective measures and list priorities.

Task 1

Survey the buildings, surroundings, and systems, and identify priorities

There is no sense in putting all this padded shelving and seismic storage in if your building is going to cave in around you.

— David Mathieson
  Supervisor of conservation
  Mystic Seaport Museum

Step 1

Evaluate the building and its systems

Damage to objects is often the result of structural damage to the building that houses those objects.[1] Yet the severest damage is usually from the fires and flooding that occur if system failures cause broken water, sewer, and fuel lines.

Review the facilities with various professionals, such as structural and seismic engineers, architectural conservators, electricians, plumbers, and emergency preparedness experts, who can help you determine the building's integrity and weaknesses. These professionals also can make recommendations for upgrading and improving the building. "You definitely need to know and understand the capabilities of the building containing the collection," advises Alissandra Cummins. She recommends an outside professional survey every five years.

Outside assessments have five main advantages:

1. They provide outside expertise your staff may not have.
2. They provide an "official" perspective for consideration by the board or governing body (especially if capital improvements are required).
3. They provide a fresh outlook.
4. Their conclusions often spark ideas and/or creative solutions by staff.
5. The surveys are usually solution-oriented (staff may know a problem exists but may not know how to solve it).

At the same time, you must call on the expertise and experience of your team members and staff. Administrators all too often will listen only to an outside voice, yet staff members are the ones who know the building best, as they work in it daily. Be sure to consult with all workers. Talk with custodians and janitors, as well as with building engineers and supervisors. "Make everyone part of this process," says David Mathieson. "No one is beneath it."

When performing assessments, be sure to ask: What types of problems would have the most serious consequences on the building? On people? On building services? On the building's contents? Below are several inspection checklist activities found in *Protecting the Past from Natural Disasters.*[2] Some depend on the building type.

Foundation and masonry

- Check foundations, masonry, basements, and exterior walls for seepage and condensation problems.
- Check foundation walls, steps, retaining walls, walks, patios, and similar areas for settling, cracks, heaving, and crumbling.
- Ensure that the foundation is attached to the structure.

Roofs and gutters

- Look for damaged, loose, or missing shingles or tiles. Check flat roofs for blisters, cracks, and other damage. Is there any sagging that might indicate previous damage covered with a new roof?
- Check for leaking, misaligned or damaged gutters, downspouts, straps, gutter guards, and strainers. All water-carrying elements should be cleared and free from obstructions. Downspouts should direct water away from the structure.
- Be sure that flashings around roof stacks, vents, skylights, and chimneys are not sources of leakage.

Doors and windows

- Check caulking and decay around doors, windows, corner boards, joints, and similar areas.
- Check glazing around windowpanes.
- Check weather stripping.

Questions to Consider

- Will structural failure block any exits?

- Are stairs, treads, and banisters secure?

- Is plastic sheeting on hand?

- Is emergency backup lighting available throughout the building and regularly tested?

- Is the institution totally dependent on a local utility for power?

- How old is the plumbing? The wiring? Is this a problem?

- Is asbestos a problem that needs to be addressed?

- Will any new construction of facilities necessitate a change in the emergency plan?

- Are electrical circuits labeled correctly, and are boxes easily accessible?

- When was the last time fire department personnel were given a tour of the facility, and was their advice sought on disaster mitigation?

According to the National Fire Protection Assocation,[3] an adequate fire safety survey considers at least the following:

Heating plant. Does it have the capacity to heat the building without overtaxing the system? Is it adequately cut off from the rest of the building by walls, floors, and ceiling having the appropriate fire resistance rating with all openings connecting the building to the heating plant properly protected with fire doors? If the plant is to be replaced, will the heating capacity provide for future museum expansion?

Electricity. Have circuits become overloaded because of additions? Has insulation become worn or deteriorated? Do fuses and circuit breakers provide protection? Has temporary wiring been eliminated? Can darkened storage areas be adequately lighted in an emergency? Are exit lights on separate circuits tied into a backup power supply, and does the building have emergency lighting in the event of power failure?

Concealed spaces. Are walls fire-stopped between floors? If not, can such defects be remedied by the introduction of noncombustible material? Do fire walls extend through the roof? Is the attic divided by fire partitions? Are attics, suspended ceilings, and other concealed spaces equipped with automatic fire detectors?

Lightning protection. Is it adequate? Is it in good repair and properly grounded?

Fire protection equipment. Are automatic sprinklers or other extinguishing systems, standpipes, and fire detection devices installed? Are they regularly inspected, tested, and maintained? Are they connected to a supervisory agency? Is the water supply adequate? Have alterations to the building or other changes nullified or reduced the effectiveness of the fire extinguishing or detection equipment?

Step 2

Evaluate the grounds and surrounding areas

If one has not already been done, consider obtaining a geological survey to help determine what the building is sitting on. Was it or is it marshland? Is it sitting on top of a landfill (which may liquefy during an earthquake)? Perhaps the site was built in what was once a riverbed (and, given enough rain, may become one again).

Your survey should include a look at whether the site is protected or threatened by trees or other buildings, or is completely exposed with no natural or human-made windbreaks. Is there a large amount of readily combustible dry grass or brush nearby? Are there risks from nearby trees, telephone poles, or buildings, such as tree limbs extending onto or over roofs? Become as familiar as possible with the activities of nature and their impact on safety.

Other questions your grounds survey should answer:

- Does landscape grading slope away from foundation walls?
- What hidden dangers exist that should be incorporated into your scenarios (e.g., gas mains near the building, nearby water mains)?
- Are lightning conductors installed?
- Are chimneys secure?
- Are there outdoor furnishings or landscape materials that could become projectiles in a tornado or hurricane? How can they be properly secured?
- Do trees near buildings need to be stabilized with guy wires?
- Is access to main roads a problem if trees come down?
- Do nearby buildings, structures, or grounds not affiliated with the institution pose any danger? If you cannot see the entire site from your grounds, request permission from the appropriate parties to go on-site to evaluate possible safety or security risks.

Set priorities for making changes. Remember that the task of preparedness can seem overwhelming unless it is taken step by step. Prioritizing needs also will help in approaching administration colleagues regarding allocation for necessary funds.

Suggested Exercise

With your team, walk through every nongallery room in your institution, staff offices included. Mentally create one big pile of the unnecessary clutter—boxes, papers, rags, trash, and so forth—that you see in all the rooms. What kind of bonfire would result if an electric wire shorted out or a careless smoker tossed a cigarette on the pile? What hazardous materials do you observe? Can you minimize the amount stored? Do you have a list of all hazardous materials stored? Is it readily available for the fire department (a legal requirement in some U.S. states)? Note and move immediately any combustibles, such as paper, wood, or textiles, that are near gas pipes or steam piping and ducts.

Step 3

Evaluate housekeeping and maintenance procedures

Cleaning up can lower the fire hazard in a building significantly. Closing the institution for a day and devoting it to clearing out and cleaning up is a step that in itself makes everyone feel good and costs nothing more than possibly rental of a dumpster to remove the rubbish.

— Barbara Roberts
 Conservator and hazard mitigation consultant

The best safeguard against building-related emergency situations is a well-managed facility program that includes regular inspection and maintenance and prompt repair and upkeep.

Step 4

Pay attention to details

The Mystic Seaport Museum consists of more than sixty buildings spread across 40 acres (16.2 hectares) of land. Its buildings encompass all types of construction and configuration possible in several different geographic plains. It is the kind of place where small details, if forgotten or not properly addressed, could create huge problems.

   In their planning phase, museum staff members measured every doorway before constructing carts designed for evacuating the collections. All oil and fuel tanks buried underground are kept full so that the tanks do not explode through the soil when the ground above becomes saturated with water.

Questions to Consider

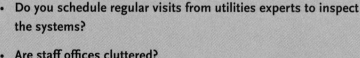

- Do you schedule regular visits from utilities experts to inspect the systems?

- Are staff offices cluttered?

- Do maintenance staff members regularly inspect the building for problems, such as leaks or birds' nests in chimneys or gutters?

- Have overgrown trees and bushes or overhanging branches near the building been cut back?

- Is equipment serviced according to manufacturer recommendations?

- Are drains clear and clean?

- Are flammable and/or hazardous materials stored properly?

Staff also gauged and recorded the distance between mean sea level and each building, discovering that many second-floor emergency evacuation locations would be underwater in a flood. The museum's experience illustrates the importance of both addressing the fine details when creating an emergency plan and testing the plan regularly to catch details that have been overlooked.

Task 2
Evaluate buildings and maintenance staff

Buildings and maintenance workers are often asked to maintain the machinery, clean drainpipes, handle electrical work, do light construction, paint, and more. Realistically, however, these are very separate trades. Listen carefully to how workers represent themselves. Find out what really is in their job descriptions. Can one person handle all aspects of a position? Does the department need to hire additional workers? Can it get by with subcontractors? What if the maintenance crew also has responsibilities elsewhere (i.e., if crew members are university employees or city workers)? What happens when maintenance employees are away on holiday or vacation? What can be done by staff members who are not engineers or electricians?

Task 3
Evaluate equipment needs

You cannot ask to purchase additional emergency equipment unless you have a realistic look at what the department currently has on hand. What is the highest priority of need, given the particular risks associated with the institution's location and based on its budget? Here are just a few items you may wish to have:

- fire detection systems
- mist systems or sprinklers to suppress fires
- fire extinguishers (and training for staff in how to use them)
- water detection devices
- water removal tools (wet-vacuum pump, squeegees, sump pump, sandbags, etc.)
- emergency generator and fuel
- portable fans, humidifiers, dehumidifiers

Questions to Consider

- **Where is the emergency standby equipment located, and who knows how to use it?**

- **Can the equipment be moved to alternative storage locations? If so, is an adequate power supply nearby?**

- **Is the heating, ventilating, and air-conditioning (HVAC) system sufficient for an emergency?**

- **Are sources of large-volume air-handling equipment listed in the emergency plan (for smoke removal or for air circulation in damp buildings)?**

- **Are supplies and equipment available to remove water and debris and to isolate affected areas?**

Task 4
Invite local agencies and individuals to participate

Do not overlook local or regional services and resources for advice and input. Fire departments, for example, are reservoirs of beneficial information and tips. Make invitations only with the agreement of the museum director and the EPC, which may itself initiate fire department visits. Initial visits should be informal to avoid code violation citations; keep in mind, though, that any identified fire hazards must be fixed. The information flow works both ways: You learn from the fire official, who in turn learns about the institution and its special needs.

Consider inviting any or all of the following to make presentations to your team. Coordinate all visits with the EPC so that other teams or all staff may benefit.

- police
- military (can be problematic in some countries)
- local chapter of the U.S. National Guard
- retired or current staff of institutions that have experienced emergencies

As a learning tool, ask presenters to bring news clippings, videotapes, and photographs of emergencies and the damage they cause. It is also helpful to talk to colleagues at other institutions around the world. The purpose, however, should be to research what those institutions did correctly and incorrectly during emergencies, not to copy their plans.

Task 5
Recommend building-related protective measures and list priorities

Protective measures are steps taken to eliminate hazards (as in fire prevention efforts) or to reduce the effects of threats to the building (as in securing buildings to their foundations in earthquake-prone areas), thereby protecting people and the collection. You and your team are to make recommendations to the EPC for both types of protection.

Protection is a long process and one that never ends. From time to time, remind the administration and your team members that protection is a priority. You also will need to remind administrators of their commitment to emergency preparedness as you lobby for funding for structural or landscape improvements. The administrators must understand that proper maintenance of the building strengthens its capacity to withstand disasters.

The priorities for protection that you set will influence the budget for resolving these problems. It is easier to request funding or to fund-raise within the community for specific projects than for the amorphous goal of achieving emergency preparedness. Set priorities for short-, medium- and long-term action and funding.

The planning phase not only yields an emergency plan, but also builds the budget to protect people and assets ahead of time, as well as reducing the institution's vulnerability. The problem in "selling" prevention is that intangibles cannot be measured. In other words, you may never know how many emergencies your prevention efforts have actually eliminated.

Suggested Exercise

Describe the following scenario to team members: Weather forecasters say a storm is headed in your direction, with gale-force winds and heavy rainfall. The storm is expected to hit tomorrow night. What is the role of buildings and maintenance staff during preparations for the storm? Who will check and stock supplies? If the power fails, will the alarm system or phones work? Will any objects be at risk if temperature control devices fail? Do windows need to be boarded up? If so, are materials on hand? Where are they stored? Are objects outside the building chained down? Are rain gutters clear? What else should be considered?

Some protection efforts may cost very little. For example, upon the recommendation of a professional structural engineer who surveyed the building, staff members at the Barbados Museum and Historical Society replaced all the nails in the roof shingles with screws and placed the screws two inches closer to each other. The project, which cost about US$200, ensured that the roof would not blow off in a strong hurricane. "Here was something practical that did not require huge amounts of money or training," reports Alissandra Cummins.

When resources for mitigation are limited, they should be directed where they will be most effective—toward the elements of the buildings that are most at risk. Your building surveys provide the data for making these decisions. Develop priorities: for example, protect people first, then collections as a whole, then storage areas, and finally display objects. Make your protection goals clear. Recognize that there may be conflicting interests within the institution, and iron these out as best as possible *before* an emergency occurs. The exercise on page 186 will help you set priorities.

The publication *Steal This Handbook!*[4] contains numerous building and maintenance protective measures. Use this information only as research in your own planning process. When you simply copy information, you lose the valuable thought process that produces an effective disaster plan.

In addition to undertaking major structural and/or landscaping improvements and establishing a good building maintenance plan, consider the following two steps as essential protective measures.

Step 1

Develop an exemplary fire protection program

It never fails. Flood alarms are put in after the flood. Fire alarms and sprinklers get put in after fires. How many times have people done things like this after *the event? They're always closing the door on the barn after the horses are out.*

— David Mathieson
  Supervisor of conservation
  Mystic Seaport Museum

The NFPA recommends that a fire protection program include the following:[5]

- selection, location, and maintenance of all fire protection equipment and devices
- indoctrination of all employees in the importance of fire safety and the necessity for complying with smoking regulations
- assignment of the best qualified personnel to fire brigade duties
- information regarding the function and operation of automatic sprinkler systems and the location of control valves

Suggested Exercise

Appoint two members of your team to play the roles of director and chief financial officer. Ask each of the remaining members to prepare a list of the ten most important repairs and/or preparations to make the building and its systems safe during an emergency. Have each person present that list to the "director" and "chief financial officer" and make a case for why the institution should spend precious resources to accomplish those items. At the end of the exercise, ask the entire group to come to a consensus as to what the top ten needs are. Now ask them to agree on the top five needs for funding.

- protection of the museum collection through cooperation with the fire department
- selection and training of night security officers
- inspection and maintenance of fire doors and exit facilities to ensure they are in working order and unobstructed
- daily inspection to ensure a high standard of housekeeping, which is one of the most important factors in the prevention of fire
- supervision of the installation and use of all electrical appliances, particularly those with extension cords
- supervision of storage and use of flammable liquids

The Mystic Seaport Museum was formerly lax about its smoking policy. Employees were allowed to smoke in staff rooms until a lit cigarette that had been tossed into the trash ignited a fire that burned down a retail shop. "Now," David Mathieson jokes, "if you want to smoke, you get in a raft in the river with water all around you." The museum no longer allows smoking anywhere on the premises.

Fire suppression systems. Nobody questions the effectiveness of sprinkler systems for putting out a fire, but there is some reluctance to install automatic sprinklers in cultural institutions for fear of water damage to the collections. In fact, extensive water damage usually results from fire department hose lines. Sprinkler systems avoid this by placing a small amount of water directly on the fire area and, in the best of cases, alerting the fire department at the same time. *Every expert consulted for this book agreed that automatic sprinkler systems are essential.* A few examples support their recommendation. Investigate the new mist systems. These use a great deal less water by volume and are probably the future of fire suppression for cultural institutions.

In May 1988, a torch being used to solder a copper downspout apparently ignited the combustible felt paper or wood in the roof during exterior renovation of the Louisiana State Museum in New Orleans. An estimated 500,000 gallons (1,892,500 liters) of water were used to control the fire. The museum lost the attic, the third floor (which was used for collections storage), and the historic building's roof. Total estimated loss was US$5 million. According to the fire chief in charge, had the museum been protected by a sprinkler system, only two sprinkler heads probably would have been necessary to control or extinguish the fire.[6]

Also in May 1988, the 185-year-old home of American statesman and former U.S. Vice President John C. Calhoun, which is now a museum in Clemson, South Carolina, was set on fire by burglars seeking to create a diversion. Three heads of the museum's sprinkler system, installed twenty years earlier, extinguished the fire before the fire department arrived. Less than 1 percent of the museum and its contents was damaged by fire or water.[7]

Alterations or reconstruction activities. The major cause of damage to cultural institutions and their collections is fire, and the majority of fires occur during renovation or construction activities. To lessen these dangers, construction contracts should specify methods and responsibility for controlling these hazards, such as the following points adapted from *Protection of Museums and Museum Collections*:[8]

- Ensure that construction and service workers are accompanied at all times. (If staff is small, a volunteer could help with this.)
- Partition off construction areas from the rest of the building.
- Allow acetylene torch or welding operations by permit only, and have security staff supervise this work, equipped with extinguishers and fire resistant blankets.
- Prohibit smoking in construction areas.
- Ensure that workers store construction materials away from the building and remove all rubbish and debris daily.
- Do not permit gasoline-powered engines inside the building.
- Limit use of paint thinners and solvents and ensure that containers are safely stored in safety cabinets. (Use water-based paints whenever possible.)
- Protect fire detection systems from operations that could cause false alarms or contaminate the detectors (e.g., keep them free of dust).
- Supervise closely all hot-tar roofing projects.

Special events. Cultural institutions often host special events, such as fundraisers, lectures, recitals, exhibition openings, and private parties. In each of these events, the institution is used for a purpose for which it was not intended. Overcrowding, catering operations, highly combustible decorations, smoking, and other associated factors can create hazardous conditions.

Work with the EPM, the collections team, and other relevant staff to establish guidelines to bring party planners and well-intentioned volunteers into the prevention and preparedness process. The following points are adapted from *Protection of Museums and Museum Collections*:[9]

- Review plans before the event to prevent overcrowding, exit blockage, introduction of hazardous materials, unsafe cooking appliances, and unsafe demonstrations. Monitor the event to ensure that the occupancy limit set by the fire marshal is not exceeded.
- Ensure that nothing visually or physically obstructs or compromises an exit or exit sign, and that wiring or cords are not placed across exit routes.
- Limit all cooking and warming to museum kitchen facilities, or off the premises if there is no kitchen. Prohibit open flames in the museum area, opting instead for electric warming pans and the like. Keep a fire extinguisher within 30 feet (9.14 meters) of any cooking, warming, or hazardous operation, and ensure that contract catering employees know how to use it.

- Prohibit smoking inside buildings, as well as any demonstrations involving flammable, explosive, or toxic material.
- Ensure that all tents and canopies are noncombustible or certified fire resistant, and that all draperies, buntings, textiles, wood, and miscellaneous support and decorative materials used inside the building are fire retardant.
- Require catering staff to remove food scraps and garbage immediately after events to avoid attracting insects or rodents.
- Ensure that key staff members (event coordinators, volunteers, etc.) are familiar with all exit routes.

Note: Some of the foregoing may already be prohibited or restricted by state or federal regulations.

Step 2
Document all protection efforts

Document protection procedures as you implement them. The two purposes of documenting are to create a powerful tool for communicating progress in emergency preparedness, and to provide evidence of the implemented protective measures for insurance or legal purposes. Use photographs, videotapes, and written records to document building interiors and exteriors and grounds. Photos should have captions, such as "Building before/after tree-trimming" and "Workers replacing roof nails." Videotaped records also work well. Remember to date all records.

Post copies of the photographs on walls or bulletin boards in staff areas to show employees the progress being made toward preparedness. Or, distribute an emergency preparedness bulletin to the entire staff. These practices build not only confidence in the emergency preparedness and response program but also morale on your team. Be sure to credit those on or off your team whose suggestions resulted in measures undertaken.

Keep additional copies of all documentation in a safe location and another set off-site, balancing the need for duplicate documentation with security concerns. Review and update documentation at least once a year.

Preparing Report 2:
Outline of Response Procedures and Techniques

In Report 2, you and your team will put together a buildings and maintenance response team and recommend related procedures and techniques for responding to any type of emergency. The report should give instructions for ensuring the safety of people and objects, including how to trigger notification of chain of command, handle emergency equipment, and relocate people and/or collections. It also should include lists of items such as emergency supplies and equipment available on-site as well as off-site, and job descriptions for response team members.

There are plenty of emergency plan templates to help you get started, but do not simply copy sections from someone else's emergency plan. It is not the *written plan* that prepares an institution for an emergency, but the *process* of planning for an emergency. The fact that you and your team are grappling with these issues now, in the comfort of a conference room, means you will be better prepared to respond to a crisis. (Note: If necessary, ask for assistance during the writing phase, or work closely with a staff member responsible for typing or computer input work.)

The following tasks, undertaken *before* an emergency happens, will help you design the buildings and maintenance team's portion of the response plan in a simple, detailed, and flexible way:

Task 1: Identify potential safe rooms and/or outside shelters.

Task 2: Develop the buildings and maintenance response team.

Task 3: Detail recovery procedures.

Task 4: Create lists of staff and resource contact information.

Task 5: Create fact sheets, maps, and plans.

Task 6: Stock emergency supplies and equipment.

Task 7: Establish routines to keep the plan viable.

Task 8: Identify and implement appropriate training.

In preparing the report, you and your team will need to address a number of important issues. Some will be general to all the team reports; others will be issues specific to buildings and maintenance. The questions below will help you address some issues and may prompt you to identify others.

Questions to Consider

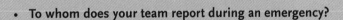

- To whom does your team report during an emergency?

- Who will be in charge of keeping your part of the plan current? (People change jobs, telephone numbers change, new equipment is purchased and old equipment is discarded, companies go out of business, and agency responsibilities change.)

- Who does the building engineer report to and take instructions from in an emergency? Outside agency personnel? The emergency response coordinator (ERC)? The director? The curators?

- Who will coordinate with collections staff regarding when the building will be safe to reenter and when damage assessment or salvage operations can be undertaken?

Task 1
Identify potential safe rooms and/or outside shelters

You and your team's input into the decision on where to establish safe rooms and/or outside shelters is invaluable. Work with the collections team and the safety and security team to identify potential locations, which may vary depending on the type of emergency. When selecting a shelter, consider the various threats facing the institution. If flooding is a potential hazard, the shelter must be on the highest point in the surrounding area. If wildfires are a possibility, make sure heavy brush and trees do not surround the shelter.

The following recommendations for emergency shelters have been adapted from *Steal This Handbook!* [10] and from interviews with advisers to this book:

Size. Ensure that the shelter is large enough to fit the maximum number of staff and visitors likely to be in the museum at any one time. Allow 5–6 square feet (0.47–0.56 square meters) per adult and 3 square feet (0.28 square meters) per child. It also should be large enough to accommodate emergency supplies and priority objects.

Accessibility. Take into account the route necessary to reach the shelter and the size of the openings through which objects must pass.

Security. The shelter must offer the highest level of security. This means a minimum of openings so the shelter can be sealed and access controlled completely.

Physical safety. The shelter should be isolated from the exterior by adjacent rooms or corridors. Walls and ceilings should be free of plumbing, pipes, and so forth.

Environmental stability. Make sure the shelter is environmentally stable and that it has good air circulation.

Lighting. Make sure adequate lighting is provided. There should be no windows or skylights if the institution is in earthquake or tornado country to avoid broken glass.

The shelter should be selected according to the likely threats. For internal shelters, choose a space on the lowest floor (e.g., basements) for tornadoes and hurricanes, and on upper floors if the institution is on a floodplain or near a river.

An ideal shelter should *not* have any of the following:

- exterior walls that are likely to be partially or completely destroyed
- roofs with windward edges (usually south and west), long spans, overhangs, or load-bearing wall supports
- corridors that have exit doors facing directly to the outside
- spaces with windows facing the likely direction of a storm or hurricane
- interior locations containing glass (display cases, doors, or skylights)

Questions to Consider

- In your institution's area, from which direction do potential natural hazards (hurricanes, windstorms, brush fires, flash floods) come?

- How does the local emergency management agency's plan for placement of civil shelters affect your plans?

- In a general area emergency, the museum itself may become a shelter. How will you protect the physical plant in such a situation?

- Does anyone other than the janitorial staff know where the toilet paper, plastic bags, and disinfectant are stored?

Task 2

Develop the buildings and maintenance response team

Step 1

Compile a list of necessary actions

The role of the buildings and maintenance response team will vary depending on the institution and on the emergency. The team's top priorities should be (1) to ensure that the weather is kept out and (2) to get systems back on-line as soon as possible. What buildings and maintenance staff members generally should *not* be expected to do is to assess the safety of the building after an emergency, unless they are structural or electrical engineers or are trained or qualified to do such an assessment. Emergency authorities and/or other building experts should make those determinations.

It is essential that the buildings and maintenance response team be allowed to concentrate on the building and its systems. Team members should not be pulled off for security or collections priorities until *they themselves* feel they have their equipment under control. Cooperation with other teams is important in making the building safe enough for people to reenter so the needs of the collections may be addressed. The director and the ERC should know buildings and maintenance staff capabilities *in advance* so that impossible requests and expectations are not made. It is also critical to ensure that team members work sensible shifts, allowing them sufficient time to rest and eat.

Here are some types of actions for which your team may be responsible (not necessarily in this order):

- Turning off the main gas valve, all electrical power, and other applicable utilities (depending on the nature and extent of the emergency).
- Conducting an initial site survey of the building and grounds as soon as possible after authorities have deemed the building safe to reenter.

- Securing shutters and/or nailing plywood sheeting to windows and doors.
- Sandbagging doors.
- Surveying the buildings and grounds for lock-down preparedness.
- Gathering emergency supplies and equipment for buildings and maintenance work.
- Topping off gasoline tanks in cars, trucks, chain saws, generators, and pumps.
- Checking all electrical equipment and unplugging if appropriate. (Staff members who use computers should be trained in what to do and when to do it.)
- Arranging for backup electricity. Coordinate with the safety and security team regarding clean water, recovery operation areas, and so forth.
- Documenting building and/or equipment damage with photographs, videotapes, and/or written records, or coordinating this task with other documentation teams.
- Contacting specialists (e.g., structural engineers, electricians, etc.) as soon as possible after discussion with the ERC.
- Shoring up damaged structural elements if team members have the appropriate knowledge.
- Trying to bring the building environment under control, while keeping the collections team updated.
- Clearing plant debris and downed trees to permit access where necessary.

At the Mystic Seaport Museum, staff members in every department—including building and ground maintenance—have a series of procedures to go through as a storm approaches, beginning forty-eight hours before a storm is expected to hit and extending until after the storm.

Step 2
Develop response team job descriptions

Designate responsibilities by position title, rather than by individual, so that if the person who is the primary designate for the response role is unavailable, the person who is next in the line of succession assumes the responsibilities of the response role. You may want to assign team leaders in the areas of grounds, utilities, and site. Group similar duties (e.g., leadership duties, assistance duties, and physical duties) so that one person is not expected to carry out too many different duties.

How many positions you assign in the line of succession will depend on how important certain skills are to the role. For example, if it is critical to have a person with engineering experience directing the buildings and maintenance response team, it would be advisable to designate a number of backups

Suggested Exercise

Describe the following scenario to team members: Imagine that the basement is under water. Who is in charge of emergency response actions in this situation? The person who can operate the pump? The collections staff members wading in the water trying to evacuate objects? The person who knows the most about how to drain out the water? The ERC? (Correct answer: the ERC.) Have team members discuss the implications of each answer given.

for the team leader. For sandbagging and boarding up windows, most people can fill the position if they have some training and are physically capable. Committing the responsibilities of each person to paper helps to define roles and familiarizes each person with his or her role and that of colleagues.

Be sure to build in flexibility. The goal in establishing a response team is to create generic positions that anyone can fill in an emergency. In other words, staff members should not be rigidly bound to a specific position. Chances are just as good that the night janitor will end up shutting off utilities and shuttering windows.

The administration and records team, which most likely is experienced in writing job descriptions as part of its human resources function, can coordinate the writing of job descriptions for each of the four departmental response teams.

The response team job description (appendix J) for the building systems supervisor position is from the Seattle Art Museum's *Emergency Planning Handbook*.[11] Note that in addition to simple and clear responsibilities, the description also lists three positions in the line of succession in the event that the person in the primary designation position is unavailable. The description also states to whom this team member reports, and provides a checklist of actions expected of the position. In short, nearly anyone could fill the position if necessary.

Task 3

Detail recovery procedures

Recovery measures occur after an event has happened. They are designed to enable the museum—and its collection—to return to normalcy in an orderly, phased, reasoned and methodical fashion. Recovery measures begin when the disaster situation has stabilized and professionals have evaluated the damage and suggested further, long-term actions. Recovery can be a long process, taking years in some cases.[12]

— John E. Hunter
  Supervisory staff curator
  National Park Service, U.S. Department of the Interior

Step 1

Consider damage assessment issues

When is it safe to enter the building? Who will make the damage assessment? How will this assessment be conducted? Working with the three other departmental preparedness teams, you and your team will build damage assessment procedures into the response plan.

One person must be responsible for assessing the condition of buildings and building systems, including the structural and nonstructural integrity of buildings; the functioning of mechanical, electrical, and plumbing systems; and the functioning of data and telecommunications systems. Consider the qualifications of your staff first, then determine whether outside expertise will need to be brought in to conduct this assessment.

If there is adequate expertise in-house, have the team develop checklists for assessing the damage. The checklist for assessing structures would include such items as "walls of primary and outlying buildings structurally sound," "roofs intact and structurally sound," and "shelving securely bolted and upright." If the institution has more than one structure, determine the order of priority for the damage assessment.

Documentation of physical damage is critical not only for salvage and conservation of historic buildings, but also for insurance purposes. If the institution has a risk manager, involve that person in the planning process. Documentation equipment, such as a camera or video camera, along with insurance damage claim forms, should be safely stored and easily accessible. If visual documentation equipment is unavailable, do the documenting in writing. Prepared checklists can make written documentation more effective.

In the United States and other countries, federal funding is available when a museum is affected by a natural emergency. *Documentation of damage, along with photographs of objects before they were damaged, is required.* In the United States, additional funding for temporary relocation of objects, equipment purchase, and so forth, may be available through the Institute of Museum and Library Services and the National Endowment for the Humanities in Washington, D.C.

Questions to Consider

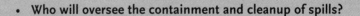

- **Who will oversee the containment and cleanup of spills?**

- **Who will mark hazards and hazardous areas? How will these areas be marked?**

- **Who prioritizes the need for repairs and restoration of essential services and repairs of damaged utilities, buildings, and equipment?**

Step 2

Determine recovery procedures

Work with the three other departmental teams to identify recovery procedures that move the institution from a state of emergency to the state of normal operations. In the aftermath of an emergency, these recovery procedures can be used as a guide in developing a recovery plan. Remember that in many emergency situations, staff can reenter the building only after it has been declared safe to do so by the relevant authorities (e.g., the fire department).

Buildings and maintenance recovery procedures include the following:

- Help determine specific recovery needs and goals.
- Organize resources, including recovery and cleanup teams, supplies, and equipment.
- Arrange for backup electricity, clean water, recovery operation areas, and so forth.
- Secure the buildings and grounds, installing barricades if necessary.
- Secure the services of structural engineers, architects, qualified contractors, and architectural conservators, as appropriate.
- Thoroughly inspect and repair power and mechanical systems and equipment before activating them.
- Monitor buildings and grounds for long-term damage.

Step 3

Address issues of mental and physical well-being

An important part of preparedness is planning for the potential long period of time before the buildings can be reoccupied. It could be hours. It could be weeks. It can be a difficult period—a time when something happens followed by another long waiting period. How do you take care of all the people in the meantime? You have to respond in a reasonable way and work that into the plan. If you do not have a plan in place, you respond emotionally.

— Jerry Podany
   Head of antiquities conservation
   The J. Paul Getty Museum

During salvage and recovery, team leaders need to pay attention to pacing and motivation. Be sure to schedule regular breaks, as well as provide food, a place to eat and rest, and bathroom facilities. Jerry Podany recalls how workers assisting in recovery efforts after an earthquake in Japan were highly organized and worked at a high energy level for extended hours. In the end, their extreme fatigue negatively affected their work.

After the same earthquake, Podany witnessed one recovery group patching one painting amid a rubble of pottery shards. "I thought it was silly to patch a painting when there was so much devastation around them," he recalls. "But it made a huge difference to that group. It really energized them."

Step 4
Require frank after-action reports

Every encounter with a disaster or an emergency is an opportunity for learning. After-action reports that detail actions taken and results observed are a key teaching tool. It is important first to emphasize and praise what went right, then to examine problems encountered or mistakes made. Do not allow these reports to be after-the-fact justifications and defenses of what the response team did; rather, they should be a candid assessment of what went on, problems and all.

Indicate to your team your desire to learn from mistakes, not to punish people for them. Encourage an atmosphere of honest self-assessment, starting with yourself. What could you have done differently? What would have worked better? How could you improve your response next time? What did you learn that could be applied to the next emergency?

Task 4
Create lists of staff and resource contact information

Once you have the list, do not rest on your laurels, thinking, Well, we have a list, so we're done. Lists go out of date quickly, so it is important to update them at least one a year.

— Gail Joice
Senior deputy director and registrar
Seattle Art Museum

You will need to furnish the EPC with the names of all your staff members, along with their work and home telephone numbers and home addresses. This information will allow staff to be reached at home during an emergency. Also, make a list of special skills at hand—for example, is an employee a former nurse, search-and-rescue team member, or National Guard member?

Put together lists of names, telephone and fax numbers, and street and e-mail addresses of individuals and organizations with which your team might have contact during and after an emergency. Update the lists regularly. Make contact with each of these organizations or individuals now, apprising them of their projected role in the institution's response plan. Coordinate your lists with those of the other departmental teams.

The following are sources you may wish to include in your lists. Check to ensure that each vendor is insured and licensed, if applicable. Work with administration to establish credit with the sources to be used in the event of an emergency.

- fire department/police/ambulance
- utility companies
- structural engineers and architects
- heating, ventilating, and air-conditioning (HVAC) and other systems service engineers
- carpenters
- fumigation companies
- equipment supply or rental companies
- locksmiths
- hardware stores, lumberyards
- roofers
- plumbers
- glaziers
- electricians
- landscape services

Questions to Consider

- **Where do you keep your resource list?**
- **Who is keeping it current?**
- **How often is it updated?**
- **Where is the off-premises copy located?**
- **Who will be responsible for contacting these people?**

Task 5

Create fact sheets, maps, and plans

Develop fact sheets, maps, and plans with other teams, particularly safety and security. Deposit duplicates of these documents in safe but accessible places inside and outside the building, and coordinate the storing of off-site copies with the administration and records team. Security concerns will need to be balanced against availability in an emergency.

Department-related fact sheets should include

- operating instructions for emergency equipment, such as generators and radios;
- location and instructions for turning off valves for gas, electricity, water, and other utilities and mechanical systems; and
- a list of hazardous materials (work with the collections team to produce this list, which must be made available to fire departments).

Maps should include

- emergency exits and evacuation routes;
- emergency shelter, supplies, and first-aid kit locations; and
- access to and location of keys to such areas as supplies, storage, and electrical circuit boxes.

Note: Carefully discuss who is authorized to hold keys for emergency events and how to override automatic closing devices or obtain access to areas with card-key entry.

Plans should include

- utility systems (electricity, water, gas, and telephone);
- architectural blueprints, with number and location of all doors, windows, and stairways ("as built" drawings are well worth the extra expense);
- mechanical system plans (heating, ventilation, and air conditioning); and
- fire detection and suppression systems.

Task 6

Stock emergency supplies and equipment

Suggested Exercise

During a meeting of the buildings and maintenance team, conduct a mental exercise. Ask members to close their eyes; then propose an emergency scenario. For example, a violent earthquake hits, or a fire breaks out in a work-room. Ask a volunteer to describe, step by step, how he or she would respond. Ask detailed questions: What do you do first? Whom do you call? What telephone do you use? Where are the keys? Where are the necessary tools, supplies, maps, and lists? Encourage others to make recommendations.

Coordinate with other teams and the EPC to acquire general supplies, such as boxes, first-aid kits, and tape. Supplies and equipment specific to the tasks of your team are also needed. Store emergency supplies in two locations: inside the institution for quick access, and outside the institution in case of evacuation or if the building is not occupied when the emergency occurs. Large quantities of expensive items or perishable materials need not be stockpiled. Instead, identify suppliers and make arrangements for emergency delivery, as needed.

Buildings and maintenance on-site emergency supplies should include the following:

- ladders
- bolt cutters
- plastic tarpaulins, duct tape
- axes
- hand saws
- nonelectric tools, as well as cordless, rechargeable hand drills (with bits)
- carts and trolleys
- emergency generator and fuel
- fire extinguishers
- plywood
- nails, screws, assorted fasteners
- rope, twine, binding wire
- crowbar
- portable humidifiers, dehumidifiers, fans (or easy access to rental equipment through a prearranged contract)
- blotting paper, towels, sponges

- buckets, shovels, rakes, hoes
- fire retardant overalls, gloves, hard hats, boots

For ideas on other supplies and equipment—for a mobile/portable first-aid box, an emergency response cart, and a disaster supply box—see appendix E.

Supplies should be based on the types of potential emergency situations identified in the risk assessment. For example, if the institution is in a flood-prone area, relevant items—such as squeegees, brooms, and pumping devices, as well as plastic tarps, sandbags, antibacterial soaps, and clean drinking water—should be stocked in sufficient quantities.

Questions to Consider

- Have you provided sufficient protection for the supplies so they will be available and undamaged in the event of a disaster?

- Are two ladders enough during an emergency? Four hammers?

- What emergency equipment can the museum borrow from local emergency authorities (e.g., barricades, tarpaulins, tents, drying or pumping equipment, vehicles, auxiliary lighting, etc.)? Remember, however, that you'll be on your own in a big event.

- What are nearby sources to replace damaged or inaccessible materials? Where is the "shopping list"? Who can purchase the materials?

- Have you communicated clearly to all staff members where these supplies are located; have you labeled them clearly; and have you posted maps showing where emergency supplies and shut-off valves and switches are located? [13]

Task 7

Establish routines to keep the plan viable

The following are a few examples of possible daily and periodic checklist activities for the buildings and maintenance team. You may be inspired to think of others. Compare lists with the other departmental preparedness teams.

Daily checklist activities:

- Electrical tools are unplugged.
- Hazardous materials are returned to appropriate storage each night.
- Construction and/or renovation areas have been fully checked to ensure that equipment is turned off and unplugged, as appropriate.
- Cigarette disposal containers have been emptied.

Periodic checklist activities:

- Check that fire extinguishers are inspected and recharged as necessary (this responsibility may be shared with or assumed by the safety and security team).

- Ensure that updated documents (revised plans, etc.) are given to the adminstration and records team for inclusion in the institution's off-site set of records.
- Ensure that equipment is inspected and serviced according to manufacturer specifications.
- Check emergency supplies and reorder if necessary.
- Verify updated contact information for outside experts and/or resources.

Task 8
Identify and implement appropriate training

Getting buildings and maintenance people to train others to help them can be difficult. They are used to working alone and being criticized for everything they do; therefore, gaining their confidence is hard.

— Barbara Roberts
Conservator and hazard mitigation consultant

After Hurricane Hugo devastated the Caribbean and the southeastern seaboard in 1989, the staff of the Barbados Museum and Historical Society actively pursued a policy of disaster preparedness. As outlined in the case history in chapter 1, the museum adopted a basic model plan in 1990 that simply outlined major activities to be taken during an emergency. "We thought we were wonderful because we had a plan," director Alissandra Cummins says. "But we had never practiced it, and we had not properly adapted it to our needs." Once the museum began practicing the plan, a multitude of deficiencies were noted, including the need for a team approach to disaster response. Now each team drills at least once a year, reporting all suggestions for improvement to the museum's central planning committee.

Training and regular drilling enables everyone on staff to react automatically in emergencies. It can make the difference between a smoldering wastebasket fire and a fire-gutted building. With regard to buildings and maintenance activities, you will need to train all staff members in activities such as

- shutdown procedures;
- location of utilities switches and how to turn them off; and
- use of specialized tools.

When training staff to shut off utilities, be sure to indicate which, if any, should not be shut off. "If you shut off water to some steam boilers, they will explode," Barbara Roberts warns. "You cannot just say, 'Shut off the systems.'" Color-coded pipes and switches can help, but training and familiarity are the most important preparedness steps.

Consider sending building managers to national training sessions, or holding a one-day brainstorming session for area building managers. The following are a few basic training methods. You may choose to employ several, either independently or simultaneously. See chapter 5 for more information on training.

Suggested Exercise

After your institution's emergency plan is in place, do impromptu tests of various staff members to see if they can follow such instructions as "Go to chiller no. 2 and turn the cog," or "Go and shut off electricity to the west wing." If they do not know what to do, walk them through the procedure. If they successfully follow the instruction, acknowledge their good work.

- group discussions conducted while standing in front of the equipment being discussed
- simulations/role-playing
- supplementary handouts
- videos
- review sessions
- self-assessment exercises
- hands-on workshops
- presentations by colleagues or consultants who have firsthand knowledge of the scenarios the institution might face

Questions to Consider

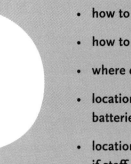

Does everyone on staff know

- **how to direct firefighters and others through local streets;**

- **how to get to the roof of the buildings and direct others to the roof;**

- **where emergency alarms and fire extinguishers are;**

- **location, both off-site and on-site, of hard hats, flashlights, fresh batteries, hoses, fire hydrants;**

- **location of supply kits for packaging the office equipment, and if staff members have access to that location;**

- **the routes to internal or external shelters;**

- **who is in charge and to whom to report; and**

- **how to evacuate computer files?**

Notes

1. John E. Hunter, "Preparing a Museum Disaster Plan," in *Southeastern Museums Conference, 1991 Disaster Preparedness Seminar Proceedings*, ed. Martha E. Battle and Pamela Meister (Baton Rouge, La.: Southeastern Museums Conference, 1991), 55.

2. Carl L. Nelson, *Protecting the Past from Natural Disasters* (Washington, D.C.: Preservation Press, National Trust for Historic Preservation, 1991), 87–88.

3. Reprinted from National Fire Protection Association (NFPA), *NFPA 911 Protection of Museums and Museum Collections* (Quincy, Mass.: National Fire Protection Association, 1991), 15–16. Copyright ©1991, National Fire Protection Association, Quincy, MA 02269. This reprinted material is not the complete and official position of the National Fire Protection Association, on the referenced subject which is represented only by the standard in its entirety. Used by permission.

4. Adapted from Allyn Lord, Carolyn Reno, and Marie Demeroukas, *Steal This Handbook! A Template for Creating a Museum's Emergency Preparedness Plan* (Columbia, S.C.: Southeastern Registrars Association, 1994).

5. NFPA, *Protection of Museums*, 8–9. Used by permission.

6. Ibid., 6. Used by permission.

7. Ibid. Used by permission.

8. Ibid., 16–17. Used by permission.

9. Ibid., 19–20. Used by permission.

10. Adapted from Lord, Reno, and Demeroukas, *Steal This Handbook!* 177–79. Used by permission.

11. Seattle Art Museum, *Emergency Planning Handbook*, rev. ed. (Seattle: Seattle Art Museum, 1994).

12. Hunter, "Preparing a Museum Disaster Plan," 58.

13. Gail Joice, "Questions to Ask Yourself When Preparing a Disaster Plan" (AAM Risk Management and Insurance Committee, American Association of Museums, Washington, D.C., April 1994, typescript).

Chapter Summary

This chapter

- outlined the role of the buildings and maintenance preparedness team in the emergency preparedness process;

- described information required in the two reports, to be delivered to the emergency planning committee;

- provided guidance through the process of assessing the vulnerability of the institution's buildings and maintenance program;

- helped define the roles and responsibilities of the buildings and maintenance response team; and

- identified tasks to guide your team through the process of developing a response plan that is simple, detailed, and flexible.

In review, the emergency preparedness process is a long-term commitment on the part of staff, teams, and committees. You cannot, and should not, expect changes quickly or easily. Interdisciplinary teamwork is difficult and requires a change in attitude that may be slow in coming at first. The payoff—in peace of mind, in the safety of staff and visitors, and in the protection of objects and irreplaceable records—will be great.

CHAPTER NINE

The Administration and Records Team

This chapter addresses issues relating to records, computer documentation, and personnel administration that must be dealt with as the institution builds its emergency plan. It is designed to be a resource for you, the leader of the administration and records team.

For an overview of the emergency preparedness and response program, please consult chapters 1–3. For training ideas, see chapter 5.

Your Role in the Process

Losing data and records in an emergency *usually* is not a threat to people or to cultural institutions; however, some natural history specimens or archaeological shards, for example, may be rendered totally irrelevant without the proper documentation. Data generally ranks far behind protection of life and safety of the collection in the hierarchy of emergency priorities. Because of this, you may consider your team's role in the emergency preparedness process less critical than that of the collections, buildings and maintenance, and safety and security teams. Keep in mind, though, that although your work may not be critical to human life, your contributions and those of your team can make a huge difference in the museum's ability to recover quickly after an emergency (Fig. 8).

The job of the administration and records preparedness team is to thoroughly evaluate administrative functions and record-keeping systems to determine where the institution is vulnerable; to evaluate personnel and legal issues related to emergency preparedness and response; and to identify their own roles during an emergency. The team will produce two reports to the emergency preparedness committee (EPC) that summarize its findings:

Report 1 is a vulnerability and asset analysis that recommends preparedness and protective measures, including what should be done to prevent damage to museum administrative functions and to prevent destruction of important data in the event of an emergency.

Figure 8   Administration staff person packing files and backing up computer records in preparation for Hurricane Georges. Courtesy of the Barbados Museum and Historical Society. Photo: Kevin Farmer.

Report 2 outlines the role of the administration and records response team during an emergency. It should include lists of service vendors and their telephone numbers, as well as equipment and supplies needed. It also should note training issues pertinent to this area.

To begin the process of compiling information and developing the administration and records team's portion of the emergency plan, you, as team leader, will perform the following tasks:

Task 1: Assemble the preparedness team.

Task 2: Interact with other teams and with the EPC.

Task 1

Assemble the preparedness team

Personnel functioning as one well-oiled machine during emergencies produce dramatically better results than scattered, chaotic responses by individuals. That is why team building is such a critical component of true emergency preparedness.

You are in charge of appointing the administration and records team and of guiding team members in gathering accurate, efficient information and in organizing a well-coordinated response to any emergency. Select team members on the basis of three categories of skills: technical and functional, problem solving, and interpersonal. All efforts at team building should focus on the process and on accomplishing the intended tasks. Building a successful team means taking risks that involve resolving conflict, establishing trust, and encouraging interdependence. Refer to chapter 5 for information on assembling and building effective teams.

As part of the recommendations in Report 2, you and your team will establish and take on the roles and responsibilities of the administration and records response team, which may or may not include all members of the preparedness team. This team—along with a team from each of the other three departments—will respond in an actual emergency situation.

Task 2

Interact with other teams and with the EPC

Competition for budgetary and personnel resources is not a luxury in an emergency. If the emergency priorities of life safety and collection protection are to be met, all of the museum's resources must be placed immediately, totally, and non-competitively at the disposal of those acting to save the collection.[1]

— John E. Hunter
   Supervisory staff curator
   National Park Service, U.S. Department of the Interior

To produce your reports for the EPC, you will need to work closely with the three other departmental teams in the following areas:

Safety and security
- Evacuation routes for equipment and/or furniture
- Volunteer screening and coordination
- Security of evacuated data
- Fire prevention efforts
- Temporary operations headquarters

Collections
- Collection insurance issues
- Volunteer coordination
- Inventory lists
- Documentation of activities

Buildings and maintenance
- Documentation during relocation or evacuation
- Repair and maintenance record keeping
- Volunteer coordination
- Building-insurance issues

In collaborating with other teams, work through the EPC to set up meetings between your team and the others to help avoid territorial disputes. It then becomes a top-down mandate rather than a lateral agreement. If necessary, you may want to include a member from the EPC during these meetings. Include on your team a member of the other departmental teams, as applicable. This works well as long as your team is discussing matters that pertain to this person's area of expertise.

Collaboration is required for the overall success of the emergency preparedness process. This process is likely to give buildings, maintenance, and security staff a higher profile in terms of both image and responsibilities. It may also require—or cause—a shift in attitudes among other professional staff.

Preparing Report 1: Vulnerability and Asset Analysis

How vulnerable are the institution's records and other operational systems to the threats of fire, flood, hurricane, earthquake, and other emergencies or hazards? For example, how quickly can you generate information on

- which artifacts were in the east wing at the time of the fire;
- the loss of value sustained; and
- the itemized cost to rehabilitate the building and reopen it to the public?

Does the biggest threat to the institution come from inadequate insurance coverage of the buildings and/or equipment? Will you be able to recover important data after an emergency? Work with the emergency preparedness manager (EPM) and the EPC to assess the institution's vulnerabilities from an administration and records point of view. The accuracy and thoroughness of your analysis will greatly affect the speed with which the institution can recover after an emergency. Report 1 should contain protective measures to reduce the vulnerabilities your team discovers.

Some examples of potential vulnerabilities are listed below. You and your department colleagues probably are already aware of some or all of these weaknesses; some may become apparent only in the analysis process. All, however, may ultimately affect the institution's preparedness and response capabilities.

- Staff members back up their individual computer files periodically, but no systemwide backup occurs. Data are backed up regularly, but not the application programs that allow staff to access and recover those data.
- The inventory of furnishings, equipment, and supplies is not complete.
- Hard-copy documents have not been duplicated for ten years.
- No system exists for tracking assets.
- Duplicate documents are stored inside the building.
- Insurance coverage is inadequate.

The following tasks will lead you and your team through the process of information gathering in order to prepare Report 1:

Task 1: Evaluate record-keeping systems and procedures.

Task 2: Anticipate financial and legal concerns.

Task 3: Review insurance coverage and procedures.

Task 4: Evaluate equipment/data safety and needs.

Task 5: Invite local agencies and individuals to participate.

Task 6: Recommend records-related protective measures.

Suggested Exercise

To get your new team thinking about vulnerabilities within the data systems, describe an emergency scenario, such as a sudden and strong earthquake. Be specific. How strong is the earthquake? What time of day is it? Details help make the exercise more real and the results more useful. Have team members close their eyes and picture the scene in their mind as you talk. Give them five minutes to list every type of possible calamity that an earthquake can cause. Were computers thrown to the ground? Did the earthquake touch off a fire? What will happen to both computer and hard-copy records? Encourage team members to share and discuss their responses. Hold a debriefing session after the exercise. Remind the team that the emergency preparedness process will make everyone safer.

Questions to Consider

- Is there a complete inventory of all furnishings, equipment, and gift shop stock?

- If the computer system goes down in a power outage, what will you lose?

- How will you recover information stored on computer tapes and drives?

- Are duplicates of legal/official documents (i.e., constitution, leases, contracts, site plans, etc.) stored safely off-site?

- Will a power outage lock up book or collections compactor stacks?

- Do you have hard copies of tour booking schedules, as well as copies of names, telephone numbers, and addresses of staff, trustees, donors, loaners, and so forth?

Task 1
Evaluate record-keeping systems and procedures

Computers are way behind art in emergency priorities, but people realize that data about the art is a close second.[2]

— Joe Shuster
Chief of information technology
Seattle Art Museum

What kind of information is being recorded and by which process? Where are the data being stored? Can the system—computer or hard copy—provide you with useful information after an emergency? These are the main questions to ask in accomplishing this task.

Step 1
Evaluate inventories

Administration inventories. Administration departments at most institutions maintain a complete inventory of the institution, including furnishings, equipment, museum store stocks, and library books. The administration and records team is responsible for all emergency preparedness and response considerations concerning these records.

To assess the adequacy of the institution's insurance coverage and of insurance reimbursement after an emergency, you need to be able to track assets. This can mean simply a file folder with furniture and equipment receipts, or vehicle papers (with duplicate copies stored off-site), or a more formal computerized database.

Up-to-date valuations for collections are required for insurance claims. Establishing values for total or partial loss payments after the object is destroyed is extremely difficult. Accurate numbers count if objects are to be grouped by type and value—for example, 500 objects at US$25 and 10,000 objects at US$150. This should be discussed with the insurance broker and underwriter; otherwise, every object that is damaged will have to be listed individually.

Collections inventories. Larger institutions have record-keeping systems for collections that are separate from the rest of the operational data. Such is the case at the Seattle Art Museum, where the collections record-keeping system contains all catalogue information, documents for objects on loan, deeds of gifts, and collections insurance. The collections team is responsible for all emergency preparedness and response considerations concerning those records.

Depending on your institution, you may need to work with the collections team to plan for collections records, or you may be in charge of evaluating all forms of records. Good documentation of the collection is vital for insurance claims and for any conservation steps following damage. How detailed the documentation should be depends on the collection and on identified priorities. In the event that the administration department is responsible for collections records, refer to chapter 7 for more information.

Step 2
Review other documentation

All administrative records need to be evaluated as part of the preparedness process. What documents must staff have in hand during the response and recovery process? These documents should be stored in a safe room for easy access in the event of an emergency. What documents must be stored safely but do not necessarily have to be readily available?

Your documentation analysis should include the following:

- payroll
- financial records
- taxation records
- legal records
- incorporation records
- contracts
- personnel files
- list of donors
- emergency fund records, including signing authorities
- valuations

Work with the buildings and maintenance team and the safety and security team to assess adequate documentation of the physical plant. These teams should have the following:

- maps that include emergency exits, evacuation routes, and the location of emergency shelters, supplies, first-aid materials, utility shut-off valves, keys and prioritized assets
- instruction sheets for emergency equipment and for turning off utilities
- a list of hazardous materials stored on the premises
- files containing plans of utility systems, mechanical systems, fire detection/suppression systems, and architectural blueprints ("as-built" plans are invaluable)

Step 3
Review computer backup procedures

Where are the computer data being stored? On the hard drive? On the disks or external drives of individual staff? In a power failure, how would you retrieve information? As businesses throughout the world know, backing up information is essential when using computers. Often overlooked in the process are the following:

- Is there a systemwide backup? Having no systemwide backup means a large amount of decentralized data, which makes it difficult to evacuate complete operational data. How often should you back up the entire system? The answer depends on how much information is input daily, hourly, or weekly.
- Are there copies or backups of the application programs? Without these, you may be unable to access the backed-up data. Copies could be kept off-site and in the safe room with other duplicate records. How often are these copies updated?
- Who checks to ensure that information is being backed up properly and regularly and that it is recoverable? How often is this done? (The Seattle Art Museum does this every week.)
- Who is authorized to remove backup tapes and disks during an emergency? Some of the information on the tapes may be sensitive, such as financial records. You may want to designate one individual for this responsibility, or several individuals, depending on the size of the institution and on the sensitivity of informaton.
- Are passwords required to obtain certain computer data? Where is the list of passwords stored, and who has access to it?
- Are surge protectors replaced and updated every three or four years?

Task 2

Anticipate financial and legal concerns

Do not ignore financial planning. A natural disaster may create a financial one. If possible, build up reserves in every budget. Disruption of business in subsequent months—and years—can cause major financial damage.[3]

— Carl L. Nelson
Protecting the Past from Natural Disasters

Your team must work with the EPC to identify potential financial and liability issues related to emergency preparedness and response. Among the questions you will need to answer are the following:

- What liabilities does the institution have for volunteers who are accepted into the cleanup process?
- What liability is faced in moving the collection off-site?
- What is the institution's liability for anyone hurt on-site during an emergency response?
- What contracts need to be put into place in advance for external consultants, contractors, and other vendors or agencies?
- How much money should be set aside to deal with an emergency?
- In the event of a regionwide disaster, are sources of funds available in another city or region?
- Are grants available for funding preemergency studies if the institution has a high potential for major damage from a natural disaster?
- Are recovery operations for cultural institutions included in the mandate of local, state, or national funding organizations?
- Have charge accounts been set up with local suppliers? Credit cards may not be usable during a large-scale emergency; you may have to operate in a "cash-only" economy.

Task 3

Review insurance coverage and procedures

Insurance coverages are designed to help restore your assets and operation when, in spite of physical prevention and protection measures, a disaster strikes. Placing property insurance coverage is, in fact, an essential part of your fiduciary responsibility to care for and preserve your institution's building and collection.[4]

— Gail E. McGiffin
"Sharing the Risks"

In reviewing and evaluating insurance coverage, work with members from the collections and the buildings and maintenance teams. Many institutions insure the structure but do not adequately insure the contents. Consult with the insurance company or agent regarding the following:

- risk assessment
- asset identification
- protection priorities
- up-to-date collections valuations and loss-of-value evaluations
- preparedness and preventive measures

- response and recovery procedures and costs
- contingency planning
- emergency plan review
- practice drills
- required damage documentation
- claim preparation, including required details

Know what the policy covers. Find out whether the policy does and/or should include the following:

- loan exhibits
- objects in the building that are awaiting setup or ship-out
- purchase or rental of prevention and/or response equipment, supplies, and resources, such as portable generators, temporary relocation costs, and cleanup services
- costs of contracting professional conservation services and/or purchasing conservation equipment and supplies
- costs to conserve objects to the claim condition only
- replacement value, where applicable
- liability for staff, board officers, and visitors
- ambulance and medical services for uninsured visitors
- valuable documents, computer data, workers' compensation
- business income insurance

A special "rider" is usually required for equipment and data. This rider will assume that data are backed up frequently and that systems are operational at an alternative site. Therefore, policies usually will not cover the reconstruction of lost data. The policy should cover drying, cleaning, and reconditioning of equipment. A "functional replacement" section is important in order to purchase newer equipment that performs the same functions and more. Computer riders usually cover a limited time, sometimes only a few months.[5]

Determine also what documents and procedures are required for filing a claim. Keep copies of insurance claims with emergency supplies both on and off the premises, along with photographic equipment and film for documentation during and after an emergency. Coordinate this with all teams. The documentation should provide evidence for an insurance claim, including the following:

- proof that the institution did all it could to prevent, or at least mitigate, the effects of the disaster
- proof that the established response and recovery procedures were followed
- fast and accurate indication of the condition and loss of value, in dollar terms, of the building and the collections following the emergency

Further information on insurance issues can be found in Smith,[6] McGiffin,[7] and Kahn.[8]

Questions to Consider

- Does insurance adequately cover the hazards identified in the risk assessment from the EPC?

- Are inventories and appraisals for collections and structures up to date?

- Are deductibles still appropriate?

- How often will the policy be reviewed and updated? Who will do it?

- Is there a building mortgage? If so, how does that affect insurance coverage and/or claims?

- What are the procedures for assessing damage (i.e., does an agent have to see a damaged object before it is moved)?

- Does the policy cover cleaning, recovery, and reconstruction of the area if the institution is located in a rented building or has rented storage space?

- If property is jointly owned, or owned by a government agency, which organization pays for damage and loss?

- Has the institution's probable maximum loss been discussed with the insurance provider? Is the probable maximum loss regularly reevaluated?

Task 4

Evaluate equipment/data safety and needs

What administrative equipment is on hand now? Typewriters? Computers? File drawers? How are they and the data they contain protected against the risks and hazards that have been identified? A few small expenditures could be all that is needed to protect costly equipment and records that could take months to re-create. For example, expensive computers should be bolted down if the institution is in an earthquake-prone area. There are inexpensive ways of securing drawers, shelves, and cabinets. Fireproof cabinets can provide extra protection for sensitive documents.

If the computer data are more important than the computers themselves—which is usually the case—your priority may be to invest in an effective automatic backup program before bolting down the computers. If the institution's records are not yet computerized, it may be time to do so. In any case, you will have to establish the highest priority of need, given the particular risks associated with the location of the institution and any budgetary restrictions. To help protect records, here are some items you may wish to have on hand:

- fire extinguishers
- fireproof file cabinets
- power-surge protectors (replace every three or four years)
- latches on cabinets

You may also wish to consult the buildings and maintenance team about fire detection and suppression systems for offices, as well as emergency generators and fuel specifically for the running of computers.

Questions to Consider

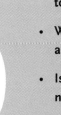

- **Have you determined what equipment and supplies are likely to be needed?**

- **What sources are nearby to replace damaged or inaccessible materials? Where is the "shopping list"? Who can purchase the materials?**

- **Is there any planned alternate on-site and/or off-site storage for noncollections objects, such as furniture, fixtures, and equipment?**

- **What equipment, materials, and documents are needed to keep administrative functions operative in the event of a relocation?**

Task 5

Invite local agencies and individuals to participate

Do not make the mistake of overlooking local or regional services and resources. Consider inviting any or all of the following professionals to make presentations to your team. Coordinate these efforts with the EPC so that other teams, and perhaps all staff members, might benefit.

- computer experts
- retired or current staff of institutions with emergency responsibilities
- business office management experts
- insurance agents

It is also helpful to solicit input and advice from colleagues at institutions around the world. The purpose, however, should be to research what they did correctly and incorrectly during emergencies, not to simply copy their plans.

Task 6

Recommend records-related protective measures

Protective measures are steps taken to eliminate hazards (as in fire prevention efforts) or to reduce the effects of threats to records and documents (as in daily backup of computer data). You and your team must make recommendations to the EPC for both types of protection.

Protection is a long process—one that never ends. From time to time, remind team members that it is a priority. You also will need to remind your administration colleagues of their commitment to emergency preparedness as you lobby for funding for good paper records, computer upgrades, or photographic records and duplication.

In setting priorities, you must decide whether the assets and/or data are worth protecting and/or evacuating in comparison with the collections.

Protecting the collections and buildings has greater priority in most cases, but there are exceptions. For example, the records and observations associated with specimens in a natural history museum may be more valuable than the easily replaceable specimens. "You have to decide what is potentially replaceable if you have to make that terrible choice," emphasizes Jerry Podany, head of antiquities conservation at the J. Paul Getty Museum.

The priorities for protection that you set will influence the budget for addressing these problems. Some protection efforts may cost next to nothing, such as photocopying paper files and storing the duplicates off-site. Others have higher price tags. The preparedness budget may be well served by protecting data in advance so that in an emergency, efforts can remain fully focused on other areas, such as collections. Bear in mind that it is easier to request funding from the community for specific projects than for the amorphous goal of achieving emergency preparedness.

Protective measures you may wish to consider include the following:

- Establish regulations confining smoking to a specific, designated area outside the premises.
- Store original records in fireproof cabinets.
- Duplicate file cards if there is only one copy.
- Work with the buildings and maintenance department to install a fire detection and suppression system in records storage areas.
- Back up computer files and systems daily.
- Ensure that computers and other office equipment are kept in well-ventilated areas and that cords and wiring are intact (i.e., not frayed).
- Unplug all office equipment during thunderstorms or if such a storm is approaching.
- Use high-quality surge protectors and change them every four years.
- Store heavy books, supplies, and related items on lower shelves; do not store anything on top of shelves or cabinets or place shelves over computers, typewriters, and other office equipment. Secure shelves to walls.
- Keep an updated medical information data sheet on all staff (who agree to volunteer the information). Include a list of emergency contacts, preferred doctors and hospitals, and medical insurance companies and account numbers for each staff member. List next of kin or out-of-state contact names and telephone numbers.
- Prohibit or limit the storage or use of documents and office equipment near plate glass windows or doors, particularly if the institution is in a tornado, hurricane, windstorm, or seismic zone.

Work with the safety and security, collections, and buildings and maintenance teams to keep duplicates of all important documents in a secure place off-site, within twenty-four hours of accessibility, and keep one set of the documents in the safe room, or in the departmental safe rooms, as appropriate. These documents should include the following:

- emergency cash, checks, credit cards, and contact information for a 24-hour bank
- acquisition and registration records
- insurance records
- financial records
- asset documentation and inventories
- ownership, rental, or lease records
- policy documents
- inventory lists
- labels for boxes and writing equipment
- computer application programs
- personnel records
- name labels for volunteers
- records of grants, donations, and museum shop sales
- library and archive inventories
- laptop computer with an adapter for using a car cigarette lighter as a power source
- membership records (for an emergency appeal, if necessary)

Records from other departments should include the following:

- acquisition and registration records
- complete, updated records of collection loans
- conservation treatment and condition reports
- hazardous materials lists
- architectural and mechanical system plans and appropriate contacts
- plans of electronic security and fire detection and suppression systems

Preparing Report 2: Outline of Response Procedures and Techniques

In Report 2, you will establish an administration and records response team and recommend administration and records-related procedures and techniques for responding to any type of emergency. The report gives instructions for ensuring the safety of staff and data. Include in the report lists of items, such as emergency supplies and equipment available on-site as well as off-site, and job descriptions for response team members.

As in all other aspects of emergency preparedness, advance planning is the key to minimizing confusion, unnecessary delays, and frustration. It also can result in significant money savings by ensuring prompt resumption of revenue-generating museum or institution activities, as well as the most efficient use of financial and staff resources in order to recover all normal operations. The following tasks, undertaken *before* an emergency event, will help you craft the administration and records portion of the response plan in a simple, detailed, and flexible way:

Suggested Exercise

With your team, brainstorm what to do in the following scenario: Weather forecasters say a storm is headed in your institution's direction, accompanied by strong winds and heavy rainfall. This is the latest in a monthlong series of such storms. The storm is expected to hit tomorrow night. What is the role of the administration and records staff during preparations for the storm? Who will check and/or stock supplies, photo equipment, and insurance paperwork? Who will move sensitive equipment to the middle of the room? Who will perform the computer backup? What else should be considered?

Task 1: Identify potential temporary operational headquarters.

Task 2: Develop the administration and records response team.

Task 3: Develop recovery procedures.

Task 4: Create lists of staff and resource contact information.

Task 5: Create relevant fact sheets and maps.

Task 6: Stock emergency supplies and equipment.

Task 7: Establish routines to keep the plan viable.

Task 8: Identify and implement appropriate training.

In preparing the report, you and your team will have to address a number of important issues. Some will be general to all the team reports, whereas others will be issues specific to administration and records. The questions below address some of these issues and may prompt you to identify others.

Questions to Consider

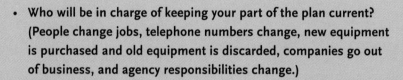

- Who will be in charge of keeping your part of the plan current? (People change jobs, telephone numbers change, new equipment is purchased and old equipment is discarded, companies go out of business, and agency responsibilities change.)

- To whom does your team report during an emergency?

- What will be the financial effect on the museum of a long-term disruption of services? A short-term disruption?

- If the institution is small, can you form an "emergency-preparedness cooperative" with other small cultural institutions? As a group, can you acquire funding to research disaster plans and/or form a central library for disaster preparedness information? Can you talk to local emergency authorities as a unified group? Can you assist one another in other ways?

- Who will handle personnel issues, such as workers' compensation claims, disability, and payroll? Do you have the forms and know the procedures?

- Who has access to immediate emergency funds and authorization for emergency expenditures?

- Who will coordinate with emergency organizations such as the Federal Emergency Management Agency (FEMA), and with the insurance company?

- Who will coordinate volunteers during and after an emergency?

Task 1

Identify potential temporary operational headquarters

During an emergency, there must be a central base of operations, or emergency command center, from which the response and recovery teams can operate following an evacuation. The location of this command post is likely to be different in anticipation of a hurricane than in response to an earthquake. In some cases, it may be the security office. In others, it could be a command post set up on or near the premises.

Work with the emergency response coordinator (ERC) and leaders of the other departmental teams to identify criteria for the emergency command center. Once established, the command post should be staffed by the ERC and the leaders of the departmental response teams.

The safety and security team may be given the responsibility for setting up the command post. Your role in regard to administrative issues for the post, and your input into the decision on where to establish temporary quarters to house operations, is invaluable. When selecting a data recovery center, consider the threats identified in your team's vulnerability assessment. If flood is a potential hazard, the center must be located on the highest point in the surrounding area.

Rapid recovery is the first priority for the administration and records team. Personnel must be accounted for and assisted, if necessary. The need for information will be great. Donors and lenders will want to know the status of their works of art and artifacts. Collections holdings may have to be moved, and it is imperative to know their current whereabouts; movement and rehousing information must be kept under full intellectual control. The insurance process must be launched. Other agencies, such as federal assistance programs, will want documentation. To function as a data recovery center and operations headquarters, the command center must

- contain at least one computer with enough power and memory to access the data and applications, if applicable;
- have access to sufficient power supply to run computers and other equipment (note: adapters are available for a car's cigarette lighter);
- be secure so as to control access to data and records;
- have a copy of the card file or accession books;
- be physically safe for those working there; and
- have adequate sanitation facilities, as well as emergency water and food supplies.

Task 2

Develop the administration and records response team

Step 1

Compile a list of needed actions

The role of the administration and records response team will vary depending on the institution and the emergency. Following are some actions for which your team may be responsible:

- Establish a base of operations that can accommodate the anticipated worker pool, and announce its location to staff.

- Provide immediate access to emergency funds and establish a contingency plan for financing recovery operations and for paying staff.
- Quickly contact trustees, board of directors, large donors, and the like—with permission from the director or the ERC—and inform them of the emergency, ideally before they hear of it on the news.
- Coordinate claims and restoration work with insurance agents, federal emergency agencies, registrars, and conservators as quickly as possible. This may require hours of detective work in the files. (Note: Accompany all insurance agents, contractors, and simliar personnel on their tour of the site. Take detailed notes of all conversations for future reference.)
- Attempt to recover data as quickly as possible.
- Evacuate records (e.g., computer disks, Rolodex files, etc.), if time permits, in the order of priority established in the emergency plan.
- Remain with evacuated records until the appropriate person can receive them.
- Recruit and screen volunteer workers.
- Create work schedules; keep staff employed part-time if they cannot be employed full-time due to the emergency situation.
- Consider purchasing or arranging for quick rental of an emergency generator for vital equipment (photocopier, computer, etc.).

Step 2
Develop response team job descriptions

Developing job descriptions should be familiar to members of your team, at least those who handle personnel files and perform human resources duties. Because of this, your team should coordinate the writing of job descriptions for each of the four departmental response teams.

Designate responsibilities by position title rather than by individual, so that if the person who is the primary designate for the role is unavailable, the person next in the line of succession will assume the responsibilities. You may want to assign response team leaders in the areas of personnel, software, and physical records. Match similar duties (e.g., leadership duties, assistance duties, and physical duties) so that one person is not handling totally different tasks. Each position on a team should have a job description.

The number of alternates—or backup positions—that you assign depends on how important certain skills are to the position. For example, if it is crucial to have a person with computer experience directing the administration and records response team, numerous alternates should be listed. Committing the responsibilities of each person to paper helps to define roles and familiarizes each person with his or her role and that of colleagues.

Be sure to build flexibility into the plan. Experts say that the goal in establishing a response team is to create generic positions that anyone can fill in an emergency. In other words, staff members should not get tied to a specific position.

The response team job description for the human resources manager in appendix K is from the Seattle Art Museum's *Emergency Planning Handbook*.[9] Note that in addition to simple and clear responsibilities, the description lists who should fill the position, and the line of succession if the designated person is unavailable. The description also states to whom this team member reports, and provides a checklist of actions expected of the position. In short, nearly anyone could fill the position if necessary.

Task 3

Develop recovery procedures

Recovery measures occur after an event has happened. They are designed to enable the museum—and its collection—to return to normalcy in an orderly, phased, reasoned and methodical fashion. Recovery measures begin when the disaster situation has stabilized and professionals have evaluated the damage and suggested further, long-term actions. Recovery can be a long process, taking years in some cases.[10]

— John E. Hunter
Supervisory staff curator
National Park Service, U.S. Department of the Interior

Step 1

Consider damage assessment issues

Working with the three other departmental preparedness teams, you and your team will build damage assessment procedures into the response plan. The institution's controller, risk manager, and general counsel should be involved in the planning process. Use their expertise to anticipate legal and financial issues or potential obstacles likely to arise in the aftermath of a large-scale emergency.

Your team should develop checklists for recovery procedures. Documentation of physical damage is critical not only for salvage and conservation of historic buildings but also for insurance purposes. Determine what role the administration and records response team will play in the documentation process.

Documentation equipment, such as a camera or video camera, should be safely stored and easily accessible, along with in-house damage assessment and object report forms and insurance claim forms. If visual documentation equipment is unavailable, do the documenting in writing. Prepared checklists can make written documentation more effective.

In the United States and other countries, federal and national funding is available when a museum is affected by a natural emergency. *Documentation of damage, along with photographs of objects before they were damaged, is required.* In the United States, additional funding for temporary relocation of objects, equipment purchase, and so forth, may be available through the Institute of Museum and Library Services and the National Endowment for the Humanities in Washington, D.C.

Step 2

Determine recovery procedures

You and your team should work with the three other teams to identify recovery procedures that move the museum from a state of emergency to the state of normal operations. In the aftermath of an emergency, these recovery procedures can be used as a guide in developing a recovery plan.

Administration and records-related recovery procedures may include the following:

- Help determine specific recovery needs and goals.
- Determine what resources are needed.
- Help prepare a written recovery plan.
- Organize resources, including recovery teams and outside experts.
- Secure funding.
- Gather emergency equipment and supplies.
- Maintain staff morale by setting a date for reopening the institution, creating work schedules, and allowing time off for staff members who have had extensive damage to their homes.
- Work with the other departmental teams to review and coordinate claims and restoration work.
- Maintain the public's goodwill by issuing news releases on the situation, and preparing a list of needs and making it available to interested organizations and members of the public.
- Reward efforts of staff, volunteers, and board members.

Step 3

Address issues of mental and physical well-being

Employees, volunteers, and others may experience secondary injuries— emotional injuries—following a disaster.[11]

— The Getty Center
"Emergency Planning Handbook"

The Getty Center's "Emergency Planning Handbook" provides information on six stages of reaction that staff may experience after an emergency:

1. Impact of the event (at the time of the event)
2. Shock (24–48 hours after the event)
3. Suggestibility (1–3 days after the event)
4. Euphoria (1–2 weeks after the event, during the initial response phase)
5. Ambivalence (when the critical response phase passes)
6. Reintegration (2–9 months after the event; routine returns, the environment is stable)

These stages are spread over a period from immediate impact to reintegration to a normal routine. The handbook recommends that follow-up support be provided to help staff deal with the impact. Support can be in the form of counseling, confidential support groups, a debriefing for all staff within forty-eight hours after an emergency, reorganization of work schedules as necessary, and reestablishment of normal operations as soon as possible.

The psychological impact of emergencies and disasters should be addressed in training exercises as well. Set aside time after a full drill or a real emergency for staff members to talk about their experiences. Drills can become total mayhem and will inevitably agitate and worry some employees. In addition to holding roundtable debriefings, consider setting up a suggestion box so that the more reticent staff members can share their feelings, comments, and observations. A debriefing should also be held after a drill. Ask participants how they are feeling. If they are doing the drill well, they are going to be almost able to smell the smoke, and will probably be anxious.

During drills and during recovery efforts in a real emergency, be sure to schedule regular breaks, as well as to provide food, a place to eat and rest, and bathroom facilities. Learn more about stress and how to manage its effects. Decision making is difficult, and tensions and tempers may be running high. A sense of humor can go a long way.

Step 4
Require frank after-action reports

Every encounter with a disaster or an emergency is an opportunity for learning. After-action reports detail actions taken and results observed, providing a useful teaching tool. It is important first to emphasize and praise what went right, then to examine problems encountered or mistakes made. Do not allow these reports to be after-the-fact justifications and defenses of what the response team did; rather, they should be a candid assessment of what went on, problems and all.

Indicate to team members your desire to learn from mistakes, not to punish people for them. Encourage an atmosphere of honest self-assessment, starting with yourself. What could you have done differently? What would have worked better? How could you improve your response next time? What did you learn that could be applied to the next emergency?

Task 4
Create lists of staff and resource contact information

You will need to furnish the emergency preparedness committee with the names of all your staff members, along with their work and home telephone numbers and addresses. This information will enable you to notify them if they happen to be at home during an emergency. Also, make a list of any special skills staff members have; for example, is any employee a nurse, a search-and-rescue team member, or an ambulance driver?

Put together lists of names, telephone and fax numbers, and street and e-mail addresses of individuals and organizations with whom your team might have contact during or after an emergency. Update the lists regularly. Coordinate your lists with those of the other teams. Contact each of these organizations or individuals now, apprising them of their projected role in your plan.

Here are some resources you may wish to include:

- local (federal) emergency relief office
- insurance company
- electronic data recovery services
- lawyer/legal adviser
- copying facility
- volunteer organizations
- banks
- board of directors, trustees, significant donors, collection lenders
- computer rental and repair firms

Questions to Consider

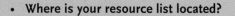

- **Where is your resource list located?**

- **Who is keeping it current? How often is it updated?**

- **Where is the off-premises copy located?**

- **Who will be responsible for contacting people identified for assistance and advice?**

- **Have you established credit lines with appropriate companies, and are they sufficient for the institution's potential needs? Will this plan work if the whole community is affected by the emergency?**

Task 5

Create relevant fact sheets and maps

Develop fact sheets and maps in collaboration with the other preparedness teams. Your department, however, will be responsible for overseeing the duplication of these documents; identifying a safe location for them on the premises, as well as off-site; and depositing all documents in these locations. In the process, you will need to balance a risk to the security of vital and confidential documents against having them available and readily accessible in an emergency. Fact sheets from your department should include the following:

- operating instructions for computer equipment
- hazardous materials in the area, including copier fluid
- data recovery location

Task 6
Stock emergency supplies and equipment

Store emergency supplies in two locations—internal for quick use, and external in case of evacuation or if the building is not occupied when the emergency occurs. Coordinate this stocking process with the EPC and other preparedness teams. Large quantities of expensive items or perishable materials need not be stockpiled. Instead, identify suppliers and make arrangements for emergency delivery, as necessary.

Emergency supplies should include the following:

- hard hats and emergency clothing (for team members who are assigned to enter a damaged building)
- workers' compensation, insurance claim, and accident report forms
- purchase orders
- emergency credit card/cash/checkbooks (vendors may not be able to verify credit card charges if telephone lines are not working)
- payroll lists
- photographic equipment (camera, lenses, accessories, flash, high-speed film) and video camera, if possible
- batteries for camera, flash, flashlights, and other equipment (replaced as necessary)
- extension cords (some of which are equipped with ground circuit interrupters)
- boxes for packing and moving records and equipment, along with sealing and strapping tape
- essential office equipment and supplies, such as a manual typewriter, pocket calculator, pencil sharpener, clipboards, stapler, rulers, pens, pencils, and waterproof notebooks
- essential stationery to ensure capability of minimal administrative operations
- a number of small carrying bags or backpacks for moving the mini-office around in what might be a damaged building
- plastic sheeting to cover exposed objects and office equipment

For further ideas on equipment and supplies that should be stocked, refer to appendix E.

Suggested Exercise

During a meeting of your team members, conduct a mental exercise. Ask them to close their eyes; then give them an emergency scenario. For example, a fire breaks out in a workroom, or a local disaster strikes. Ask a volunteer to describe, step by step, how he or she would respond to the emergency. Ask detailed questions: What do you do first? Who has a flashlight? Whom do you call? What telephone do you use? Where are the keys? Where are the necessary supplies, maps, and lists? Encourage others to make recommendations.

Questions to Consider

- Have you provided sufficient protection for the supplies so they will be available and undamaged in the event of an emergency?

- Have you communicated clearly to all staff where these supplies are located, have you labeled them clearly and have you posted maps showing where the supplies are located?

- What are nearby sources to replace damaged or inaccessible materials? Where is the "shopping list"? Who can purchase the materials?

- Is someone responsible for being sure supply levels are maintained? [13]

Task 7

Establish routines
to keep the plan viable

The following are a few examples of possible daily and periodic checklist activities for the administration and records team. Compare your list with those of the other preparedness teams to learn about other important activities you may have overlooked.

Daily checklist activities:

- Computer system and files are backed up daily.
- Copier and other equipment are turned off, unplugged, or put on power-saving mode, as appropriate.
- The safe and confidential file cabinets are locked and the keys deposited in the designated location.
- Doors and windows in the administration areas are locked.
- Waste disposal containers are emptied.

Periodic checklist activities:

- Check emergency supplies, and reorder if necessary.
- Have fire extinguishers in the administration areas inspected, and recharged if necessary.
- Coordinate with other departments the duplication and off-site storage of new documents.
- Verify and update information on the contact list of emergency resources.
- Update the duty roster with changes in staff and administrative operations.

Task 8

Identify and implement appropriate training

During a large-scale disaster, your team may be in charge of handling the community volunteers, docents, trustees, members of the military or National Guard, and other emergency workers available to help. Training some of these individuals in advance can provide an additional layer of support in an emergency. It also can aid in community awareness and in fund-raising for prevention efforts. Use untrained volunteers on work on tasks that do not involve collections.

Aside from handling volunteers and performing evacuation procedures, you may also need to train staff to retrieve backup computer tapes and/or disks and to perform other activities specific to administration and records. Coordinate training activities with the EPC, as many of these activities will be relevant to other departmental staff and teams.

Some basic training methods are listed below. You may choose to employ several, either independently or simultaneously. Please see chapter 5 for more information on training.

- group discussions
- simulations/role-playing
- supplementary handouts
- video tapes
- review sessions
- self-assessment exercises
- hands-on workshops
- presentations by colleagues with firsthand experience in the types of scenarios that might be expected at your institution

Questions to Consider

Does everyone on your staff know

- how to direct firefighters and others through local streets;

- how to get to the roof of the buildings and direct others to the roof;

- where emergency alarms and fire extinguishers are;

- the location, both off-site and on-site, of emergency supplies and equipment;

- where supply kits for packaging the office equipment are, and if staff members have access to that location;

- the routes to internal or external shelters;

- who is in charge and to whom to report; and

- how to evacuate computer files (do these need to be evacuated if backup files are maintained)?

While your team may be asked to document response and recovery efforts for the entire institution during execution of the emergency plan, do not forget to keep good written and photographic records of your team activities, as well. Hold regular team meetings as soon as possible to communicate how work is progressing and how to make response and recovery efforts easier and less stressful.

After normal operations have resumed following a disaster, subject the emergency plan and the performance of all team members to a candid critique as soon as possible. Encourage feedback from all persons involved through written reports, interviews, and group meetings.

When possible, following a major emergency, schedule time off for staff members, particularly if any of them have sustained injuries, or damage or loss to their homes. Contact counselors if necessary, and assure staff that such counseling is entirely confidential.

Notes

1. John E. Hunter, "Preparing a Museum Disaster Plan," in *Southeastern Museums Conference, 1991 Disaster Preparedness Seminar Proceedings*, ed. Martha E. Battle and Pamela Meister (Baton Rouge, La.: Southeastern Museums Conference, 1991), 64.

2. Joe Shuster, telephone interview with Sharon Jones, 1993.

3. Carl L. Nelson, *Protecting the Past from Natural Disasters* (Washington, D.C.: Preservation Press, National Trust for Historic Preservation, 1991), 78.

4. Gail E. McGiffin, "Sharing the Risks," *History News* 48, no. 1 (1993): 16–19. Used by permission of the American Association for State and Local History.

5. Adapted from Miriam Kahn, *Disaster Response and Prevention for Computers and Data* (Columbus, Ohio: MBK Consulting, 1994), 43. Used by permission.

6. Scott E. Smith, "Insurance Planning," *History News* 48, no. 1 (1993): 18, 37.

7. McGiffin, "Sharing the Risks."

8. Kahn, *Disaster Response for Computers*, 41–44.

9. Seattle Art Museum, *Emergency Planning Handbook*, rev. ed. (Seattle: Seattle Art Museum, 1994).

10. Hunter, "Preparing a Museum Disaster Plan," 58.

11. Getty Center, "Emergency Planning Handbook" (J. Paul Getty Trust, Los Angeles, 1997, photocopy), Fact Sheets section.

12. Excerpted from Gail Joice, "Questions to Ask Yourself When Preparing a Disaster Plan" (AAM Risk Management and Insurance Committee, American Association of Museums, Washington, D.C., April 1994, typescript), with additional information provided by the advisers in the development of this book.

Chapter Summary

This chapter

- outlined the role of the administration and records preparedness team in the emergency preparedness process;

- described information required in the two reports to be delivered to the emergency planning committee;

- provided guidance in assessing the vulnerability and assets of the administration and records program;

- helped define the roles and responsibilities of the administration and records response team; and

- identified tasks to guide you through the process of designing a response plan that is simple, detailed, and flexible.

In review, the emergency preparedness process is a long-term commitment on the part of the institution's staff, teams, and committees. You cannot, and should not, expect changes to happen quickly or easily. Interdisciplinary teamwork is difficult and requires a change in attitude that may be slow in coming at first. The payoff—in peace of mind, in the safety of staff and visitors, and in the protection of objects and irreplaceable records—will be great.

Appendixes

Appendix A   Emergency Teams at the Barbados Museum

EMERGENCY TEAMS

Our response to emergency situations is centred around a number of teams. These teams are outlined below :

1.   CORE TEAMS (6)

One Curator
One person from the Administrative or Security Staff
One person from Technical Staff
At least two volunteers

When it appears that a threat to the security of the Museum is likely, and when there is adequate time to do so, the role of the CORE TEAMS is to secure the institution's <u>COL</u>LECTIONS and <u>RE</u>CORDS. Each member of staff is assigned to a CORE TEAM.

2.   DISASTER TEAM

Director
Curators
Executive Officer
Librarian
Special Events Manager
Structural Engineer
Architect

After an emergency, the DISASTER TEAM will enter the buildings and ascertain the physical condition of the buildings and the collections. The DISASTER TEAM determines if and how the RECOVERY TEAM is to be activated.

3.   RECOVERY TEAM

Director
Curators
Executive Officer
Librarian
Marketing Officer
Administration Staff
Technical Staff

After an emergency, the RECOVERY TEAM will survey the facility and the collections and begin to take the appropriate steps. The person in charge will decide when the other staff members can enter the building to assist in the RECOVERY PROGRAMME.

A   Emergency teams list from the Barbados Museum and Historical Society's "Emergency Plan" (Barbados Museum and Historical Society, St. Michael, 1994, photocopy). Used by permission.

Appendix B   Tables of Contents from Emergency Planning Manuals

GETTY CENTER EMERGENCY PLANNING HANDBOOK
TABLE OF CONTENTS

INTRODUCTION

STAFF EMERGENCY PROCEDURES

ORGANIZATIONAL RESPONSE

EVACUATION

COMMUNICATIONS

ORGANIZATION CHART

CHECKLISTS

FACT SHEETS - Introduction and Index
  1   Evacuation
  2   General Security
  3   Visitors and Staff
  4   Collections and Valuable Equipment
  5   Building Assessment
  6   Specific Emergencies
  7   Communications and Documentation
  8   Mechanical Equipment
  9   Life/Safety
  10   Technical Systems
  11   Tram and Helipad

ON-SITE SUPPLIES

OFF-SITE RESOURCES

RECOVERY
  1   Collections
  2   Data and Telecommunications Systems
  3   Financial Systems

B.1 Table of contents from the Getty Center's "Emergency Planning Handbook" (J. Paul Getty Trust, Los Angeles, 1997, photocopy).

TABLE OF CONTENTS

B.2 Table of contents from the Seattle Art Museum's *Emergency Planning Handbook,* rev. ed. (Seattle: Seattle Art Museum, 1994). Used by permission.

TABLE OF CONTENTS

B.3 Table of contents from the Barbados Museum and Historical Society's "Emergency Plan" (Barbados Museum and Historical Society, St. Michael, 1994, photocopy). Used by permission.

SEVERE WEATHER PREPARATION MANUAL
TABLE OF CONTENTS

DEPARTMENTS AND DIVISIONS

BOAT OPERATORS - NEXT OF KIN FORM T 6-7

B.4 Table of contents from the Mystic Seaport Museum's "Severe Weather Preparation Manual" (Mystic Seaport Museum, Mystic, Conn., 1994, photocopy). Used by permission.

POWER SHUT DOWN M 6-7

VHF RADIO INFORMATION S 11-12
EXHIBIT BOAT SHIP AND WHITE BOAT SHOP

Appendix C   Evacuation Procedures for Staff and the Public

Employee Evacuation Procedures

When you hear the evacuation alarm, see the strobe lights, hear the voice evacuation system, or are told to evacuate the building by your Floor Warden:

1. **Immediately shut down all hazardous operations:** seal chemicals, turn off equipment, etc. **Shut all doors and windows behind you** if safe to do so, but do not lock.

2. **Leave quickly by the nearest safe exit.**

3. Go directly to the nearest safe designated Evacuation Assembly Area (see map, back cover of this booklet).

Additional Information:

4. Your Floor Warden will ensure that occupants evacuate the area. All employees should **help each other leave as instructed.** As you exit, quickly check nearby restrooms, copier rooms, closets, etc. for other staff.

5. Accompany and help any people with disabilities, visitors and any co-worker who appears to need calm direction or assistance. Stairwell, Elevator, and Assistance monitors will facilitate your evacuation.

6. Take your car keys, purse, and/or wallet if safe to do so. Do not attempt to take large or heavy objects.

7. Proceed as quickly as possible, but in an orderly manner. Do not push or shove. Hold handrails when you are walking on stairs. Remove high heels to avoid tripping. Move to the right if you encounter emergency personnel.

8. Once out of the building, **move away from the structure.** Do not block streets or driveways.

9. Group with other members of your department and remain in the assembly area. Assist your department head in completing a head count of your department and be prepared to relay the information to Security or others.

If instructed to leave the premises:

1. Ridesharers: contact your rideshare partners immediately. All others needing rides, see your rideshare coordinator for assistance.

2. **Drive carefully.** Extra caution is required anytime you are excited, worried, or distracted by an emergency situation. Watch for pedestrians, obstructions and emergency vehicles.

3. Where roads intersect, merge alternately with vehicles from the other road. Expect traffic back-ups. Be patient. Follow traffic directions from Security or other safety officials. If normal exits are blocked, you will be directed to an alternate route.

4. If you are in doubt about whether to report back to work, call the Getty hotline at (800) 899-5506. This number will have recorded messages on the status of closings and reopenings at all Getty locations.

C.1 Employee evacuation procedures from the Getty Center's "Emergency Planning Handbook" (J. Paul Getty Trust, Los Angeles, 1997, photocopy), Staff Emergency Procedures section.

EVACUATION OF STAFF AND VISITORS

If it becomes necessary to evacuate the Museum, only the person in charge (Director or her appointee) will give the order to carry out evacuation procedures. The following action will be taken by Museum staff, adhering to a "people first" policy.

1. The person in charge will call the appropriate police, security or emergency officials.

2. The person in charge will notify all staff using the telephone intercom system, and keep groups together if possible, (i.e. reception, administration, Cafe staff working at the same location).

3. Designate staff at each exit to monitor walkie-talkies and to maintain contact.

4. The Museum staff will:

    a.   Oversee the evacuation of Museum visitors through front and rear exits. Evacuation should be conducted calmly. Staff should assist visitors to follow appropriate evacuation route.

    b.   Lock away any valuables if time permits.

    c.   Turn off any appliances, lights and extinguish all smoking materials.

    d.   Gather all personal belongings, if time permits.

    e.   Gather all important museum files, e.g. computer disks, rolodex files, etc.

    f.   Lock doors to offices and work areas. In the event of fire, office doors should be closed but left **unlocked**.

    g.   Assign staff to check all areas to ensure complete evacuation.

5.   **EVACUATION PROCEDURES:**

      Evacuation through Front Exit:

Evacuation of staff and visitors through the front entrance to the designated area: Museum carpark near bus stop, will include all individuals located in the following areas:

      -- Library
      -- Shop
      -- Reception

C.2 "Evacuation of Staff and Visitors" document from the Barbados Museum and Historical Society's "Emergency Plan" (Barbados Museum and Historical Society, St. Michael, 1994, photocopy). Used by permission.

- -- Cafe
- -- Security
- -- Exhibition Galleries
- -- Storage Areas
- -- Lower Courtyard - Grounds

* Cafe staff will evacuate through the North Gate, circle the building and join group in Playing Area next to CXC carpark.

-- Security Guard will act as person in charge, and maintain radio contact with other members in the group.

Evacuation through Rear Exit:

Evacuation of staff and visitors through rear entrance to the designated area: CXC Carpark will include all individuals located in the following areas:

- -- Administrative Building
- -- Garrison House
- -- Maintenance worksheds
- -- Staff Hut
- -- Associated Storage areas
- -- Upper Courtyard areas

* Executive Officer will act as person in charge, and maintain radio contact with other group.

General:

a. Notify the person in charge when you have arrived safely at the designated area.

b. Check if everyone is in the designated area. Do not block traffic.

c. Await instructions from the person in charge. Do not leave meeting area unless otherwise instructed. Complete list of evacuees.

6. If fire or police officials require access to the storage areas, the person in charge will provide access or direction as necessary.

Appendix D   Safety and Welfare Supervisor Job Description

SAFETY AND WELFARE SUPERVISOR

RESPONSIBILITIES: Responsible for general safety and welfare of all employees and visitors during emergency operations.

REPORTS TO: PROTECTIVE SERVICES MANAGER

LINE OF SUCCESSION

1.   Security Supervisor
2.   Assistant Chief of Security

ACTION CHECKLIST:

____   Quickly gathers information and develops initial strategy based on personnel available and the nature of the emergency.

____   Obtains the Safety and Welfare Supervisor's Emergency Supply Kit and a portable radio; obtains additional radios as available.

____   Assembles and directs a team of workers, primarily using Security Department personnel and others trained in first aid when possible. Coordinates with Security, Equipment and Transportation and Building Systems Supervisors.

LIFE SAFETY

____   Establishes and maintains first aid station(s).

____   Supervises evacuation of the sick and injured as possible.

____   Reports hospitalization needs of the injured to Protective Services Manager.

____   Conducts search and rescue operations.

____   Coordinates identification, removal and storage of the deceased. See attached Fact Sheet.

WELFARE

____   Establishes food and shelter station(s).

____   Provides special services as required for the care of unaccompanied children, the aged and the handicapped.

____   Arranges for sanitation and disposal of human waste. See attached Fact Sheet.

D   Safety and welfare supervisor job description from the Seattle Art Museum's *Emergency Planning Handbook*, rev. ed. (Seattle: Seattle Art Museum, 1994). Used by permission.

____   Maintains ongoing inventory of all emergency supplies including food, water, first aid supplies, etc. See Chapter V (On-site Resources) and Chapter VI (Off-site Resources).

____   Coordinates equipment and supplies needs with Equipment and Transportation Supervisor.

____   Investigates all accidents, injuries or deaths related to the emergency and maintains accurate chronological records including confidential lists of the injured and dead, citing causes when known. Reports this information to Human Resources Manager.

____   Coordinates with Media Manager to facilitate outside communications with or concerning, staff and visitors.

____   Coordinates with Red Cross as appropriate.

OTHER

____   Arranges for chronological documentation of significant events, using an assistant is possible.

____   Regularly reports to Protective Services Manager on progress/problems.

____   Thoroughly briefs his/her replacement.

Fact Sheets: Safety and Welfare Supervisor

1. Portable Radios
2. Organizational Chart

D   *continued*

Appendix E   Emergency Response Supply Lists

GETTY CENTER EMERGENCY PLAN

Mobile/Portable First Aid Box

Contents

Knuckle bandages	5	Burn sheet	1
Fingertip bandages	5	4" stretch gauze	2
2" x 3" adhesive pads	15	3" stretch gauze	2
3/4" x 3" bandages	25	2" stretch gauze	2
1" x 3" plastic bandages	25	Coban wrap bandages	3
1" x 3" woven bandages	25	Bloodstoppers	3
Betadine swabs	25	Kwick-Cold packs	3
Wound wipes	25	Comfort masks	3
Alcohol pads	50	PTP valve masks	1
Bacitracin	25	Emergency water	2
Towelettes	10	Trauma dressing	1
4-oz. eye wash	1	Micro shield	1
4-oz. hydrogen peroxide	1	Scissors	1
First aid spray	1	Large tweezers	1
Tongue depressors	12	Forceps with magnifier	1
6" cotton-tipped applicators	10	Magnifying glass	1
3" x 3" gauze pads	10	Snake bite kit	1
4" x 4" gauze pads	10	Flashlight	1
2" x 2" gauze pads	10	Pairs vinyl gloves	10
Ammonia inhalants	10	Blood Borne Pathegon kit	1
Eye dressings	4	Large Kerlix roll	1
Nox-a-Sting	20	Pens	2
Triangular bandages	2	Pencil	1
Bandage compress	1	Emergency report forms	6
Rescue blankets	2	Body Fluids Protection kit	1

Swift 68-PM 20-7 Special Fill Trauma Kit - 5/9/96

E.1 List of contents for the mobile/portable first-aid box from the Getty Center's "Emergency Planning Handbook" (J. Paul Getty Trust, Los Angeles, 1997, photocopy), Fact Sheets section.

Emergency Response Cart

Contents:

1.	6 wheeled cart with folding platform and lockable cabinet	1
2.	Lock and key for cabinet, with break box	1
3.	Plastic rolls	2
4.	Spill kit	1
5.	Plastic bucket (in Spill kit)	1
6.	Plastic boot covers (in Spill kit)	3
7.	Coveralls (Tyvek) (L-1, XL-1, XXL-1) (in Spill kit)	3
8.	Rubber gloves (chemical resistant - pairs (in Spill kit)	1
9.	Rigid plastic containers with lid 29"x18"x15"	1
10.	Wet/Dry Vac (in container)	1
11.	Sponges - assorted (in container)	9
12.	Paper towels rolls/packets (in container)	1
13.	Cotton towel rags (in container)	6
14.	Clear eye goggles	1
15.	Dust masks	6
16.	Heavy duty Nitrile gloves (pairs)	12
17.	Leather gloves (pairs)	1
18.	Caution tape rolls	1
19.	Duct tape rolls	1
20.	Door wedges	2
21.	Hammer	1
22.	Scissors	1
23.	Pliers	1
24.	Cutter	1
25.	Quick Link	4
26.	Flash light (complete with batteries) and spare batteries	1
27.	Power pack light (complete with batteries)	1
28.	Emergency floor lamp 500 watt	1
29.	Spare bulb for floor lamp 500 watt	1
30.	Electric heavy duty power cable 100' on reel	1
31.	Electric heavy duty power cable 50' on reel	1
32.	Electric power strip	1
33.	Dust pan and brush	1
34.	Truckers rope 100'	1
35.	Floor prop-up signs "Closed/Caution"	2
36.	Signs for traffic cone (Do Not Enter and Caution - 1 each)	2
37.	Traffic cones 18"	2
38.	Crow bar (wrecking tool)	1
39.	Combination tool (spade/pick/ax/rake/mattock)	1
40.	Squeegee 18" curved with handle	1
41.	Small first aid kit	1
42.	Fire extinguisher	1
43.	Bungee cord fasteners	6

E.2 List of contents for the emergency response cart from the Getty Center's "Emergency Planning Handbook" (J. Paul Getty Trust, Los Angeles, 1997, photocopy), Fact Sheets section.

Cart's exterior contents:		
1.	Plastic rolls	2
2.	Spill kit complete	1
	Plastic bucket	1
	Plastic boot covers	3
	Tyvek coveralls	4
	Rubber gloves (chem. resist)	1
3.	Plastic box container	1
	Wet/Dry Vac	1
	Sponges, assorted	6
	Paper towels/rolls	2
	Cotton towel rags	6
4.	Floor sign - Caution/Do not enter	1
5.	Traffic cones	2
6.	Cone signs - Caution/Do not enter	2
7.	Crow bar/wrecking tool	1
8.	Combination tool set, complete	1
9.	Squeegee, rubber, 18" curved	1
10.	Squeegee sponge, 9"	1
11.	First Aid kit	1
12.	Fire extinguisher	1
13.	Bungee cord fasteners	6
14.	Electrical power distribution strip	1

Cabinet upper shelf:		
1.	Clear eye goggles	1
2.	Dust masks	6
3.	Heavy duty Nitrile gloves	12
4.	Leather gloves (pairs)	1
5.	Caution tape rolls	1
6.	Duct tape rolls	1
7.	Door wedges	2
8.	Hammer	1
9.	Scissors	1
10.	Pliers	1
11.	Cutter	1
12.	Quick Link	4
13.	Flash light with spare batteries	1
14.	Power pack with battery	1

Cabinet Middle Shelf:		
1.	Trucker's rope 100'	1
2.	Dust pan and brush	1
3.	Parts for combination tool set	1

Cabinet lower shelf:		
1.	Emergency floor lamp 500 watt	1
2.	Electric power cable 100'	2
3.	Electric power cable 50'	1
4.	Spare bulb 500 watt	1

E.2 *continued*

FACT SHEET: DISASTER SUPPLY BOX (DOWNTOWN)

The disaster supply box is located in the first aid room on the first floor adjacent to the freight elevator, along with emergency medical equipment, including "First Response" kit, Infection Control kit, and inflatable splints.

Contents:

1.   One roll plastic sheeting, 12'x100', 4ml
2.   One 10-lb. sledge hammer
3.   One 31-lb. drill hammer
4.   One 36" goose neck bar
5.   One 24" goose neck bar
6.   One 14" utility bar
7.   Four adjustable wrenches (10", 15", 10", 8")
8.   One 10" T&G pliers
9.   One 9" lineman's pliers
10. One side cutting dikes
11. One needle-nose pliers
12. Two four-in-one screw drivers
13. One slotted screw driver
14. One Phillips type screw driver
15. Two utility knives
16. One hacksaw
17. One putty knife
18. Six pair leather palm gloves
19. Six two-cell (D) flashlights
20. Six sets of D-cell batteries
21. One roll caution tape
22. Two rolls duct tape
23. One roll electrical tape
24. One roll 2" masking tape
25. Twelve pair cotton gloves
26. One box (100) latex exam gloves
27. Six clipboards with pads
28. One box each permanent markers, ballpoint pens
29. One box (20) dust/mist respirators
30. One box (200) sterile alcohol prep pads
31. One coil 3/8"x50' rope
32. One coil fiber twine
33. One box (25) 33x43 bio hazard bags
34. One bag diaper cloth
35. Four boxes (120 each) pre-moistened anti-bacterial towelettes

E.3 Fact sheet for a disaster supply box from the Seattle Art Museum's *Emergency Planning Handbook,* rev. ed. (Seattle: Seattle Art Museum, 1994). Used with permission.

Appendix F   Collection Safety Manager Job Description

COLLECTION SAFETY MANAGER

RESPONSIBILITIES: Directs all aspects of emergency operations involving the museum art collections; assures that aggressive action is taken for the salvage, preservation, and restoration of the collections. Is responsible for general supervision of technical areas involving art work, including conservation assessment and treatment, transportation and packing activities, storage arrangement, and documentation of movement and treatment.

REPORTS TO: EMERGENCY PLAN COORDINATOR

LINE OF SUCCESSION

1. Registrar
2. Associate Registrar
3. Associate Registrar
4. Exhibition Designer
5. Curator of <u>unaffected department</u>:

ACTION CHECKLIST:

____ Quickly gathers information and develops initial strategy based on personnel available and the nature of the emergency.

____ Immediately appoints Conservation, Art Registration, and Art Relocation Supervisors, using attached work sheet and Emergency Plan Organizational Chart.

____ Receives the Collections Manager's Emergency Supply Kit and a portable radio from Protective Services.

____ Establishes a base of operations and clearly announces its location.

____ Receives initial damage assessment reports from all Conservation, Art Registration and Art Relocation Supervisors and establishes priorities with them.

____ Arranges for chronological documentation of significant events, using an assistant if possible.

____ Receives recommendations from Conservation Supervisor(s) and Art Relocation Manager for on-site storage locations. Designates safe room(s) for emergency art storage.

____ Approves off-site art storage location(s) upon recommendations of Art Registration and Art Relocation Supervisors.

F   Collection safety manager job description from the Seattle Art Museum's *Emergency Planning Handbook*, rev. ed. (Seattle: Seattle Art Museum, 1994). Used by permission.

_____ Coordinates the use of arriving staff through Human Resources Manager, ensuring that all needs are met by priority.

_____ Establishes priority lists for all further salvage efforts.

_____ Continually reevaluates state of emergency and priorities.

_____ Thoroughly briefs his/her replacement.

Fact Sheets: Collections Manager

1.   Portable Radios
2.   Assignment Work sheet
3.   Organizational Chart

Appendix G   Evacuation Procedures for Collections

EVACUATION OF COLLECTIONS

1. In the event of an emergency, Museum collections will be removed from the premises only under the following circumstances:

    a. When the safe evacuation of staff and visitors is completed and staff are not endangered.

    b. If conditions within the Museum are an immediate threat to the collections. Such conditions might occur in events such as fires and floods.

    c. If conditions outside of the Museum are more favourable to the preservation of the collections than existing conditions within the building.

    d. If removal of the collections can be carried out without undue hindrance to fire and police officials.

2. Only the Director or person in charge will give the order to remove the collections from the building. All available staff will assist with the evacuation and the protection of the collections.

    a. Removal of the designated objects will be supervised by the curatorial staff. Objects in immediate danger and those on the **Collections** Priorities list will be removed first.

    b. If conditions allow, objects should be properly wrapped and packed in cartons prior to moving. Use padded carts to move objects if possible.

    c. The curators will maintain a current list of priority objects and their locations. It is the responsibility of each curator to maintain and update the list of priority objects. This list will be located in the Emergency Plan File in the Administrator's office. A copy will also be filed with our Insurance Company.

    d. The Curatorial staff will advise on the removal of :
        *   valuable items on loan to the Museum
        *   objects in temporary exhibitions.

3. Removal of the collections will be accomplished in the following manner:

    a. Collections will be placed in Museum and staff vehicles. A list will be maintained by the Curators of collections that have been evacuated and their location.

    b. Works evacuated will be transported to locations previously designated for storage.

4. If the museum facility cannot be secured after the emergency, temporary storage will be found in another structure until permanent arrangements can be made. The accession numbers and location of collections items going into storage will be recorded by the curators.

G   "Evacuation of Collections" document from the Barbados Museum and Historical Society's "Emergency Plan" (Barbados Museum and Historical Society, St. Michael, 1994, photocopy), 28–29. Used by permission.

Appendix H   Fact Sheet List

INDEX OF FACT SHEETS

1- EVACUATION
Evacuation Procedures: General Instructions
Evacuation Procedures: Security Department
Evacuation Horns
Fire Response: Evacuation Team

2 - GENERAL SECURITY
Command Post: Establishing
Command Post: Mobile
Off-Shirt Emergency Procedures: Security Department
Maps
Personnel Rescue: Hills and Surrounding Brush

3 - VISITORS AND STAFF
Children: Special Assistance
Disabled and Elderly People: Special Assistance
Emotional Response to a Disaster
Gallery Groups

4 - COLLECTIONS AND VALUABLE EQUIPMENT
Art Protection and Handling
Art Relocation Form
Art Condition/Damage Report
Scientific Equipment Protection

5 - BUILDING ASSESSMENT
Post-Earthquake Assessment of Buildings

6 - SPECIFIC EMERGENCIES
Bomb Search Procedures
Bombs: Identifying Mail or Suspicious Packages
Brush Fire: Security
Brush Fire: Emergency Response Executive
Flooding - Exterior
Flooding - Interior

H   Index of fact sheets from the Getty Center's "Emergency Planning Handbook" (J. Paul Getty Trust, Los Angeles, 1997, photocopy), Fact Sheets section.

7 - COMMUNICATIONS AND DOCUMENTATION
Camera: Still
Camera: Polaroid
Camera: Video
Cellular Telephones: Use
HAM Radio
Radios: Channels
Radios: Motorola MTS2000
Radios: Motorola HT600
Radio Unit Numbering

8 - MECHANICAL EQUIPMENT
Elevators: Locations
Elevators: Rescue Procedures
Gate Operation: Loading Dock Roll-up
Gate Operation: NEP Roll-up
Gate Operation: South Entry
Generator: Honda 1000 Watt Unit
Generator: Caterpillar Diesel-Fueled Units
Mechanical Equipment Checklist
Utility Shutoffs: Gas
Utility Shutoffs: Electrical
Utility Shutoffs: Water
Utility Shutoffs: Fire System
Ventilation System Emergency Operation: North Entry Parking
Water Heaters: Location and Response

9 - LIFE/SAFETY
Emergency Bins: Contents
Emergency Response Carts: Locations and Contents
Emergency Response Team: Back Pack Contents
First Aid Box: Locations and Contents
Medical Status Summary Report
Morgue: Temporary
Sanitation of Human Waste
Search and Rescue Backpack Inventory
Search and Rescue Basics
Search and Rescue Team Assignments
Toilets: Portable/Chemical
Treatment Area/Field Hospital Roster

10 - TECHNICAL SYSTEMS
Fire Command Room: System Operations and Shutoffs
Fire Fighting Equipment: Fire Extinguishers
Fire Hydrants: Location
Fire Pump Room
Key Distribution: Emergency Override
Keying System: Nomenclature
Sprinkler Systems: Operation
Standpipe: Connection Locations
Uninterruptible Power Supplies
Water Detection Systems: Procedures and Locations
Won-Door: Locations, Activation and Manual Reset

11 - TRAM AND HELIPAD
Emergency Operation
Evacuation of Occupants
"Blue Light" Station Operation
Firefighter Helipad Bridge

Appendix I   Procedures for Handling Art in an Emergency

PROTECTION OF ART IN EMERGENCY SITUATIONS

The purpose of this section is to inform all staff of the basic procedures to be followed in the protection of art during an emergency, **in the absence of any staff who are specially trained to handle works of art**. The fundamental principle to be observed is that all art should be moved <u>only</u> by trained personnel at all times, even in an emergency, unless the art is in imminent danger of loss, damage, or destruction.

Most art objects require special expertise for safe handling.. Therefore, in the absence of a clear and present danger to the artwork, it is preferable to await direction and assistance from the appropriate registration, conservation, preparation, or curatorial staff.

Before moving any art object:

1.   Select the nearest safe location.

2.   Determine how the art object can be most safely handled.

3.   Do not drag or push a work of art.

4.   Do not try to lift more than you can handle. Get help.

5.   If the object is broken already and cannot be left where it is without risk of further damage, collect and save <u>all</u> the pieces.

Emergency Handling of Paintings

Special tools and equipment are required for moving paintings which are on display. Displayed paintings cannot be lifted from the walls and moved to another location. If the damage has already occurred and the situation is now under control, paintings should, unless absolutely necessary, be left until professional help arrives.

If displayed paintings <u>must</u> be moved to prevent further damage, the following procedures will apply.

1.   Never insert finger between the canvas and the stretcher bars.

2.   Do not touch the front or back of a painting. Move the painting by holding the frame or stretcher bars.

3.   Never allow any object to touch or rest against the front <u>or</u> back of the painting, however lightly.

I.1   "Protection of Art in Emergency Situations" from the Seattle Art Museum's *Emergency Planning Handbook*, rev. ed. (Seattle: Seattle Art Museum, 1994). Used by permission.

4.   Do not carry a painting by the top of the frame. Carry it with one hand under the frame and one hand to the side, or with a hand on either side of the frame.

5.   Hold the frame where it is strongest, never by the fragile gesso decoration.

6.   If there appears to be loose paint present, carry the painting flat, painted surface up, to prevent flakes from falling off.

7.   Paintings should never be stacked. However, when rapid response is necessary and safe space is limited, paintings may need be leaned together against a wall. If this is the case, place the paintings face-to-face and back-to-back, ensuring that the frames overlap and that nothing is in direct contact with the painting surfaces, front or back. Watch for screw-eyes and wires on the backs of frames that could damage the paintings.

Emergency Handling of Small Objects, Vases, Sculpture

Particular care must be observed in the handling of small, fragile are objects. Before moving, determine a safe, out-of-the-way location where they cannot be bumped or hit.

1.   Do not lift or carry a fragile object by its handles, spout, rim, finials, or by any projecting part.

2.   Use one hand to support the bottom of the object and the other hand and arm (like a gentle hug) to support the sides.

3.   Never lift a sculpture by a projecting member such as a hand, arm, foot or head.

4.   Ensure that the earthquake safety wire, if any, has been removed before attempting to move a small object.

Emergency Handling of Furniture

Furniture is particularly vulnerable to damage by water or excessive humidity. If the exposure to water or other danger has already occurred and no further danger is present, the furniture should not be moved until conservators or registrars advise.

1.   Do not drag or push furniture.

2.   Do not lift furniture by arms, legs, back, finials, or other projecting parts.

3.   If possible, remove marble tops before moving furniture.

I.1   *continued*

Emergency Handling of Drawings and Manuscripts

Drawings and prints are particularly vulnerable to damage by water or excessive humidity. The cases and cabinets in the storage area provide protection from water and smoke.

In case of ceiling leaks in drawings and manuscripts storage:

1.   Cover solander shelves and print drawers with plastic sheeting.

2.   Do not open drawing or print cabinets or drawers.

If damage occurs within storage area, the drawings and prints should be moved only if leaving them in the cases and cabinets will cause further damage. When moving them:

1.   Do not open cabinets unless situation is fully under control.

2.   Do not open solander boxes. Under no circumstances should objects be removed from their storage boxes.

3.   Always carry boxed prints with two hands. Carry box horizontally at all times. Do not tilt box or tuck box under arm.

4.   Do not move objects abruptly.

5.   Do not stack large unframed works on paper.

6.   For oversize prints lacking storage boxes, wrap with protective paper or plastic before moving (time permitting), being careful not to snag metal attachments on the binding.

7.   Objects should be moved to a safe, dry, protected area, as prolonged exposure to excess humidity will cause further damage.

If damage occurs in galleries:

1.   Leave objects in display cases until registrar arrives.

2.   Do not attempt to open cabinets or move cases.

I.1   *continued*

HANDLING COLLECTIONS IN EMERGENCIES

A.   PAINTINGS

1. Use common sense.
2. Use extreme care in handling paintings.
3. Always carry only one painting at a time.
4. Always have two or more people lift or move any painting which one person finds even slightly difficult to manage alone.
5. Always carry framed paintings by the frame, with two hands on opposite sides of the painting. Never hold a frame by the ornate deceptions at the corners or centres of the sides.
6. Always hold the face of a painting toward your body when you are carrying it.
7. Never touch the surface of a painting with your fingers.
8. Never hold an unframed painting with your knuckles pressing into the reverse of the canvas.
9. Always be very careful of where you put your hands when holding a frame. Gold leaf is very fragile and can easily be knocked off by the pressure of your hands.
10. Walk smoothly when carrying a painting so that you don't jar or vibrate the canvas and paint layers.
11. Know where you plan to put the painting and where you are going before you lift it. Do not move it unnecessarily.
12. Put paintings where they will not be accidentally knocked into, or be in the way of emergency crews.
13. Always rest paintings vertically against a wall and not flat on the floor, unless there is no other alternative. Use non-skid pads. If none are available, place paintings at a safe angle, from which they will neither fall over nor slide flat. If possible, rest single frame paintings face against the wall.
14. Paintings should not be stacked vertically against each other. If necessary, stack them back-to-back and front-to-front. Always make sure that any wire, screws or protruding pieces on the reverse of frames cannot cause damage. If possible, use cardboard/soft foam pieces to separate stacked paintings.

B.   OBJECTS

1. Use common sense.
2. Use extreme care in handling collections.
3. Move every object by itself.
4. Do not lift by handles, spouts, arms, rims, tails, heads or projecting parts. Use two hands and lift from the base or secure area only. Separate jars and lids whenever

I.2   "Handling Collections in Emergencies" from the Barbados Museum and Historical Society's "Emergency Plan" (Barbados Museum and Historical Society, St. Michael, 1994, photocopy), Appendix 1. Used by permission.

possible and transport individually. Carry with one hand at bottom and one hand at side or near bottom for support and balance.

5. Transfer small objects to boxes or trays, wrapping in tissue paper.
6. Use a cart if possible to move more than one object at a time. Use protective pads, wedges, or blankets to stabilize objects on cards and prevent them from abrading each other.   Be aware of projecting parts - they may require extra padding and extra precaution.
7. Lift, do not drag.
8. Know how a piece is to be handled before lifting; know where you are going and where you plan to put it.
9. Always be careful of where hands are placed as paint, gold leaf, feathers, etc., are easily knocked off.
10. Collect and preserve fragments broken off of any of the collections.   Save all pieces.
11. Place objects where there is no chance of their getting accidentally knocked into or being in the way of the emergency crews.
12. No piece should touch another.
13. Do not allow parts of objects to protrude beyond the edge of shelving, where they might be bumped into.
14. When moving objects to new areas, store heavier objects on lower shelves to lower the centre of gravity and minimize danger of a rack toppling over.
15. Place padding underneath if you must place an object on a palette, on the floor.

C. PAPER DOCUMENTS

E.g. books, unframed photographs, parchment document and files.

1. Use common sense.
2. Use extreme care in handling paper documents. Wear gloves if possible.
3. Lay unmounted sheets between clean sheets of cardboard.
4. Unframed graphics should never be placed against each other. If this is necessary, always place tissue between each piece.
5. Objects other than flat graphics should be maintained in approximately the same horizontal or vertical position in which they were exhibited.
6. Know where you are going and where you plan to place the work of art before you lift it.
7. Walk smoothly when carrying a print or drawing so that you don't jar or vibrate it.
8. Put works of art where there is no chance of their being accidentally knocked into or in the way of emergency crews.
9. Support books well. Do not hold by the spine only. Carry in container if possible.

Appendix J   Building Systems Supervisor Job Description

BUILDING SYSTEMS SUPERVISOR

RESPONSIBILITIES: Maintains maximum functioning of all physical plant systems. Reduces or eliminates risk to people, buildings, and objects through repair work and anticipation of structural, electrical, mechanical, and other problems.

REPORTS TO: PROTECTIVE SERVICES MANAGER

LINE OF SUCCESSION:

1.   Maintenance Superintendent
2.   Maintenance Engineer
3.   Chief of Security

ACTION CHECKLIST:

____   Quickly gathers information and develops initial strategy based on personnel available and the nature of the emergency.

____   Receives the Building Systems Supervisor's Emergency Supply Kit and a portable radio from Protective Services.

____   Assembles and directs a team of workers, primarily from Engineering Department, to immediately conduct initial structural, systems and utility damage assessments. Reports location(s) and severity of problems to Protective Services Manager.

____   Provides emergency power. Coordinates use of emergency generator(s) with Equipment and Transportation Supervisor.

____   Directs necessary emergency shutdown procedures for heating, ventilation, air conditioning, water, and electrical systems.

____   Shuts off water heaters and gas supply lines as necessary.

____   Restores and maintains essential services.

____   Repairs emergency equipment by priority.

____   Inspects and clearly marks hazards and hazardous areas.

____   Constructs emergency facilities as needed, in coordination with Safety and Welfare Supervisor.

____   Provides mechanical maintenance as necessary.

J   Building systems supervisor job description from the Seattle Art Museum's *Emergency Planning Handbook*, rev. ed. (Seattle: Seattle Art Museum, 1994). Used by permission.

____ Maintains and distributes maps and diagrams of systems and equipment locations.

____ Secures contractor support to supplement staff in the repair of damaged utilities, buildings, fire protection systems, equipment, etc.

____ Develops checklist for structural safety in museum, such as:
Fire sprinkler system intact and functional
Natural gas supply lines intact and functional
Walls structurally sound
Roof intact and structurally sound.

OTHER

____ Arranges for chronological documentation of significant events, using an assistant is possible.

____ Regularly reports to Protective Services Manager on progress/problems.

____ Thoroughly briefs his/her replacement.

Fact Sheets: Building Systems Supervisor

1. Portable Radios
2. Organizational Chart

Appendix K   Human Resources Manager Job Description

HUMAN RESOURCES MANAGER

RESPONSIBILITIES: Under the direction of the Emergency Plan Coordinator, is responsible for the efficient deployment and re-deployment of all personnel on Museum property. This included utilizing essential personnel and establishing a safe area for non-essential personnel outside of the emergency area(s). Must make rapid decision based on existing conditions and available staff.

REPORTS TO: EMERGENCY PLAN COORDINATOR

LINE OF SUCCESSION:

1.   Assistant Chief of Security
2.   Assistant to the Director

ACTION CHECKLIST:

____ Quickly gathers information and develops initial strategy based on personnel available and the nature of the emergency.

____ Receives the Human Resources Manager's Emergency Supply Kit and a portable radio from Protective Services.

____ Establishes a base of operations which can accommodate the anticipated manpower pool, and clearly announces its location.

____ Assembles all available personnel and deploys them individually or in teams to report to other managers or supervisors as needed, based on primary skills.

____ Under the direction of the Emergency Plan Coordinator, establishes and continually revises the relative manpower priorities of various teams.

____ Maintains a status board of all current deployment of on-site personnel.

____ Arranges for chronological documentation of significant events, using an assistant if possible.

____ Clearly instructs all personnel to return to the personnel pool for reassignment upon completion of task and release by the requesting manager or supervisor.

____ Identifies whether any personnel are missing and believed trapped in hazardous areas, and informs Protective Services Manager.

K   Human resources manager job description from the Seattle Art Museum's *Emergency Planning Handbook*, rev. ed. (Seattle: Seattle Art Museum, 1994). Used by permission.

___ Coordinates the use of arriving staff with Collections, Protective Services and Media Managers, ensuring that all needs are met by priority.

___ Surveys available visitors, volunteers and docents for special skills (medical, etc.). NOTE: Use only in non-security-risk areas/roles. Screen carefully. Coordinate with Docent and/or Volunteer Coordinator when possible.

___ Recruits outside medical personnel as required; coordinates with Protective Services Manager. See Section V, Off-Site Resources, for listing of local hospitals.

___ Regularly reports to Emergency Plan Coordinator on progress/problems.

___ Establishes records of known missing, injured or dead persons, and coordinates information with Media Manager.

___ Thoroughly briefs his/her replacement.

Fact Sheets: Human Resources Manager

1.   Portable Radios
2.   Organizational Charts

Directory of Selected Organizations

International Conservation Organizations

American Institute for Conservation of Historic and Artistic Works (AIC)
1717 K Street NW, Suite 301
Washington, DC 20006
Tel. (202) 452-9545
Fax (202) 452-9328
E-mail: InfoAic@aol.com
Web: palimpsest.stanford.edu/aic

Association for Preservation Technology International (APT)
PO Box 3511
Williamsburg, VA 23187
Tel. (540) 373-1621
Fax (888) 723-4242
Web: www.apti.org

Australian Institute for the Conservation of Cultural Material (AICCM)
Robyn Sloggett, President
GPO Box 1638
Canberra ACT 2601, Australia
Tel. (61 3) 9344 7989
Fax (61 3) 9347 7448
E-mail:
r.sloggett@artmseum.unimelb.edu.au
Web: avoca.vicnet.net.au/~conserv/
aiccmhc.htm

Canadian Association for Conservation (CAC)
280 Metcalfe Street, Suite 400
Ottawa, Ontario, K2P 1R7, Canada
Tel. (613) 567-0099
Fax (613) 233-5438
E-mail: mhmyre@museums.ca
Web: www.cac-accr.ca

Canadian Conservation Institute
1030 Innes Road
Ottawa, Ontario, K1A 0M5, Canada
Tel. (613) 998-3721
Fax (613) 998-4721
E-mail: cci_library@pch.gc.ca
Web: www.pch.gc.ca/cci-icc

Grupo Español del IIC
Museo Nacional Centro
de Arte Reina Sofia
Departamento de Restauración
C/ Santa Isabel 52
28012 Madrid, Spain

Heritage Preservation
1730 K Street NW, Suite 566
Washington, DC 20006-3836
Tel. (202) 634-1422
Fax (202) 634-1435
E-mail: kdixon@heritagepreservation.org
Web: www.heritagepreservation.org

IIC Hellenic Group
PO Box 27031
117 02 Athens, Greece

IIC Japan
Tokyo National Research Institute
of Cultural Properties
13-27 Ueno Park
Taito-ku
Tokyo 110, Japan

IIC Nederland
Robien van Gulik, Secretariar
Ruys de Beerenbroucklaan 54
1181 XT Amstelveen, Netherlands

The Institute of Paper Conservation
Leigh Lodge, Leigh
Worcester WR6 5LB, United Kingdom
Tel. (44 1886) 832 323
Fax (44 1886) 833 688
E-mail: clare@ipc.org.uk
Web: www.palimpsest.stanford.edu/ipc

International Centre for the Study of the Preservation and Restoration of Cultural Property (ICCROM)
Via de San Michele 13
00153 Rome, Italy
Tel. (39 06) 585-531
Fax (39 06) 5855-3349
E-mail: iccrom@iccrom.org
Web: www.iccrom.org

International Council of Museums— Committee for Conservation (ICOM-CC)
Secretariat, Institut Royal du Patrimoine
Artistique
1, Parc de Cinquanteinaire
B-1000 Brussels, Belgium
Tel. (32) 2 739 6711
Fax (32) 2 732 0105
E-mail: francoise.rosier@kikirpa.be
Web: www.natmus.dk/cons/icom_cc

International Council on Monuments and Sites (ICOMOS)
Secrétariat général
49-51 , rue de la Fédération
75015 Paris, France
Tel. (33 1) 45 67 67 70
Fax (33 1) 45 66 06 22
E-mail: secretariat@icomos.org
Web: www.international.icomos.org

International Institute for Conservation of Historic and Artistic Works (IIC)
6 Buckingham Street
London WC2N 6BA, United Kingdom
Tel. (44 171) 839 5975
Fax (44 171) 976 1564
E-mail: iicon@compuserve.com
Web: www.natmus.dk/cons/iic

Museums & Galleries Commission Conservation Unit
16 Queen Anne's Gate
London SW1H 9AA, United Kingdom
Tel. (44 171) 233 4200
Fax (44 171) 233 3686
Web: www.antiquesworld.co.uk/
Restoration/cons_register.html

National Center for Preservation Technology and Training (NCPTT)
NSU Box 5682
Natchitoches, LA 71497
Tel. (318) 357-6464
Fax: (318) 357-6421
E-mail: ncptt@ncptt.nps.gov
Web: www.ncptt.nps.gov

National Council of Structural Engineers Associations (NCSEA)
203 North Wabash Avenue, Suite 1000
Chicago, IL 60610
Tel. (312) 372-8035
Fax (312) 372-5673
E-mail: office@seaoi.com
Web: www.ncsea.com

National Park Service Division of Conservation
Harpers Ferry Center
PO Box 50
Harpers Ferry, WV 25425-0050
Tel. (304) 535-6205
Fax (304) 535-6295

National Park Service Technical Preservation Services for Historic Buildings
1849 C Street NW, NC330
Washington, DC 20240
Tel. (202) 343-9594
Fax (202) 343-3921
E-mail: hps-info@nps.gov
Web: www2.cr.nps.gov/tps

National Trust for Historic Preservation
1785 Massachusetts Avenue NW
Washington, DC 20036
Tel. (800) 944-6847; (202) 588-6000
Fax (202) 588-6038
E-mail: resource@nthp.org
Web: www.nationaltrust.org

Nordisk Konservatorforbund– IIC Nordic Group
c/o Kari Greve
Nasjonalgalleriet
Postboks 8157-Dep
0033 Oslo, Norway

Österreichische Sektion des IIC Bundesdenkmalamt
Restaurier-Werkstätten
Arsenal Objekt 15/Tor 4
1030 Vienna, Austria

Scottish Society for Conservation and Restoration
The Glasite Meeting House
33 Barony Street
Edinburgh EH3 6NX, Scotland, United Kingdom
Tel. (44 131) 556 8417
Fax (44 131) 557 5977
E-mail: admin@sscr.demon.co.uk
Web: www.sscr.demon.co.uk

Section Française de l'IIC
29 rue de Paris
77420 Champs sur Marne, France
Tel. (33 1) 60 37 77 97
Fax (33 1) 60 37 77 99
E-mail: sfiic@lrmh.fr
Web: www.fnet.fr/sfiic

Society for the Preservation of Natural History Collections (SPNHC)
PO Box 797
Washington, DC 20044-0797
Tel. (202) 786-2426
Fax (202) 357-2986
E-mail: palmer.lisa@nmnh.si.edu
Web: www.spnhc.org

United Kingdom Institute for Conservation (UKIC)
109 The Chandlery
50 Westminster Bridge Road
London SE1 7QY, United Kingdom
Tel. (44 171) 721 8721
Fax (44 171) 721 8722
E-mail: ukic@ukic.org.uk
Web: www.ukic.org.uk

Emergency-Related Organizations

Asian Disaster Preparedness Center
Asian Institute of Technology
PO Box 4, Klong Luang
Pathumthani, 12120, Thailand
Tel. (66 2) 524 5353
Fax (66 2) 524 5360
E-mail: adpc@ait.ac.th
Web: www.adpc.ait.ac.th

Canadian National Committee for the IDNDR
Jannis Klein, Coordinator
Royal Society of Canada
225 Metcalfe Street, Suite 308
Ottawa, Ontario, K2P 1P9, Canada
Tel. (613) 991-9007
Fax (613) 991-6996
E-mail: jklein@rsc.ca
Web: www.rsc.ca/idndr

Caribbean Disaster Emergency Response Agency (CDERA)
The Garrison, St. Michael
Barbados
Tel. (246) 436-9651
Fax (246) 437-7649
E-mail: CDERA@Caribsurf.com
Web: www.cdera.org

Emergency Preparedness Canada
122 Bank Street
Ottawa, Ontario, K1A 0W6, Canada
Tel. (613) 991-7034
Fax (613) 998-9589
E-mail:
communications@epc-pcc.x400.gc.ca
Web: www.epc-pcc.gc.ca

Federal Emergency Management Agency (FEMA)
500 C Street SW
Washington, DC 20472-0001
Tel. (202) 646-4600
Fax (202) 646-4060
E-mail: eipa@fema.gov
Web: www.fema.gov

Fire Protection Association of Australia
PO Box 1049
Box Hill, VIC 3128, Australia
Tel. (61 3) 9890-1544
Fax (61 3) 9890-1577
Web: www.fpaa.com.au

**International Committee
for Museum Security (ICMS)**
Günther Dembski, Chair
Kunsthistorisches Museum
Burgring 5
1010 Vienna, Austria
Tel: (43 1) 525 24 380
Fax: (43 1) 525 24 501
E-mail: icms@icms.org.pl
Web: www.cims.org.pl

**International Committee
of the Blue Shield (ICBS)**
Blue Shield Coordinator
ICOMOS
75 rue du Temple
75005 Paris, France
Tel. (33 1) 42 77 35 76
Fax (33 1) 42 77 57 42
E-mail: leovn@xs4all.nl
Web: www.icomos.org/blue_shield

**International Decade of Natural Disaster
Reduction (IDNDR)**
United Nations Department of
Humanitarian Affairs
Palais des Nations
CH-1211 Geneva 10, Switzerland
Tel. (41 22) 798 6894
Fax (41 22) 733 8695
E-mail: idndr@dha.unicc.org
Web: hoshi.cic.sfu.ca/idndr

**National Fire Protection Association
(NFPA)**
One Batterymarch Park
Quincy, MA 02269-9101
Tel. (617) 770-3000
Fax (617) 770-0700
E-mail: public_affairs@nfpa.org
Web: www.nfpa.org

NFPA International
Tel. (1 617) 984-7700
Fax (1 617) 984-7777
E-mail: NCandee@NFPA.org

Museum and Other Related Professional Organizations

**American Association for State and Local
History (AASLH)**
1717 Church Street
Nashville, TN 37203-2991
Tel. (615) 320-3203
Fax (615) 327-9013
E-mail: history@aaslh.org
Web: www.aaslh.org

American Association of Museums (AAM)
1575 Eye Street NW, Suite 400
Washington, DC 20005-3943
Tel. (202) 289-1818
Fax (202) 289-6578
E-mail: americas@aam.us.org
Web: www.aam-us.org

American Institute of Architects (AIA)
1735 New York Avenue NW
Washington, DC 20006
Tel. (202) 626-7300
Fax: (202) 626-7587
Web: www.aiaonline.com

Association of Art Museum Directors
41 E. 65th Street
New York, NY 10021
Tel. (212) 249-4423
Fax: (212) 535-5039
E-mail: aamd@amn.org
Web: www.aamd.net

Canadian Museums Association (CMA)
280 Metcalfe Street, Suite 400
Ottawa, Ontario, K2P 1R7, Canada
Tel. (613) 567-0099
Fax (613) 233-5438
E-mail: info@museums.ca
Web: www.museums.ca

Conseil de l'Europe/Council of Europe
Point I
67075 Strasbourg Cedex, France
Tel. (33 3) 88 41 20 00
Fax (33 3) 88 41 27 81
E-mail: point_i@coe.fr
Web: www.coe.fr

ICOM—ARAB
M. A. Nur El Din, Chair
Faculty of Archaeology
Cairo University
Giza, Egypt
Fax (20 2) 572 8108

ICOM—Asia and Pacific (ASPAC)
Dr. Amareswar Galla, Chair
Director, Australian Centre for Cultural
Diversity Research & Development
University of Canberra
PO Box 1, Belconnen
ACT 2616, Australia
Tel. (61 6) 201 2199
Fax (61 6) 201 5999
E-mail: galla@science.canberra.edu.au

ICOM—Central Africa (ICOMAC)
Mme Shaje Tshiluila, Chair
Professeur à l'Université de Kinshasa
B.P. 13933
Kinsha I,
République démocratique du Congo
Tel. (243 12) 60 263

ICOM—Europe
Jack Kock, Chair
Department of Medieval Archaeology
University of Aarhus
Moesgard, DK-8270
Hojbjerg, Denmark
Tel. (45) 89 42 4606
Fax (45) 86 27 2378

**ICOM—Latin America and the Caribbean
(ICOM-LAC)**
Sra. L. San Román, Chair
Ministerio de Cultura, Juventud y
Deportes, Dirección General de Museos
Apdo. 10277-1000 San José, Costa Rica
Tel. (506) 255 3051
Fax (506) 255 2197
E-mail: lsanroma@terra.ccouncil.sc.cr

ICOM—Maghreb
M. H. Ben Hassan, Chair
Directeur de la Planification
et du Suivi des Projets
Agence nationale de Mise en Valeur du
Patrimoine Archéologique et Historique
20 rue 8010, Monplaisir 1002 Belvédère
Tunis, Tunisia
Tel. (216 1) 796 168
Fax (216 1) 781 993

ICOM—West Africa (CIAO)
M. Samuel Sidibe
Directeur de Musée National
B.P. 159
Bamako, Mali
Tel. (223) 231 486
Fax (233) 231 909

Institute of Museum and Library Services (IMLS)
11000 Pennyslvania Avenue NW
Washington, DC 20506
Tel. (202) 606-8536
Fax (202) 606-8591
E-mail: imlsinfo@imls.fed.us
Web: www.imls.fed.us

International Commitee for Documentation (ICOM-CIDOC)
Pat Young, Chair
c/o CHIN
15 Eddy Street, 4th Floor
Ottawa, Ontario, K1A 0M5, Canada
Tel. (819) 994-1200
Fax (819) 994-9555
E-mail: pyoung@chin.gc.ca
Web: www.cidoc.icom.org

International Council of Museums (ICOM)
Maison de l'Unesco
1, rue Miollis
F-75732 Paris Cedex 15, France
Tel. (33 1) 47 34 05 00
Fax (33 1) 43 06 78 62
E-mail: secretariat@icom.org
Web: www.icom.org

International Council on Archives (ICA)
60, rue des Francs-Bourgeois
75003 Paris, France
Tel. (33 1) 40 27 63 49
Fax (33 1) 42 72 20 65
E-mail: 100650.54@compuserve.com
Web: www.archives.ca/ica

International Federation of Library Associations and Institutions (IFLA)
PO Box 95312
2509 CH The Hague, Netherlands
Tel. (31 70) 314 0884
Fax (31 70) 383 4827
E-mail: IFLA@ifla.org
Web: www.ifla.org

Museums Association of the Caribbean (MAC)
MAC Secretariat
PO Box 112
Bridgetown, Barbados
Tel. (1 246) 228 2024
Fax (1 246) 429 8483
E-mail: gill@candw.lc

Parks Canada National Office
25 Eddy Street
Hull, Quebec, K1A 0M5, Canada
Tel. (819) 997-0055
Fax (819) 953-8770
E-mail: parks_webmaster@pch.gc.ca
Web: www.parkscanada.pch.gc.ca

Scottish Museums Council
20/22 Torpichen Street
Edinburgh EH3 8JB, Scotland, United Kingdom
Tel. (44 131) 229 7465
Fax (44 131) 229 2728
E-mail: inform@scottishmuseums.org.uk
Web: www.scottishmuseums.org.uk

Unesco
7, place de Fontenoy
75352 Paris 07 SP, France
Tel. (33 1) 45 68 10 00
Fax (33 1) 45 67 16 90
E-mail: wh-info@unesco.org
Web: www.unesco.org/whc

Index

About the Compilers

Valerie Dorge is a project specialist at the Getty Conservation Institute, providing conservation, training, and project-management expertise to GCI projects. As a training coordinator from 1992 to 1997, she organized a variety of courses for the institute nationally and internationally. She was an adviser for the AIC Task Force on Disaster Mitigation, Response, and Recovery, which developed a draft workshop curriculum on this topic. Previously, she was a conservator at the Canadian Conservation Institute (CCI), where her responsibilities also included participation in the institute's emergency response team activities. She has organized a number of conference programs, was coeditor of *Painted Wood: History and Conservation* (Getty Conservation Institute, 1998), and has been published in a number of professional journals. Dorge is a professional associate of the American Institute for Conservation of Historic and Artistic Works (AIC), and a Fellow of the International Institute for Conservation of Historic and Artistic Works (IIC).

Sharon L. Jones is a journalist-turned-technologist with more than sixteen years' experience in newspapers, educational products, and hypermedia publishing. She has received two master's degrees, one in journalism from Columbia University and one in educational technology from San Diego State University. She began her writing career with the Associated Press, the wire service, and spent the majority of her journalism career with the *San Diego Union-Tribune*. She has worked as a general assignment reporter, where she covered a variety of emergencies (bombings, earthquakes, brush fires, arson fires) and learned firsthand about the devastation they can bring. She has also worked as an education writer and has developed training materials for IBM Corporation and other companies.